Advanced Python Programming
Second Edition

Accelerate your Python programs using proven
techniques and design patterns

Quan Nguyen

BIRMINGHAM—MUMBAI

Advanced Python Programming
Second Edition

Group Product Manager: Richa Tripathi
Publishing Product Manager: Gebin George
Senior Editor: Ruvika Rao
Content Development Editor: Nithya Sadanandan
Technical Editor: Maran Fernandes
Copy Editor: Safis Editing
Project Coordinator: Manisha Singh
Proofreader: Safis Editing
Indexer: Subalakshmi Govindhan
Production Designer: Aparna Bhagat
Marketing Coordinator: Sonakshi Bubbar

First published: February 2019

Second edition: March 2022

Production reference: 1180222

Published by Packt Publishing Ltd.
Livery Place
35 Livery Street
Birmingham
B3 2PB, UK.

ISBN 978-1-80181-401-0

www.packt.com

To Julie. Please learn Python—it's better than R, I promise.

– Quan Nguyen

Contributors

About the author

Quan Nguyen is a Python programmer and machine learning enthusiast. He is interested in solving decision-making problems under uncertainty. Quan has authored several books on Python programming and scientific computing. He is currently pursuing a Ph.D. degree in computer science at Washington University in St. Louis, researching Bayesian methods in machine learning.

About the reviewers

Dhruv Thakkar is a full-stack developer with 7+ years of experience working in multiple Fortune 500 companies in industries such as telecoms, information technology, and finance. He holds a masters in computer science from the University of Bridgeport, Connecticut, and a Bachelor of Science (information technology) from the University of Mumbai.

Having started his career working as a frontend developer, he later transitioned to backend technologies such as Python, PHP, Perl, and Node.js to name a few. He also has experience working on DevOps tools such as Git, Jenkins, Ansible, and Docker. He is always open to learning new skills and is also passionate about open source and blockchain technologies.

Marius Iulian Mihailescu, Ph.D. is an associate professor at Spiru Haret University and a software project manager at the company Institute for Computers, both based in Bucharest, Romania. As an associate professor at Spiru Haret University, Marius is responsible for information security, functional programming, and developing IoT application courses. For more than 6 years, he has served as a lecturer at well-known national and international universities and different companies.

His main activity involves fields such as information security and cryptography related business/industry and research projects, ethical hacking, and developing software projects using the latest technologies, such as DevOps, IoT, cloud computing, big data, C#, F#, Java, Haskell, and Python.

Marius has authored and coauthored more than 30 articles in conference proceedings, 25 articles in journals, and 6 books.

Table of Contents

3

Fast Array Operations with NumPy, Pandas, and Xarray

4

C Performance with Cython

5
Exploring Compilers

6
Automatic Differentiation and Accelerated Linear Algebra for Machine Learning

Section 2: Concurrency and Parallelism

7
Implementing Concurrency

8
Parallel Processing

9
Concurrent Web Requests

10
Concurrent Image Processing

11
Building Communication Channels with asyncio

12
Deadlocks

13
Starvation

14
Race Conditions

15

The Global Interpreter Lock

Section 3: Design Patterns in Python

16

The Factory Pattern

17

The Builder Pattern

18

Other Creational Patterns

19

The Adapter Pattern

20

The Decorator Pattern

Preface

Advanced Python Programming serves as a guide for you to take your Python skills to the next level. To beginners, Python is a great option for fast prototyping and software development due to its simple syntax, but some tend to lean toward other languages when they want to speed up and scale their code. However, this mindset is not necessarily correct. As this book will show us, Python comes with a wide range of support for optimizing, scaling, and overall high-performance computing.

This second edition includes both updated and new content from the first. Many chapters with overlapping materials have been combined to make a succinct, logical flow throughout the text. Further, a new chapter on JAX, the state-of-the-art high-performance computing tool in machine learning, has been added. These adjustments promise to make the book a high-quality text for all Python users who are looking to get the most out of their programs.

By the end of this book, you will have been exposed to a variety of techniques and libraries that are designed to streamline, protect, and optimize your software. You will gain practical skills on how to make your Python applications robust, efficient, and scalable.

Who this book is for

This book is for intermediate to experienced Python programmers who are looking to scale up their applications in a systematic and robust manner. Programmers from a range of backgrounds will find this book useful, including software engineers, scientific programmers, and software architects.

What this book covers

Chapter 1, Benchmarking and Profiling, teaches you how to assess the performance of Python programs and practical strategies on how to identify and isolate slow sections of your code.

Chapter 2, Pure Python Optimizations, discusses how to improve your running times by orders of magnitude using the efficient data structures and algorithms available in the Python standard library and pure-Python third-party modules.

Chapter 3, Fast Array Operations with NumPy, Pandas, and Xarray, offers a guide to the NumPy and pandas packages. Mastery of these packages will allow you to implement fast numerical algorithms with an expressive, concise interface.

Chapter 4, *C Performance with Cython*, is a tutorial on Cython, a language that uses a Python-compatible syntax to generate efficient C code.

Chapter 5, *Exploring Compilers*, covers tools that can be used to compile Python to efficient machine code. The chapter will teach you how to use Numba, an optimizing compiler for Python functions, and PyPy, an alternative interpreter that can execute and optimize Python programs on the fly.

Chapter 6, *Automatic Differentiation and Accelerated Linear Algebra for Machine Learning*, covers high-performance Python programming, which is essential in scientific computing and machine learning. JAX implements many compiler-related optimizations under the hood, which speeds up NumPy operations by a significant amount. Further, the tool can automatically differentiate native Python functions, allowing for the wide application of gradient-based optimization routines.

Chapter 7, *Implementing Concurrency*, offers a guide to asynchronous and reactive programming. We will learn about key terms and concepts, and demonstrate how to write clean, concurrent code using the asyncio and RxPy frameworks.

Chapter 8, *Parallel Processing*, provides an introduction to parallel programming on multi-core processors and GPUs. In this chapter, you will learn how to achieve parallelism using the multiprocessing module and by expressing your code using Theano and TensorFlow.

Chapter 9, *Concurrent Web Requests*, covers one of the main applications of concurrent programming: web scraping. It also covers other relevant elements of web scraping, before discussing how threading can be applied to parallelize this process.

Chapter 10, *Concurrent Image Processing*, goes into a specific application of concurrency: image processing. The basic ideas behind image processing, in addition to some of the most common processing techniques, are discussed. We will, of course, see how concurrency, specifically multiprocessing, can speed up the task of image processing.

Chapter 11, *Building Communication Channels with asyncio*, combines the knowledge obtained regarding asynchronous programming covered in previous chapters with the topic of network communication. Specifically, we will look into using the aiohttp module as a tool to make asynchronous HTTP requests to web servers, as well as the aiofile module that implements asynchronous file reading/writing.

Chapter 12, Deadlocks, introduces the first of the problems that are commonly faced in concurrent programming. We will learn about the classical dining philosophers problem as an example of how deadlocks can cause concurrent programs to stop functioning. This chapter also covers a number of potential approaches to deadlocks as well as relevant concepts, such as livelocks and distributed deadlocks.

Chapter 13, Starvation, considers another common problem in concurrent applications. The chapter uses the narrative of the classical readers-writers problem to explain the concept of starvation and its causes. We will, of course, also discuss potential solutions to these problems via hands-on examples in Python.

Chapter 14, Race Conditions, addresses arguably the most well-known concurrency problem: race conditions. We will also discuss the concept of a critical section, which is an essential element in the context of race conditions specifically, and concurrent programming in general. The chapter then covers mutual exclusion as a potential solution for this problem.

Chapter 15, The Global Interpreter Lock, introduces the infamous GIL, which is considered the biggest challenge in concurrent programming in Python. We will learn about the reason behind the GIL's implementation and the problems that it raises. This chapter concludes with some thoughts regarding how Python programmers and developers should think about and interact with the GIL.

Chapter 16, The Factory Pattern, teaches you how to use the Factory design pattern (Factory Method and Abstract Factory) to initialize objects, and also covers the benefits of using the Factory design pattern instead of direct object instantiation.

Chapter 17, The Builder Pattern, teaches you how to simplify the object creation process for cases typically composed of several related objects. We will review real-world examples and use cases, and then implement the builder pattern in developing a pizza-ordering application.

Chapter 18, Other Creational Patterns, teaches you how to handle other object creation situations with techniques such as creating a new object that is a full copy (a named clone) of an existing object, a technique offered by the Prototype pattern. You will also learn about the Singleton pattern.

Chapter 19, The Adapter Pattern, teaches you how to make your existing code compatible with a foreign interface (for example, an external library) with minimal changes. Specifically, you will see how you can achieve interface conformance using the Adapter pattern without modifying the source code of the incompatible model.

Chapter 20, The Decorator Pattern, teaches you how to enhance the functionality of an object without using inheritance. We will mention several categories of cross-cutting concerns and specifically demonstrate memoization in this view. We will also describe how decorators can help us to keep our functions clean, without sacrificing performance.

Chapter 21, The Bridge Pattern, teaches you how to externalize an object's implementation details from its class hierarchy to another object class hierarchy. This chapter encourages the idea of preferring composition over inheritance.

Chapter 22, The Façade Pattern, teaches you how to create a single entry point to hide the complexity of a system. We will cover the basic use cases of facade and the implementation of the interface used by a multiserver operating system.

Chapter 23, Other Structural Patterns, teaches you about the Flyweight, **Model-View-Controller** (**MVC**), and Proxy patterns. With the Flyweight pattern, you will learn how to reuse objects from an object pool to improve the memory usage and possibly the performance of your applications. The MVC pattern is used in application development (desktop and the web) to improve maintainability by avoiding mixing the business logic with the user interface. And with the Proxy pattern, you provide a special object that acts as a surrogate or placeholder for another object to control access to it and reduce complexity and/or improve performance.

Chapter 24, The Chain of Responsibility Pattern, teaches you another technique to improve the maintainability of your applications by avoiding mixing the business logic with the user interface.

Chapter 25, The Command Pattern, teaches you how to encapsulate operations (such as undo, copy, and paste) as objects, to improve your application. Among the advantages of this technique, the object that invokes the command is decoupled from the object that performs it.

Chapter 26, The Observer Pattern, teaches you how to send a request to multiple receivers.

To get the most out of this book

The code used in this book has been tested on Python version 3.8 on macOS Big Sur, Windows, Ubuntu, and Monterey.

You should first have Python installed, preferably in a virtual environment. The recommended way to do this is via Anaconda, which can be downloaded from `https://www.anaconda.com/products/individual`. Individual chapters may discuss various external libraries and tools that have to be installed via a package manager, and specific instructions on how to do so are included in the corresponding text.

> **Note**
>
> If you are using the digital version of this book, we advise you to type the code yourself or access the code from the book's GitHub repository (a link is available in the next section). Doing so will help you avoid any potential errors related to the copying and pasting of code.

Download the example code files

You can download the example code files for this book from GitHub at `https://github.com/PacktPublishing/Advanced-Python-Programming-Second-Edition`. If there's an update to the code, it will be updated in the GitHub repository.

We also have other code bundles from our rich catalog of books and videos available at `https://github.com/PacktPublishing/`. Check them out!

Download the color images

We also provide a PDF file that has color images of the screenshots and diagrams used in this book. You can download it here: `https://static.packt-cdn.com/downloads/9781801814010_ColorImages.pdf`.

Conventions used

There are a number of text conventions used throughout this book.

`Code in text`: Indicates code words in text, database table names, folder names, filenames, file extensions, pathnames, dummy URLs, user input, and Twitter handles. Here is an example: "In our main program, we create the fork as a lock object first; then, we create two `Spouse` thread objects, which are each other's `partner` attributes."

A block of code is set as follows:

```
fork = threading.Lock()

partner1 = Spouse('Wife', None)
partner2 = Spouse('Husband', partner1)
partner1.partner = partner2

partner1.start()
```

```
partner2.start()

partner1.join()
partner2.join()

print('Finished.')
```

When we wish to draw your attention to a particular part of a code block, the relevant lines or items are set in bold:

```
fork = threading.Lock()

partner1 = Spouse('Wife', None)
partner2 = Spouse('Husband', partner1)
partner1.partner = partner2

partner1.start()
partner2.start()

partner1.join()
partner2.join()

print('Finished.')
```

Any command-line input or output is written as follows:

```
pip install numpy
```

Bold: Indicates a new term, an important word, or words that you see onscreen. For instance, words in menus or dialog boxes appear in **bold**. Here is an example: "The **Coordinates** section shows the values that each of these dimensions can take on."

> **Tips or important notes**
> Appear like this.

Get in touch

Feedback from our readers is always welcome.

General feedback: If you have questions about any aspect of this book, email us at customercare@packtpub.com and mention the book title in the subject of your message.

Errata: Although we have taken every care to ensure the accuracy of our content, mistakes do happen. If you have found a mistake in this book, we would be grateful if you would report this to us. Please visit www.packtpub.com/support/errata and fill in the form.

Piracy: If you come across any illegal copies of our works in any form on the internet, we would be grateful if you would provide us with the location address or website name. Please contact us at copyright@packt.com with a link to the material.

If you are interested in becoming an author: If there is a topic that you have expertise in and you are interested in either writing or contributing to a book, please visit authors.packtpub.com.

Share Your Thoughts

Once you've read *Advanced Python Programming*, we'd love to hear your thoughts! Scan the QR code below to go straight to the Amazon review page for this book and share your feedback.

https://packt.link/r/1801814015

Your review is important to us and the tech community and will help us make sure we're delivering excellent quality content.

Section 1: Python-Native and Specialized Optimization

Python, along with its many libraries and packages, offers specialized data structures and classes that facilitate highly optimized operations. You will learn how to navigate through these different tools and use them appropriately to accelerate your Python program.

This section contains the following chapters:

- *Chapter 1, Benchmarking and Profiling*
- *Chapter 2, Pure Python Optimizations*
- *Chapter 3, Fast Array Operations with NumPy, Pandas, and Xarray*
- *Chapter 4, C Performance with Cython*
- *Chapter 5, Exploring Compilers*
- *Chapter 6, Automatic Differentiation and Accelerated Linear Algebra for Machine Learning*

1
Benchmarking and Profiling

Recognizing the slow parts of your program is the single most important task when it comes to speeding up your code. In most cases, the code that causes the application to slow down is a very small fraction of the program. By identifying these critical sections, you can focus on the parts that need the most improvement without wasting time in micro-optimization.

Profiling is a technique that allows us to pinpoint the most resource-intensive parts of an application. A **profiler** is a program that runs an application and monitors how long each function takes to execute, thus detecting the functions on which your application spends most of its time.

Python provides several tools to help us find these bottlenecks and measure important performance metrics. In this chapter, we will learn how to use the standard `cProfile` module and the `line_profiler` third-party package. We will also learn how to profile the memory consumption of an application through the `memory_profiler` tool. Another useful tool that we will cover is **KCachegrind**, which can be used to graphically display the data produced by various profilers.

Finally, **benchmarks** are small scripts used to assess the total execution time of your application. We will learn how to write benchmarks and use them to accurately time your programs.

The topics we will cover in this chapter are listed here:

- Designing your application
- Writing tests and benchmarks
- Writing better tests and benchmarks with `pytest-benchmark`
- Finding bottlenecks with `cProfile`
- Optimizing our code
- Using the `dis` module
- Profiling memory usage with `memory_profiler`

By the end of the chapter, you will have gained a solid understanding of how to optimize a Python program and will be armed with practical tools that facilitate the optimization process.

Technical requirements

To follow the content of this chapter, you should have a basic understanding of Python programming and be familiar with core concepts such as variables, classes, and functions. You should also be comfortable with working with the command line to run Python programs. Finally, the code for this chapter can be found in the following GitHub repository: `https://github.com/PacktPublishing/Advanced-Python-Programming-Second-Edition/tree/main/Chapter01`.

Designing your application

In the early development stages, the design of a program can change quickly and may require large rewrites and reorganizations of the code base. By testing different prototypes without the burden of optimization, you are free to devote your time and energy to ensure that the program produces correct results and that the design is flexible. After all, who needs an application that runs fast but gives the wrong answer?

The mantras that you should remember when optimizing your code are outlined here:

- **Make it run**: We have to get the software in a working state and ensure that it produces the correct results. This exploratory phase serves to better understand the application and to spot major design issues in the early stages.

- **Make it right**: We want to ensure that the design of the program is solid. Refactoring should be done before attempting any performance optimization. This really helps separate the application into independent and cohesive units that are easy to maintain.

- **Make it fast**: Once our program is working and well structured, we can focus on performance optimization. We may also want to optimize memory usage if that constitutes an issue.

In this section, we will write and profile a *particle simulator* test application. A **simulator** is a program that considers some particles and simulates their movement over time according to a set of laws that we impose. These particles can be abstract entities or correspond to physical objects—for example, billiard balls moving on a table, molecules in a gas, stars moving through space, smoke particles, fluids in a chamber, and so on.

Building a particle simulator

Computer simulations are useful in fields such as physics, chemistry, astronomy, and many other disciplines. The applications used to simulate systems are particularly performance-intensive, and scientists and engineers spend an inordinate amount of time optimizing their code. In order to study realistic systems, it is often necessary to simulate a very high number of bodies, and every small increase in performance counts.

In our first example, we will simulate a system containing particles that constantly rotate around a central point at various speeds, just like the hands of a clock.

The necessary information to run our simulation will be the starting positions of the particles, the speed, and the rotation direction. From these elements, we have to calculate the position of the particle in the next instant of time. An example system is shown in the following diagram. The origin of the system is the (0, 0) point, the position is indicated by the *x, y* vector, and the velocity is indicated by the *vx, vy* vector:

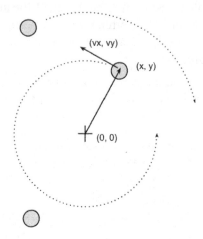

Figure 1.1 – An example of a particle system

The basic feature of a circular motion is that the particles always move perpendicular to the direction connecting the particle and the center. To move the particle, we simply change the position by taking a series of very small steps (which correspond to advancing the system for a small interval of time) in the direction of motion, as shown in the following diagram:

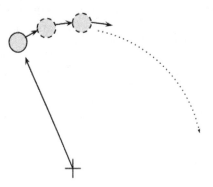

Figure 1.2 – Movement of a particle

We will start by designing the application in an **object-oriented (OO)** way. According to our requirements, it is natural to have a generic `Particle` class that stores the particle positions, x and y, and their angular velocity, ang_vel, as illustrated in the following code snippet:

```
class Particle:
    def __init__(self, x, y, ang_vel):
        self.x = x
        self.y = y
        self.ang_vel = ang_vel
```

Note that we accept positive and negative numbers for all the parameters (the sign of ang_vel will simply determine the direction of rotation).

Another class, called `ParticleSimulator`, will encapsulate the laws of motion and will be responsible for changing the positions of the particles over time. The __init__ method will store a list of `Particle` instances, and the evolve method will change the particle positions according to our laws. The code is illustrated in the following snippet:

```
class ParticleSimulator:
    def __init__(self, particles):
        self.particles = particles
```

We want the particles to rotate around the position corresponding to the x=0 and y=0 coordinates, at a constant speed. The direction of the particles will always be perpendicular to the direction from the center (refer to *Figure 1.1* in this chapter). To find the direction of the movement along the *x* and *y* axes (corresponding to the Python v_x and v_y variables), it is sufficient to use these formulae:

```
v_x = -y / (x**2 + y**2)**0.5
v_y = x / (x**2 + y**2)**0.5
```

If we let one of our particles move, after a certain time *t*, it will reach another position following a circular path. We can approximate a circular trajectory by dividing the time interval, *t*, into tiny time steps, *dt*, where the particle moves in a straight line tangentially to the circle. (Note that higher-order curves could be used rather than straight lines for better accuracy, but we will stick with lines as the simplest approximation.) The final result is just an approximation of a circular motion.

In order to avoid a strong divergence, such as the one illustrated in the following diagram, it is necessary to take very small time steps:

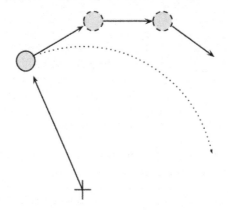

Figure 1.3 – Undesired divergence in particle motion due to large time steps

In a more schematic way, we have to carry out the following steps to calculate the particle position at time *t*:

1. Calculate the direction of motion (v_x and v_y).

2. Calculate the displacement (d_x and d_y), which is the product of the time step, angular velocity, and direction of motion.

3. Repeat *Steps 1* and *2* enough times to cover the total time *t*.

The following code snippet shows the full ParticleSimulator implementation:

```
class ParticleSimulator:

    def __init__(self, particles):
        self.particles = particles

    def evolve(self, dt):
        timestep = 0.00001
        nsteps = int(dt/timestep)

        for i in range(nsteps):
            for p in self.particles:
                # 1. calculate the direction
                norm = (p.x**2 + p.y**2)**0.5
```

```
v_x = -p.y/norm
v_y = p.x/norm


# 2. calculate the displacement
d_x = timestep * p.ang_vel * v_x
d_y = timestep * p.ang_vel * v_y


p.x += d_x
p.y += d_y
# 3. repeat for all the time steps
```

And with that, we have finished building the foundation of our particle simulator. Next, we will see it in action by visualizing the simulated particles.

Visualizing the simulation

We can use the `matplotlib` library here to visualize our particles. This library is not included in the Python standard library, but it can be easily installed using the `pip install matplotlib` command.

Alternatively, you can use the Anaconda Python distribution (`https://store.continuum.io/cshop/anaconda/`), which includes `matplotlib` and most of the other third-party packages used in this book. Anaconda is free and is available for Linux, Windows, and Mac.

To make an interactive visualization, we will use the `matplotlib.pyplot.plot` function to display the particles as points and the `matplotlib.animation.FuncAnimation` class to animate the evolution of the particles over time.

The `visualize` function takes a `ParticleSimulator` particle instance as an argument and displays the trajectory in an animated plot. The steps necessary to display the particle trajectory using the `matplotlib` tools are outlined here:

1. Set up the axes and use the `plot` function to display the particles. The `plot` function takes a list of *x* and *y* coordinates.
2. Write an initialization function, `init`, and a function, `animate`, that updates the *x* and *y* coordinates using the `line.set_data` method. Note that in `init`, we need to return the line data in the form of `line`, due to syntactic reasons.
3. Create a `FuncAnimation` instance by passing the `init` and `animate` functions and the `interval` parameters, which specify the update interval, and `blit`, which improves the update rate of the image.

4. Run the animation with `plt.show()`, as illustrated in the following code snippet:

```python
from matplotlib import pyplot as plt
from matplotlib import animation

def visualize(simulator):

    X = [p.x for p in simulator.particles]
    Y = [p.y for p in simulator.particles]

    fig = plt.figure()
    ax = plt.subplot(111, aspect='equal')
    line, = ax.plot(X, Y, 'ro')

    # Axis limits
    plt.xlim(-1, 1)
    plt.ylim(-1, 1)

    # It will be run when the animation starts
    def init():
        line.set_data([], [])
        return line, # The comma is important!

    def animate(i):
        # We let the particle evolve for 0.01 time
          units
        simulator.evolve(0.01)
        X = [p.x for p in simulator.particles]
        Y = [p.y for p in simulator.particles]

        line.set_data(X, Y)
        return line,

    # Call the animate function each 10 ms
    anim = animation.FuncAnimation(fig,
      animate,init_func=init,blit=True,
        interval=10)
    plt.show()
```

To test this code, we define a small function, `test_visualize`, that animates a system of three particles rotating in different directions. Note in the following code snippet that the third particle completes a round three times faster than the others:

```python
def test_visualize():
    particles = [
                    Particle(0.3, 0.5, 1),
                    Particle(0.0, -0.5, -1),
                    Particle(-0.1, -0.4, 3)
    ]

    simulator = ParticleSimulator(particles)
    visualize(simulator)

if __name__ == '__main__':
    test_visualize()
```

The `test_visualize` function is helpful to graphically understand the system time evolution. Simply close the animation window when you'd like to terminate the program. With this program in hand, in the following section, we will write more test functions to properly verify program correctness and measure performance.

Writing tests and benchmarks

Now that we have a working simulator, we can start measuring our performance and tune up our code so that the simulator can handle as many particles as possible. As a first step, we will write a test and a benchmark.

We need a test that checks whether the results produced by the simulation are correct or not. Optimizing a program commonly requires employing multiple strategies; as we rewrite our code multiple times, bugs may easily be introduced. A solid test suite ensures that the implementation is correct at every iteration so that we are free to go wild and try different things with the confidence that, if the test suite passes, the code will still work as expected. More specifically, what we are implementing here are called unit tests, which aim to verify the intended logic of the program regardless of the implementation details, which may change during optimization.

Our test will take three particles, simulate them for 0.1 time units, and compare the results with those from a reference implementation. A good way to organize your tests is using a separate function for each different aspect (or unit) of your application. Since our current functionality is included in the evolve method, our function will be named test_evolve. The following code snippet shows the test_evolve implementation. Note that, in this case, we compare floating-point numbers up to a certain precision through the fequal function:

```python
def test_evolve():
    particles = [Particle( 0.3,  0.5, +1),
                 Particle( 0.0, -0.5, -1),
                 Particle(-0.1, -0.4, +3)
                 ]

    simulator = ParticleSimulator(particles)

    simulator.evolve(0.1)

    p0, p1, p2 = particles

    def fequal(a, b, eps=1e-5):
        return abs(a - b) < eps

    assert fequal(p0.x,  0.210269)
    assert fequal(p0.y,  0.543863)

    assert fequal(p1.x, -0.099334)
    assert fequal(p1.y, -0.490034)

    assert fequal(p2.x,  0.191358)
    assert fequal(p2.y, -0.365227)

if __name__ == '__main__':
    test_evolve()
```

The assert statements will raise an error if the included conditions are not satisfied. Upon running the test_evolve function, if you notice no error or output printed out, that means all the conditions are met.

A test ensures the correctness of our functionality but gives little information about its running time. A **benchmark** is a simple and representative use case that can be run to assess the running time of an application. Benchmarks are very useful to keep score of how fast our program is with each new version that we implement.

We can write a representative benchmark by instantiating a thousand `Particle` objects with random coordinates and angular velocity and feeding them to a `ParticleSimulator` class. We then let the system evolve for `0.1` time units. The code is illustrated in the following snippet:

```python
from random import uniform


def benchmark():
    particles = [
        Particle(uniform(-1.0, 1.0), uniform(-1.0, 1.0),
            uniform(-1.0, 1.0))
        for i in range(1000)]

    simulator = ParticleSimulator(particles)
    simulator.evolve(0.1)

if __name__ == '__main__':
    benchmark()
```

With the benchmark program implemented, we now need to run it and keep track of the time needed for the benchmark to complete execution, which we will see next. (Note that when you run these tests and benchmarks on your own system, you are likely to see different numbers listed in the text, which is completely normal and dependent on your system configurations and Python version.)

Timing your benchmark

A very simple way to time a benchmark is through the Unix `time` command. Using the `time` command, as follows, you can easily measure the execution time of an arbitrary process:

```
$ time python simul.py
real    0m1.051s
user    0m1.022s
sys     0m0.028s
```

The `time` command is not available for Windows. To install Unix tools such as `time` on Windows, you can use the `cygwin` shell, downloadable from the official website (`http://www.cygwin.com/`). Alternatively, you can use similar PowerShell commands, such as `Measure-Command` (`https://msdn.microsoft.com/en-us/powershell/reference/5.1/microsoft.powershell.utility/measure-command`), to measure execution time.

By default, `time` displays three metrics, as outlined here:

- `real`: The actual time spent running the process from start to finish, as if it were measured by a human with a stopwatch.

- `user`: The cumulative time spent by all the **central processing units** (**CPUs**) during the computation.

- `sys`: The cumulative time spent by all the CPUs during system-related tasks, such as memory allocation.

> **Note**
>
> Sometimes, `user` and `sys` might be greater than `real`, as multiple processors may work in parallel.

`time` also offers richer formatting options. For an overview, you can explore its manual (using the `man time` command). If you want a summary of all the metrics available, you can use the `-v` option.

The Unix `time` command is one of the simplest and most direct ways to benchmark a program. For an accurate measurement, the benchmark should be designed to have a long enough execution time (in the order of seconds) so that the setup and teardown of the process are small compared to the execution time of the application. The `user` metric is suitable as a monitor for the CPU performance, while the `real` metric also includes the time spent on other processes while waiting for **input/output** (**I/O**) operations.

Another convenient way to time Python scripts is the `timeit` module. This module runs a snippet of code in a loop for *n* times and measures the total execution time. Then, it repeats the same operation *r* times (by default, the value of *r* is 3) and records the time of the best run. Due to this timing scheme, `timeit` is an appropriate tool to accurately time small statements in isolation.

The `timeit` module can be used as a Python package, from the command line or from *IPython*.

IPython is a Python shell design that improves the interactivity of the Python interpreter. It boosts tab completion and many utilities to time, profile, and debug your code. We will use this shell to try out snippets throughout the book. The IPython shell accepts **magic commands**—statements that start with a % symbol—that enhance the shell with special behaviors. Commands that start with %% are called **cell magics**, which can be applied on multiline snippets (termed as **cells**).

IPython is available on most Linux distributions through `pip` and is included in Anaconda. You can use IPython as a regular Python shell (`ipython`), but it is also available in a Qt-based version (`ipython qtconsole`) and as a powerful browser-based interface (`jupyter notebook`).

In IPython and **command-line interfaces** (**CLIs**), it is possible to specify the number of loops or repetitions with the `-n` and `-r` options. If not specified, they will be automatically inferred by `timeit`. When invoking `timeit` from the command line, you can also pass some setup code, through the `-s` option, which will execute before the benchmark. In the following snippet, the `IPython` command line and Python module version of `timeit` are demonstrated:

```
# IPython Interface
$ ipython
In [1]: from simul import benchmark
In [2]: %timeit benchmark()
1 loops, best of 3: 782 ms per loop


# Command Line Interface
$ python -m timeit -s 'from simul import benchmark'
'benchmark()'
10 loops, best of 3: 826 msec per loop


# Python Interface
# put this function into the simul.py script

import timeit
result = timeit.timeit('benchmark()',
  setup='from __main__ import benchmark', number=10)
```

```
# result is the time (in seconds) to run the whole loop
result = timeit.repeat('benchmark()',
  setup='from __main__ import benchmark', number=10, \
    repeat=3)
# result is a list containing the time of each repetition
(repeat=3 in this case)
```

Note that while the command line and IPython interfaces automatically infer a reasonable number of loops n, the Python interface requires you to explicitly specify a value through the number argument.

Writing better tests and benchmarks with pytest-benchmark

The Unix time command is a versatile tool that can be used to assess the running time of small programs on a variety of platforms. For larger Python applications and libraries, a more comprehensive solution that deals with both testing and benchmarking is pytest, in combination with its pytest-benchmark plugin.

In this section, we will write a simple benchmark for our application using the pytest testing framework. For those who are, the pytest documentation, which can be found at http://doc.pytest.org/en/latest/, is the best resource to learn more about the framework and its uses.

You can install pytest from the console using the pip install pytest command. The benchmarking plugin can be installed, similarly, by issuing the pip install pytest-benchmark command.

A testing framework is a set of tools that simplifies writing, executing, and debugging tests, and provides rich reports and summaries of the test results. When using the pytest framework, it is recommended to place tests separately from the application code. In the following example, we create a test_simul.py file that contains the test_evolve function:

```
from simul import Particle, ParticleSimulator

def test_evolve():
    particles = [
                Particle( 0.3,  0.5, +1),
                Particle( 0.0, -0.5, -1),
```

```
                    Particle(-0.1, -0.4, +3)
    ]

    simulator = ParticleSimulator(particles)

    simulator.evolve(0.1)

    p0, p1, p2 = particles

    def fequal(a, b, eps=1e-5):
        return abs(a - b) < eps

    assert fequal(p0.x,  0.210269)
    assert fequal(p0.y,  0.543863)

    assert fequal(p1.x, -0.099334)
    assert fequal(p1.y, -0.490034)

    assert fequal(p2.x,  0.191358)
    assert fequal(p2.y, -0.365227)
```

The `pytest` executable can be used from the command line to discover and run tests contained in Python modules. To execute a specific test, we can use the `pytest path/to/module.py::function_name` syntax. To execute `test_evolve`, we can type the following command in a console to obtain simple but informative output:

```
$ pytest test_simul.py::test_evolve

platform linux -- Python 3.5.2, pytest-3.0.5, py-1.4.32,
pluggy-0.4.0
rootdir: /home/gabriele/workspace/hiperf/chapter1, inifile:
plugins:
collected 2 items

test_simul.py .

=========================== 1 passed in 0.43 seconds
===========================
```

Once we have a test in place, it is possible for you to execute your test as a benchmark using the `pytest-benchmark` plugin. If we change our `test` function so that it accepts an argument named `benchmark`, the `pytest` framework will automatically pass the `benchmark` resource as an argument (in `pytest` terminology, these resources are called **fixtures**). The `benchmark` resource can be called by passing the function that we intend to benchmark as the first argument, followed by the additional arguments. In the following snippet, we illustrate the edits necessary to benchmark the `ParticleSimulator.evolve` function:

```
from simul import Particle, ParticleSimulator


def test_evolve(benchmark):
    # ... previous code
    benchmark(simulator.evolve, 0.1)
```

To run the benchmark, it is sufficient to rerun the `pytest test_simul.py::test_evolve` command. The resulting output will contain detailed timing information regarding the `test_evolve` function, as shown here:

```
==================================== test session starts ====================================
platform linux -- Python 3.5.2, pytest-3.0.5, py-1.4.32, pluggy-0.4.0
benchmark: 3.0.0 (defaults: timer=time.perf_counter disable_gc=False min_rounds=5 min_time=5.00us max_time=1.00s cal
ibration_precision=10 warmup=False warmup_iterations=100000)
rootdir: /home/gabriele/workspace/hiperf/chapter1, inifile:
plugins: benchmark-3.0.0
collected 2 items

test_simul.py .

------------------------------ benchmark: 1 tests ------------------------------
Name (time in ms)        Min      Max     Mean  StdDev   Median      IQR  Outliers(*)  Rounds  Iterations
--------------------------------------------------------------------------------
test_evolve          29.4716  41.1791  30.4622  2.0234  29.9630   0.7376          2;2      34           1
--------------------------------------------------------------------------------

(*) Outliers: 1 Standard Deviation from Mean; 1.5 IQR (InterQuartile Range) from 1st Quartile and 3rd Quartile.
==================================== 1 passed in 2.52 seconds ====================================
```

Figure 1.4 – Output from pytest

For each test collected, `pytest-benchmark` will execute the `benchmark` function several times and provide a statistic summary of its running time. The preceding output shown is very interesting as it shows how running times vary between runs.

In this example, the benchmark in `test_evolve` was run 34 times (Rounds column), its timings ranged between 29 and 41 **milliseconds (ms)** (Min and Max), and the Average and Median times were fairly similar at about 30 ms, which is actually very close to the best timing obtained. This example demonstrates how there can be substantial performance variability between runs and that, as opposed to taking timings with one-shot tools such as time, it is a good idea to run the program multiple times and record a representative value, such as the minimum or the median.

`pytest-benchmark` has many more features and options that can be used to take accurate timings and analyze the results. For more information, consult the documentation at `http://pytest-benchmark.readthedocs.io/en/stable/usage.html`.

Finding bottlenecks with cProfile

After assessing the correctness and timing of the execution time of the program, we are ready to identify the parts of the code that need to be tuned for performance. We typically aim to identify parts that are small compared to the size of the program.

Two profiling modules are available through the Python standard library, as outlined here:

- **The profile module**: This module is written in pure Python and adds significant overhead to the program execution. Its presence in the standard library is due to its vast platform support and the ease with which it can be extended.

- **The cProfile module**: This is the main profiling module, with an interface equivalent to `profile`. It is written in C, has a small overhead, and is suitable as a general-purpose profiler.

The `cProfile` module can be used in three different ways, as follows:

- From the command line
- As a Python module
- With IPython

`cProfile` does not require any change in the source code and can be executed directly on an existing Python script or function. You can use `cProfile` from the command line in this way:

```
$ python -m cProfile simul.py
```

This will print a long output containing several profiling metrics of all of the functions called in the application. You can use the `-s` option to sort the output by a specific metric. In the following snippet, the output is sorted by the `tottime` metric, which will be described here:

```
$ python -m cProfile -s tottime simul.py
```

The data produced by `cProfile` can be saved in an output file by passing the `-o` option. The format that `cProfile` uses is readable by the `stats` module and other tools. The usage of the `-o` option is shown here:

```
$ python -m cProfile -o prof.out simul.py
```

The usage of `cProfile` as a Python module requires invoking the `cProfile.run` function in the following way:

```
from simul import benchmark
import cProfile


cProfile.run("benchmark()")
```

You can also wrap a section of code between method calls of a `cProfile.Profile` object, as shown here:

```
from simul import benchmark
import cProfile

pr = cProfile.Profile()
pr.enable()
benchmark()
pr.disable()
pr.print_stats()
```

`cProfile` can also be used interactively with IPython. The `%prun` magic command lets you profile an individual function call, as illustrated in the following screenshot:

```
IPython: chapter1/codes
(hperf) → codes ipython
Python 3.5.2 |Continuum Analytics, Inc.| (default, Jul  2 2016, 17:53:06)
Type "copyright", "credits" or "license" for more information.

IPython 5.1.0 -- An enhanced Interactive Python.
?         -> Introduction and overview of IPython's features.
%quickref -> Quick reference.
help      -> Python's own help system.
object?   -> Details about 'object', use 'object??' for extra details.

In [1]: from simul import benchmark

In [2]: %prun benchmark()
        707 function calls in 1.231 seconds

  Ordered by: internal time

  ncalls  tottime  percall  cumtime  percall filename:lineno(function)
       1    1.230    1.230    1.230    1.230 simul.py:21(evolve)
       1    0.000    0.000    0.001    0.001 simul.py:118(<listcomp>)
     300    0.000    0.000    0.000    0.000 random.py:342(uniform)
     100    0.000    0.000    0.000    0.000 simul.py:10(__init__)
     300    0.000    0.000    0.000    0.000 {method 'random' of '_random.Random' objects}
       1    0.000    0.000    1.231    1.231 {built-in method builtins.exec}
       1    0.000    0.000    1.231    1.231 <string>:1(<module>)
       1    0.000    0.000    1.231    1.231 simul.py:117(benchmark)
       1    0.000    0.000    0.000    0.000 simul.py:18(__init__)
       1    0.000    0.000    0.000    0.000 {method 'disable' of '_lsprof.Profiler' objects}

In [3]:
```

Figure 1.5 – Using cProfile within IPython

The `cProfile` output is divided into five columns, as follows:

- `ncalls`: The number of times the function was called.

- `tottime`: The total time spent in the function without taking into account the calls to other functions.

- `cumtime`: The time spent in the function including other function calls.

- `percall`: The time spent for a single call of the function—this can be obtained by dividing the total or cumulative time by the number of calls.

- `filename:lineno`: The filename and corresponding line numbers. This information is not available when calling C extension modules.

The most important metric is `tottime`, the actual time spent in the function body excluding subcalls, which tells us exactly where the bottleneck is.

Unsurprisingly, the largest portion of time is spent in the `evolve` function. We can imagine that the loop is the section of the code that needs performance tuning. `cProfile` only provides information at the function level and does not tell us which specific statements are responsible for the bottleneck. Fortunately, as we will see in the next section, the `line_profiler` tool is capable of providing line-by-line information of the time spent in the function.

Analyzing the `cProfile` text output can be daunting for big programs with a lot of calls and subcalls. Some visual tools aid the task by improving navigation with an interactive, graphical interface.

Graphically analyzing profiling results

KCachegrind is a **graphical user interface** (**GUI**) useful for analyzing the profiling output emitted by `cProfile`.

KCachegrind is available in the Ubuntu 16.04 official repositories. The Qt port, QCacheGrind, can be downloaded for Windows from `http://sourceforge.net/projects/qcachegrindwin/`. Mac users can compile QCacheGrind using MacPorts (`http://www.macports.org/`) by following the instructions present in the blog post at `http://blogs.perl.org/users/rurban/2013/04/install-kachegrind-on-macosx-with-ports.html`.

KCachegrind can't directly read the output files produced by `cProfile`. Luckily, the `pyprof2calltree` third-party Python module is able to convert the `cProfile` output file into a format readable by KCachegrind.

You can install `pyprof2calltree` from the **Python Package Index** (**PyPI**) using the `pip install pyprof2calltree` command.

To best show the KCachegrind features, we will use another example with a more diversified structure. We define a recursive function, `factorial`, and two other functions that use `factorial`, named `taylor_exp` and `taylor_sin`. They represent the polynomial coefficients of the Taylor approximations of `exp(x)` and `sin(x)` and are illustrated in the following code snippet:

```
def factorial(n):
    if n == 0:
        return 1.0
    else:
        return n * factorial(n-1)
```

```python
def taylor_exp(n):
    return [1.0/factorial(i) for i in range(n)]


def taylor_sin(n):
    res = []
    for i in range(n):
        if i % 2 == 1:
            res.append((-1)**((i-1)/2)/
                float(factorial(i)))
        else:
            res.append(0.0)
    return res


def benchmark():
    taylor_exp(500)
    taylor_sin(500)


if __name__ == '__main__':
    benchmark()
```

To access profile information, we first need to generate a cProfile output file, as follows:

```
$ python -m cProfile -o prof.out taylor.py
```

Then, we can convert the output file with pyprof2calltree and launch KCachegrind by running the following code:

```
$ pyprof2calltree -i prof.out -o prof.calltree
$ kcachegrind prof.calltree # or qcachegrind prof.calltree
```

The output is shown in the following screenshot:

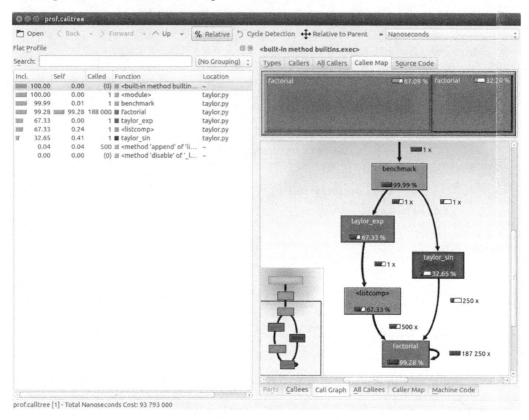

Figure 1.6 – Profiling output generated by pyprof2calltree and displayed by KCachegrind

The screenshot shows the KCachegrind UI. On the left, we have an output fairly similar to cProfile. The actual column names are slightly different: **Incl.** translates to the cProfile module's cumtime value and **Self** translates to tottime. The values are given in percentages by clicking on the **Relative** button on the menu bar. By clicking on the column headers, you can sort them by the corresponding property.

On the top right, a click on the **Callee Map** tab will display a diagram of the function costs. In the diagram shown in *Figure 1.6*, the time percentage spent by the function is proportional to the area of the rectangle. Rectangles can contain sub-rectangles that represent subcalls to other functions. In this case, we can easily see that there are two rectangles for the factorial function. The one on the left corresponds to the calls made by taylor_exp and the one on the right to the calls made by taylor_sin.

On the bottom right, you can display another diagram, a **call graph**, by clicking on the **Call Graph** tab. A call graph is a graphical representation of the calling relationship between the functions; each square represents a function and the arrows imply a calling relationship. For example, `taylor_exp` calls `factorial` **500** times, and `taylor_sin` calls `factorial` **250** times. KCachegrind also detects recursive calls: `factorial` calls itself **187250** times.

You can navigate to the **Call Graph** or the **Callee Map** tab by double-clicking on the rectangles; the interface will update accordingly, showing that the timing properties are relative to the selected function. For example, double-clicking on `taylor_exp` will cause the graph to change, showing only the contribution of `taylor_exp` to the total cost.

Gprof2Dot (`https://github.com/jrfonseca/gprof2dot`) is another popular tool used to produce call graphs. Starting from output files produced by one of the supported profilers, it will generate a `.dot` diagram representing a call graph.

Profiling line by line with line_profiler

Now that we know which function we have to optimize, we can use the `line_profiler` module that provides information on how time is spent in a line-by-line fashion. This is very useful in situations where it's difficult to determine which statements are costly. The `line_profiler` module is a third-party module that is available on PyPI and can be installed by following the instructions at `https://github.com/rkern/line_profiler`.

In order to use `line_profiler`, we need to apply a `@profile` decorator to the functions we intend to monitor. Note that you don't have to import the `profile` function from another module as it gets injected into the global namespace when running the `kernprof.py` profiling script. To produce profiling output for our program, we need to add the `@profile` decorator to the `evolve` function, as follows:

```
@profile
def evolve(self, dt):
    # code
```

The `kernprof.py` script will produce an output file and print the result of the profiling on the standard output. We should run the script with two options, as follows:

- `-l` to use the `line_profiler` function
- `-v` to immediately print the results on screen

The usage of `kernprof.py` is illustrated in the following line of code:

```
$ kernprof.py -l -v simul.py
```

It is also possible to run the profiler in an IPython shell for interactive editing. You should first load the `line_profiler` extension that will provide the `lprun` magic command. Using that command, you can avoid adding the `@profile` decorator, as illustrated in the following screenshot:

```
        IPython: chapter1/codes

In [1]: %load_ext line_profiler

In [2]: from simul import benchmark, ParticleSimulator

In [3]: %lprun -f ParticleSimulator.evolve benchmark()
Timer unit: 1e-06 s

Total time: 8.66675 s
File: /home/gabriele/workspace/hiperf/chapter1/codes/simul.py
Function: evolve at line 21

Line #      Hits         Time  Per Hit   % Time  Line Contents
==============================================================
    21                                           def evolve(self, dt):
    22           1            2      2.0      0.0      timestep = 0.00001
    23           1            4      4.0      0.0      nsteps = int(dt/timestep)
    24
    25       10001        12561      1.3      0.1      for i in range(nsteps):
    26     1010000       867457      0.9     10.0          for p in self.particles:
    27
    28     1000000      1859312      1.9     21.5              norm = (p.x**2 + p.y**2)**0.5
    29     1000000       972028      1.0     11.2              v_x = (-p.y)/norm
    30     1000000       921008      0.9     10.6              v_y = p.x/norm
    31
    32     1000000       982441      1.0     11.3              d_x = timestep * p.ang_vel * v_x
    33     1000000       974838      1.0     11.2              d_y = timestep * p.ang_vel * v_y
    34
    35     1000000      1058183      1.1     12.2              p.x += d_x
    36     1000000      1018915      1.0     11.8              p.y += d_y

In [4]:
```

Figure 1.7 – Using line_profiler within IPython

The output is quite intuitive and is divided into six columns, as follows:

- `Line #`: The number of the line that was run
- `Hits`: The number of times that line was run
- `Time`: The execution time of the line in microseconds (`Time`)
- `Per Hit`: Time/hits
- `% Time`: Fraction of the total time spent executing that line
- `Line Contents`: The content of the line

By looking at the **% Time** column, we can get a pretty good idea of where the time is spent. In this case, there are a few statements in the `for` loop body with a cost of around 10-20 percent each.

Optimizing our code

Now that we have identified where exactly our application is spending most of its time, we can make some changes and assess the resulting improvement in performance.

There are different ways to tune up our pure Python code. The way that typically produces the most significant results is to improve the *algorithms* used. In this case, instead of calculating the velocity and adding small steps, it will be more efficient (and correct, as it is not an approximation) to express the equations of motion in terms of radius, r, and angle, `alpha`, (instead of x and y), and then calculate the points on a circle using the following equation:

```
x = r * cos(alpha)
y = r * sin(alpha)
```

Another optimization method lies in minimizing the number of instructions. For example, we can precalculate the `timestep * p.ang_vel` factor that doesn't change with time. We can exchange the loop order (first, we iterate on particles, then we iterate on time steps) and put the calculation of the factor outside the loop on the particles.

The line-by-line profiling also showed that even simple assignment operations can take a considerable amount of time. For example, the following statement takes more than 10 percent of the total time:

```
v_x = (-p.y)/norm
```

We can improve the performance of the loop by reducing the number of assignment operations performed. To do that, we can avoid intermediate variables by rewriting the expression into a single, slightly more complex statement (note that the right-hand side gets evaluated completely before being assigned to the variables), as follows:

```
p.x, p.y = p.x - t_x_ang*p.y/norm, p.y + t_x_ang *
p.x/norm
```

This leads to the following code:

```
def evolve_fast(self, dt):
    timestep = 0.00001
    nsteps = int(dt/timestep)

    # Loop order is changed
    for p in self.particles:
        t_x_ang = timestep * p.ang_vel
        for i in range(nsteps):
            norm = (p.x**2 + p.y**2)**0.5
            p.x, p.y = (p.x - t_x_ang * p.y/norm,
                        p.y + t_x_ang * p.x/norm)
```

After applying the changes, we should verify that the result is still the same by running our test. We can then compare the execution times using our benchmark, as follows:

```
$ time python simul.py # Performance Tuned
real    0m0.756s
user    0m0.714s
sys     0m0.036s

$ time python simul.py # Original
real    0m0.863s
user    0m0.831s
sys     0m0.028s
```

As you can see, we obtained only a modest increment in speed by making a pure Python micro-optimization.

Using the dis module

In this section, we will dig into the Python internals to estimate the performance of individual statements. In the CPython interpreter, Python code is first converted to an intermediate representation, the **bytecode**, and then executed by the Python interpreter.

To inspect how the code is converted to bytecode, we can use the dis Python module (dis stands for **disassemble**). Its usage is really simple; all we need to do is call the dis.dis function on the ParticleSimulator.evolve method, like this:

```
import dis
from simul import ParticleSimulator
dis.dis(ParticleSimulator.evolve)
```

This will print, for each line in the function, a list of bytecode instructions. For example, the v_x = (-p.y)/norm statement is expanded in the following set of instructions:

29	85	LOAD_FAST	5 (p)
	88	LOAD_ATTR	4 (y)
	91	UNARY_NEGATIVE	
	92	LOAD_FAST	6 (norm)
	95	BINARY_TRUE_DIVIDE	
	96	STORE_FAST	7 (v_x)

LOAD_FAST loads a reference of the p variable onto the stack and LOAD_ATTR loads the y attribute of the item present on top of the stack. The other instructions, UNARY_ NEGATIVE and BINARY_TRUE_DIVIDE, simply do arithmetic operations on top-of-stack items. Finally, the result is stored in v_x (STORE_FAST).

By analyzing the dis output, we can see that the first version of the loop produces 51 bytecode instructions, while the second gets converted into 35 instructions.

The dis module helps discover how the statements get converted and serves mainly as an exploration and learning tool of the Python bytecode representation. For a more comprehensive introduction and discussion on the Python bytecode, refer to the *Further reading* section at the end of this chapter.

To improve our performance even further, we can keep trying to figure out other approaches to reduce the number of instructions. It's clear, however, that this approach is ultimately limited by the speed of the Python interpreter, and it is probably not the right tool for the job. In the following chapters, we will see how to speed up interpreter-limited calculations by executing fast specialized versions written in a lower-level language (such as C or Fortran).

Profiling memory usage with memory_profiler

In some cases, high memory usage constitutes an issue. For example, if we want to handle a huge number of particles, we will incur a memory overhead due to the creation of many `Particle` instances.

The `memory_profiler` module summarizes, in a way similar to `line_profiler`, the memory usage of a process.

The `memory_profiler` package is also available on PyPI. You should also install the `psutil` module (`https://github.com/giampaolo/psutil`) as an optional dependency that will make `memory_profiler` considerably faster.

Just as with `line_profiler`, `memory_profiler` also requires the instrumentation of the source code by placing a `@profile` decorator on the function we intend to monitor. In our case, we want to analyze the `benchmark` function.

We can slightly change `benchmark` to instantiate a considerable amount (`100000`) of `Particle` instances and decrease the simulation time, as follows:

```
def benchmark_memory():
    particles = [
                Particle(uniform(-1.0, 1.0),
                         uniform(-1.0, 1.0),
                         uniform(-1.0, 1.0))
                for i in range(100000)
        ]

    simulator = ParticleSimulator(particles)
    simulator.evolve(0.001)
```

We can use `memory_profiler` from an IPython shell through the `%mprun` magic command, as shown in the following screenshot:

```
IPython: chapter1/codes

IPython 5.1.0 -- An enhanced Interactive Python.
?            -> Introduction and overview of IPython's features.
%quickref -> Quick reference.
help         -> Python's own help system.
object?    -> Details about 'object', use 'object??' for extra details.

In [1]: %load_ext memory_profiler

In [2]: from simul import benchmark_memory

In [3]: %mprun -f benchmark_memory benchmark_memory()
Filename: /home/gabriele/workspace/hiperf/chapter1/codes/simul.py

Line #     Mem usage     Increment    Line Contents
================================================================
   142     37.8 MiB      0.0 MiB     def benchmark_memory():
   143     61.5 MiB     23.7 MiB         particles = [Particle(uniform(-1.0, 1.0),
   144                                                  uniform(-1.0, 1.0),
   145                                                  uniform(-1.0, 1.0))
   146     61.5 MiB      0.0 MiB                        for i in range(100000)]
   147
   148     61.5 MiB      0.0 MiB         simulator = ParticleSimulator(particles)
   149     61.5 MiB      0.0 MiB         simulator.evolve(0.001)

In [4]:
```

Figure 1.8 – Output from memory_profiler

It is possible to run `memory_profiler` from the shell using the `mprof run` command after adding the `@profile` decorator.

From the `Increment` column, we can see that 100,000 `Particle` objects take `23.7 MiB` of memory.

1 **mebibyte** (**MiB**) is equivalent to 1,048,576 bytes. It is different from 1 **megabyte** (**MB**), which is equivalent to 1,000,000 bytes.

We can use `__slots__` on the `Particle` class to reduce its memory footprint. This feature saves some memory by avoiding storing the variables of the instance in an internal dictionary. This strategy, however, has a small limitation—it prevents the addition of attributes other than the ones specified in `__slots__`. You can see this feature in use in the following code snippet:

```python
class Particle:
    __slots__ = ('x', 'y', 'ang_vel')

    def __init__(self, x, y, ang_vel):
        self.x = x
```

```
        self.y = y
        self.ang_vel = ang_vel
```

We can now rerun our benchmark to assess the change in memory consumption. The result is displayed in the following screenshot:

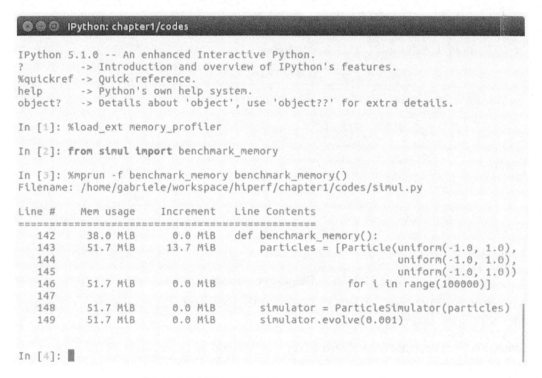

Figure 1.9 – Improvement in memory consumption

By rewriting the Particle class using __slots__, we can save about 10 MiB of memory.

Summary

In this chapter, we introduced the basic principles of optimization and applied those principles to a test application. When optimizing an application, the first thing to do is test and identify the bottlenecks in the application. We saw how to write and time a benchmark using the time Unix command, the Python timeit module, and the full-fledged pytest-benchmark package. We learned how to profile our application using cProfile, line_profiler, and memory_profiler, and how to analyze and navigate the profiling data graphically with KCachegrind.

Speed is undoubtedly an important component of any modern software. The techniques we have learned in this chapter will allow you to systematically tackle the problem of making your Python programs more efficient from different angles. Further, we have seen that these tasks can take advantage of Python built-in/native packages and do not require any special external tools.

In the next chapter, we will explore how to improve performance using algorithms and data structures available in the Python standard library. We will cover scaling and sample usage of several data structures, and learn techniques such as caching and memorization. We will also introduce Big O notation, which is a common computer science tool to analyze the running time of algorithms and data structures.

Questions

1. Arrange the following three items in order of importance when building a software application: correctness (the program does what it is supposed to do), efficiency (the program is optimized in speed and memory management), and functionality (the program runs).

2. How could `assert` statements be used in Python to check for the correctness of a program?

3. What is a benchmark in the context of optimizing a software program?

4. How could `timeit` magic commands be used in Python to estimate the speed of a piece of code?

5. List three different types of information that are recorded and returned by `cProfile` (included as output columns) in the context of profiling a program.

6. On a high level, what is the role of the `dis` module in optimization?

7. In the `exercise.py` file, we write a simple function, `close()`, that checks whether a pair of particles are close to each other (with 1e-5 tolerance). In `benchmark()`, we randomly initialize two particles and call `close()` after running the simulation. Make a guess of what takes most of the execution time in `close()`, and profile the function via `benchmark()` using `cProfile`; does the result confirm your guess?

Further reading

- Profilers in Python: `https://docs.python.org/3/library/profile.html`

- Using PyCharm's profiler: `https://www.jetbrains.com/help/pycharm/profiler.html`

- A beginner-friendly introduction to bytecode in Python: `https://opensource.com/article/18/4/introduction-python-bytecode`

2
Pure Python Optimizations

As mentioned in the previous chapter, one of the most effective ways of improving the performance of applications is through the use of better algorithms and data structures. The Python standard library provides a large variety of ready-to-use algorithms and data structures that can be directly incorporated into your applications. With the tools learned from this chapter, you will be able to use the right algorithm for the task and achieve massive speed gains.

Even though many algorithms have been around for quite a while, they are especially relevant in today's world as we continuously produce, consume, and analyze ever-increasing amounts of data. Buying a larger server or micro-optimizing can work for some time, but achieving better scaling through algorithmic improvement can solve the problem once and for all.

In this chapter, we will learn how to achieve better scaling using standard algorithms and data structures. More advanced use cases where we take advantage of third-party libraries will also be covered. We will also learn about tools to implement caching, a technique used to achieve faster response times by sacrificing some space in memory or on disk.

The list of topics to be covered in this chapter is as follows:

- Using the right algorithms and data structures
- Improved efficiency with caching and memoization
- Efficient iteration with comprehensions and generators

Technical requirements

You will find the code files for this chapter here: `https://github.com/ PacktPublishing/Advanced-Python-Programming-Second-Edition/ tree/main/Chapter02`.

Using the right algorithms and data structures

Algorithmic improvements are especially effective in increasing performance because they typically allow the application to scale better with increasingly large inputs.

Algorithm running times can be classified according to their computational complexity, a characterization of the resources required to perform a task.

Such classification is expressed through the *Big O notation*, an upper bound on the operations required to execute the task, which usually depends on the input size. Specifically, Big O notation describes how the runtime or memory requirement of an algorithm grows in terms of the input size. For this reason, a lower Big O denotes a more efficient algorithm, which is what we aim for.

For example, incrementing each element of a list can be implemented using a `for` loop, as follows:

```
input = list(range(10))
for i, _ in enumerate(input):
    input[i] += 1
```

If the operation does not depend on the size of the input (for example, accessing the first element of a list), the algorithm is said to take constant, or $O(1)$, time. This means that, no matter how much data we have, the time to run the algorithm will always be the same.

In this simple algorithm, the `input[i] += 1` operation will be repeated 10 times, which is the size of the input. If we double the size of the input array, the number of operations will increase proportionally. Since the number of operations is proportional to the input size, this algorithm is said to take $O(N)$ time, where N is the size of the input array.

In some instances, the running time may depend on the structure of the input (for example, if the collection is sorted or contains many duplicates). In these cases, an algorithm may have different best-case, average-case, and worst-case running times. Unless stated otherwise, the running times presented in this chapter are considered to be average running times.

In this section, we will examine the running times of algorithms and data structures that are implemented in the Python standard library and understand how improving running times results in massive gains and allows us to solve large-scale problems with elegance.

You can find the code used to run the benchmarks in this chapter in the `Algorithms.ipynb` notebook, which can be opened using *Jupyter*.

First, we will examine **lists** and **deques**.

Lists and deques

Python lists are ordered collections of elements and, in Python, are implemented as resizable arrays. An **array** is a basic data structure that consists of a series of contiguous memory locations, and each location contains a reference to a Python object.

Lists shine in accessing, modifying, and appending elements. Accessing or modifying an element involves fetching the object reference from the appropriate position of the underlying array and has $O(1)$ complexity. Appending an element is also very fast. When an empty list is created, an array of fixed size is allocated and, as we insert elements, the slots in the array are gradually filled up. Once all the slots are occupied, the list needs to increase the size of its underlying array, thus triggering a memory reallocation that can take $O(N)$ time. Nevertheless, those memory allocations are infrequent, and the time complexity for the append operation is referred to as amortized $O(1)$ time.

The list operations that may have efficiency problems are those that add or remove elements at the beginning (or somewhere in the middle) of the list. When an item is inserted or removed from the beginning of a list, all the subsequent elements of the array need to be shifted by a position, thus taking $O(N)$ time.

In the following table, the timings for different operations on a list of 10,000 size are shown; you can see how insertion and removal performances vary quite dramatically if performed at the beginning or the end of the list:

Code	N=10000 (µs)	N=20000 (µs)	N=30000 (µs)	Time
list.pop()	0.50	0.59	0.58	O(1)
list.pop(0)	4.20	8.36	12.09	O(N)
list.append(1)	0.43	0.45	0.46	O(1)
list.insert(0, 1)	6.20	11.97	17.41	O(N)

Table 1.1 – The speed of different list operations

In some cases, it is necessary to efficiently perform the insertion or removal of elements both at the beginning and the end of the collection. Python provides a data structure with those properties in the collections.deque class. The word *deque* stands for **double-ended queue** because this data structure is designed to efficiently put and remove elements at the beginning and the end of the collection, as it is in the case of queues. In Python, deques are implemented as doubly linked lists.

Deques, in addition to pop and append, expose the popleft and appendleft methods that have O(1) running time:

Code	N=10000 (µs)	N=20000 (µs)	N=30000 (µs)	Time
deque.pop()	0.41	0.47	0.51	O(1)
deque.popleft()	0.39	0.51	0.47	O(1)
deque.append(1)	0.42	0.48	0.50	O(1)
deque.appendleft(1)	0.38	0.47	0.51	O(1)

Table 1.2 – The speed of different deque operations

Despite these advantages, deques should not be used to replace regular lists in most cases. The efficiency gained by the appendleft and popleft operations comes at a cost – accessing an element in the middle of a deque is an O(N) operation, as shown in the following table:

Code	N=10000 (µs)	N=20000 (µs)	N=30000 (µs)	Time
deque[0]	0.37	0.41	0.45	O(1)
deque[N - 1]	0.37	0.42	0.43	O(1)
deque[int(N / 2)]	1.14	1.71	2.48	O(N)

Table 1.3 – The inefficiency of deques in accessing the middle element

Searching for an item in a list is generally an $O(N)$ operation and is performed using the `list.index` method. A simple way to speed up searches in lists is to keep the array sorted and perform a binary search using the `bisect` module.

The `bisect` module allows fast searches on sorted arrays. The `bisect.bisect` function can be used on a sorted list to find the index to place an element while maintaining the array in sorted order. In the following example, we can see that if we want to insert the 3 element in the array while keeping `collection` in sorted order, we should put 3 in the third position (which corresponds to index 2):

```
insert bisect
collection = [1, 2, 4, 5, 6]
bisect.bisect(collection, 3)
# Result: 2
```

This function uses the binary search algorithm that has $O(log(N))$ running time. Such a running time is exceptionally fast and, basically, means that your running time will increase by a constant amount every time you *double* your input size. This means that if, for example, your program takes 1 second to run on an input of 1000 size, it will take 2 seconds to process an input of 2000 size, 3 seconds to process an input of 4000 size, and so on. If you had 100 seconds, you could theoretically process an input of 10^33 size, which is larger than the number of atoms in your body!

If the value we are trying to insert is already present in the list, the `bisect.bisect` function will return the location *after* the already present value. Therefore, we can use the `bisect.bisect_left` variant, which returns the correct index in the following way (taken from the module documentation at `https://docs.python.org/3.5/library/bisect.html`):

```
def index_bisect(a, x):
    'Locate the leftmost value exactly equal to x'
    i = bisect.bisect_left(a, x)
    if i != len(a) and a[i] == x:
    return i
    raise ValueError
```

In the following table, you can see how the running time of the `bisect` solution is barely affected by these input sizes, making it a suitable solution when searching through very large collections:

Code	N=10000 (µs)	N=20000 (µs)	N=30000 (µs)	Time
`list.index(a)`	87.55	171.06	263.17	$O(N)$
`index_bisect(list, a)`	3.16	3.20	4.71	$O(\log(N))$

Table 1.4 – The efficiency of the bisect function

Dictionaries

Dictionaries are extremely versatile and extensively used in the Python language, for example, in package-, module-, and class-level namespaces, as well as object and class annotations. Dictionaries are implemented as hash maps and are very good at element insertion, deletion, and access; all these operations have an average $O(1)$ time complexity.

> **Important Note**
>
> In Python versions up to 3.5, dictionaries are *unordered collections*. Since Python 3.6, dictionaries are capable of maintaining their elements by order of insertion.

Hash map

A **hash map** is a data structure that associates a set of key-value pairs. The principle behind hash maps is to assign a specific index to each key so that its associated value can be stored in an array. The index can be obtained through the use of a `hash` function; Python implements `hash` functions for several data types. As a demonstration, the generic function to obtain hash codes is `hash`. In the following example, we show you how to obtain the hash code when given the `"hello"` string:

```
hash("hello")
# Result: -1182655621190490452


# To restrict the number to be a certain range you can
use
# the modulo (%) operator
hash("hello") % 10
# Result: 8
```

Hash maps can be tricky to implement because they need to handle collisions that happen when two different objects have the same hash code. However, all the complexity is elegantly hidden behind the implementation and the default collision resolution works well in most real-world scenarios.

The access to, insertion, and removal of an item in a dictionary scales as $O(1)$ with the size of the dictionary. However, note that the computation of the hash function still needs to happen and, for strings, the computation scales with the length of the string. As string keys are usually relatively small, this doesn't constitute a problem in practice.

A dictionary can be used to efficiently count unique elements in a list. In this example, we define the counter_dict function that takes a list and returns a dictionary containing the number of occurrences of each value in the list:

```python
def counter_dict(items):
    counter = {}
    for item in items:
        if item not in counter:
            counter[item] = 1
        else:
            counter[item] += 1
    return counter
```

The code can be somewhat simplified using collections.defaultdict, which can be used to produce dictionaries where each new key is automatically assigned a default value. In the following code, the defaultdict(int) call produces a dictionary where every new element is automatically assigned a zero value and can be used to streamline the counting:

```python
from collections import defaultdict
def counter_defaultdict(items):
    counter = defaultdict(int)
    for item in items:
        counter[item] += 1
    return counter
```

The `collections` module also includes a `Counter` class that can be used for the same purpose with a single line of code:

```
from collections import Counter
counter = Counter(items)
```

Speed-wise, all these ways of counting have the same time complexity, but the `Counter` implementation is the most efficient, as shown in the following table:

Code	N=1000 (μs)	N=2000 (μs)	N=3000 (μs)	Time
Counter(items)	51.48	96.63	140.26	O(N)
counter_dict(items)	111.96	197.13	282.79	O(N)
counter_defaultdict(items)	120.90	238.27	359.60	O(N)

Table 1.5 – The different methods of computing counters

Building an in-memory search index using a hash map

Dictionaries can be used to quickly search for a word in a list of documents, similar to a search engine. In this subsection, we will learn how to build an inverted index based on a dictionary of lists. Let's say we have a collection of four documents:

```
docs = ["the cat is under the table",
        "the dog is under the table",
        "cats and dogs smell roses",
        "Carla eats an apple"]
```

A simple way to retrieve all the documents that match a query is to scan each document and test for the presence of a word. For example, if we want to look up the documents where the word `table` appears, we can employ the following filtering operation:

```
matches = [doc for doc in docs if "table" in doc]
```

This approach is simple and works well when we have one-off queries; however, if we need to query the collection very often, it can be beneficial to optimize querying time. Since the per-query cost of the linear scan is O(N), you can imagine that better scaling will allow us to handle much larger document collections.

A better strategy is to spend some time preprocessing the documents so that they are easier to find at query time. We can build a structure, called the **inverted index**, that associates each word in our collection with the list of documents where that word is present. In our earlier example, the word `"table"` will be associated with the `"the cat is under the table"` and `"the dog is under the table"` documents; they correspond to `0` and `1` indices.

Such a mapping can be implemented by going over our collection of documents and storing in a dictionary the index of the documents where that term appears. The implementation is similar to the `counter_dict` function, except that, instead of incrementing a counter, we are growing the list of documents that match the current term:

```python
# Building an index
index = {}
for i, doc in enumerate(docs):
    # We iterate over each term in the document
    for word in doc.split():
        # We build a list containing the indices
        # where the term appears
        if word not in index:
            index[word] = [i]
        else:
            index[word].append(i)
```

Once we have built our index, doing a query involves a simple dictionary lookup. For example, if we want to return all the documents containing the `table` term, we can simply query the index and retrieve the corresponding documents:

```python
results = index["table"]
result_documents = [docs[i] for i in results]
```

Since all it takes to query our collection is dictionary access, the index can handle queries with $O(1)$ time complexity! Thanks to the inverted index, we are now able to query any number of documents (as long as they fit in memory) in constant time. Needless to say, indexing is a technique widely used to quickly retrieve data, not only in search engines but also in databases and any system that requires fast searches.

> **Important Note**
>
> Building an inverted index is an expensive operation and requires you to encode every possible query. This is a substantial drawback, but the benefits are great, and it may be worthwhile to pay the price in terms of decreased flexibility.

Sets

Sets are unordered collections of elements, with the additional restriction that the elements must be unique. The main use cases where sets are a good choice are membership tests (testing whether an element is present in the collection) and, unsurprisingly, set operations such as union, difference, and intersection.

In Python, sets are implemented using a hash-based algorithm, just like dictionaries; therefore, the time complexities for addition, deletion, and testing for membership scale as $O(1)$ with the size of the collection.

Sets contain only *unique elements*. An immediate use case of sets is the removal of duplicates from a collection, which can be accomplished by simply passing the collection through the `set` constructor, as follows:

```
# create a list that contains duplicates
x = list(range(1000)) + list(range(500))
# the set *x_unique* will contain only
# the unique elements in x
x_unique = set(x)
```

The time complexity for removing duplicates is $O(N)$, as it requires reading the input and putting each element in the set.

Sets offer a number of operations, such as union, intersection, and difference. The union of two sets is a new set containing all the elements of both the sets; the intersection is a new set that contains only the elements in common between the two sets, and the difference is a new set containing the elements of the first set that are not contained in the second set. The time complexities for these operations are shown in the following table. Note that since we have two different input sizes, we will use the letter `S` to indicate the size of the first set (called `s`), and `T` to indicate the size of the second set (called `t`):

Code	Time
`s.union(t)`	$O(S + T)$
`s.intersection(t)`	$O(min(S, T))$
`s.difference(t)`	$O(S)$

Table 1.6 – The running time of set operations

An application of set operations is, for example, Boolean queries. Going back to the inverted index example of the previous subsection, we may want to support queries that include multiple terms. For example, we may want to search for all the documents that contain the words `cat` and `table`. This kind of query can be efficiently computed by taking the intersection between the set of documents containing `cat` and the set of documents containing `table`.

In order to efficiently support those operations, we can change our indexing code so that each term is associated with a set of documents (rather than a list). After applying this change, calculating more advanced queries is a matter of applying the right set operation. In the following code, we show the inverted index based on sets and the query using set operations:

```python
# Building an index using sets
index = {}
for i, doc in enumerate(docs):
    # We iterate over each term in the document
    for word in doc.split():
        # We build a set containing the indices
        # where the term appears
        if word not in index:
            index[word] = {i}
        else:
            index[word].add(i)


# Querying the documents containing both "cat" and
    "table"
index['cat'].intersection(index['table'])
```

Heaps

Heaps are data structures designed to quickly find and extract the maximum (or minimum) value in a collection. A typical use case for heaps is to process a series of incoming tasks in order of maximum priority.

You can theoretically use a sorted list using the tools in the `bisect` module; however, while extracting the maximum value will take $O(1)$ time (using `list.pop`), insertion will still take $O(N)$ time (remember that, even if finding the insertion point takes $O(log(N))$ time, inserting an element in the middle of a list is still an $O(N)$ operation). A heap is a more efficient data structure that allows for the insertion and extraction of maximum values with $O(log(N))$ time complexity.

In Python, heaps are built using the procedures contained in the `heapq` module on an underlying list. For example, if we have a list of 10 elements, we can reorganize it into a heap with the `heapq.heapify` function:

```
import heapq

collection = [10, 3, 3, 4, 5, 6]
heapq.heapify(collection)
```

To perform the insertion and extraction operations on the heap, we can use the `heapq.heappush` and `heapq.heappop` functions. The `heapq.heappop` function will extract the minimum value in the collection in $O(log(N))$ time and can be used in the following way:

```
heapq.heappop(collection)
# Returns: 3
```

Similarly, you can push the 1 integer with the `heapq.heappush` function, as follows:

```
heapq.heappush(collection, 1)
```

Another easy-to-use option is the `queue.PriorityQueue` class, which as a bonus, is thread- and process-safe. The `PriorityQueue` class can be filled up with elements using the `PriorityQueue.put` method, while `PriorityQueue.get` can be used to extract the minimum value in the collection:

```
from queue import PriorityQueue

queue = PriorityQueue()
for element in collection:
```

```
        queue.put(element)
```

```
    queue.get()
    # Returns: 3
```

If the maximum element is required, a simple trick is to multiply each element of the list by -1. In this way, the order of the elements will be inverted. Also, if you want to associate an object (for example, a task to run) with each number (which can represent the priority), you can insert tuples of the (number, object) form; the comparison operator for the tuple will be ordered with respect to its first element, as shown in the following example:

```
    queue = PriorityQueue()
    queue.put((3, "priority 3"))
    queue.put((2, "priority 2"))
    queue.put((1, "priority 1"))
```

```
    queue.get()
    # Returns: (1, "priority 1")
```

Tries

A perhaps less popular data structure, but very useful in practice, is the **trie** (sometimes called **prefix tree**). Tries are extremely fast at matching a list of strings against a prefix. This is especially useful when implementing features such as *search as you type* and *autocompletion*, where the list of available completions is very large and short response times are required.

Unfortunately, Python does not include a trie implementation in its standard library; however, many efficient implementations are readily available through *PyPI*. The one we will use in this subsection is patricia-trie, a single-file, pure Python implementation of trie. As an example, we will use patricia-trie to perform the task of finding the longest prefix in a set of strings (just like autocompletion).

Here, we can demonstrate how fast a trie is able to search through a list of strings. In order to generate a large amount of unique random strings, we can define a function, `random_string`. The `random_string` function will return a string composed of random uppercase characters and, while there is a chance to get duplicates, we can greatly reduce the probability of duplicates to the point of being negligible if we make the string long enough. The implementation of the `random_string` function is shown as follows:

```python
from random import choice
from string import ascii_uppercase

def random_string(length):
  """Produce a random string made of *length* uppercase \
    ascii characters"""
  return ''.join(choice(ascii_uppercase) for i in \
    range(length))
```

We can build a list of random strings and time how fast it searches for a prefix (in our case, the `"AA"` string) using the `str.startswith` function:

```python
strings = [random_string(32) for i in range(10000)]
matches = [s for s in strings if s.startswith('AA')]
```

List comprehension and `str.startwith` are already very optimized operations and, on this small dataset, the search takes only a millisecond or so:

```python
%timeit [s for s in strings if s.startswith('AA')]

1000 loops, best of 3: 1.76 ms per loop
```

Now, let's try using a trie for the same operation. In this example, we will use the `patricia-trie` library that is installable through `pip`. The `patricia.trie` class implements a variant of the trie data structure with an interface similar to a dictionary. We can initialize our trie by creating a dictionary from our list of strings, as follows:

```python
from patricia import trie
strings_dict = {s:0 for s in strings}
# A dictionary where all values are 0
strings_trie = trie(**strings_dict)
```

To query `patricia-trie` for a matching prefix, we can use the `trie.iter` method, which returns an iterator over the matching strings:

```
matches = list(strings_trie.iter('AA'))
```

Now that we know how to initialize and query a trie, we can time the operation:

```
%timeit list(strings_trie.iter('AA'))
10000 loops, best of 3: 60.1 µs per loop
```

The timing for this input size is **60.1 µs**, which is about 30 times faster (1.76 ms = 1760 µs) than linear search! This impressive speedup is because of the better computational complexity of the trie prefix search. Querying a trie has an $O(S)$ time complexity, where S is the length of the longest string in the collection, while the time complexity of a simple linear scan is $O(N)$, where N is the size of the collection.

Note that if we want to return all the prefixes that match, the running time will be proportional to the number of results that match the prefix. Therefore, when designing timing benchmarks, care must be taken to ensure that we are always returning the same number of results.

The scaling properties of a trie versus a linear scan for datasets of different sizes that contains 10 prefix matches are shown in the following table:

Algorithm	N=10000 (µs)	N=20000 (µs)	N=30000 (µs)	Time
Trie	17.12	17.27	17.47	$O(S)$
Linear scan	1978.44	4075.72	6398.06	$O(N)$

Table 1.7 – The running time of a trie versus a linear scan

An interesting fact is that the implementation of `patricia-trie` is actually a single Python file; this clearly shows how simple and powerful a clever algorithm can be. For extra features and performance, other C-optimized trie libraries are also available, such as `datrie` and `marisa-trie`.

At this point, we have considered most of the important data structures that are native to Python. Appropriate use of these data structures will speed up your application by a significant degree. In addition to data structures, there are other computing techniques and concepts that we could utilize in order to make our programs even faster. In the next section, we will take a look at caching and memoization, which are common practices when you expect the same computations to be repeated multiple times.

Improved efficiency with caching and memoization

Caching is a great technique used to improve the performance of a wide range of applications. The idea behind caching is to store expensive results in a temporary location, called a **cache**, that can be located in memory, on disk, or in a remote location.

Web applications make extensive use of caching. In a web application, it is often the case that multiple users request a certain page at the same time. In this case, instead of recomputing the page for each user, the web application can compute it once and serve the user the already rendered page. Ideally, caching also needs a mechanism for invalidation so that if the page needs to be updated, we can recompute it before serving it again. Intelligent caching allows web applications to handle the increasing number of users with fewer resources. Caching can also be done preemptively, such as the later sections of a video getting buffered when watching a video online.

Caching is also used to improve the performance of certain algorithms. A great example is computing the Fibonacci sequence. Since computing the next number in the Fibonacci sequence requires the previous number in the sequence, you can store and reuse previous results, dramatically improving the running time. Storing and reusing the results of the previous function calls in an application is usually termed **memoization** and is one of the forms of caching. Several other algorithms can take advantage of memoization to gain impressive performance improvements, and this programming technique is commonly referred to as **dynamic programming**, where you aim to solve a large problem by breaking it into smaller ones.

The benefits of caching, however, do not come for free. What we are actually doing is sacrificing some space to improve the speed of the application. Additionally, if the cache is stored in a location on the network, we may incur transfer costs and the general time needed for communication. You should evaluate when it is convenient to use a cache and how much space you are willing to trade for an increase in speed.

Given the usefulness of this technique, the Python standard library includes a simple in-memory cache out of the box in the `functools` module. The `functools.lru_cache` decorator can be used to easily cache the results of a function.

In the following example, we create a function, `sum2`, that prints a statement and returns the sum of two numbers. By running the function twice, you can see that the first time the `sum2` function is executed, the `"Calculating ..."` string is produced, while the second time, the result is returned without running the function:

```
from functools import lru_cache


@lru_cache()
```

```
def sum2(a, b):
    print("Calculating {} + {}".format(a, b))
    return a + b

print(sum2(1, 2))
# Output:
# Calculating 1 + 2
# 3

print(sum2(1, 2))
# Output:
# 3
```

The `lru_cache` decorator also provides other basic features. To restrict the size of the cache, you can set the number of elements that we intend to maintain through the `max_size` argument. If we want our cache size to be unbounded, we can specify a value of `None`. An example of `max_size` usage is shown here:

```
@lru_cache(max_size=16)
def sum2(a, b):
    ...
```

In this way, as we execute `sum2` with different arguments, the cache will reach a maximum size of `16` and, as we keep requesting more calculations, new values will replace older values in the cache. The `lru` prefix originates from this strategy, which means *least recently used*.

The `lru_cache` decorator also adds extra functionalities to the decorated function. For example, it is possible to examine the cache performance using the `cache_info` method, and it is possible to reset the cache using the `cache_clear` method, as follows:

```
sum2.cache_info()
# Output: CacheInfo(hits=0, misses=1, maxsize=128,
    currsize=1)
sum2.cache_clear()
```

As an example, we can see how a problem, such as computing the Fibonacci series, may benefit from caching. We can define a `fibonacci` function and time its execution:

```
def fibonacci(n):
    if n < 1:
        return 1
    else:
        return fibonacci(n - 1) + fibonacci(n - 2)


# Non-memoized version
%timeit fibonacci(20)
100 loops, best of 3: 5.57 ms per loop
```

The execution takes 5.57 milliseconds, which is very long. The scaling of the function written in this way has poor performance; the previously computed Fibonacci sequences are not reused, causing this algorithm to have an exponential scaling of roughly $O(2N)$.

Caching can improve this algorithm by storing and reusing the already-computed Fibonacci numbers. To implement the cached version, it is sufficient to apply the `lru_cache` decorator to the original `fibonacci` function. Also, to design a proper benchmark, we need to ensure that a new cache is instantiated for every run; to do this, we can use the `timeit.repeat` function, as shown in the following example:

```
import timeit
setup_code = '''
from functools import lru_cache
from __main__ import fibonacci
fibonacci_memoized = lru_cache(maxsize=None)(fibonacci)'''

results = timeit.repeat('fibonacci_memoized(20)',
                        setup=setup_code,
                        repeat=1000,
                        number=1)
print("Fibonacci took {:.2f} us".format(min(results)))
# Output: Fibonacci took 0.01 us
```

Even though we changed the algorithm by adding a simple decorator, the running time now is much less than a microsecond. The reason is, thanks to caching, we now have a linear time algorithm instead of an exponential one.

The `lru_cache` decorator can be used to implement simple in-memory caching in your application. For more advanced use cases, third-party modules can be used for more powerful implementation and on-disk caching.

Joblib

A simple library that, among other things, provides a simple on-disk cache is `joblib`. The package can be used in a similar way as `lru_cache`, except that the results will be stored on disk and will persist between runs.

The `joblib` module can be installed from PyPI using the `pip install joblib` command.

The `joblib` module provides the `Memory` class, which can be used to memoize functions using the `Memory.cache` decorator:

```
from joblib import Memory
memory = Memory(cachedir='/path/to/cachedir')


@memory.cache
def sum2(a, b):
    return a + b
```

The function will behave similarly to `lru_cache`, with the exception that the results will be stored on disk in the directory specified by the `cachedir` argument during `Memory` initialization. Additionally, the cached results will persist over subsequent runs!

The `Memory.cache` method also allows limiting recomputation to only when certain arguments change, and the resulting decorated function supports basic functionalities to clear and analyze the cache.

Perhaps the best `joblib` feature is, thanks to intelligent hashing algorithms, providing efficient memoization of functions that operate on `numpy` arrays, which is particularly useful in scientific and engineering applications.

At this point, we have seen that by using caching and memoization, our program can reuse computations in an efficient way. Another common strategy to improve running time is to utilize specifically designed techniques as appropriate. In the next section, we will see how we can take advantage of comprehensions and generators when working with Python loops.

Efficient iteration with comprehensions and generators

In this section, we will explore a few simple strategies to speed up Python loops using **comprehensions** and **generators**. In Python, comprehension and generator expressions are fairly optimized operations and should be preferred in place of explicit `for` loops, as they are designed to avoid many unnecessary computational overheads during their construction. Another reason to use this construct is readability; even if the speedup over a standard loop is modest, the comprehension and generator syntax is more compact and (most of the time) more intuitive.

In the following example, we can see that both the list comprehension and generator expressions are faster than an explicit loop when combined with the `sum` function:

```python
def loop():
    res = []
    for i in range(100000):
        res.append(i * i)
    return sum(res)


def comprehension():
    return sum([i * i for i in range(100000)])


def generator():
    return sum(i * i for i in range(100000))


%timeit loop()
100 loops, best of 3: 16.1 ms per loop
%timeit comprehension()
100 loops, best of 3: 10.1 ms per loop
%timeit generator()
100 loops, best of 3: 12.4 ms per loop
```

Just like lists, it is possible to use `dict` comprehension to build dictionaries slightly more efficiently and compactly, as shown in the following code:

```python
def loop():
    res = {}
    for i in range(100000):
```

```
            res[i] = i
        return res


def comprehension():
    return {i: i for i in range(100000)}
%timeit loop()
100 loops, best of 3: 13.2 ms per loop
%timeit comprehension()
100 loops, best of 3: 12.8 ms per loop
```

Efficient looping (especially in terms of memory) can be implemented using iterators and functions such as `filter` and `map`. As an example, consider the problem of applying a series of operations to a list using list comprehension and then taking the maximum value:

```
def map_comprehension(numbers):
    a = [n * 2 for n in numbers]
    b = [n ** 2 for n in a]
    c = [n ** 0.33 for n in b]
    return max(c)
```

The problem with this approach is that for every list comprehension, we are allocating a new list, increasing memory usage. Instead of using list comprehension, we can employ generators. Generators are objects that, when iterated upon, compute a value on the fly and return the result.

For example, the `map` function takes two arguments – a function and an iterator – and returns a generator that applies the function to every element of the collection. The important point is that the operation happens only *while we are iterating*, and not when `map` is invoked!

We can rewrite the previous function using `map` and by creating intermediate generators, rather than lists, thus saving memory by computing the values on the fly:

```
def map_normal(numbers):
    a = map(lambda n: n * 2, numbers)
    b = map(lambda n: n ** 2, a)
    c = map(lambda n: n ** 0.33, b)
    return max(c)
```

We can profile the memory of the two solutions using the `memory_profiler` extension from an IPython session. The extension provides a small utility, `%memit`, that will help us evaluate the memory usage of a Python statement in a way similar to `%timeit`, as illustrated in the following details:

```
%load_ext memory_profiler
numbers = range(1000000)
%memit map_comprehension(numbers)
peak memory: 166.33 MiB, increment: 102.54 MiB
%memit map_normal(numbers)
peak memory: 71.04 MiB, increment: 0.00 MiB
```

As you can see, the memory used by the first version is `102.54 MiB`, while the second version consumes `0.00 MiB`! For those who are interested, more functions that return generators can be found in the `itertools` module, which provides a set of utilities designed to handle common iteration patterns.

Summary

Algorithmic optimization can improve how your application scales as we process increasingly large data. In this chapter, we demonstrated use cases and running times of the most common data structures available in Python, such as lists, deques, dictionaries, heaps, and tries. We also covered caching, a technique that can be used to trade some space, in memory or on disk, in exchange for the increased responsiveness of an application. We also demonstrated how to get modest speed gains by replacing `for` loops with fast constructs, such as list comprehensions and generator expressions.

Overall, we have seen that by utilizing a specifically designed data structure or technique that is appropriate in certain situations, the efficiency of our program can be greatly improved. The topics covered in this chapter offer us the ability to do just that across a wide range of use cases.

In the subsequent chapters, we will learn how to improve performance further using numerical libraries such as `numpy` and how to write extension modules in a lower-level language with the help of *Cython*.

Questions

1. Identify the best/most appropriate from the data structures covered in this chapter concerning the following use cases:

    A. Mapping items to another *set* of items (*set* being used in the most general sense)

    B. Accessing, modifying, and appending elements

    C. Maintaining a collection of unique elements

    D. Keeping track of the minimum/maximum of a *set* (in the most general sense)

    E. Appending and removing elements at the endpoints of a *sequence* (in the most general sense).

    F. Fast searching according to some similarity criterion (for example, being used by autocompletion engines).

2. What is the difference between caching and memoization?

3. Why are comprehensions and generators (in most situations) more preferred than explicit `for` loops?

4. Consider the problem of representing a pairwise association between a set of letters and a set of numbers (for example, a → 2, b → 1, c → 3, and so on), where we need to look at what number a given letter is associated with in our application.

    A. Is a list an appropriate data structure for this task, and if not, what is?

    B. What if each number represented the number of instances of a given letter in a text document? What would the best data structure for this task be?

Further reading

- Lazy evaluation in Python: `https://towardsdatascience.com/what-is-lazy-evaluation-in-python-9efb1d3bfed0`

- The `yield` statement in Python: `https://realpython.com/introduction-to-python-generators/`

3
Fast Array Operations with NumPy, Pandas, and Xarray

NumPy is the *de facto* standard for scientific computing in Python. It offers flexible multidimensional arrays that allow you to perform fast and concise mathematical calculations.

NumPy provides common data structures and algorithms designed to express complex mathematical operations using a concise syntax. The multidimensional array, `numpy.ndarray`, is internally based on C arrays. Apart from the performance benefits, this choice allows NumPy code to easily interface with the existing C and FORTRAN routines; NumPy helps bridge the gap between Python and the legacy code written using those languages.

In this chapter, we will learn how to create and manipulate NumPy arrays. We will also explore the NumPy broadcasting feature, which is used to rewrite complex mathematical expressions efficiently and succinctly.

pandas is a tool that relies heavily on NumPy and provides additional data structures and algorithms targeted toward data analysis. We will introduce the main pandas features and their usage. We will also learn how to achieve high performance using pandas data structures and vectorized operations.

Both NumPy and pandas are insufficient in many use cases concerning labeled, multidimensional data. The xarray library combines the best features from the other two tools and offers further optimized data processing functionalities. We will discuss the motivation for this tool and study the performance improvements it offers via explicit examples.

In this chapter, we will be covering the following topics:

- Getting started with NumPy
- Rewriting the particle simulator in NumPy
- Reaching optimal performance with numexpr
- Working with database-style data with pandas
- High-performance labeled data with xarray

Technical requirement

The code files for this chapter can be accessed by going to this book's GitHub repository at `https://github.com/PacktPublishing/Advanced-Python-Programming-Second-Edition/Chapter03`.

Getting started with NumPy

The NumPy library revolves around its multidimensional array object, `numpy.ndarray`. NumPy arrays are collections of elements of the same data type; this fundamental restriction allows NumPy to pack the data in a way that allows for high-performance mathematical operations.

Creating arrays

Let's explore NumPy's functionalities by following these steps:

1. You can create NumPy arrays using the `numpy.array` function. It takes a list-like object (or another array) as input and, optionally, a string expressing its data type. You can interactively test array creation using an IPython shell, as follows:

    ```
    import numpy as np
    a = np.array([0, 1, 2])
    ```

2. Every NumPy array has an associated data type that can be accessed using the `dtype` attribute. If we inspect the `a` array, we will find that its `dtype` is `int64`, which stands for 64-bit integer:

```
a.dtype
# Result:
# dtype('int64')
```

3. We may decide to convert those integer numbers into the `float` type. To do this, we can either pass the `dtype` argument at array initialization or cast the array to another data type using the `astype` method. These two ways to select a data type are shown in the following code:

```
a = np.array([1, 2, 3], dtype='float32')
a.astype('float32')
# Result:
# array([ 0.,   1.,   2.], dtype=float32)
```

4. To create an array with two dimensions (an array of arrays), we can perform the required initialization using a nested sequence, as follows:

```
a = np.array([[0, 1, 2], [3, 4, 5]])
print(a)
# Output:
# [[0 1 2]
#  [3 4 5]]
```

5. An array that's created in this way has two dimensions, which are called **axes** in terms of NumPy's jargon. An array that's formed in this way is like a table that contains two rows and three columns. We can access the axes using the `ndarray.shape` attribute:

```
a.shape
# Result:
# (2, 3)
```

6. Arrays can also be reshaped, so long as the product of the shape dimensions is equal to the total number of elements in the array (that is, the total number of elements is conserved). For example, we can reshape an array containing 16 elements in the following ways: `(2, 8)`, `(4, 4)`, or `(2, 2, 4)`. To reshape an array, we can either use the `ndarray.reshape` method or assign a new value to the `ndarray.shape` tuple. The following code illustrates the use of the `ndarray.reshape` method:

```
a = np.array([0, 1, 2, 3, 4, 5, 6, 7, 8,
              9, 10, 11, 12, 13, 14, 15])
a.shape
# Output:
# (16,)


a.reshape(4, 4) # Equivalent: a.shape = (4, 4)
# Output:
# array([[ 0,  1,  2,  3],
#        [ 4,  5,  6,  7],
#        [ 8,  9, 10, 11],
#        [12, 13, 14, 15]])
```

Thanks to this property, you can freely add dimensions of size 1. You can reshape an array with 16 elements to `(16, 1)`, `(1, 16)`, `(16, 1, 1)`, and so on. In the next section, we will extensively use this feature to implement complex operations through *broadcasting*.

7. NumPy provides convenience functions, as shown in the following code, to create arrays filled with zeros, ones, or with no initial value (in this case, their actual value is meaningless and depends on the memory state). Those functions take the array shape as a tuple and, optionally, its `dtype`:

```
np.zeros((3, 3))
np.empty((3, 3))
np.ones((3, 3), dtype='float32')
```

In our examples, we will use the `numpy.random` module to generate random floating-point numbers in the `(0, 1)` interval. `numpy.random.rand` will take a shape and return an array of random numbers with that shape:

```
np.random.rand(3, 3)
```

8. Sometimes, it is convenient to initialize arrays that have the same shape as that of some other array. For that purpose, NumPy provides some handy functions, such as `zeros_like`, `empty_like`, and `ones_like`. These functions can be used as follows:

```
np.zeros_like(a)
np.empty_like(a)
np.ones_like(a)
```

These functions will return arrays with the specified values, whose shapes match exactly with that of array a.

Accessing arrays

The NumPy array interface is, at a shallow level, similar to that of Python lists. NumPy arrays can be indexed using integers and iterated using a `for` loop:

```
A = np.array([0, 1, 2, 3, 4, 5, 6, 7, 8])
A[0]
# Result:
# 0

[a for a in A]
# Result:
# [0, 1, 2, 3, 4, 5, 6, 7, 8]
```

However, explicitly looping over an array is, most of the time, not the most efficient way to access its elements. In this section, we will learn how to take advantage of NumPy's API to fully utilize its efficiency.

Indexing and slicing

Indexing and slicing refer to the act of accessing elements within an array that are at certain locations or satisfy some condition that we are interested in. In NumPy, array elements and sub-arrays can be conveniently accessed by using multiple values separated by commas inside the subscript operator, []. Let's get started:

1. If we take a (3,3) array (an array containing three triplets) and we access the element with an index of 0, we can obtain the first row, as follows:

```
A = np.array([[0, 1, 2], [3, 4, 5], [6, 7, 8]])
A[0]
```

```
# Result:
# array([0, 1, 2])
```

2. We can index the row again by adding another index separated by a comma. To get the second element of the first row, we can use the (0, 1) index. An important observation is that the A[0, 1] notation is shorthand for A[(0, 1)]; that is, we are indexing using a *tuple*! Both versions are shown in the following snippet:

```
A[0, 1]
# Result:
# 1


# Equivalent version using tuple
A[(0, 1)]
```

3. NumPy allows you to slice arrays into multiple dimensions. If we slice on the first dimension, we can obtain a collection of triplets, as follows:

```
A[0:2]
# Result:
# array([[0, 1, 2],
#        [3, 4, 5]])
```

4. If we slice the array again on the second dimension with 0:2, we are extracting the first two elements from the collection of triplets shown earlier. This results in an array whose shape is (2, 2), as shown in the following code:

```
A[0:2, 0:2]
# Result:
# array([[0, 1],
#        [3, 4]])
```

5. Intuitively, you can update the values in the array using both *numerical indexes* and *slices*. An example of this is illustrated in the following code snippet:

```
A[0, 1] = 8
A[0:2, 0:2] = [[1, 1], [1, 1]]
```

6. Indexing with the slicing syntax is very fast because, unlike lists, it doesn't produce a copy of the array. In NumPy's terminology, it returns a *view* of the same memory area. If we take a slice of the original array, and then we change one of its values, the original array will be updated as well. The following code illustrates an example of this feature:

```
a= np.array([1, 1, 1, 1])
a_view = a[0:2]
a_view[0] = 2
print(a)
# Output:
# [2 1 1 1]
```

It is important to be extra careful when mutating NumPy arrays. Since views share data, changing the values of a view can result in hard-to-find bugs. To prevent side effects, you can set the a.flags.writeable = False flag, which will prevent the array or any of its views from being accidentally mutated.

7. Let's look at another example that shows how the slicing syntax can be used in a real-world setting. Let's define an r_i array, as shown in the following line of code, which contains a set of 10 coordinates (x, y). Its shape will be (10, 2):

```
r_i = np.random.rand(10, 2)
```

If you have a hard time distinguishing arrays that differ in the axes order, for example, between an array of shape (10, 2) and shape (2, 10), it is useful to think that every time you say the word *of*, you should introduce a new dimension. An array with 10 elements *of* size two will be (10, 2). Conversely, an array with two elements *of* size 10 will be (2, 10).

A typical operation we may be interested in is extracting the x component from each coordinate. In other words, you want to extract the (0, 0), (1, 0), and (2, 0), items, resulting in an array with a shape of (10,). It is helpful to think that the first index is *moving* while the second one is *fixed* (at 0). With this in mind, we will slice every index on the first axis (the moving one) and take the first element (the fixed one) on the second axis, as shown in the following line of code:

```
x_i = r_i[:, 0]
```

On the other hand, the following expression will keep the first index fixed and the second index moving, returning the first (x, y) coordinate:

```
r_0 = r_i[0, :]
```

Slicing all the indexes over the last axis is optional; using `r_i[0]` has the same effect as using `r_i[0, :]`.

Fancy indexing

NumPy allows you to index an array using another NumPy array made up of either integer or Boolean values. This is a feature called **fancy indexing**:

1. If you index an array (say, a) with another array of integers (say, `idx`), NumPy will interpret the integers as indexes and will return an array containing their corresponding values. If we index an array containing 10 elements with `np.array([0, 2, 3])`, we obtain an array of shape `(3,)` containing the elements at positions 0, 2, and 3. The following code illustrates this concept:

```
a = np.array([9, 8, 7, 6, 5, 4, 3, 2, 1, 0])
idx = np.array([0, 2, 3])
a[idx]
# Result:
# array([9, 7, 6])
```

2. You can use fancy indexing on multiple dimensions by passing an array for each dimension. If we want to extract the `(0, 2)` and `(1, 2)` elements, we have to pack all the indexes acting on the first axis in one array, and the ones acting on the second axis in another. This can be seen in the following code:

```
a = np.array([[0, 1, 2], [3, 4, 5], \
              [6, 7, 8], [9, 10, 11]])
idx1 = np.array([0, 1])
idx2 = np.array([2, 2])
a[idx1, idx2]
```

3. You can also use normal lists as index arrays, but not tuples. For example, the following two statements are equivalent:

```
a[np.array([0, 1])] # is equivalent to
a[[0, 1]]
```

However, if you use a tuple, NumPy will interpret the following statement as an index on multiple dimensions:

```
a[(0, 1)] # is equivalent to
a[0, 1]
```

4. The index arrays are not required to be one-dimensional; we can extract elements from the original array in any shape. For example, we can select elements from the original array to form a (2,2) array, as shown here:

```
idx1 = [[0, 1], [3, 2]]
idx2 = [[0, 2], [1, 1]]
a[idx1, idx2]
# Output:
# array([[ 0,   5],
#        [10,   7]])
```

5. The array slicing and fancy indexing features can be combined. This is useful, for instance, when we want to swap the *x* and *y* columns in a coordinate array. In the following code, the first index will be running over all the elements (a slice) and, for each of those, we extract the element in position 1 (the *y*) first and then the one in position 0 (the *x*):

```
r_i = np.random.rand(10, 2)
r_i[:, [0, 1]] = r_i[:, [1, 0]]
```

6. When the index array is of the bool type, the rules are slightly different. The bool array will act as a *mask*; every element corresponding to True will be extracted and put in the output array. This is shown in the following code:

```
a = np.array([0, 1, 2, 3, 4, 5])
mask = np.array([True, False, True, False, \
    False, False])
a[mask]
# Output:
# array([0, 2])
```

The same rules apply when dealing with multiple dimensions. Furthermore, if the index array has the same shape as the original array, the elements corresponding to True will be selected and put in the resulting array.

7. Indexing in NumPy is a reasonably fast operation. When speed is critical, you can use the slightly faster `numpy.take` and `numpy.compress` functions to squeeze out a little more performance. The first argument of `numpy.take` is the array we want to operate on, while the second is the list of indexes we want to extract. The last argument is `axis`; if this is not provided, the indexes will act on the flattened array; otherwise, they will act along the specified axis:

```
r_i = np.random.rand(100, 2)
idx = np.arange(50) # integers 0 to 50

%timeit np.take(r_i, idx, axis=0)
1000000 loops, best of 3: 962 ns per loop

%timeit r_i[idx]
100000 loops, best of 3: 3.09 us per loop
```

8. The similar but faster version for Boolean arrays is `numpy.compress`, which works in the same way. The use of `numpy.compress` is shown here:

```
In [51]: idx = np.ones(100, dtype='bool') # all
    True values
In [52]: %timeit np.compress(idx, r_i, axis=0)
1000000 loops, best of 3: 1.65 us per loop
In [53]: %timeit r_i[idx]
100000 loops, best of 3: 5.47 us per loop
```

As we can see, `compress` gives us a slight speed improvement, which will prove useful if you are dealing with large-sized arrays.

Broadcasting

The true power of NumPy lies in its fast mathematical operations. The approach that's used by NumPy is to avoid stepping into the Python interpreter by performing element-wise calculations using optimized C code. **Broadcasting** is a clever set of rules that enables fast array calculations for arrays of similar (but not equal!) shapes. Let's see how that goes.

Whenever you perform an arithmetic operation on two arrays (such as a product), if the two operands have the same shape, the operation will be applied in an element-wise fashion. For example, upon multiplying two (2,2) arrays, the operation will be done between pairs of corresponding elements, producing another (2, 2) array, as shown in the following code:

```
A = np.array([[1, 2], [3, 4]])
B = np.array([[5, 6], [7, 8]])
A * B
# Output:
# array([[ 5, 12],
#        [21, 32]])
```

If the shapes of the operands don't match, NumPy will attempt to match them using broadcasting rules. If one of the operands is a *scalar* (for example, a number), it will be applied to every element of the array, as shown in the following code:

```
A * 2
# Output:
# array([[2, 4],
#        [6, 8]])
```

If the operand is another array, NumPy will try to match the shapes starting from the last axis. For example, if we want to combine an array of shape (3, 2) with one of shape (2,), the second array will be repeated three times to generate a (3, 2) array. In other words, the array is *broadcasted* along a dimension to match the shape of the other operand, as shown in the following diagram:

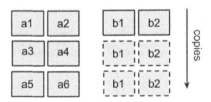

Figure 3.1 – Illustration of array broadcasting

If the shapes don't match – for example, when combining a (3, 2) array with a (2, 2) array – NumPy will throw an exception.

If one of the axis's sizes is 1, the array will be repeated over this axis until the shapes match. To illustrate this point, let's consider that we have an array of the following shape:

```
5, 10, 2
```

Now, let's consider that we want to broadcast it with an array of shape (5, 1, 2); the array will be repeated on the second axis 10 times, as shown here:

```
5, 10, 2
5,  1, 2 → repeated
- - - -
5, 10, 2
```

Earlier, we saw that it is possible to freely reshape arrays to add axes of size 1. Using the numpy.newaxis constant while indexing will introduce an extra dimension. For instance, if we have a (5, 2) array and we want to combine it with one of shape (5, 10, 2), we can add an extra axis in the middle, as shown in the following code, to obtain a compatible (5, 1, 2) array:

```
A = np.random.rand(5, 10, 2)
B = np.random.rand(5, 2)
A * B[:, np.newaxis, :]
```

This feature can be used, for example, to operate on all possible combinations of the two arrays. One of these applications is the *outer product*. Let's consider that we have the following two arrays:

```
a = [a1, a2, a3]
b = [b1, b2, b3]
```

The outer product is a matrix containing the product of all the possible combinations *(i, j)* of the two array elements, as shown in the following snippet:

```
a x b = a1*b1, a1*b2, a1*b3
        a2*b1, a2*b2, a2*b3
        a3*b1, a3*b2, a3*b3
```

To calculate this using NumPy, we will repeat the [a1, a2, a3] elements in one dimension, the [b1, b2, b3] elements in another dimension, and then take their element-wise product, as shown in the following diagram:

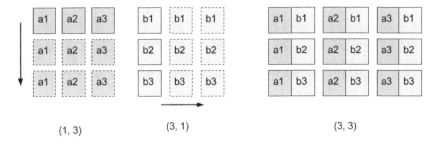

Figure 3.2 – Illustration of an outer product

Using code, our strategy will be to transform the a array from shape (3,) into shape (3, 1), and the b array from shape (3,) into shape (1, 3). These two arrays are broadcasted in the two dimensions and get multiplied together using the following code:

```
AB = a[:, np.newaxis] * b[np.newaxis, :]
```

This operation is very fast and extremely effective as it avoids Python loops and can process a high number of elements at speeds comparable with pure C or FORTRAN code.

Mathematical operations

NumPy includes the most common mathematical operations available for broadcasting by default, ranging from simple algebra to trigonometry, rounding, and logic.

For instance, to take the square root of every element in the array, we can use numpy.sqrt, as shown in the following code:

```
np.sqrt(np.array([4, 9, 16]))
# Result:
# array([2., 3., 4.])
```

The comparison operators are useful when we're trying to filter certain elements based on a condition. Imagine that we have an array of random numbers from 0 to 1, and we want to extract all the numbers greater than 0.5. We can use the > operator on the array to obtain a bool array, as follows:

```
a = np.random.rand(5, 3)
a > 0.3
```

```
# Result:
# array([[ True, False,   True],
#        [ True,  True,   True],
#        [False,  True,   True],
#        [ True,  True, False],
#        [ True,  True, False]], dtype=bool)
```

The resulting `bool` array can then be reused as an index to retrieve the elements that are greater than `0.5`:

```
a[a > 0.5]
print(a[a>0.5])
# Output:
# [ 0.9755  0.5977  0.8287  0.6214  0.5669  0.9553
    0.5894  0.7196  0.9200  0.5781  0.8281 ]
```

NumPy also implements methods such as `ndarray.sum`, which takes the sum of all the elements on an axis. If we have an array of shape `(5, 3)`, we can use the `ndarray.sum` method to sum the elements on the first axis, the second axis, or over all the elements of the array, as illustrated in the following snippet:

```
a = np.random.rand(5, 3)
a.sum(axis=0)
# Result:
# array([ 2.7454,  2.5517,  2.0303])

a.sum(axis=1)
# Result:
# array([ 1.7498,  1.2491,  1.8151,  1.9320,  0.5814])

a.sum() # With no argument operates on flattened array
# Result:
# 7.3275
```

Note that by summing the elements over an axis, we eliminate that axis. From the preceding example, the sum on axis `0` produces an array of shape `(3,)`, while the sum on axis `1` produces an array of shape `(5,)`.

Calculating the norm

We can review the basic concepts illustrated in this section by calculating the *norm* of a set of coordinates. The norm of a pair of coordinates is an important concept in linear algebra and is often interpreted as the magnitude of the corresponding line segment. For a two-dimensional vector, the norm is defined as follows:

```
norm = sqrt(x**2 + y**2)
```

Given an array of 10 coordinates (x, y), we want to find the norm of each coordinate. We can calculate the norm by performing these steps:

1. Square the coordinates, obtaining an array that contains (x**2, y**2) elements.
2. Sum those with numpy.sum over the last axis.
3. Take the square root, element-wise, with numpy.sqrt.

The final expression can be compressed into a single line:

```
r_i = np.random.rand(10, 2)
norm = np.sqrt((r_i ** 2).sum(axis=1))
print(norm)
# Output:
# [ 0.7314   0.9050   0.5063   0.2553   0.0778   0.9143
    1.3245   0.9486   1.010    1.0212]
```

We can verify that this method of calculating norm gives us the correct answer while having compact code.

Rewriting the particle simulator in NumPy

In this section, we will optimize our particle simulator by rewriting some parts of it in NumPy. From the profiling we did in *Chapter 1, Benchmarking and Profiling*, we found that the slowest part of our program is the following loop, which is contained in the ParticleSimulator.evolve method:

```
for i in range(nsteps):
    for p in self.particles:

        norm = (p.x**2 + p.y**2)**0.5
```

```
v_x = (-p.y)/norm
v_y = p.x/norm

d_x = timestep * p.ang_vel * v_x
d_y = timestep * p.ang_vel * v_y

p.x += d_x
p.y += d_y
```

You may have noticed that the body of the loop acts solely on the current particle. If we had an array containing the particle positions and angular speed, we could rewrite the loop using a broadcasted operation. In contrast, the loop's steps depend on the previous step and cannot be parallelized in this way.

So, it is natural to store all the array coordinates in an array of shape (nparticles, 2) and the angular speed in an array of shape (nparticles,), where nparticles is the number of particles. We'll call those arrays r_i and ang_vel_i:

```
r_i = np.array([[p.x, p.y] for p in self.particles])
ang_vel_i = np.array([p.ang_vel for p in \
    self.particles])
```

The velocity direction, which is perpendicular to the vector (x, y), was defined as follows:

```
v_x = -y / norm
v_y = x / norm
```

The norm can be calculated using the strategy illustrated in the *Calculating the norm* section under the *Getting started with NumPy* heading:

```
norm_i = ((r_i ** 2).sum(axis=1))**0.5
```

For the $(-y, x)$ components, we need to swap the x and y columns in r_i and then multiply the first column by -1, as shown in the following code:

```
v_i = r_i[:, [1, 0]] / norm_i
v_i[:, 0] *= -1
```

To calculate the displacement, we need to compute the product of v_i, ang_vel_i, and timestep. Since ang_vel_i is of shape (nparticles,), it needs a new axis to operate with v_i of shape (nparticles, 2). We will do that using numpy.newaxis, as follows:

```
d_i = timestep * ang_vel_i[:, np.newaxis] * v_i
r_i += d_i
```

Outside the loop, we have to update the particle instances with the new coordinates, x and y, as follows:

```
for i, p in enumerate(self.particles):
    p.x, p.y = r_i[i]
```

To summarize, we will implement a method called ParticleSimulator. evolve_numpy and benchmark it against the pure Python version, renamed as ParticleSimulator.evolve_python:

```
def evolve_numpy(self, dt):
    timestep = 0.00001
    nsteps = int(dt/timestep)

    r_i = np.array([[p.x, p.y] for p in self.particles])
    ang_vel_i = np.array([p.ang_vel for p in \
        self.particles])

    for i in range(nsteps):

        norm_i = np.sqrt((r_i ** 2).sum(axis=1))
        v_i = r_i[:, [1, 0]]
        v_i[:, 0] *= -1
        v_i /= norm_i[:, np.newaxis]
        d_i = timestep * ang_vel_i[:, np.newaxis] * v_i
        r_i += d_i

        for i, p in enumerate(self.particles):
            p.x, p.y = r_i[i]
```

We will also update the benchmark to conveniently change the number of particles and the simulation method, as follows:

```python
def benchmark(npart=100, method='python'):
    particles = [Particle(uniform(-1.0, 1.0),
                          uniform(-1.0, 1.0),
                          uniform(-1.0, 1.0))
                            for i in range(npart)]

    simulator = ParticleSimulator(particles)

    if method=='python':
      simulator.evolve_python(0.1)

    elif method == 'numpy':
      simulator.evolve_numpy(0.1)
```

Let's run the benchmark in an IPython session:

```
from simul import benchmark
%timeit benchmark(100, 'python')
1 loops, best of 3: 614 ms per loop
%timeit benchmark(100, 'numpy')
1 loops, best of 3: 415 ms per loop
```

We have made some improvements, but it doesn't look like a huge speed boost. The power of NumPy is revealed when handling big arrays. If we increase the number of particles, we will note a more significant performance boost:

```
%timeit benchmark(1000, 'python')
1 loops, best of 3: 6.13 s per loop
%timeit benchmark(1000, 'numpy')
1 loops, best of 3: 852 ms per loop
```

The plot in the following diagram was produced by running the benchmark with different particle numbers:

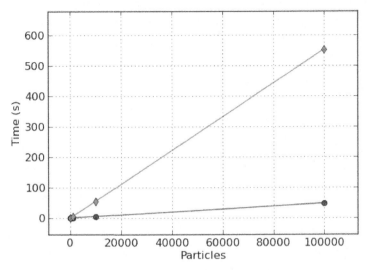

Figure 3.3 – The running time growth of pure Python versus NumPy

The plot shows that both implementations scale linearly with particle size, but the runtime in the pure Python version grows much faster than the NumPy version; at greater sizes, we have a greater NumPy advantage. In general, when using NumPy, you should try to pack things into large arrays and group the calculations using the broadcasting feature.

Reaching optimal performance with numexpr

When handling complex expressions, NumPy stores intermediate results in memory. David M. Cooke wrote a package called numexpr, which optimizes and compiles array expressions on the fly. It works by optimizing the usage of the CPU cache and by taking advantage of multiple processors.

Its usage is generally straightforward and is based on a single function: numexpr. evaluate. The function takes a string containing an array expression as its first argument. The syntax is basically identical to that of NumPy. For example, we can calculate a simple a + b * c expression in the following way:

```
a = np.random.rand(10000)
b = np.random.rand(10000)
c = np.random.rand(10000)
d = ne.evaluate('a + b * c')
```

The `numexpr` package increases performance in almost all cases, but to get a substantial advantage, you should use it with large arrays. An application that involves a large array is the calculation of a *distance matrix*. In a particle system, a distance matrix contains all the possible distances between the particles. To calculate it, we should calculate all the vectors connecting any two particles, `(i,j)`, as follows:

```
x_ij = x_j - x_i
y_ij = y_j - y_i.
```

Then, we must calculate the length of this vector by taking its norm, as shown in the following code:

```
d_ij = sqrt(x_ij**2 + y_ij**2)
```

We can write this in NumPy by employing the usual broadcasting rules (the operation is similar to the outer product):

```
r = np.random.rand(10000, 2)
r_i = r[:, np.newaxis]
r_j = r[np.newaxis, :]
d_ij = r_j - r_i
```

Finally, we must calculate the norm over the last axis using the following line of code:

```
d_ij = np.sqrt((d_ij ** 2).sum(axis=2))
```

Rewriting the same expression using the `numexpr` syntax is extremely easy. The `numexpr` package (aliased `ne` in our following code) doesn't support slicing in its array expression; therefore, we first need to prepare the operands for broadcasting by adding an extra dimension, as follows:

```
r = np.random.rand(10000, 2)
r_i = r[:, np.newaxis]
r_j = r[np.newaxis, :]
```

At this point, we should try to pack as many operations as possible into a single expression to allow significant optimization.

Most of the NumPy mathematical functions are also available in numexpr. However, there is a limitation – the reduction operations (the ones that reduce an axis, such as sum) have to happen last. Therefore, we have to calculate the sum first, then step out of numexpr, and finally calculate the square root in another expression:

```
import numexpr as ne

d_ij = ne.evaluate('sum((r_j - r_i)**2, 2)')
d_ij = ne.evaluate('sqrt(d_ij)')
```

The numexpr compiler will avoid redundant memory allocation by not storing intermediate results. When possible, it will also distribute the operations over multiple processors. In the distance_matrix.py file, you will find two functions that implement the two versions – distance_matrix_numpy and distance_matrix_numexpr:

```
from distance_matrix import (distance_matrix_numpy, \
    distance_matrix_numexpr)
%timeit distance_matrix_numpy(10000)
1 loops, best of 3: 3.56 s per loop
%timeit distance_matrix_numexpr(10000)
1 loops, best of 3: 858 ms per loop
```

By simply converting the expressions to use numexpr, we were able to obtain a 4.5x increase in performance over standard NumPy. The numexpr package can be used every time you need to optimize a NumPy expression that involves large arrays and complex operations, and you can do so while making minimal changes to the code.

Overall, we have seen that NumPy, in combination with numexpr, offers powerful APIs when it comes to working with multidimensional data. However, in many use cases, data is only two-dimensional but is *labeled* in the sense that the data axes include explicit information about the type of data they contain. This is the case for data extracted from database tables. In such situations, pandas is the most popular and one of the best libraries in Python for this, as we will see next.

Working with database-style data with pandas

pandas is a library that was originally developed by Wes McKinney. It was designed to analyze datasets in a seamless and performant way. In recent years, this powerful library has seen incredible growth and a huge adoption by the Python community. In this section, we will introduce the main concepts and tools provided in this library, and we will use them to increase the performance of various use cases that can't otherwise be addressed with NumPy's vectorized operations and broadcasting.

pandas fundamentals

While NumPy deals mostly with arrays, pandas's main data structures are `pandas.Series`, `pandas.DataFrame`, and `pandas.Panel`. In the rest of this chapter, we will abbreviate `pandas` to pd.

The main difference between a `pd.Series` object and an `np.array` is that a `pd.Series` object associates a specific *key* with each element of an array. Let's see how this works in practice with an example.

Let's assume that we are trying to test a new blood pressure drug and we want to store, for each patient, whether the patient's blood pressure improved after administering the drug. We can encode this information by associating each subject ID (represented by an integer) with `True` if the drug was effective and `False` otherwise:

1. We can create a `pd.Series` object by associating an array of keys – the patients – to the array of values that represent the drug's effectiveness. This array of keys can be passed to the `Series` constructor using the `index` argument, as shown in the following snippet:

    ```
    import pandas as pd
    patients = [0, 1, 2, 3]
    effective = [True, True, False, False]


    effective_series = pd.Series(effective, \
        index=patients)
    ```

2. Associating a set of integers from *0* to *N* with a set of values can technically be implemented with `np.array` since, in this case, the key will simply be the position of the element in the array. In pandas, keys are not limited to integers; they can also be strings, floating-point numbers, and generic (hashable) Python objects. For example, we can easily turn our IDs into strings with little effort, as shown in the following code:

    ```
    patients = ["a", "b", "c", "d"]
    effective = [True, True, False, False]
    ```

```
effective_series = pd.Series(effective, \
    index=patients)
```

An interesting observation is that, while NumPy arrays can be thought of as a contiguous collection of values similar to Python lists, the pandas `pd.Series` object can be thought of as a structure that maps keys to values, similar to Python dictionaries.

3. What if you want to store the initial and final blood pressure for each patient? In pandas, you can use a `pd.DataFrame` object to associate multiple data with each key.

    `pd.DataFrame` can be initialized, similarly to a `pd.Series` object, by passing a dictionary of columns and an index. In the following example, we will see how to create `pd.DataFrame` containing four columns that represent the initial and final measurements of systolic and diastolic blood pressure for our patients:

```
patients = ["a", "b", "c", "d"]

columns = {
    "sys_initial": [120, 126, 130, 115],
    "dia_initial": [75, 85, 90, 87],
    "sys_final": [115, 123, 130, 118],
    "dia_final": [70, 82, 92, 87]
}

df = pd.DataFrame(columns, index=patients)
```

4. Equivalently, you can think of `pd.DataFrame` as a collection of `pd.Series`. It is possible to directly initialize `pd.DataFrame` using a dictionary of `pd.Series` instances:

```
columns = {
    "sys_initial": pd.Series([120, 126, 130, 115], \
        index=patients),
    "dia_initial": pd.Series([75, 85, 90, 87], \
        index=patients),
    "sys_final": pd.Series([115, 123, 130, 118], \
        index=patients),
```

```
        "dia_final": pd.Series([70, 82, 92, 87], \
            index=patients)
    }

    df = pd.DataFrame(columns)
```

5. To inspect the content of a pd.DataFrame or pd.Series object, you can use the pd.Series.head and pd.DataFrame.head methods, which print the first few rows of the dataset:

```
effective_series.head()
# Output:
# a  True
# b  True
# c  False
# d  False
# dtype: bool


df.head()
# Output:
#     dia_final  dia_initial  sys_final sys_initial
# a          70           75        115
120
# b          82           85        123
126
# c          92           90        130
130
# d          87           87        118
115
```

Just like a pd.DataFrame can be used to store a collection of pd.Series, you can use a pd.Panel to store a collection of pd.DataFrames. We will not cover the usage of pd.Panel as it is not used as often as pd.Series and pd.DataFrame. To learn more about pd.Panel, make sure that you refer to the excellent documentation at http://pandas.pydata.org/pandas-docs/stable/dsintro.html#panel.

Indexing Series and DataFrame objects

In many instances, we might want to access certain elements stored inside a pd.Series or a pd.DataFrame object. In the following steps, we will see how we can index these objects:

1. Retrieving data from a pd.Series, given its *key*, can be done intuitively by indexing the pd.Series.loc attribute:

```
effective_series.loc["a"]
# Result:
# True
```

2. It is also possible to access the elements, given their *position* in the underlying array, using the pd.Series.iloc attribute:

```
effective_series.iloc[0]
# Result:
# True
```

3. Indexing pd.DataFrame works similarly. For example, you can use pd.DataFrame.loc to extract a row by key, and you can use pd.DataFrame.iloc to extract a row by position:

```
df.loc["a"]
df.iloc[0]
# Result:
# dia_final 70
# dia_initial 75
# sys_final 115
# sys_initial 120
# Name: a, dtype: int64
```

4. An important aspect is that the return type in this case is a pd.Series, where each column is a new key. To retrieve a specific row and column, you can use the following code. The loc attribute will index both the row and the column by key, while the iloc version will index the row and the column by an integer:

```
df.loc["a", "sys_initial"] # is equivalent to
df.loc["a"].loc["sys_initial"]
```

```
df.iloc[0, 1] # is equivalent to
df.iloc[0].iloc[1]
```

5. Retrieving a column from a pd.DataFrame by name can be achieved by regular indexing or attribute access. To retrieve a column by position, you can either use iloc or use the pd.DataFrame.column attribute to retrieve the name of the column:

```
# Retrieve column by name
df["sys_initial"] # Equivalent to
df.sys_initial


# Retrieve column by position
df[df.columns[2]] # Equivalent to
df.iloc[:, 2]
```

These methods also support more advanced indexing, similar to those of NumPy, such as bool, lists, and int arrays.

Now, it's time for some performance considerations. There are some differences between an index in pandas and a dictionary. For example, while the keys of a dictionary cannot contain duplicates, pandas indexes can contain repeated elements. This flexibility, however, comes at a cost – if we try to access an element in a non-unique index, we may incur substantial performance loss – the access will be $O(N)$, like a linear search, rather than $O(1)$, like a dictionary.

A way to mitigate this effect is to sort the index; this will allow pandas to use a binary search algorithm with a computational complexity of $O(log(N))$, which is much better. This can be accomplished using the pd.Series.sort_index function, as shown in the following code (the same applies for pd.DataFrame):

```
# Create a series with duplicate index
index = list(range(1000)) + list(range(1000))


# Accessing a normal series is a O(N) operation
series = pd.Series(range(2000), index=index)


# Sorting the will improve look-up scaling to O(log(N))
series.sort_index(inplace=True)
```

The timings for the different versions are summarized in the following table. If you'd like to rerun this benchmarking yourself, please refer to `Chapter03/Pandas.ipynb`:

Index type	N=10000	N=20000	N=30000	Time
Unique	12.30	12.58	13.30	$O(1)$
Non-unique	494.95	814.10	1129.95	$O(N)$
Non-unique (sorted)	145.93	145.81	145.66	$O(log(N))$

Table 3.1 – Performance analysis for pandas indexing

Database-style operations with pandas

You may have noted that the *tabular* data is similar to what is usually stored in a database. A database is usually indexed using a primary key, and the various columns can have different data types, just like in a `pd.DataFrame`.

The efficiency of the index operations in pandas makes it suitable for database-style manipulations, such as counting, joining, grouping, and aggregations.

Mapping

pandas supports element-wise operations, just like NumPy (after all, `pd.Series` stores their data using `np.array`).

For example, it is possible to apply transformation very easily to both `pd.Series` and `pd.DataFrame`:

```
np.log(df.sys_initial) # Logarithm of a series
df.sys_initial ** 2     # Square a series
np.log(df)              # Logarithm of a dataframe
df ** 2                 # Square of a dataframe
```

You can also perform element-wise operations between two `pd.Series` objects in a way similar to NumPy. An important difference is that the operands will be matched by key, rather than by position; if there is a mismatch in the index, the resulting value will be set to NaN. Both scenarios are exemplified in the following example:

```
# Matching index
a = pd.Series([1, 2, 3], index=["a", "b", "c"])
b = pd.Series([4, 5, 6], index=["a", "b", "c"])
```

```
a + b
# Result:
# a 5
# b 7
# c 9
# dtype: int64


# Mismatching index
b = pd.Series([4, 5, 6], index=["a", "b", "d"])
a + b
# Result:
# a 5.0
# b 7.0
# c NaN
# d NaN
# dtype: float64
```

For added flexibility, pandas offers the `map`, `apply`, and `applymap` methods, which can be used to apply specific transformations.

The `pd.Series.map` method can be used to execute a function for each value and return a `pd.Series` containing each result. In the following example, we can see how to apply the `superstar` function to each element of a `pd.Series`:

```
a = pd.Series([1, 2, 3], index=["a", "b", "c"])
def superstar(x):
    return '*' + str(x) + '*'
a.map(superstar)

# Result:
# a *1*
# b *2*
# c *3*
# dtype: object
```

The pd.DataFrame.applymap function is the equivalent of pd.Series.map, but for DataFrames:

```
df.applymap(superstar)
# Result:
#     dia_final  dia_initial  sys_final  sys_initial
# a       *70*         *75*      *115*         *120*
# b       *82*         *85*      *123*         *126*
# c       *92*         *90*      *130*         *130*
# d       *87*         *87*      *118*         *115*
```

Finally, the pd.DataFrame.apply function can apply the passed function to each column or each row, rather than element-wise. This selection can be performed with the argument axis, where a value of 0 (the default) corresponds to columns and 1 corresponds to rows. Also, note that the return value of apply is a pd.Series:

```
df.apply(superstar, axis=0)
# Result:
# dia_final *a 70nb 82nc 92nd 87nName: dia...
# dia_initial *a 75nb 85nc 90nd 87nName: dia...
# sys_final *a 115nb 123nc 130nd 118nName:...
# sys_initial *a 120nb 126nc 130nd 115nName:...
# dtype: object


df.apply(superstar, axis=1)
# Result:
# a *dia_final 70ndia_initial 75nsys_f...
# b *dia_final 82ndia_initial 85nsys_f...
# c *dia_final 92ndia_initial 90nsys_f...
# d *dia_final 87ndia_initial 87nsys_f...
# dtype: object
```

pandas also supports efficient numexpr-style expressions with the convenient eval method. For example, if we want to calculate the difference between the final and initial blood pressure, we can write the expression as a string, as shown in the following code:

```
df.eval("sys_final - sys_initial")
# Result:
# a -5
```

```
# b -3
# c 0
# d 3
# dtype: int64
```

It is also possible to create new columns using the assignment operator in the
`pd.DataFrame.eval` expression. Note that if the `inplace=True` argument is used, the
operation will be applied directly to the original `pd.DataFrame`; otherwise, the function
will return a new DataFrame. In the following example, we are computing the difference
between `sys_final` and `sys_initial`, and we store it in the `sys_delta` column:

```
df.eval("sys_delta = sys_final - sys_initial", \
   inplace=False)
# Result:
#       dia_final    dia_initial    sys_final    sys_initial
   sys_delta
# a          70            75           115          120
-5
# b          82            85           123          126
   -3
# c          92            90           130          130
   0
# d          87            87           118          115
   3
```

Grouping, aggregations, and transforms

One of the most appreciated features of pandas is its simple and concise method of
grouping, transforming, and aggregating data. To demonstrate this concept, let's extend
our dataset by adding two new patients that we didn't administer the treatment to
(this is usually called a *control group*). We will also include a column, `drug_admst`,
which records whether the patient was administered the treatment:

```
patients = ["a", "b", "c", "d", "e", "f"]

columns = {
    "sys_initial": [120, 126, 130, 115, 150, 117],
    "dia_initial": [75, 85, 90, 87, 90, 74],
    "sys_final": [115, 123, 130, 118, 130, 121],
```

```
        "dia_final": [70, 82, 92, 87, 85, 74],
        "drug_admst": [True, True, True, True, False, False]
    }

    df = pd.DataFrame(columns, index=patients)
```

At this point, we may be interested to know how the blood pressure changed between the two groups. You can group the patients according to `drug_amst` using the `pd.DataFrame.groupby` function. The return value will be the `DataFrameGroupBy` object, which can be iterated to obtain a new `pd.DataFrame` for each value of the `drug_admst` column:

```
    df.groupby('drug_admst')
    for value, group in df.groupby('drug_admst'):
        print("Value: {}".format(value))
        print("Group DataFrame:")
        print(group)
# Output:
# Value: False
# Group DataFrame:
#     dia_final    dia_initial    drug_admst    sys_final
    sys_initial
# e          85             90         False          130
    150
# f          74             74         False          121
    117
# Value: True
# Group DataFrame:
#     dia_final    dia_initial    drug_admst    sys_final
    sys_initial
# a          70             75          True          115
    120
# b          82             85          True          123
    126
# c          92             90          True          130
    130
# d          87             87          True          118
    115
```

Iterating the `DataFrameGroupBy` object is rarely necessary because, thanks to method chaining, it is possible to calculate group-related properties directly. For example, we may want to calculate the mean, max, or standard deviation for each group. All those operations that summarize the data in some way are called aggregations and can be performed using the `agg` method. The result of `agg` is another `pd.DataFrame` that relates the grouping variables and the result of the aggregation, as illustrated in the following code:

```
df.groupby('drug_admst').agg(np.mean)
#                  dia_final    dia_initial    sys_final    sys_in
   itial
# drug_admst
# False              79.50         82.00         125.5
   133.50
# True               82.75         84.25         121.5
   122.75
```

> **Note**
>
> It is also possible to perform processing on the DataFrame groups that do not represent a summarization. One common example of such an operation is filling in missing values. Those intermediate steps are called **transforms**.

We can illustrate this concept with an example. Let's assume that we have a few missing values in our dataset, and we want to replace those values with the average of the other values in the same group. This can be accomplished using a transform, as follows:

```
df.loc['a','sys_initial'] = None
df.groupby('drug_admst').transform(lambda df: \
   df.fillna(df.mean()))
#        dia_final    dia_initial    sys_final    sys_initial
# a          70           75            115        123.666667
# b          82           85            123        126.000000
# c          92           90            130        130.000000
# d          87           87            118        115.000000
# e          85           90            130        150.000000
# f          74           74            121        117.000000
```

Joining

Joins are useful for aggregating data that is scattered among different tables. Let's say that we want to include the location of the hospital in which patient measurements were taken in our dataset. We can reference the location for each patient using the H1, H2, and H3 labels, and we can store the address and identifier of the hospital in a `hospital` table:

```
hospitals = pd.DataFrame(
    { "name" : ["City 1", "City 2", "City 3"],
        "address" : ["Address 1", "Address 2", "Address \
        3"],
        "city": ["City 1", "City 2", "City 3"] },
    index=["H1", "H2", "H3"])


hospital_id = ["H1", "H2", "H2", "H3", "H3", "H3"]
df['hospital_id'] = hospital_id
```

Now, we want to find the city where the measure was taken for each patient. We need to *map* the keys from the `hospital_id` column to the city stored in the `hospitals` table.

This can be implemented in Python using dictionaries:

```
hospital_dict = {
  "H1": ("City 1", "Name 1", "Address 1"),
  "H2": ("City 2", "Name 2", "Address 2"),
  "H3": ("City 3", "Name 3", "Address 3")
}
cities = [hospital_dict[key][0]
            for key in hospital_id]
```

This algorithm runs efficiently with an $O(N)$ time complexity, where N is the size of `hospital_id`. pandas allows you to encode the same operation using simple indexing; the advantage is that the join will be performed in heavily optimized Cython and with efficient hashing algorithms. The preceding simple Python expression can easily be converted into pandas in this way:

```
cities = hospitals.loc[hospital_id, "city"]
```

More advanced joins can also be performed with the pd.DataFrame.join method, which will produce a new pd.DataFrame that will attach the hospital information for each patient:

```
result = df.join(hospitals, on='hospital_id')
result.columns
# Result:
# Index(['dia_final', 'dia_initial', 'drug_admst',
# 'sys_final', 'sys_initial',
# 'hospital_id', 'address', 'city', 'name'],
# dtype='object')
```

This concludes our discussion on pandas. In the next section, we will talk about xarray, the state-of-the-art tool for working with multidimensional labeled data in Python.

High-performance labeled data with xarray

With NumPy, we can manipulate multidimensional numerical data and perform mathematical computations that are highly optimized by low-level C and FORTRAN code. On the other hand, we have seen that pandas allows us to work with labeled, categorical data that resembles data tables using database-like operations.

These two tools complement each other: NumPy does not allow categorical data to be mixed in with numerical values, while pandas is mostly limited to two-dimensional, database-like datasets. Combining these tools can help address many data processing needs, but when we are faced with big, multidimensional data that is also labeled, many performance-related problems arise.

In the last section of this chapter, we will discuss xarray, a library that combines the best of both the NumPy and the pandas worlds and offers one of the best tools for working with labeled multidimensional data. We will explore some of its most prominent features while noting the improvements we achieve with xarray over other Python libraries.

Analyzing CO_2 concentration

To guide our discussion, we will be using the carbon dioxide concentration data, which was collected concerning the volcano Mauna Loa in Hawaii. The dataset is a time series of monthly measurements of the CO_2 level, starting from 1958 to this day. We have prepared a cleaned version of this dataset for you, which is included in the code repository for this book in the monthly_co2.csv file.

The data has three simple columns:

- The year of measurement
- The month of measurement
- The measurement itself

Our goal is to analyze this dataset and visualize any time-related trends. Since we are already familiar with using pandas to work with a .csv file, let's proceed with the library to start:

```
import pandas as pd
df = pd.read_csv('monthly_co2.csv', index_col=[0, 1])
df.head()
```

Make sure that the data file is in the same directory as this code. You may remember that this will read in the file and store the data in a DataFrame object. Here, we are using the first two columns (by using the index_col=[0, 1] argument) as the index of this DataFrame object. Finally, we print out the first five rows of this dataset, which look as follows:

year	month	co2
1958	3	315.70
	4	317.45
	5	317.51
	6	317.24
	7	315.86

Here, we can see that in March 1958, the CO_2 level was 315.70, and that the following month's measurement was 317.45.

The first thing we'd like to look at is a simple line graph corresponding to the co2 column, which is simply the graph of the CO_2 level as a function of time (in month). With the help of Matplotlib, the go-to plotting tool in Python, we can do this very easily:

```
import matplotlib.pyplot as plt

plt.plot(df.co2.values);
```

The preceding code will produce the following output:

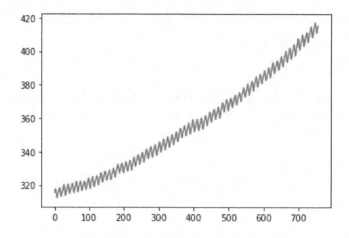

Figure 3.4 – Monthly CO_2 level

We can notice two very distinct trends:

- The first is the *global* increasing trend, which roughly goes from 320 to 420 during our timeline.

- The second looks like a *seasonal* zigzag trend, which is present locally and repeats itself every year.

To verify this intuition, we can inspect the average data across the years, which will tell us that the CO_2 level has been rising as a global trend. We can also compute the average measurement for each month and consider how the data changed from January to December. To accomplish this, we will utilize the groupby function by computing the yearly averages and plotting them:

```
by_year = df.groupby('year').mean().co2
plt.plot(by_year);
```

This gives us the following output:

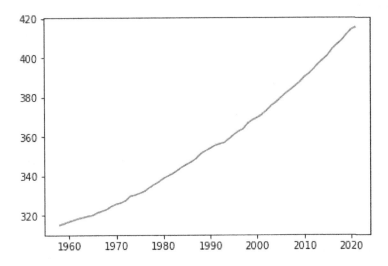

Figure 3.5 – Yearly CO_2 level, averaged across months

Just as we expected, we can see the global rising trend of the CO_2 level:

```
by_month = df.groupby('month').mean().co2
plt.plot(by_month);
```

Similarly, the preceding code generates the following average-by-month data:

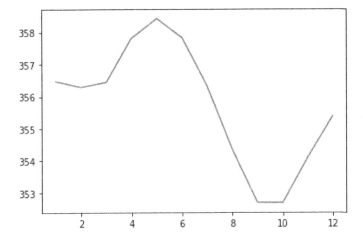

Figure 3.6 – Monthly CO_2 level, averaged across years

The seasonal trend we suspected now becomes clear: the CO_2 level tends to rise during the summer and fall between fall and winter.

So far, we have been using pandas to manipulate our data. Even with this minimal example, we can notice a few things:

- Loading the data, specifically the `co2` column, as a NumPy array would be inappropriate since we would lose information about the year and month each measurement was made. pandas is the better choice here.

- On the other hand, the `groupby` function can be unintuitive and costly to work with. Here, we simply want to compute the *average-by-month and average-by-year measurements*, but that requires us to group our data by the `month` column and then by `year`. Although pandas takes care of this grouping for us behind the scenes, it is an expensive operation, especially if we are working with a significantly large dataset.

- To bypass this inefficiency, we can think of representing the `co2` column as a two-dimensional NumPy array, where the rows represent years and the columns represent months, and each cell in the array holds the measurement. Now, to compute the averages we want, we could simply calculate the mean along each of the two axes, which we know NumPy can do efficiently. However, once again, we lose the expressiveness of the labeled `month` and `year` data we have under pandas.

This dilemma we are currently facing is similar to the one that motivated the development of xarray, the premiere tool in Python for working with labeled, multidimensional data. The idea is to extend NumPy's support for fast, multidimensional array computations and allow dimensions (or axes) to have labels, which is one of the main selling points of pandas.

The xarray library

xarray is developed and actively maintained by PyData and a part of the NumFOCUS project. To use the library, you must head to `http://xarray.pydata.org/en/stable/installing.html` for more details on how to install it. To continue with our example of the CO_2 concentration level, we will feed the data we have into a `Dataset` object in xarray using the following code:

```
import xarray as xr

ds = xr.Dataset.from_dataframe(df)
```

If we were to print this object out in a Jupyter notebook, the output would be formatted nicely:

```
[7]:  ds = xr.Dataset.from_dataframe(df)
      ds
```

```
[7]:  xarray.Dataset
```

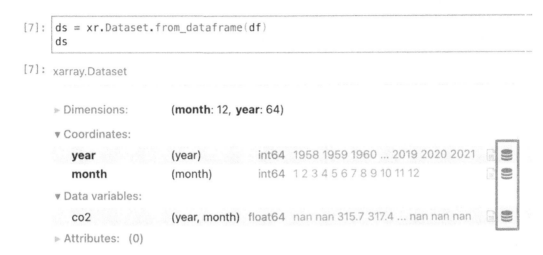

Figure 3.7 – A Dataset instance of xarray, printed in Jupyter

xarray was able to infer that `month` and `year` (the index columns in `DataFrame`) should be the dimension, as indicated by the **Dimensions** section of the output. The **Coordinates** section shows the values that each of these dimensions can take on; in our case, the year could be anything between **1958** and **2021**, while the month could be anything between **1** and **12**. The **Data variables** section shows the actual `co2` data we care about, which is now a two-dimensional array indexed by `year` and `month`.

xarray makes interacting and inspecting its objects easy and interactive; you can inspect the values of the coordinates and data variables further by clicking on the icons highlighted in the preceding screenshot.

We mentioned earlier that xarray combines the best features of NumPy and pandas; this is best illustrated via the slicing/indexing interface it provides. For example, let's say that we'd like to extract the measurements within the first 10 years of the dataset. For the first 5 months, we could apply NumPy-style slicing to the `'co2'` variable of the `ds` object:

```
ds['co2'][:10, :5]
```

This gives us a `DataArray` object containing the requested values:

```
[9]: ds['co2'][:10, :5]
```

```
[9]: xarray.DataArray  'co2'  (year: 10, month: 5)
```

```
array([[   nan,    nan, 315.7 , 317.45, 317.51],
       [315.58, 316.49, 316.65, 317.72, 318.29],
       [316.43, 316.98, 317.58, 319.03, 320.04],
       [316.89, 317.7 , 318.54, 319.48, 320.58],
       [317.94, 318.55, 319.68, 320.57, 321.02],
       [318.74, 319.07, 319.86, 321.38, 322.25],
       [319.57, 320.01, 320.74, 321.84, 322.26],
       [319.44, 320.44, 320.89, 322.14, 322.17],
       [320.62, 321.6 , 322.39, 323.7 , 324.08],
       [322.33, 322.5 , 323.04, 324.42, 325.  ]])
```

▼ Coordinates:

| **year** | (year) | int64 | 1958 1959 1960 ... 1965 1966 1967 |
| **month** | (month) | int64 | 1 2 3 4 5 |

▶ Attributes: (0)

Figure 3.8 – A DataArray instance of xarray, printed in Jupyter

While NumPy slicing can be flexible, it does not offer much expressiveness for labeled data: we would have to know that the first axis of the implied multidimensional array is `year`, that the second is `month`, and that `ds['co2'][:10, :5]` doesn't explicitly say which years we are selecting for.

As such, we could use the `sel` function, which roughly offers the same functionality as pandas filtering. To select the values within the example year of `1960`, we can simply use the following code:

```
ds['co2'].sel(year=1960)
```

This explicitly tells us that we are selecting `1960` along the `year` axis. For more examples of the different APIs the library offers, you can check out the documentation at `http://xarray.pydata.org/en/stable/api.html`.

Improved performance

Now, we will consider the performance improvements that xarray offers. Recall that our goal is to compute the average measurement, first for each year to visualize the global trend, and then for each month for the seasonal trend. To do this, we can simply call the `mean` function while specifying the appropriate (labeled!) dimension.

First, to obtain the average-by-year, we must compute the mean across the `month` dimension:

```
ds.mean(dim='month')
```

This returns another `Dataset` object containing the computed values:

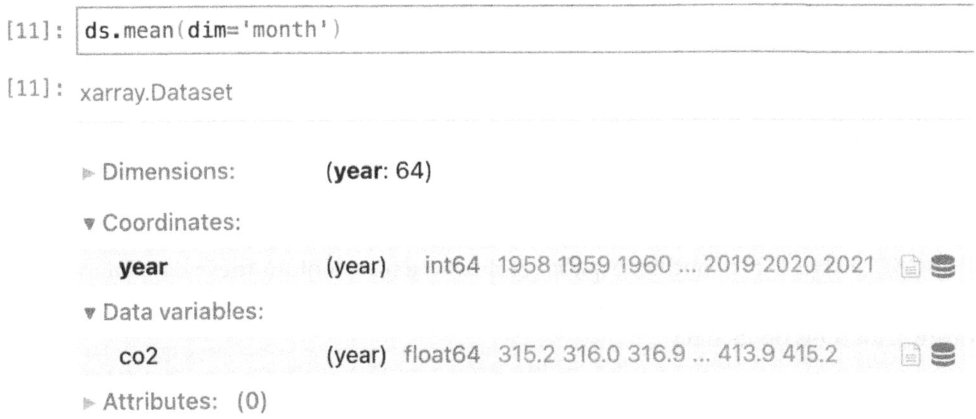

[11]:   `ds.mean(dim='month')`

[11]:   xarray.Dataset

  ► Dimensions: **(year**: 64)

  ▼ Coordinates:

    year   (year)   int64   1958 1959 1960 ... 2019 2020 2021 📄 🗄

  ▼ Data variables:

    co2   (year) float64   315.2 316.0 316.9 ... 413.9 415.2   📄 🗄

  ► Attributes: (0)

Figure 3.9 – Taking the average across a dimension in xarray

From here, we can simply access the `co2` variable and pass the array to the `plot` function of Matplotlib to replicate *Figure 3.5*. For *Figure 3.6*, we can follow the same procedure using `ds.mean(dim='year')`.

The advantage we are gaining here is the expressiveness in our code. If we were using NumPy, we would need to specify the **axis number** (for example, 0, 1, 2, and so on), not the **dimension name**, (for example, `'month'`, `'year'`). This might lead to hard-to-find bugs if you confuse which axis is which type of data in NumPy.

Furthermore, the code is simpler and can take advantage of the optimized mean operation, which is managed under the hood by xarray, compared to the expensive `groupby` function from pandas. To see this, we can benchmark the two ways of computing the average-by-year that we have. First, we have the pandas way:

```
%timeit df.groupby('year').mean().co2
# Result:
# 534 µs ± 10.8 µs per loop (mean ± std. dev. of 7 runs,
  1000 loops each)
```

Then, we have the xarray way:

```
%timeit ds.mean(dim='month').co2.values
# Result:
# 150 µs ± 1.27 µs per loop (mean ± std. dev. of 7 runs,
    10000 loops each)
```

Here, we can see a clear performance improvement, achieved almost for free by passing our data to xarray!

Plotting with xarray

Labeled multidimensional arrays are ubiquitous in time series (where one of the dimensions is time), geospatial data (where some dimensions represent the coordinates on a map), or data that is both geospatial and time-dependent. In these data analysis tasks, data visualization is crucial; as such, xarray makes it easy to implement and call complex plotting functions on its data.

Let's look at this through a quick example. First, we will read in an example dataset we have prepared for you, saved in a file named 2d_measurement.npy, which can be read into a Python program using NumPy:

```
measures = np.load('2d_measure.npy')
measures.shape
# Result:
# (100, 100, 3)
```

As you can see, it is a 100x100x3 array. Let's say that this dataset contains a specific type of measurement, taken over a 100x100 grid of a two-dimensional space (corresponding to the first two axes) at three specific timestamps (corresponding to the third axis).

We would like to visualize these measurements as three squares, where each square represents a specific time stamp, and each pixel in each square represents the intensity of the corresponding measurement.

To do this in Matplotlib, we could use the imshow function, which takes in a two-dimensional array and plots it as an image. So, we would iterate through the three timestamps that we have and plot the corresponding grids one by one, as follows:

```
fig, ax = plt.subplots(1, 3, figsize=(10, 3))


for i in range(3):
```

```
    c = ax[i].imshow(measures[:, :, i], origin='lower')
    plt.colorbar(c, ax=ax[i])

plt.show()
```

> **Note**
>
> The index, i, iterates through the three indices of the third axis in the measures array. Again, we can see that this indexing scheme is not very expressive and readable. Here, we are also using the colorbar function to add a color bar to each of the plots.

The preceding code produces the following output:

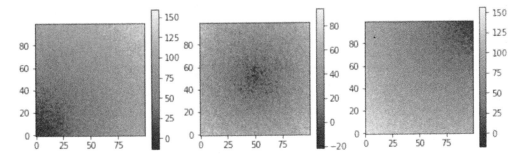

Figure 3.10 – Regular imshow from Matplotlib

Although there is noise in the measurements, we can observe some global trends; specifically, we seem to have low-intensity measurements in the lower-left corner in the first plot, in the center in the second, and in the top-right corner in the third. As the final note, something we might want to change about this plot is making the three color bars have the same range, which may be hard to do with Matplotlib.

Now, let's see how we can produce this plot using xarray. First, we must convert the NumPy array into a DataArray object:

```
da = xr.DataArray(measures, dims=['x', 'y', 'time'])
```

Here, we are also specifying the names for the three dimensions: 'x', 'y', and 'time'. This will allow us to manipulate the data more expressively, as we saw previously. To plot out the 2D grids, we can use the similarly named imshow method:

```
da.plot.imshow(x='x', y='y', col='time', robust=True);
```

This results in the following output:

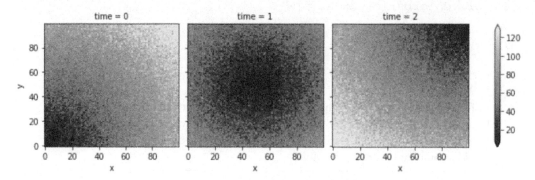

Figure 3.11 – Specialized imshow from xarray

The plotting function is much simpler than the for loop we had earlier. Furthermore, with minimal code, xarray has taken care of many different aesthetics-related aspects of this plot:

- First, the plots have their titles and x- and y-axis labels automatically created.

- Second, by using a common color range, the fact that the measurements at the second timestamp are lower than those in the other two is now more obvious. This demonstrates that functions and methods in xarray are optimized to make working with labeled multidimensional data more efficient.

On the topic of plotting, many data scientists work with map data. xarray nicely integrates with the popular Cartopy library for geospatial data processing and offers many plotting functionalities that incorporate world and country maps. More details can be found in their documentation: http://xarray.pydata.org/en/stable/plotting.html.

Summary

In this chapter, we learned how to manipulate NumPy arrays and how to write fast mathematical expressions using array broadcasting. This knowledge will help you write more concise, expressive code and, at the same time, obtain substantial performance gains. We also introduced the numexpr library to further speed up NumPy calculations with minimal effort.

pandas implements efficient data structures that are useful when analyzing large datasets. In particular, pandas shines when the data is indexed by non-integer keys and provides very fast hashing algorithms.

NumPy and pandas work well when handling large, homogenous inputs, but they are not suitable when the expressions become complex and the operations cannot be expressed using the tools provided by these libraries. xarray comes in handy as an alternative option where we need to work with labeled, multidimensional data.

In combination, the three libraries offer Python users powerful APIs and flexible functionalities to work with a wide range of data. By keeping them in your toolbox, you are well situated to tackle most data processing and engineering tasks using Python.

In other cases, we can also leverage Python capabilities as a glue language by interfacing it with C using the Cython package, as we will see in the next chapter.

Questions

1. Name the advantages NumPy has over Python-native lists when working with multidimensional data.

2. What are some of the database-style operations that pandas offers in its API?

3. What problems does xarray address and why can they not be addressed by NumPy or pandas?

Further reading

- An overview tutorial on NumPy and pandas: `https://cloudxlab.com/blog/numpy-pandas-introduction/`

- Data structures in xarray: `https://towardsdatascience.com/basic-data-structures-of-xarray-80bab8094efa`

4

C Performance with Cython

Cython is a language that extends Python by supporting the declaration of types for functions, variables, and classes. These typed declarations enable Cython to compile Python scripts to efficient C code. Cython can also act as a bridge between Python and C as it provides easy-to-use constructs to write interfaces to external C and C++ routines.

In this chapter, we will learn about the following topics:

- Compiling Cython extensions
- Adding static types
- Sharing declarations
- Working with arrays
- Using a particle simulator in Cython
- Profiling Cython
- Using Cython with Jupyter

Through this chapter, we will learn how to leverage Cython to improve the efficiency of our programs. While a minimum knowledge of C is helpful, this chapter focuses only on Cython in the context of Python optimization. Therefore, it doesn't require any C background.

Technical requirements

You can access the code used in this chapter on GitHub at `https://github.com/PacktPublishing/Advanced-Python-Programming-Second-Edition/tree/main/Chapter04`.

Compiling Cython extensions

The Cython syntax is, by design, a superset of Python. Cython can compile, with a few exceptions, most Python modules without requiring any change. Cython source files have the `.pyx` extension and can be compiled to produce a C file using the `cython` command.

All that is required to convert Python code to Cython is some syntactic modifications that we will see throughout this chapter (such as when declaring variables and functions) as well as compilation. While this procedure may seem intimidating at first, Cython will more than make up for itself via the computational benefits that it offers.

First off, to install Cython, we can simply run the `pip` command, like this:

```
$pip install cython
```

Refer to the documentation at `https://pypi.org/project/Cython/` for more details. Our first Cython script will contain a simple function that prints `Hello, World!` as the output. Follow these next steps:

1. Create a new `hello.pyx` file containing the following code:

   ```
   def hello():
       print('Hello, World!')
   ```

2. The `cython` command will read `hello.pyx` and generate a `hello.c` file, as follows:

   ```
   $ cython hello.pyx
   ```

3. To compile `hello.c` to a Python extension module, we will use the **GNU Compiler Collection (GCC)** compiler (more details on how to install it can be found at `https://gcc.gnu.org/install/`). We need to add some Python-specific compilation options that depend on the operating system. It's important to specify the directory that contains the header files; in the following example, the directory is `/usr/include/python3.5/`:

   ```
   $ gcc -shared -pthread -fPIC -fwrapv -O2 -Wall -fno-
   strict-aliasing -lm -I/usr/include/python3.5/ -o
   hello.so hello.c
   ```

> **Note**
>
> To find your Python `include` directory, you can use the `distutils` utility and run `sysconfig.get_python_inc`. To execute it, you can simply issue the following command: `python -c "from distutils import sysconfig; print(sysconfig.get_python_inc())"`.

4. This will produce a file called `hello.so`, a C extension module that is directly importable into a Python session. The code is illustrated in the following snippet:

```
>>> import hello
>>> hello.hello()
Hello, World!
```

5. Cython accepts both Python 2 and Python 3 as **input and output (I/O)** languages. In other words, you can compile a Python 3 script `hello.pyx` file using the `-3` option, as illustrated in the following code snippet:

```
$ cython -3 hello.pyx
```

6. The generated `hello.c` file can be compiled without any changes to Python 2 and Python 3 by including the corresponding headers with the `-I` option, as follows:

```
$ gcc -I/usr/include/python3.5 # ... other options
$ gcc -I/usr/include/python2.7 # ... other options
```

7. A Cython program can be compiled in a more straightforward way using `distutils`, the standard Python packaging tool. By writing a `setup.py` script, we can compile the `.pyx` file directly to an extension module. To compile our `hello.pyx` example, we can write a minimal `setup.py` script containing the following code:

```
from distutils.core import setup
from Cython.Build import cythonize

setup(
    name='Hello',
    ext_modules = cythonize('hello.pyx')
)
```

In the first two lines of the preceding code snippet, we import the `setup` function and the `cythonize` helper. The `setup` function contains a few key-value pairs that specify the name of the application and the extensions that need to be built.

8. The `cythonize` helper takes either a string or a list of strings containing the Cython modules we want to compile. You can also use glob patterns by running the following code:

```
cythonize(['hello.pyx', 'world.pyx', '*.pyx'])
```

9. To compile our extension module using `distutils`, you can execute the `setup.py` script using the following code:

```
$ python setup.py build_ext --inplace
```

The `build_ext` option tells the script to build the extension modules indicated in `ext_modules`, while the `--inplace` option tells the script to place the `hello.so` output file in the same location as the source file (instead of a build directory).

10. Cython modules can also be automatically compiled using `pyximport`. All that's needed is a call to `pyximport.install()` at the beginning of your script (or you need to issue the command in your interpreter), as illustrated in the following code snippet. After doing that, you can import `.pyx` files directly and `pyximport` will transparently compile the corresponding Cython modules:

```
>>> import pyximport
>>> pyximport.install()
>>> import hello # This will compile hello.pyx
```

Unfortunately, `pyximport` will not work for all kinds of configurations (for example, when they involve a combination of C and Cython files), but it comes in handy for testing simple scripts.

11. Since version 0.13, IPython includes the `cythonmagic` extension to interactively write and test a series of Cython statements. You can load the extensions in an IPython shell using `load_ext`, as follows:

```
%load_ext Cython
```

Once the extension is loaded, you can use the `%%cython` *cell magic* to write a multiline Cython snippet. In the following example, we define a `hello_snippet` function that will be compiled and added to the IPython session namespace:

```
%%cython
def hello_snippet():
    print("Hello, Cython!")


hello_snippet()
Hello, Cython!
```

It is that simple to work with Cython source code. In the next section, we will see how we can add static types to our program, getting it closer to C code.

Adding static types

In Python, a variable can be associated with objects of different types during the execution of the program. While this feature is desirable as it makes the language flexible and dynamic, it also adds significant overhead to the interpreter as it needs to look up the type and methods of the variables at runtime, making it difficult to perform various optimizations. Cython extends the Python language with explicit type declarations so that it can generate efficient C extensions through compilation.

The main way to declare data types in Cython is through `cdef` statements. The `cdef` keyword can be used in multiple contexts, such as variables, functions, and extension types (statically typed classes). We will see how to do this in the following subsections.

Declaring variables

In Cython, you can declare the type of a variable by prepending the variable with `cdef` and its respective type. For example, we can declare the `i` variable as a 16-bit integer in the following way:

```
cdef int i
```

The `cdef` statement supports multiple variable names on the same line along with optional initialization, as seen in the following line of code:

```
cdef double a, b = 2.0, c = 3.0
```

Typed variables are treated differently from regular variables. In Python, variables are often described as *labels* that refer to objects in memory. For example, we could assign the value `'hello'` to the a variable at any point in the program without restriction, as illustrated here:

```
a = 'hello'
```

The a variable holds a reference to the `'hello'` string. We can also freely assign another value (for example, the integer `1`) to the same variable later in the code, as follows:

```
a = 1
```

Python will assign the integer `1` to the a variable without any problem.

Typed variables behave quite differently and are usually described as *data containers*:
we can only store values that fit into the container that is determined by its data type.
For example, if we declare the a variable as `int`, and then we try to assign it to a `double`
data type, Cython will trigger an error, as shown in the following code snippet:

```
%%cython
cdef int i
i = 3.0


# Output has been cut
...cf4b.pyx:2:4 Cannot assign type 'double' to 'int'
```

Static typing makes it easy for the compiler to perform useful optimizations. For example,
if we declare a loop index as `int`, Cython will rewrite the loop in pure C without needing
to step into the Python interpreter. The typing declaration guarantees that the type of the
index will always be `int` and cannot be overwritten at runtime so that the compiler is free
to perform optimizations without compromising the program's correctness.

We can assess the speed gain in this case with a small test case. In the following example,
we implement a simple loop that increments a variable `100` times. With Cython, the
`example` function can be coded as follows:

```
%%cython
def example():
    cdef int i, j=0
    for i in range(100):
        j += 1
    return j

example()
# Result:
# 100
```

We can compare the speed of an analogous, untyped, pure Python loop, as follows:

```
def example_python():
    j=0
    for i in range(100):
        j += 1
```

```
    return j
```

```
%timeit example()
10000000 loops, best of 3: 25 ns per loop
%timeit example_python()
100000 loops, best of 3: 2.74 us per loop
```

The speedup obtained by implementing this simple type declaration is a whopping 100 times! This works because the Cython loop has first been converted to pure C and then to efficient machine code, while the Python loop still relies on the slow interpreter.

In Cython, it is possible to declare a variable to be of any standard C type, and it is also possible to define custom types using classic C constructs, such as struct, enum, and typedef.

An interesting example is that if we declare a variable to be of the object type, the variable will accept any kind of Python object, as illustrated in the following code snippet:

```
cdef object a_py
# both 'hello' and 1 are Python objects
a_py = 'hello'
a_py = 1
```

Note that declaring a variable as object has no performance benefits, as accessing and operating on the object will still require the interpreter to look up the underlying type of the variable and its attributes and methods.

Sometimes, certain data types (such as float and int numbers) are compatible in the sense that they can be converted into each other. In Cython, it is possible to convert (*cast*) between types by surrounding the destination type with pointy brackets, as shown in the following code snippet:

```
cdef int a = 0
cdef double b
b = <double> a
```

Together with static types for variables, we can provide information about functions, which we will learn how to do next.

Declaring functions

You can add type information to the arguments of a Python function by specifying the type in front of each of the argument names. Functions specified in this way will work and perform like regular Python functions, but their arguments will be type-checked. We can write a max_python function that returns the greater value between two integers, as follows:

```
def max_python(int a, int b):
    return a if a > b else b
```

A function specified in this way will perform type checking and treat the arguments as typed variables, just as in cdef definitions. However, the function will still be a Python function, and calling it multiple times will still need to switch back to the interpreter. To allow Cython for function call optimizations, we should declare the type of the return type using a cdef statement, as follows:

```
cdef int max_cython(int a, int b):
    return a if a > b else b
```

Functions declared in this way are translated to native C functions and have much less overhead compared to Python functions. A substantial drawback is that they can't be used from Python but only from Cython, and their scope is restricted to the same Cython file unless they're exposed in a definition file (refer to the *Sharing declarations* section).

Fortunately, Cython allows you to define functions that are both callable from Python and translatable to performant C functions. If you declare a function with a cpdef statement, Cython will generate two versions of the function: a Python version available to the interpreter, and a fast C function usable from Cython. The cpdef syntax is equivalent to cdef, shown as follows:

```
cpdef int max_hybrid(int a, int b):
    return a if a > b else b
```

Sometimes, the call overhead can be a performance issue even with C functions, especially when the same function is called many times in a critical loop. When the function body is small, it is convenient to add the inline keyword in front of the function definition; the function call will be replaced by the function body itself. Our max function is a good candidate for *inlining*, as illustrated in the following code snippet:

```
cdef inline int max_inline(int a, int b):
    return a if a > b else b
```

Finally, we will see how to work with class types next.

Declaring classes

We can define an extension type using the cdef class statement and declare its attributes in the class body. For example, we can create a Point extension type, as shown in the following code snippet, which stores two coordinates (x, y) of the double type:

```
cdef class Point:
    cdef double x
    cdef double y
    def __init__(self, double x, double y):
        self.x = x
        self.y = y
```

Accessing the declared attributes in the class methods allows Cython to bypass expensive Python attribute lookups by direct access to the given fields in the underlying C struct. For this reason, attribute access in typed classes is an extremely fast operation.

To use the cdef class statement in your code, you need to explicitly declare the type of the variables you intend to use at compile time. You can use the extension type name (such as Point) in any context where you will use a standard type (such as double, float, and int). For example, if we want a Cython function that calculates the distance from the origin (in the example, the function is called norm) of a Point, we have to declare the input variable as Point, as shown in the following code snippet:

```
cdef double norm(Point p):
    return (p.x**2 + p.y**2)**0.5
```

Just as with typed functions, typed classes have some limitations. If you try to access an extension type attribute from Python, you will get an AttributeError warning, as follows:

```
>>> a = Point(0.0, 0.0)
>>> a.x
AttributeError: 'Point' object has no attribute 'x'
```

In order to access attributes from Python code, you have to use the public (for read/write access) or readonly specifiers in the attribute declaration, as shown in the following code snippet:

```
cdef class Point:
    cdef public double x
```

Additionally, methods can be declared with the `cpdef` statement, just as with regular functions.

Extension types do not support the addition of extra attributes at runtime. To do that, a solution is defining a Python class that is a subclass of the typed class and extends its attributes and methods in pure Python.

And with that, we have seen how to add static types to various objects in Cython. In the next section, we will begin our discussion regarding declarations.

Sharing declarations

When writing your Cython modules, you may want to reorganize your most-used functions and classes declaration in a separate file so that they can be reused in different modules. Cython allows you to put these components in a *definition file* and access them with `cimport` statements.

Let's say that we have a module with the `max` and `min` functions, and we want to reuse those functions in multiple Cython programs. If we simply write a bunch of functions in a `.pyx` file, the declarations will be confined to the same file.

> **Note**
>
> Definition files are also used to interface Cython with external C code. The idea is to copy (or, more accurately, translate) the types and function prototypes in the definition file and leave the implementation in the external C code that will be compiled and linked in a separate step.

To share the `max` and `min` functions, we need to write a definition file with a `.pxd` extension. Such a file only contains the types and function prototypes that we want to share with other modules—a *public* interface. We can declare the prototypes of our `max` and `min` functions in a file named `mathlib.pxd`, as follows:

```
cdef int max(int a, int b)
cdef int min(int a, int b)
```

As you can see, we only write the function name and arguments without implementing the function body.

The function implementation goes into the implementation file with the same base name but the `.pyx` extension `mathlib.pyx`, as follows:

```
cdef int max(int a, int b):
    return a if a > b else b

cdef int min(int a, int b):
    return a if a < b else b
```

The `mathlib` module is now importable from another Cython module.

To test our new Cython module, we will create a file named `distance.pyx` containing a function named `chebyshev`. The function will calculate the Chebyshev distance between two points, as shown in the following code snippet. The Chebyshev distance between two coordinates— `(x1, y1)` and `(x2, y2)`—is defined as the maximum value of the difference between each coordinate:

```
max(abs(x1 - x2), abs(y1 - y2))
```

To implement the `chebyshev` function, we will use the `max` function declared in `mathlib.pxd` by importing it with the `cimport` statement, as shown in the following code snippet:

```
from mathlib cimport max

def chebyshev(int x1, int y1, int x2, int y2):
    return max(abs(x1 - x2), abs(y1 - y2))
```

The `cimport` statement will read `mathlib.pxd` and the `max` definition will be used to generate a `distance.c` file.

Along with static types and declarations, one factor that allows C to be generally faster than Python is its highly optimized array operations, which we will examine in the next section.

Working with arrays

Numerical and high-performance calculations often make use of arrays. Cython provides an easy way to interact with different types of arrays, using directly low-level C arrays, or the more general *typed memoryviews*. We will see how to do this in the following subsections.

C arrays and pointers

C arrays are a collection of items of the same type, stored contiguously in memory. Before digging into the details, it is helpful to understand (or review) how memory is managed in C.

Variables in C are like containers. When creating a variable, a space in memory is reserved to store its value. For example, if we create a variable containing a 64-bit floating-point number (double), the program will allocate 64 bits (16 bytes) of memory. This portion of memory can be accessed through an address to that memory location.

To obtain the address of a variable, we can use the *address operator* denoted by the & symbol. We can also use the printf function, as follows, available in the libc.stdio Cython module to print the address of this variable:

```
%%cython
cdef double a
from libc.stdio cimport printf
printf("%p", &a)
# Output:
# 0x7fc8bb611210
```

> **Note**
>
> The output will only be generated when the code is run from a standard Python terminal. This limitation of IPython is detailed at https://github.com/ipython/ipython/issues/1230.

Memory addresses can be stored in special variables, *pointers*, that can be declared by putting a * prefix in front of the variable name, as follows:

```
from libc.stdio cimport printf
cdef double a
cdef double *a_pointer
a_pointer = &a # a_pointer and &a are of the same type
```

If we have a pointer and we want to grab the value contained in the address it's pointing at, we can use the zero-index notation shown here:

```
cdef double a
cdef double *a_pointer
```

```
a_pointer = &a

a = 3.0
print(a_pointer[0]) # prints 3.0
```

When declaring a C array, the program allocates enough space to accommodate all the elements requested. For instance, to create an array that has 10 `double` values (16 bytes each), the program will reserve *16 * 10 = 160* bytes of contiguous space in memory. In Cython, we can declare such arrays using the following syntax:

```
cdef double arr[10]
```

We can also declare a multidimensional array, such as an array with 5 rows and 2 columns, using the following syntax:

```
cdef double arr[5][2]
```

The memory will be allocated in a single block of memory, row after row. This order is commonly referred to as *row-major* and is depicted in the following screenshot. Arrays can also be *column-major* ordered, as is the case for the Fortran programming language:

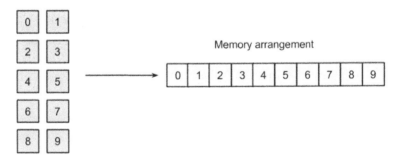

Figure 4.1 – Row-major order

Array ordering has important consequences. When iterating a C array over the last dimension, we access contiguous memory blocks (in our example, 0, 1, 2, 3 ...), while when we iterate on the first dimension, we skip a few positions (0, 2, 4, 6, 8, 1 ...). You should always try to access memory sequentially as this optimizes cache and memory usage.

We can store and retrieve elements from the array using standard indexing, as shown here; C arrays don't support fancy indexing or slices:

```
arr[0] = 1.0
```

C arrays have many of the same behaviors as pointers. The arr variable, in fact, points to the memory location of the first element of the array. We can verify that the address of the first element of the array is the same as the address contained in the arr variable using the dereference operator, as follows:

```
%%cython
from libc.stdio cimport printf
cdef double arr[10]
printf("%p\n", arr)
printf("%p\n", &arr[0])
# Output
# 0x7ff6de204220
# 0x7ff6de204220
```

> **Note**
>
> The output will only be generated when the aforementioned code is run from a standard Python terminal. This limitation of IPython is detailed at https://github.com/ipython/ipython/issues/1230.

You should use C arrays and pointers when interfacing with existing C libraries or when you need fine control over the memory (also, they are very performant). This level of fine control is also prone to mistakes as it doesn't prevent you from accessing the wrong memory locations. For more common use cases and improved safety, you can use NumPy arrays or typed memoryviews.

Working with NumPy arrays

NumPy arrays can be used as normal Python objects in Cython, using their already optimized broadcasted operations. However, Cython provides a numpy module with better support for direct iteration.

When we normally access an element of a NumPy array, a few other operations take place at the interpreter level, causing a major overhead. Cython can bypass those operations and checks by acting directly on the underlying memory area used by NumPy arrays, thus obtaining impressive performance gains.

NumPy arrays can be declared as the `ndarray` data type. To use the data type in our code, we first need to `cimport` the numpy Cython module (which is not the same as the Python numpy module). We will bind the module to the `c_np` variable to make the difference with the Python numpy module more explicit, as follows:

```
cimport numpy as c_np
import numpy as np
```

We can now declare a NumPy array by specifying its type and the number of dimensions between square brackets (this is called *buffer syntax*). To declare a **two-dimensional (2D)** array of type `double`, we can use the following code:

```
cdef c_np.ndarray[double, ndim=2] arr
```

Access to this array will be performed by directly operating on the underlying memory area; the operation will avoid stepping into the interpreter, giving us a tremendous speed boost.

In the next example, we will show the usage of typed NumPy arrays and compare them with the normal Python version.

We first write a `numpy_bench_py` function that increments each element of `py_arr`. We declare the `i` index as an integer so that we avoid the `for` loop overhead, as follows:

```
%%cython
import numpy as np
def numpy_bench_py():
    py_arr = np.random.rand(1000)
    cdef int i
    for i in range(1000):
        py_arr[i] += 1
```

Then, we write the same function using the `ndarray` type. Note that after we define the `c_arr` variable using `c_np.ndarray`, we can assign to it an array from the numpy Python module. The code is illustrated in the following snippet:

```
%%cython
import numpy as np
cimport numpy as c_np
```

```
def numpy_bench_c():
    cdef c_np.ndarray[double, ndim=1] c_arr
    c_arr = np.random.rand(1000)
    cdef int i

    for i in range(1000):
        c_arr[i] += 1
```

We can time the results using `timeit`, and we can see here how the typed version is 50 times faster:

```
%timeit numpy_bench_c()
100000 loops, best of 3: 11.5 us per loop
%timeit numpy_bench_py()
1000 loops, best of 3: 603 us per loop
```

This gives us a significant speedup from the Python code!

Working with typed memoryviews

C and NumPy arrays, as well as the built-in `bytes`, `bytearray`, and `array.array` objects, are similar in the sense that they all operate on a contiguous memory area (also called a memory *buffer*). Cython provides a universal interface—a *typed memoryview*—that unifies and simplifies access to all these data types.

A **memoryview** is an object that maintains a reference on a specific memory area. It doesn't actually own the memory, but it can read and change its contents; in other words, it is a *view* of the underlying data. Memoryviews can be defined using a special syntax. For example, we can define a memoryview of `int` and a 2D memoryview of `double` in the following way:

```
cdef int[:] a
cdef double[:, :] b
```

The same syntax applies to the declaration of any type in variables, function definitions, class attributes, and so on. Any object that exposes a buffer interface (for example, NumPy arrays, `bytes`, and `array.array` objects) will be bound to the memoryview automatically. For example, we can bind the memoryview to a NumPy array using a simple variable assignment, as follows:

```
import numpy as np

cdef int[:] arr
```

```
arr_np = np.zeros(10, dtype='int32')
arr = arr_np # We bind the array to the memoryview
```

It is important to note that the memoryview does not *own* the data, but it only provides a way to *access* and *change* the data it is bound to; the ownership, in this case, is left to the NumPy array. As you can see in the following example, changes made through the memoryview will act on the underlying memory area and will be reflected in the original NumPy structure (and vice versa):

```
arr[2] = 1 # Changing memoryview
print(arr_np)
# [0 0 1 0 0 0 0 0 0 0]
```

In a certain sense, the mechanism behind memoryviews is similar to what NumPy produces when we slice an array. As we have seen in *Chapter 3, Fast Array Operations with NumPy, Pandas, and Xarray*, slicing a NumPy array does not copy the data but returns a view on the same memory area, and changes to the view will reflect on the original array.

Memoryviews also support array slicing with the standard NumPy syntax, as illustrated in the following code snippet:

```
cdef int[:, :, :] a
arr[0, :, :] # Is a 2-dimensional memoryview
arr[0, 0, :] # Is a 1-dimensional memoryview
arr[0, 0, 0] # Is an int
```

To copy data between one memoryview and another, you can use syntax similar to slice assignment, as shown in the following code snippet:

```
import numpy as np

cdef double[:, :] b
cdef double[:] r
b = np.random.rand(10, 3)
r = np.zeros(3, dtype='float64')

b[0, :] = r # Copy the value of r in the first row of b
```

In the next section, we will use typed memoryviews to declare types for the arrays in our particle simulator.

Using a particle simulator in Cython

Now that we have a basic understanding of how Cython works, we can rewrite the `ParticleSimulator.evolve` method. Thanks to Cython, we can convert our loops in C, thus removing the overhead introduced by the Python interpreter.

In *Chapter 3, Fast Array Operations with NumPy, Pandas, and Xarray*, we wrote a fairly efficient version of the `evolve` method using NumPy. We can rename the old version `evolve_numpy` to differentiate it from the new version. The code is illustrated in the following snippet:

```python
def evolve_numpy(self, dt):
    timestep = 0.00001
    nsteps = int(dt/timestep)

    r_i = np.array([[p.x, p.y] for p in \
        self.particles])
    ang_speed_i = np.array([p.ang_speed for p in \
        self.particles])
    v_i = np.empty_like(r_i)

    for i in range(nsteps):
        norm_i = np.sqrt((r_i ** 2).sum(axis=1))

        v_i = r_i[:, [1, 0]]
        v_i[:, 0] *= -1
        v_i /= norm_i[:, np.newaxis]

        d_i = timestep * ang_speed_i[:, np.newaxis] * \
            v_i

        r_i += d_i
    for i, p in enumerate(self.particles):
        p.x, p.y = r_i[i]
```

We want to convert this code to Cython. Our strategy will be to take advantage of the fast indexing operations by removing the NumPy array broadcasting, thus reverting to an indexing-based algorithm. Since Cython generates efficient C code, we are free to use as many loops as we like without any performance penalty.

As a design choice, we can decide to encapsulate the loop in a function that we will rewrite in a Cython module called `cevolve.pyx`. The module will contain a single Python function, `c_evolve`, that will take the particle positions, angular velocities, timestep, and the number of steps as input.

At first, we are not adding typing information; we just want to isolate the function and ensure that we can compile our module without errors. The code is illustrated in the following snippet:

```python
# file: simul.py
def evolve_cython(self, dt):
    timestep = 0.00001
    nsteps = int(dt/timestep)

    r_i = np.array([[p.x, p.y] for p in \
        self.particles])
    ang_speed_i = np.array([p.ang_speed for p in \
        self.particles])

    c_evolve(r_i, ang_speed_i, timestep, nsteps)

    for i, p in enumerate(self.particles):
        p.x, p.y = r_i[i]

# file: cevolve.pyx
import numpy as np

def c_evolve(r_i, ang_speed_i, timestep, nsteps):
    v_i = np.empty_like(r_i)

    for i in range(nsteps):
        norm_i = np.sqrt((r_i ** 2).sum(axis=1))

        v_i = r_i[:, [1, 0]]
        v_i[:, 0] *= -1
        v_i /= norm_i[:, np.newaxis]
```

```
        d_i = timestep * ang_speed_i[:, np.newaxis] *
            v_i


        r_i += d_i
```

Note that we don't need a return value for `c_evolve` as values are updated in place in the `r_i` array. We can benchmark the untyped Cython version against the old NumPy version by slightly changing our `benchmark` function, as follows:

```
def benchmark(npart=100, method='python'):
    particles = [
                Particle(uniform(-1.0, 1.0),
                        uniform(-1.0, 1.0),
                        uniform(-1.0, 1.0))
                        for i in range(npart)
        ]
    simulator = ParticleSimulator(particles)
    if method=='python':
        simulator.evolve_python(0.1)
    elif method == 'cython':
        simulator.evolve_cython(0.1)
    elif method == 'numpy':
        simulator.evolve_numpy(0.1)
```

We can time the different versions in an IPython shell, as follows:

```
%timeit benchmark(100, 'cython')
1 loops, best of 3: 401 ms per loop
%timeit benchmark(100, 'numpy')
1 loops, best of 3: 413 ms per loop
```

The two versions have the same speed. Compiling the Cython module without static typing doesn't have any advantage over pure Python. The next step is to declare the type of all the important variables so that Cython can perform its optimizations.

We can start adding types to the function arguments and see how the performance changes. We can declare the arrays as typed memoryviews containing `double` values. It's worth mentioning that if we pass an array of the `int` or `float32` type, the casting won't happen automatically and we will get an error. The code is illustrated in the following snippet:

```
def c_evolve(double[:, :] r_i,
             double[:] ang_speed_i,
             double timestep,
             int nsteps):
```

At this point, we can rewrite the loops over the particles and timesteps. We can declare the `i` and `j` iteration indices and the `nparticles` particle number as `int`, as follows:

```
cdef int i, j
cdef int nparticles = r_i.shape[0]
```

The algorithm is very similar to the pure Python version; we iterate over the particles and timesteps, and we compute the velocity and displacement vectors for each particle coordinate using the following code:

```
for i in range(nsteps):
    for j in range(nparticles):
        x = r_i[j, 0]
        y = r_i[j, 1]
        ang_speed = ang_speed_i[j]

        norm = sqrt(x ** 2 + y ** 2)

        vx = (-y)/norm
        vy = x/norm

        dx = timestep * ang_speed * vx
        dy = timestep * ang_speed * vy

        r_i[j, 0] += dx
        r_i[j, 1] += dy
```

In the preceding code snippet, we added the x, y, ang_speed, norm, vx, vy, dx, and dy variables. To avoid the Python interpreter overhead, we have to declare them with their corresponding types at the beginning of the function, as follows:

```
cdef double norm, x, y, vx, vy, dx, dy, ang_speed
```

We also used a function called sqrt to calculate the norm. If we use the sqrt function present in the math module or the one in numpy, we will again include a slow Python function in our critical loop, thus killing our performance. A fast sqrt function is available in the standard C library, already wrapped in the libc.math Cython module. Run the following code to import it:

```
from libc.math cimport sqrt
```

We can rerun our benchmark to assess our improvements, as follows:

```
In [4]: %timeit benchmark(100, 'cython')
100 loops, best of 3: 13.4 ms per loop
In [5]: %timeit benchmark(100, 'numpy')
1 loops, best of 3: 429 ms per loop
```

For small particle numbers, the speedup is massive as we obtained a 40 times faster performance over the previous version. However, we should also try to test the performance scaling with a larger number of particles, as follows:

```
In [2]: %timeit benchmark(1000, 'cython')
10 loops, best of 3: 134 ms per loop
In [3]: %timeit benchmark(1000, 'numpy')
1 loops, best of 3: 877 ms per loop
```

As we increase the number of particles, the two versions get closer in speed. By increasing the particle size to 1000, we already decreased our speedup to a more modest 6 times. This is likely because, as we increase the number of particles, the Python for loop overhead becomes less and less significant compared to the speed of other operations.

The topic of benchmarking naturally transitions us to our next section: profiling.

Profiling Cython

Cython provides a feature called *annotated view* that helps find which lines are executed in the Python interpreter and which are good candidates for ulterior optimizations. We can turn this feature on by compiling a Cython file with the - a option. In this way, Cython will generate a **HyperText Markup Language** (**HTML**) file containing our code annotated with some useful information. The usage of the - a option is shown here:

```
$ cython -a cevolve.pyx
$ firefox cevolve.html
```

The HTML file displayed in the following screenshot shows our Cython file line by line:

```
generated for it.

Raw output: cevolve.c

+01: import numpy as np
 02: cimport cython
 03: from libc.math cimport sqrt
 04:
+05: def c_evolve(double[:, :] r_i,double[:] ang_speed_i,
 06:              double timestep,int nsteps):
 07:     cdef int i
 08:     cdef int j
+09:     cdef int nparticles = r_i.shape[0]
 10:     cdef double norm, x, y, vx, vy, dx, dy, ang_speed
 11:
 12:
+13:     for i in range(nsteps):
+14:         for j in range(nparticles):
+15:             x = r_i[j, 0]
+16:             y = r_i[j, 1]
+17:             ang_speed = ang_speed_i[j]
 18:
+19:             norm = sqrt(x ** 2 + y ** 2)
 20:
+21:             vx = (-y)/norm
+22:             vy = x/norm
      if (unlikely(__pyx_v_norm == 0)) {
        #ifdef WITH_THREAD
        PyGILState_STATE __pyx_gilstate_save = PyGILState_Ensure();
        #endif
        PyErr_SetString(PyExc_ZeroDivisionError, "float division");
        #ifdef WITH_THREAD
        PyGILState_Release(__pyx_gilstate_save);
        #endif
        {__pyx_filename = __pyx_f[0]; __pyx_lineno = 22; __pyx_clineno = __LINE__; goto __pyx_L1_error;}
      }
      __pyx_v_vy = (__pyx_v_x / __pyx_v_norm);
 23:
+24:             dx = timestep * ang_speed * vx
+25:             dy = timestep * ang_speed * vy
 26:
+27:             r_i[j, 0] += dx
+28:             r_i[j, 1] += dy
 29:
```

Figure 4.2 – Generated HTML containing annotated code

Each line in the source code can appear in different shades of yellow. A more intense color corresponds to more interpreter-related calls, while white lines are translated to regular C code. Since interpreter calls substantially slow down execution, the objective is to make the function body as white as possible. By clicking on any of the lines, we can inspect the code generated by the Cython compiler. For example, the `v_y = x/norm` line checks that the norm is not `0` and raises a `ZeroDivisionError` error if the condition is not verified. The `x = r_i[j, 0]` line shows that Cython checks whether the indexes are within the bounds of the array. You may have noted that the last line is of a very intense color; by inspecting the code, we can see that this is actually a glitch—the code refers to a boilerplate related to the end of the function.

Cython can shut down checks such as division by zero so that it can remove those extra interpreter-related calls; this is usually accomplished through compiler directives. There are a few different ways to add compiler directives, as outlined here:

- Using a decorator or a context manager
- Using a comment at the beginning of the file
- Using the Cython command-line options

For a complete list of the Cython compiler directives, you can refer to the official documentation at `http://docs.cython.org/src/reference/compilation.html#compiler-directives`.

For example, to disable bounds checking for arrays, it is sufficient to decorate a function with `cython.boundscheck`, in the following way:

```
cimport cython


@cython.boundscheck(False)
def myfunction():
    # Code here
```

Alternatively, we can use `cython.boundscheck` to wrap a block of code into a context manager, as follows:

```
with cython.boundscheck(False):
    # Code here
```

If we want to disable bounds checking for a whole module, we can add the following line of code at the beginning of the file:

```
# cython: boundscheck=False
```

To alter the directives with the command-line options, you can use the -X option, as follows:

```
$ cython -X boundscheck=True
```

To disable the extra checks in our c_evolve function, we can disable the boundscheck directive and enable cdivision (this prevents checks for ZeroDivisionError), as in the following code snippet:

```
cimport cython


@cython.boundscheck(False)
@cython.cdivision(True)
def c_evolve(double[:, :] r_i,double[:] ang_speed_i, \
             double timestep,int nsteps):
```

If we look at the annotated view again, the loop body has become completely white—we removed all traces of the interpreter from the inner loop. In order to recompile, just type python setup.py build_ext --inplace again. By running the benchmark, however, we note that we didn't obtain a performance improvement, suggesting that those checks are not part of the bottleneck, as we can see here:

```
In [3]: %timeit benchmark(100, 'cython')
100 loops, best of 3: 13.4 ms per loop
```

Another way to profile Cython code is using the cProfile module. As an example, we can write a simple function that calculates the Chebyshev distance between coordinate arrays. Create a cheb.py file, as follows:

```
import numpy as np
from distance import chebyshev

def benchmark():
    a = np.random.rand(100, 2)
    b = np.random.rand(100, 2)
    for x1, y1 in a:
        for x2, y2 in b:
            chebyshev(x1, x2, y1, y2)
```

If we try profiling this script as-is, we won't get any statistics regarding the functions that we implemented in Cython. If we want to collect profiling information for the max and min functions, we need to add the `profile=True` option to the `mathlib.pyx` file, as shown in the following code snippet:

```
# cython: profile=True


cdef int max(int a, int b):
    # Code here
```

We can now profile our script with `%prun` using IPython, as follows:

```
import cheb
%prun cheb.benchmark()


# Output:
2000005 function calls in 2.066 seconds

  Ordered by: internal time

  ncalls tottime percall cumtime percall
  filename:lineno(function)
       1    1.664    1.664    2.066    2.066
cheb.py:4(benchmark)
 1000000    0.351    0.000    0.401    0.000
{distance.chebyshev}
 1000000    0.050    0.000    0.050    0.000 mathlib.pyx:2(max)
       2    0.000    0.000    0.000    0.000 {method 'rand' of
'mtrand.RandomState' objects}
       1    0.000    0.000    2.066    2.066
<string>:1(<module>)
       1    0.000    0.000    0.000    0.000 {method 'disable'
  of          '_lsprof.Profiler' objects}
```

From the output, we can see that the max function is present and is not a bottleneck. Most of the time seems to be spent in the benchmark function, meaning that the bottleneck is likely a pure Python for loop. In this case, the best strategy will be rewriting the loop in NumPy or porting the code to Cython.

One feature in Python that many users enjoy is the ability to work with Jupyter Notebooks. When working with Cython, you don't have to give up on this feature. In the next and last section of this chapter, we will see how we can use Cython with Jupyter.

Using Cython with Jupyter

Optimizing Cython code requires substantial trial and error. Fortunately, Cython tools can be conveniently accessed through Jupyter Notebooks for a more streamlined and integrated experience.

You can launch a notebook session by typing `jupyter notebook` in the command line, and you can load the Cython magic by typing `%load_ext cython` in a cell.

As mentioned earlier, the `%%cython` magic can be used to compile and load the Cython code inside the current session. As an example, we may copy the contents of the `cheb.py` file into a notebook cell, like this:

```
%%cython
import numpy as np

cdef int max(int a, int b):
    return a if a > b else b

cdef int chebyshev(int x1, int y1, int x2, int y2):
    return max(abs(x1 - x2), abs(y1 - y2))

def c_benchmark():
    a = np.random.rand(1000, 2)
    b = np.random.rand(1000, 2)

    for x1, y1 in a:
        for x2, y2 in b:
            chebyshev(x1, x2, y1, y2)
```

A useful feature of the `%%cython` magic is the `-a` option that will compile the code and produce an annotated view (just as with the `-a` command-line option) of the source code directly in the notebook, as shown in the following screenshot:

```
In [15]:  %%cython -a
          import numpy as np

          cdef int max(int a, int b):
              return a if a > b else b

          cdef int chebyshev(int x1, int y1, int x2, int y2):
              return max(abs(x1 - x2), abs(y1 - y2))

          def c_benchmark():
              a = np.random.rand(1000, 2)
              b = np.random.rand(1000, 2)

              for x1, y1 in a:
                  for x2, y2 in b:
                      chebyshev(x1, x2, y1, y2)
```

```
Out[15]:
          Generated by Cython 0.25.2

          Yellow lines hint at Python interaction.
          Click on a line that starts with a "+" to see the C code that Cython generated for it.
           01: # cython: profile=True
          +02: import numpy as np
           03:
          +04: cdef int max(int a, int b):
          +05:     return a if a > b else b
           06:
          +07: cdef int chebyshev(int x1, int y1, int x2, int y2):
          +08:     return max(abs(x1 - x2), abs(y1 - y2))
           09:
          +10: def c_benchmark():
          +11:     a = np.random.rand(1000, 2)
          +12:     b = np.random.rand(1000, 2)
           13:
          +14:     for x1, y1 in a:
          +15:         for x2, y2 in b:
          +16:             chebyshev(x1, x2, y1, y2)
```

Figure 4.3 – Generated annotated code

This allows you to quickly test different versions of your code and use the other integrated tools available in Jupyter. For example, we can time and profile the code (provided that we activate the profile directive in the cell) in the same session using tools such as `%prun` and `%timeit`. We can also inspect the profiling results by taking advantage of the `%prun` magic, as shown in the following screenshot:

```
In [22]: %prun c_benchmark()
```

```
         2000005 function calls in 1.370 seconds

   Ordered by: internal time

   ncalls  tottime  percall  cumtime  percall filename:lineno(function)
        1    1.127    1.127    1.370    1.370 _cython_magic_c7d6eab16ab5658137c9af8534d5cafb.pyx:10(c_benchma
rk)
  1000000    0.191    0.000    0.243    0.000 _cython_magic_c7d6eab16ab5658137c9af8534d5cafb.pyx:7(chebyshev)
  1000000    0.052    0.000    0.052    0.000 _cython_magic_c7d6eab16ab5658137c9af8534d5cafb.pyx:4(max)
        1    0.000    0.000    1.370    1.370 <string>:1(<module>)
        1    0.000    0.000    1.370    1.370 {built-in method builtins.exec}
        1    0.000    0.000    1.370    1.370 {_cython_magic_c7d6eab16ab5658137c9af8534d5cafb.c_benchmark}
        1    0.000    0.000    0.000    0.000 {method 'disable' of '_lsprof.Profiler' objects}
```

Figure 4.4 – Profiling output

It is also possible to use the line_profiler tool we discussed in *Chapter 1, Benchmarking and Profiling*, directly in the notebook. To support line annotations, it is necessary to do the following things:

- Enable the linetrace=True and binding=True compiler directives.

- Enable the CYTHON_TRACE=1 flag at compile time.

This can be easily accomplished by adding the respective arguments to the %%cython magic and by setting the compiler directives, as shown in the following code snippet:

```
%%cython -a -f -c=-DCYTHON_TRACE=1
# cython: linetrace=True
# cython: binding=True

import numpy as np

cdef int max(int a, int b):
    return a if a > b else b

def chebyshev(int x1, int y1, int x2, int y2):
    return max(abs(x1 - x2), abs(y1 - y2))

def c_benchmark():
    a = np.random.rand(1000, 2)
    b = np.random.rand(1000, 2)
```

```
        for x1, y1 in a:
            for x2, y2 in b:
                chebyshev(x1, x2, y1, y2)
```

Once the code is instrumented, we can install the `line_profiler` package via `pip install line_profiler` and profile using the `%lprun` magic, as follows:

```
%load_ext line_profiler
%lprun -f c_benchmark c_benchmark()
# Output:
Timer unit: 1e-06 s

Total time: 2.322 s
File: /home/gabriele/.cache/ipython/cython/_cython_
magic_18ad8204e9d29650f3b09feb48ab0f44.pyx
Function: c_benchmark at line 11
```

Line #	Hits	Time	Per Hit	% Time	Line Contents
11					def c_benchmark():
12	1	226	226.0	0.0	a = np.random.rand...
13	1	67	67.0	0.0	b = np.random.rand...
14					
15	1001	1715	1.7	0.1	for x1, y1 in a:
16	1001000	1299792	1.3	56.0	for x2, y2 in b:
17	1000000	1020203	1.0	43.9	chebyshev...

As you can see, a good chunk of time is spent in *line 16*, which is a pure Python loop and a good candidate for further optimization.

The tools available in Jupyter Notebook allow for a fast edit-compile-test cycle so that you can quickly prototype and save time when testing different solutions.

Summary

Cython is a tool that bridges the convenience of Python with the speed of C. Compared to C bindings, Cython programs are much easier to maintain and debug, thanks to the tight integration and compatibility with Python and the availability of excellent tools.

In this chapter, we introduced the basics of the Cython language and how to make our programs faster by adding static types to our variables and functions. We also learned how to work with C arrays, NumPy arrays, and memoryviews.

We optimized our particle simulator by rewriting the critical `evolve` function, obtaining a tremendous speed gain. Finally, we learned how to use the annotated view to spot hard-to-find interpreter-related calls and how to enable `cProfile` support in Cython. Also, we learned how to take advantage of the Jupyter Notebook for integrated profiling and analysis of Cython code.

All these tasks provide us with the high level of flexibility, which we already enjoy with Python, when working with Cython, while allowing our programs to be more optimized with low-level C code.

In the next chapter, we will explore other tools that can generate fast machine code on the fly, without requiring the compilation of our code to C **ahead of time (AOT)**.

Questions

1. What is the benefit of implementing static types?
2. What is the benefit of a memoryview?
3. Which tools for profiling Cython were introduced in this chapter?

5

Exploring Compilers

Python is a mature and widely used language, and there is great interest in improving its performance by compiling functions and methods directly to machine code rather than executing instructions in the interpreter. We have already seen a compiler example in *Chapter 4*, *C Performance with Cython*, where Python code is enhanced with types, compiled to efficient C code, and the interpreter calls are sidestepped.

In this chapter, we will explore two projects, Numba and PyPy, that approach compilation in a slightly different way. **Numba** is a library designed to compile small functions on the fly. Instead of transforming Python code to C, Numba analyzes and compiles Python functions directly to machine code. **PyPy** is a replacement interpreter that works by analyzing the code at runtime and optimizing the slow loops automatically.

These tools are called **Just-In-Time** (**JIT**) compilers because the compilation is performed at runtime rather than before running the code (in other cases, the compiler is called **Ahead-Of-Time** or **AOT**).

The list of topics to be covered in this chapter is as follows:

- Getting started with Numba
- The PyPy project
- Other interesting projects

Overall, Numba and PyPy offer us flexibility in leveraging JIT compilation to accelerate our programs. This chapter adds another instrument to our toolbox for improving the speed of Python applications.

Technical requirements

The code files for this chapter can be accessed through this link: `https://github.com/PacktPublishing/Advanced-Python-Programming-Second-Edition/tree/main/Chapter05`.

Getting started with Numba

Numba was started in 2012 by Travis Oliphant, the original author of NumPy, as a library for compiling individual Python functions at runtime using the **Low-Level Virtual Machine** (**LLVM**) toolchain.

LLVM is a set of tools designed to write compilers. LLVM is language-agnostic and is used to write compilers for a wide range of languages (an important example is the Clang compiler). One of the core aspects of LLVM is the intermediate representation (the LLVM IR), a very low-level, platform-agnostic language-like assembly, that can be compiled to machine code for the specific target platform.

Numba works by inspecting Python functions and compiling them, using LLVM, to the IR. As we saw in the last chapter, speed gains can be obtained when we introduce types for variables and functions. Numba implements clever algorithms to guess the types (this is called **type inference**) and compiles type-aware versions of the functions for fast execution.

Note that Numba was developed to improve the performance of numerical code. The development efforts often prioritize the optimization of applications that intensively use NumPy arrays.

> **Important Note**
> Numba is evolving fast and can have substantial improvements between releases and, sometimes, backward-incompatible changes. To keep up, ensure that you refer to the release notes for each version. In the rest of this chapter, we will use Numba version 0.53.1; ensure that you install the correct version to avoid any error by using `pip install numba==0.53.1`. The complete code examples in this chapter can be found in the `Numba.ipynb` notebook.

For the rest of this section, we will explore different aspects of Numba usage such as type specializations and JIT classes, as well as its limitations. First, we will discuss how to integrate Numba into a Python program via decorators.

Using Numba decorators

In most cases, the way we point Numba to specific Python functions is via decorators. Let's see how to do this:

1. As a first example, we will implement a function that calculates the sum of the squares of an array. The function definition is as follows:

```
def sum_sq(a):
    result = 0
    N = len(a)
    for i in range(N):
        result += a[i]
    return result
```

2. To set up this function with Numba, it is sufficient to apply the nb.jit decorator:

```
from numba import nb


@nb.jit
def sum_sq(a):
    ...
```

The nb.jit decorator won't do much when applied. However, when the function is invoked for the first time, Numba will detect the type of the input argument, a, and compile a specialized, performant version of the original function.

3. To measure the performance gain obtained by the Numba compiler, we can compare the timings of the original and the specialized functions. The original, undecorated function can be easily accessed through the py_func attribute. The timings for the two functions are as follows:

```
import numpy as np


x = np.random.rand(10000)


# Original
%timeit sum_sq.py_func(x)
```

```
4.3 ms ± 81.6 µs per loop
# Numba
%timeit sum_sq(x)
12.8 µs ± 5.41 µs per loop
```

From the previous code, you can see how the Numba version (12.8 µs) is one order of magnitude faster than the Python version (4.3 ms).

4. We can also compare how this implementation stacks up against NumPy standard operators:

```
%timeit (x**2).sum()
9.44 µs ± 93.7 ns per loop
```

In this case, the Numba compiled function is marginally slower than NumPy vectorized operations, although this difference might change across different runs.

Considering that all we needed to do was apply a simple decorator to obtain an incredible speed up over different data types, it's no wonder that what Numba does looks like magic. In the following sections, we will dig deeper to understand how Numba works and evaluate the benefits and limitations of the Numba compiler.

Type specializations

As shown earlier, the nb.jit decorator works by compiling a specialized version of the function once it encounters a new argument type. To better understand how this works, we can inspect the decorated function in the sum_sq example:

1. Numba exposes the specialized types using the signatures attribute. Right after the sum_sq definition, we can inspect the available specialization by accessing sum_sq.signatures, as follows:

```
sum_sq.signatures
# Output:
# []
```

2. If we call this function with a specific argument, for instance, an array of float64 numbers, we can see how Numba compiles a specialized version on the fly. If we also apply the function on an array of float32, we can see how a new entry is added to the sum_sq.signatures list:

```
x = np.random.rand(1000).astype('float64')
sum_sq(x)
```

```
sum_sq.signatures
# Result:
# [(array(float64, 1d, C),)]


x = np.random.rand(1000).astype('float32')
sum_sq(x)
sum_sq.signatures
# Result:
# [(array(float64, 1d, C),), (array(float32, 1d,
    C),)]
```

It is possible to explicitly compile the function for certain types by passing a signature to the nb.jit function.

3. An individual signature can be passed as a tuple that contains the type we would like to accept. Numba provides a great variety of types that can be found in the nb.types module, and they are also available in the top-level nb namespace. If we want to specify an array of a specific type, we can use the slicing operator, [:], on the type itself. In the following example, we demonstrate how to declare a function that takes an array of float64 as its only argument:

```
@nb.jit((nb.float64[:],))
def sum_sq(a):
```

4. Note that when we explicitly declare a signature, we are prevented from using other types, as demonstrated in the following example. If we try to pass an array, x, as float32, Numba will raise a TypeError exception:

```
sum_sq(x.astype('float32'))
# TypeError: No matching definition for argument
    type(s)
array(float32, 1d, C)
```

5. Another way to declare signatures is through type strings. For example, a function that takes float64 as input and returns float64 as output can be declared with the float64(float64) string. Array types can be declared using a [:] suffix. To put this together, we can declare a signature for our sum_sq function, as follows:

```
@nb.jit("float64(float64[:])")
def sum_sq(a):
```

6. You can also pass multiple signatures by passing a list:

```
@nb.jit(["float64(float64[:])",
         "float64(float32[:])"])
def sum_sq(a):
```

These APIs ensure that Numba has the correct information about what data type a function works with.

Object mode versus native mode

So far, we have shown how Numba behaves when handling a simple function. In this case, Numba worked exceptionally well, and we obtained great performance on arrays and lists.

The degree of optimization obtainable from Numba depends on how well Numba can infer the variable types and how well it can translate those standard Python operations to fast type-specific versions. If this happens, the interpreter is sidestepped, and we can get performance gains such as those of Cython.

When Numba cannot infer variable types, it will still try and compile the code, reverting to the interpreter when the types can't be determined or when certain operations are unsupported. In Numba, this is called **object mode** and contrasts with the interpreter-free scenario called **native mode**.

Numba provides a function called inspect_types that helps understand how effective the type inference was and which operations were optimized. Let's see how to use the following function:

1. As an example, we can look at the types inferred for our sum_sq function:

```
sum_sq.inspect_types()
```

2. When this function is called, Numba will print the type inferred for each specialized version of the function. The output consists of blocks that contain information about variables and types associated with them. For example, we can examine the N = len(a) line:

```
# --- LINE 4 ---
#  label  0
#    a = arg(0, name=a)   :: array(float64, 1d, A)
#    $2load_global.0 = global(len: <built-in \
        function len>) :: Function (<built-in \
        function len>)
```

```
#    N = call $2load_global.0(a, func= \
        $2load_global.0, args=[Var(a, \
            <ipython-in put-19-4687c4bff0ac>:4)], \
            kws=(), vararg=None)   :: (array( \
                float64, 1d, A),) -> int64
N = len(a)
```

For each line, Numba prints a thorough description of variables, functions, and intermediate results. In the preceding example, you can see (on the second line) that the a argument is correctly identified as an array of float64 numbers. At LINE 4, the input and return type of the len function is also correctly identified (and likely optimized) as taking an array of float64 numbers and returning int64.

If you scroll through the output, you can see how all the variables have a well-defined type. Therefore, we can be certain that Numba is able to compile the code quite efficiently. This form of compilation is called **native mode**.

As a counterexample, we can see what happens if we write a function with unsupported operations. For example, as of version 0.53.1, Numba has limited support for string operations.

3. We can implement a function that concatenates a series of strings and compiles it as follows:

```
@nb.jit
def concatenate(strings):
    result = ''
    for s in strings:
        result += s
    return result
```

4. Now, we can invoke this function with a list of strings and inspect the types:

```
concatenate(['hello', 'world'])
concatenate.signatures
# Output: concatenate (reflected
   list(unicode_type)<iv=None>,)
concatenate.inspect_types()
```

5. Numba will return the output of the function for the `reflected list` (`unicode type`) type. We can, for instance, examine how the third line gets inferred. The output of `concatenate.inspect_types()` is reproduced here:

```
# --- LINE 3 ---
# label 0
#   strings = arg(0, name=strings)  :: reflected \
 list(unicode_type)<iv=None>
#   result = const(str, )  :: Literal[str]()

result = ''
```

You can see that this time, each variable, or function is of the `unicode` or `str` type. Once again by timing the original and compiled function, we can note a significant improvement in performance:

```
x = ['hello'] * 1000
%timeit concatenate.py_func(x)
81.9 µs ± 1.25 µs per loop

%timeit concatenate(x)
1.27 ms ± 23.3 µs per loop
```

This is because the Numba compiler is not able to optimize the code and adds some extra overhead to the function call.

> **An Equivalent Decorator**
>
> Note that from version 0.12, the more concise `@nb.njit` decorator could be used instead.

Numba and NumPy

Numba was originally developed to easily increase the performance of code that uses NumPy arrays. Currently, many NumPy features are implemented efficiently by the compiler. Here, we will see how to combine the two tools to achieve even better performance for universal functions.

Universal functions with Numba

Universal functions are special functions defined in NumPy that can operate on arrays of different sizes and shapes according to the broadcasting rules. One of the best features of Numba is the implementation of fast `ufunc` instances.

We have already seen some `ufunc` examples in *Chapter 3, Fast Array Operations with NumPy, Pandas, and Xarray*. For instance, the `np.log` function is a `ufunc` instance because it can accept scalars and arrays of different sizes and shapes. Also, universal functions that take multiple arguments still work according to the broadcasting rules. Examples of universal functions that take multiple arguments are `np.sum` and `np.difference`.

Universal functions can be defined in standard NumPy by implementing the scalar version and using the `np.vectorize` function to enhance the function with the broadcasting feature. As an example, let's see how to write the *Cantor pairing function*:

1. A pairing function is a function that encodes two natural numbers into a single natural number so that you can easily interconvert between the two representations. The Cantor pairing function can be written as follows:

```
import numpy as np

def cantor(a, b):
    return  int(0.5 * (a + b)*(a + b + 1) + b)
```

2. As already mentioned, it is possible to create a `ufunc` instance in pure Python using the `np.vectorized` decorator:

```
@np.vectorize
def cantor(a, b):
    return  int(0.5 * (a + b)*(a + b + 1) + b)

cantor(np.array([1, 2]), 2)
# Result:
# array([ 8, 12])
```

Except for the convenience, defining universal functions in pure Python is not very useful, as it requires a lot of function calls affected by interpreter overhead. For this reason, `ufunc` implementation is usually done in C or Cython, but Numba beats all these methods with its convenience.

All that is needed in order to perform the conversion is to use the equivalent decorator, `nb.vectorize`.

3. We can compare the speed of the standard np.vectorized version, which, in the following code, is called cantor_py, and the same function is implemented using standard NumPy operations:

```
# Pure Python
%timeit cantor_py(x1, x2)
2.4 ms ± 23.7 µs per loop
# Numba
%timeit cantor(x1, x2)
9.1 µs ± 204 ns per loop
# NumPy
%timeit (0.5 * (x1 + x2)*(x1 + x2 + 1) + \
    x2).astype(int)
33.2 µs ± 1.12 µs per loop
```

You can see how the Numba version beats all the other options by a large margin! Numba works extremely well because the function is simple and type inference is possible.

> **Important Note**
> An additional advantage of universal functions is that, since they depend on individual values, their evaluation can also be executed in parallel. Numba provides an easy way to parallelize such functions by passing the target="cpu" or target="gpu" keyword argument to the nb.vectorize decorator.

Generalized universal functions

One of the main limitations of universal functions is that they must be defined on scalar values. A **generalized universal function**, abbreviated as gufunc, is an extension of universal functions to procedures that take arrays. Let's see how we can apply Numba to these functions:

1. A classic example is matrix multiplication. In NumPy, matrix multiplication can be applied using the np.matmul function, which takes two 2D arrays and returns another 2D array. An example of the usage of np.matmul is as follows:

```
a = np.random.rand(3, 3)
b = np.random.rand(3, 3)
```

```
c = np.matmul(a, b)
c.shape
# Result:
# (3, 3)
```

As we saw in the previous subsection, a `ufunc` instance broadcasts the operation over arrays of *scalars*; its natural generalization will be to broadcast over an array of *arrays*. If, for instance, we take two arrays of 3 by 3 matrices, we will expect `np.matmul` to match the matrices and take their product.

2. In the following example, we take two arrays containing 10 matrices of the `(3, 3)` shape. If we apply `np.matmul`, the product will be applied *matrix-wise* to obtain a new array containing the 10 results (which are, again, `(3, 3)` matrices):

```
a = np.random.rand(10, 3, 3)
b = np.random.rand(10, 3, 3)

c = np.matmul(a, b)
c.shape
# Output
# (10, 3, 3)
```

3. The usual rules for broadcasting will work in a similar way. For example, if we have an array of `(3, 3)` matrices, which will have a shape of `(10, 3, 3)`, we can use `np.matmul` to calculate the matrix multiplication of each element with a single `(3, 3)` matrix. According to the broadcasting rules, we find that the single matrix will be repeated to obtain a size of `(10, 3, 3)`:

```
a = np.random.rand(10, 3, 3)
b = np.random.rand(3, 3) # Broadcasted to shape
  (10, 3, 3)
c = np.matmul(a, b)
c.shape
# Result:
# (10, 3, 3)
```

Numba supports the implementation of efficient generalized universal functions through the `nb.guvectorize` decorator. As an example, we will implement a function that computes the Euclidean distance between two arrays as a `gufunc` instance. To create a `gufunc` instance, we must define a function that takes the input arrays, plus an output array where we will store the result of our calculation.

The nb.guvectorize decorator requires two arguments:

- The types of input and output – two 1D arrays as input and a scalar as output.

- The so-called layout string, which is a representation of the input and output sizes; in our case, we take two arrays of the same size (denoted arbitrarily by n) and output a scalar.

4. In the following example, we can see the implementation of the euclidean function using the nb.guvectorize decorator:

```
@nb.guvectorize(['float64[:], float64[:], \
    float64[:]'], '(n), (n) -> ()')
def euclidean(a, b, out):
    N = a.shape[0]
    out[0] = 0.0
    for i in range(N):
        out[0] += (a[i] - b[i])**2
```

There are a few very important points to be made. Predictably, we declared the a and b input types as float64[:] because they are 1D arrays. However, what about the output argument? Wasn't it supposed to be a scalar? Yes, but *Numba treats a scalar argument as arrays of size 1*. That's why it was declared as float64[:].

Similarly, the layout string indicates that we have two arrays of size (n) and the output is a scalar, denoted by empty brackets – (). However, the array out will be passed as an array of size 1. Also, note that we don't return anything from the function; all the output must be written in the out array.

> **Important Note**
>
> The letter n in the layout string is completely arbitrary; you may choose to use k or other letters of your liking. Also, if you want to combine arrays of uneven sizes, you can use layout strings, such as (n, m).

5. Our brand-new euclidean function can be conveniently used on arrays of different shapes, as shown in the following example:

```
a = np.random.rand(2)
b = np.random.rand(2)
c = euclidean(a, b) # Shape: (1,)
```

```
a = np.random.rand(10, 2)
b = np.random.rand(10, 2)
c = euclidean(a, b) # Shape: (10,)
```

```
a = np.random.rand(10, 2)
b = np.random.rand(2)
c = euclidean(a, b) # Shape: (10,)
```

6. How does the speed of euclidean compare to standard NumPy? In the following code, we will benchmark a NumPy vectorized version with our previously defined euclidean function:

```
a = np.random.rand(10000, 2)
b = np.random.rand(10000, 2)

%timeit ((a - b)**2).sum(axis=1)
153 µs ± 13.2 µs per loop

%timeit euclidean(a, b)
47.1 µs ± 3.19 µs per loop
```

The Numba version, again, beats the NumPy version by a large margin!

JIT classes

As of today, Numba doesn't support the optimization of generic Python objects. This limitation, however, doesn't have a huge impact on numerical codes, as they usually involve arrays and math operations exclusively.

Nevertheless, certain data structures are much more naturally implemented using objects; therefore, Numba provides support for defining classes that can be used and compiled to fast native code. Bear in mind that this is one of the newest (and almost experimental) features, and it is extremely useful, as it allows us to extend Numba to support fast data structures that are not easily implemented with arrays.

As an example, we will show how to implement a simple linked list using *JIT classes*. A linked list can be implemented by defining a Node class that contains two fields – a value and the next item in the list. As you can see in the following figure, each **Node** connects to the next and holds a value, and the last **Node** contains a broken link, to which we assign a value of **None**:

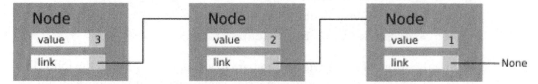

Figure 5.1 – An illustration of a linked list

We will explore various JIT-related features in the following steps:

1. In Python, we can define the Node class as follows:

```
class Node:
    def __init__(self, value):
        self.next = None
        self.value = value
```

2. We can manage the collection of Node instances by creating another class, called LinkedList. This class will keep track of the head of the list (in the preceding figure, this corresponds to the **Node** instance with **value 3**). To insert an element in the front of the list, we can simply create a new Node instance and link it to the current head.

    In the following code, we develop the initialization function for LinkedList and the LinkedList.push_back method that inserts an element in the front of the list using the strategy outlined earlier:

```
class LinkedList:

    def __init__(self):
        self.head = None

    def push_front(self, value):
        if self.head == None:
            self.head = Node(value)
        else:
            # We replace the head
```

```
        new_head = Node(value)
        new_head.next = self.head
        self.head = new_head
```

3. For debugging purposes, we can also implement the `LinkedList.show` method that traverses and prints each element in the list. The method is shown in the following snippet:

```
def show(self):
    node = self.head
    while node is not None:
        print(node.value)
        node = node.next
```

4. At this point, we can test our `LinkedList` and see whether it behaves correctly. We can create an empty list, add a few elements, and print its content. Note that since we are pushing elements to the front of the list, the last elements inserted will be the first to be printed:

```
lst = LinkedList()
lst.push_front(1)
lst.push_front(2)
lst.push_front(3)
lst.show()
# Output:
# 3
# 2
# 1
```

5. Finally, we can implement a function, `sum_list`, that returns the sum of the elements in the linked list. We will use this method to time differences between the Numba and pure Python versions:

```
@nb.jit
def sum_list(lst):
    result = 0
    node = lst.head
    while node is not None:
        result += node.value
        node = node.next
    return result
```

6. If we measure the execution time of the original `sum_list` version and the `nb.jit` version, we see that there is not much difference. The reason is that Numba cannot infer the type of classes:

```
lst = LinkedList()
[lst.push_front(i) for i in range(10000)]


%timeit sum_list(lst)
1.73 ms ± 159 µs per loop


%timeit sum_list.py_func(lst)
1.01 ms ± 175 µs per loop
```

7. We can improve the performance of `sum_list` by compiling the `Node` and `LinkedList` classes using the `nb.jitclass` decorator.

    The `nb.jitclass` decorator takes a single argument that contains the attribute types. In the `Node` class, the attribute types are `int64` for `value` and `Node` for `next`. The `nb.jitclass` decorator will also compile all the methods defined for the class. Before delving into the code, we need to make two observations.

    First, the attribute declaration must be done before the class is defined, but how do we declare a type that we haven't defined yet? Numba provides the `nb.deferred_type()` function that can be used for this purpose.

    Second, the `next` attribute can be either `None` or a `Node` instance. This is what is called an optional type, and Numba provides a utility called `nb.optional` that lets you declare variables that can be (optionally) `None`.

    This `Node` class is illustrated in the following code sample. As you can see, `node_type` is predeclared using `nb.deferred_type()`. The attributes are declared as a list of pairs containing the attribute name and the type (also note the use of `nb.optional`). After the class declaration, we are required to declare the deferred type:

```
node_type = nb.deferred_type()


node_spec = [
    ('next', nb.optional(node_type)),
    ('value', nb.int64)
]
```

```
@nb.jitclass(node_spec)
class Node:
    # Body of Node is unchanged


node_type.define(Node.class_type.instance_type)
```

8. The LinkedList class can be easily compiled, as follows. All that's needed is to define the head attribute and to apply the nb.jitclass decorator:

```
ll_spec = [
    ('head', nb.optional(Node.class_type. \
        instance_type))
]

@jitclass(ll_spec)
class LinkedList:
    # Body of LinkedList is unchanged
```

9. We can now measure the execution time of the sum_list function when we pass a JIT LinkedList:

```
lst = LinkedList()
[lst.push_front(i) for i in range(10000)]

%timeit sum_list(lst)
106 µs ± 2.64 µs per loop

%timeit sum_list.py_func(lst)
2.42 ms ± 51.8 µs per loop
```

Interestingly, when using a JIT class from a compiled function, we obtain a substantial performance improvement against the pure Python version. However, using the JIT class from the original sum_list.py_func actually results in a worse performance. Ensure that you use JIT classes only inside compiled functions!

Limitations in Numba

There are some instances where Numba cannot properly infer the variable types. In the following example, we define a function that takes a nested list of integers and returns the sum of the element in every sublist. In this case, Numba will raise a warning:

```
a = [[0, 1, 2],
     [3, 4],
     [5, 6, 7, 8]]


@nb.jit
def sum_sublists(a):
    result = []
    for sublist in a:
        result.append(sum(sublist))
    return result


sum_sublists(a)


# NumbaWarning: Compilation is falling back to object
    mode WITH looplifting enabled because Function
        "sum_sublists" failed type inference...
```

The problem with this code is that Numba is not able to determine the list type and fails. A way to fix this problem is to help the compiler determine the right type by initializing the list with a sample element and removing it at the end:

```
@nb.jit
def sum_sublists(a):
    result = [0]
    for sublist in a:
        result.append(sum(sublist))
    return result[1:]
```

Among other features that are not yet implemented in the Numba compiler are function and class definitions, list, set, and dict comprehensions, generators, the with statement, and try and except blocks. Note, however, that many of these features may become supported in the future.

Overall, we have seen multiple approaches of working with Numba to speed up our applications, such as type specializations, NumPy's universal functions, and JIT classes. We will now move on to our second main topic in this chapter – PyPy.

The PyPy project

PyPy is a very ambitious project at improving the performance of the Python interpreter. The way PyPy improves performance is by automatically compiling slow sections of the code at runtime.

PyPy is written in a special language called **RPython** (rather than C) that allows developers to implement advanced features and improvements quickly and reliably. RPython means **Restricted Python** because it implements a restricted subset of the Python language targeted to the compiler development.

As of today, PyPy version 7.3.5 supports a lot of Python features and is a possible choice for a large variety of applications, such as game and web development. PyPy compiles code using a very clever strategy called **tracing JIT compilation**. At first, the code is executed normally using interpreter calls. PyPy then starts to profile the code and identifies the most intensive loops. After the identification takes place, the compiler then observes (*traces*) the operations and can compile its optimized, interpreter-free version.

Once an optimized version of the code is present, PyPy can run the slow loop much faster than the interpreted version.

This strategy can be contrasted with what Numba does. In Numba, the units of compilation are methods and functions, while the PyPy focus is just slow loops. Overall, the focus of the projects is also very different, as Numba has limited scope for numerical code and requires a lot of instrumentation, while PyPy aims at replacing the CPython interpreter.

In this section, we will demonstrate and benchmark PyPy on our particle simulator application. We will begin by setting up Python and then look at running a particle simulator in PyPy.

Setting up PyPy

PyPy is distributed as a precompiled binary that can be downloaded from http://pypy.org/download.html, and it currently supports Python versions 2.7 and 3.7. In this chapter, we will demonstrate the usage of the 3.7 version.

Once PyPy is downloaded and unpacked, you can locate the interpreter in the `bin/pypy` directory relative to the unpacked archive. You can initialize a new virtual environment, where we can install additional packages using the following command:

```
$ /path/to/bin/pypy -m ensurepip
$ /path/to/bin/pypy -m pip install virtualenv
$ /path/to/bin/virtualenv my-pypy-env
```

To activate the environment, we will use the following command:

```
$ source my-pypy-env/bin/activate
```

At this point, you can verify that the binary Python is linked to the PyPy executable by typing `python -V`. At this point, we can go ahead and install some packages we may need. Note that PyPy may have limited support for software that uses the Python C API (most notably, packages such as `numpy` and `matplotlib`). We can go ahead and install them in the usual way:

```
(my-pypy-env) $ pip install numpy matplotlib
```

On certain platforms, the installation of `numpy` and `matplotlib` can be tricky. You can skip the installation step and remove any imports on these two packages from the scripts we will run.

Running a particle simulator in PyPy

Now that we have successfully set up the PyPy installation, we can go ahead and run our particle simulator. As a first step, we will time the particle simulator from *Chapter 1, Benchmarking and Profiling*, on the standard Python interpreter. If the virtual environment is still active, you can issue the `deactivate` command to exit the environment:

```
(my-pypy-env) $ deactivate
```

At this point, we can time our code using the `timeit` command-line interface:

```
$ python -m timeit --setup "from simul import benchmark"
  "benchmark()"
10 loops, best of 3: 886 msec per loop
```

We can reactivate the environment and run the exact same code from PyPy. On Ubuntu, you may have problems importing the `matplotlib.pyplot` module. You can try issuing the following `export` command to fix the issue or removing the `matplotlib` imports from `simul.py`:

```
$ export MPLBACKEND='agg'
```

Now, we can go ahead and time the code using PyPy:

```
$ source my-pypy-env/bin/activate
(my-pypy-env) $ python -m timeit --setup "from simul import
  benchmark" "benchmark()"
WARNING: timeit is a very unreliable tool. use perf or
something else for real measurements
10 loops, average of 7: 106 +- 0.383 msec per loop (using
standard deviation)
```

Note that we obtained a large (more than eight times) speed-up! PyPy, however, warns us that the `timeit` module can be unreliable. We can confirm our timings using the `perf` module, as suggested by PyPy:

```
(my-pypy-env) $ pip install perf
(my-pypy-env) $ python -m perf timeit --setup 'from simul
  import benchmark' 'benchmark()'
.......
Median +- std dev: 97.8 ms +- 2.3 ms
```

This gives us a more reliable assurance that our speed-up is consistent. Overall, we can see that with a simple reinstallation of Python, we are able to achieve significant speed-up via PyPy.

Advanced PyPy

Although not within the scope of this chapter, for more advanced usage of PyPy, one could integrate it with Pyglet for game development and PyLongs and Django for web development.

Overall, Numba and PyPy together offer us many options regarding how we might want to go about leveraging JIT compilers to supercharge our Python programs. In the next section, we examine several other options that may be of interest.

Other interesting projects

Over the years, many projects attempted to improve Python performance through several strategies, and, sadly, many of them failed. As of today, there are a few projects that survive and hold the promise for a faster Python.

Numba and PyPy are mature projects that are steadily improving over the years. Features are continuously being added, and they hold great promise for the future of Python:

- **Nuitka** is a program developed by Kay Hayen that compiles Python code to C. At the time of writing (version 0.6.15), it provides extreme compatibility with the Python language and produces efficient code that results in moderate performance improvements over CPython.

  Nuitka is quite different than Cython in the sense that it focuses on extreme compatibility with the Python language, and it doesn't extend the language with additional constructs.

- **Pyston** is a new interpreter developed by Dropbox that powers JIT compilers. It differs substantially from PyPy as it doesn't employ a tracing JIT but rather a method-at-a-time JIT (similar to what Numba does). Pyston, like Numba, is also built on top of the LLVM compiler infrastructure.

  Pyston is in active development and supports both **Python 2.7** and **3.8**. Benchmarks show that it is faster than CPython but slower than PyPy; that said, it is still an interesting project to follow as new features are added and compatibility is increased.

At this point, we have been introduced to four different JIT compilers. You may find in your own experience that, when developing an application, different situations and use cases may call for different compilers. It is, therefore, important to explore our options when it comes to using a JIT compiler to speed up our Python code.

Summary

Numba is a tool that compiles fast, specialized versions of Python functions at runtime. In this chapter, we learned how to compile, inspect, and analyze functions compiled by Numba. We also learned how to implement fast NumPy universal functions that are useful in a wide array of numerical applications. Finally, we implemented more complex data structures using the `nb.jitclass` decorator. Overall, Numba is built to accelerate numeric loops that are common in scientific computing. As we have seen, Numba works seamlessly with the popular NumPy library.

Tools such as PyPy allow us to run Python programs unchanged to obtain significant speed improvements. We demonstrated how to set up PyPy, and we assessed the performance improvements on our particle simulator application. We have also seen that, unlike Numba, PyPy doesn't operate on a function level but instead seeks to implement a more efficient interpreter for a whole Python program.

We also, briefly, described the current ecosystem of the Python compilers and compared them with each other. These discussions will give you the confidence to explore and work with different JIT compilers and select the most appropriate for your applications. In the next chapter, we will see a specialized version of a JIT compiler that is optimized for machine learning operations and tasks.

Questions

1. What are JIT compilers and why are they useful?
2. How does Numba determine the types of variables in a Python program? What happens when these variables are not of the type that Numba works well with?
3. What is the high-level idea of tracing a JIT compilation of PyPy?

Further reading

- More on JIT compilers: `https://www.freecodecamp.org/news/just-in-time-compilation-explained/`

6

Automatic Differentiation and Accelerated Linear Algebra for Machine Learning

With the recent explosion of data and data generating systems, machine learning has grown to be an exciting field, both in research and industry. However, implementing a machine learning model might prove to be a difficult endeavor. Specifically, common tasks in machine learning, such as deriving the loss function and its derivative, using gradient descent to find the optimal combination of model parameters, or using the kernel method for nonlinear data, demand clever implementations to make predictive models efficient.

In this chapter, we will discuss the JAX library, the premier high-performance machine learning tool in Python. We will explore some of its most powerful features, such as automatic differentiation, JIT compilation, and automatic vectorization. These features streamline the tasks that are central to machine learning mentioned previously, making training a predictive model as simple and accessible as possible. All these discussions will revolve around a hands-on example of a binary classification problem.

By the end of the chapter, you will be able to use JAX to power your machine learning applications and explore the more advanced features that it offers.

The list of topics covered in this chapter is as follows:

- A crash course in machine learning
- Getting JAX up and running
- Automatic differentiation for loss minimization
- Just-In-Time compilation for improved efficiency
- Automatic vectorization for efficient kernels

A crash course in machine learning

To fully appreciate the functionalities that JAX offers, let's first talk about the principal components of a typical workflow of training a machine learning model. If you are already familiar with the basics, feel free to skip to the next section, where we begin discussing JAX.

In machine learning, we set out to solve the problem of predicting an unknown target value of interest of a data point by considering its observable features. The goal is to design a predictive model that processes the observable features and outputs an estimate of what the target value might be. For example, image recognition models analyze the pixel values of an image to predict which object the image depicts, while a model processing weather data could predict the probability of rainy weather for tomorrow by accounting for temperature, wind, and humidity.

In general, a machine learning model could be viewed as a general mathematical function that takes in the observable features, typically referred to as X, and produces a prediction about the target value, Y. Implicitly assumed by the model is the fact that there is a certain mathematical relationship between the features (input) and the target values (output). Machine learning models in turn aim to learn about this relationship by studying a large number of examples. As such, data is crucial in any machine learning workflow.

A **dataset** is a collection of *labeled* examples – data points whose observable features, X, and target values, Y, are both available. It is through these labeled points that a model will attempt to uncover the relationship between X and Y; this is known as *training* the model. After training, the learned model can then take in the features of *unlabeled* data points, whose target values are unknown to us, and output its predictions. These predictions are what the model believes the target values of the unlabeled data points to be, given the observable features that they have.

In this section, we will talk about how training is facilitated for many common machine learning models. Specifically, it consists of three core components—the model's parameters, the model's loss function, and the minimization of that loss function—which we will consider one by one.

We will ground our discussions with an explicit example problem. Assume that we have a number of points in a two-dimensional space (which is simply the xy plane), each of which belongs to either the positive class or the negative class. The following is an example where the yellow points are the positives, and the purple ones are the negatives:

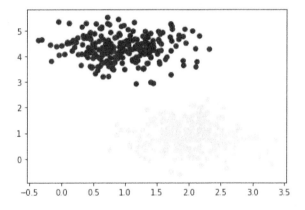

Figure 6.1 – An example binary classification problem

In this case, the observable features are the x and y coordinates of the points, so X consists of two features, while the target value y is their class membership, a positive or a negative. Our goal is to train a machine learning model on a set of labeled data and make predictions on unlabeled points. For example, after training, our model should be able to predict whether point $(2, 1)$ is positive or negative.

It is quite clear to us what the separation between the positives and the negatives is, where the lower-right corner corresponds to the positive class, and the upper-left corner corresponds to the negative class. Point $(2, 1)$ specifically is likely a positive (a yellow point). But how does a machine learning model do this automatically, without humans having to hardcode such a classification rule? We will see this in the next section.

Model parameters

A predictive model starts out with a formula that attempts to explain the relationship between the observable features and the target value. We will consider the class of linear models (one of the most common and simplest types of machine learning models), which assume that the target value is a linear combination of the features (hence the model's name)

$$y = w_0 + w_1 x_1 + w_2 x_2$$

where x_1 and x_2 are the x and y coordinates of the points, and the numbers w_i are the model's *parameters*.

We do not know the values of these parameters, and each combination of values for these parameters defines a unique relationship between x and y, a unique hypothesis. It is the values of these parameters that we need to identify during the training phase, such that the aforementioned relationship fits the labeled data that we have access to.

In our classification model, we constrain the target values y to be either positive (+1) or negative (-1), but y as defined by the linear relationship discussed earlier can take on any real value. As such, it is customary to transform a real-valued y to be either +1 or -1 by simply taking the sign of the value. In other words, the actual model we are working with is:

$$y = sign(w_0 + w_1 x_1 + w_2 x_2)$$

Performing predictions is at the heart of a common machine learning task. Given the linear relationship between features X and the target value y, predicting the target value y_* of a new data point with features x_{*1} and x_{*2} simply involves applying the mathematical model we have:

$$y_* = sign(w_0 + w_1 x_{*1} + w_2 x_{*2})$$

The only missing piece of our puzzle is how to identify the correct values for our parameters w_i. Again, we need to determine the values for the model's parameters to fit our training data. But how can we exactly quantify how well a specific value combination for the parameters explains a given labeled dataset? This question leads to the next component of a machine learning workflow: the model's loss function.

Loss function

A model's loss function quantifies a property about the model that we'd like to minimize. This could, in general, be the cost incurred when the model is trained a certain way. Within our context, the loss function is specifically the amount of predictive error that the model makes on the training dataset. This quantity approximates the error made on future unseen data, which is what we really care about. (In different settings, you might encounter **utility functions**, which, most of the time, are simply the negative of corresponding loss functions, which are to be maximized.) The lower the loss, the better our model is likely to perform (barring technical problems such as overfitting).

In a classification problem like ours, there are many ways to design an appropriate loss function. For example, the 0-1 loss simply counts how many instances there are in which the model makes an incorrect prediction, while the binary cross-entropy loss is a more popular choice as the function is smoother than 0-1 and thus easy to optimize (we will come back to this point later).

For our example, we will use a version of the support-vector loss function, which is formalized as:

$$L = \frac{1}{n} \sum_{i=1}^{n} \max(0, 1 - y_i \bar{y}_i)$$

where i, indicating the index of unique examples in the training set, ranges from 1 to n, the training set size. y_i is the true label of the i-th example, while $\bar{y}_i$ is the corresponding label predicted by the learning model.

This non-negative function calculates the average of the $\max(0, 1 - y_i \bar{y}_i)$ term across all training examples. It is easy to see that for each example i, if y_i and $\bar{y}_i$ are similar to each other, the max term will evaluate to a small value. On the other hand, if y_i and $\bar{y}_i$ have opposite signs (in other words, if the model misclassifies the example), the max term will increase. As such, this function is appropriate to quantify the error that our predictive model is making for a given parameter combination.

Given this loss function, the problem of training our linear model reduces to finding the optimal parameter w_i that minimizes the loss (preferably at 0). Of course, the search space of w_i is very large—each parameter could be any real-valued number—so exhaustively trying out all possible combinations of values for w_i is out of the question. This leads us to the final subsection: intelligently minimizing a loss function.

Loss minimization

Without going into too much technical detail, you can mathematically find the minimum of a given function by utilizing its *derivative* information. Derivates of a function denote the rate of change in the function value with respect to the rate of change of its input. By analyzing the value of the derivative, or more commonly referred to in machine learning as the *gradient*, we could algorithmically identify input locations at which the objective function is likely to be low-valued.

However, derivatives are only informative in helping us locate the function minimum if the function itself is *smooth*. Smoothness is a mathematical property that states that if the input value of a function only changes by a little, the function value (output) should not change by too much. Notable examples of non-smooth functions include the step function and the absolute value function, but most functions that you will encounter are likely to be smooth. The smoothness property explains our preference for the binary cross-entropy loss over the 0-1 loss, the latter of which is a non-smooth function. The support vector-style loss function we will be using is also smooth.

The overall takeaway is that if we have access to the derivate of a smooth function, finding its minimum will be easy to do. But how do we do this exactly? Many gradient-based optimization routines have been studied, but we will consider arguably the most common method: *gradient descent*. The high-level idea is to inspect the gradient of the loss function at a given location and move in the direction *opposite* to that gradient (in other words, descending the gradient, hence the name), illustrated next:

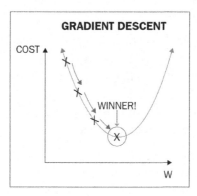

Figure 6.2 – Illustration of gradient descent

Due to the definition of the gradient, the function value $f(x')$ evaluated at the point x' that is immediately in the opposite direction of the gradient with respect to a given point x is lower than $f(x)$. As such, by using the gradient of the loss function as a guide and incrementally moving in the opposite direction, we can theoretically arrive at the function minimum. One important consideration is that, if we move our evaluation by a large amount, even in the correct direction, we could end up missing the true minimum. To address this, we typically adjust our step to be only a fraction of the loss gradient.

Concretely, denote ∇L_i as the gradient of the loss function L with respect to the i-th parameter w_i, so the gradient descent *update rule* is to adjust the value of w_i as:

$$w_i \leftarrow w_i - \gamma \nabla L_i$$

where γ is a small number (much lower than 1) that acts as a step size. By repeatedly applying this update rule, we could incrementally adjust the values of the model's parameters to lower the model's loss, thereby improving its predictive performance.

And with that, we have finished sketching out the main components of a typical machine learning workflow. As a summary, we work with a predictive model (in our case, a linear one) that has a certain number of adjusting parameters that seek to explain the data we have. Each parameter combination leads to a different hypothesis whose validity is quantified by the loss function. Finally, by taking the derivative of the loss function and using gradient descent, we have a way to incrementally update the model's parameters to achieve better performance.

We will now begin the main topic of this chapter: the JAX library.

Getting JAX up and running

As briefly mentioned, JAX is a combination of different tools for developing accelerated, high-performance computations with a focus on machine learning applications. Remember from the last chapter that the NumPy library offers optimized computation for numerical operations such as finding the min/max or taking the sum of the average along an axis. We can think of JAX as the NumPy equivalent for machine learning, where common tasks in machine learning could be done in highly optimized code. These, as we will see, include automatic differentiation, accelerated linear algebra using a Just-In-Time compiler, and efficient vectorization and parallelization of code, among other things.

JAX offers these functionalities through what's known as **functional transformations**. In the simplest sense, a functional transformation in JAX converts a function, typically one that we build ourselves, to an optimized version where different functionalities are facilitated. This is done via a simple API, as we will see later.

But first, we will talk about installing the library on a local system.

Installing JAX

A barebones version of JAX could be simply installed using the regular Python package manager `pip`:

```
pip install --upgrade pip
pip install --upgrade jax jaxlib
```

These commands will install a CPU-only version of JAX, which is recommended if you are planning to try it out on a local system such as a laptop. The full version of JAX, with support for NVIDIA GPUs (commonly used by deep learning models), could also be installed via a more involved procedure, outlined in their documentation: `https://jax.readthedocs.io/en/latest/developer.html`.

Furthermore, note that JAX can only be installed on Linux (Ubuntu 16.04 or above) or macOS (10.12 or above). To run JAX on a Windows machine, you would need the Windows Subsystem for Linux, which lets you run a GNU/Linux environment on Windows. If you typically run your machine learning jobs on a cluster, you should talk to your system administrator about finding the correct way to install JAX.

If you are an independent machine learning practitioner, you might find these technical requirements to install the full version of JAX intimidating. Luckily, there is a free platform that we could use to see JAX in action: *Google Colab*.

Using Google Colab

Generally, Google Colab is a free Jupyter notebook platform that is integrated with a high-performance backend and machine learning tools on which you could build prototypes of machine learning models with ease.

There are two main advantages to using Google Colab. First, the platform comes with most machine learning-related libraries (for example, TensorFlow, PyTorch, and scikit-learn) and tools preinstalled, including a **GPU (graphics processing unit)** and a **TPU (tensor processing unit)**, free of charge! This allows independent machine learning researchers and students to try out expensive hardware on their machine learning pipelines at no cost. Second, Google Colab allows collaborative editing between different users, enabling streamlined group work when building models.

To utilize this platform, all you need is a Google/Gmail account when signing in at `https://colab.research.google.com/`. Using this platform is generally simple and intuitive, but you can also refer to several readings included at the end of this chapter for further content relating to Google Colab. Note that the code presented in the remainder of this chapter is run on Google Colab, which means you could go to **[INSERT LINK]** and simply run the code yourself to follow along with our later discussions.

And with that, we are ready to begin talking about the functionalities that JAX offers.

Automatic differentiation for loss minimization

Recall from our previous discussion that to fit a predictive model to a training dataset, we first analyze an appropriate loss function, derive the gradient of this loss, and then adjust the parameters of the model in the opposite direction of the gradient to achieve a lower loss. This procedure is only possible if we have access to the derivative of the loss function.

Earlier machine learning models were able to do this because researchers derived the derivatives of common loss functions by hand using calculus, which were then hardcoded into the training algorithm so that a loss function could be minimized. Unfortunately, taking the derivative of a function could be difficult to do at times, especially if the loss function being used is not well behaved. In the past, you would have to choose a different, more mathematically convenient loss function to make your model run even if the new function was less appropriate, potentially sacrificing some of the expressiveness of the original function.

Recent advances in computational algebra have resulted in the technique called **automatic differentiation**. Exactly as it sounds, this technique allows for an automated process to numerically evaluate the derivative of a given function, expressed in computer code, without relying on a human to provide the closed-form solution for that derivative. On the highest level, automatic differentiation traces the order in which the considered function is computed and which arithmetic operations (for example, addition, multiplication, and exponentiation) were involved, and then applies the chain rule to obtain the numerical value of the derivative in an automated manner. By intelligently taking advantage of the information present in the computational calculation of the function itself, automatic differentiation can compute its derivative efficiently and accurately.

Recall that in our running toy problem, we would like to minimize the loss function:

$$L = \frac{1}{n} \sum_{i=1}^{n} \max(0, 1 - y_i \, \overline{y}_i)$$

where $\overline{y}_i$ is the prediction made by our linear predictive model for the i-th data point. Of course, we could derive the gradient of this loss function when implementing gradient descent (which would require us to brush up on our calculus!), but with automatic differentiation, we will not have to.

The technique is widely used in deep learning tools such as TensorFlow and PyTorch, where computing the gradient of a loss function is a central task. We could use the API for automatic differentiation from these libraries to compute the loss gradient, but by using JAX's API, we will be able to utilize other powerful functionalities that we will get to later. For now, let's build our model and the gradient descent algorithm using JAX's automatic differentiation tool.

Making the dataset

First, we need to generate the toy dataset shown in *Figure 6.1*. To do this, we will make use of the `make_blobs` function from the `datasets` module in scikit-learn. If you are running your code locally, you would need to install scikit-learn using the `pip` command:

```
pip install sklearn
```

Otherwise, if you are using Google Colab, scikit-learn, as well as all the other external libraries used in this chapter's code, already comes preinstalled, so you only need to import it into your program.

The `make_blobs` function, as the name suggests, generates blobs (in other words, clusters) of data points. Its API is simple and readable:

```
X, y = make_blobs(
    n_samples=500, n_features=2, centers=2, \
        cluster_std=0.5, random_state=0
)
```

Here we are creating a two-dimensional (specified by n_features) dataset of 500 points (specified by n_samples). These data points should belong to one of two classes (specified by centers). The cluster_std argument controls how tightly the points belonging to the same class cluster together; in this case, we are setting it to 0.5. At this point, we have a dataset of 500 points, each of which has two features and belongs to either the positive class or the negative class. The variable X is a NumPy array that contains the features, having a shape of (500, 2), while y is a 500-long, one-dimensional, binary array containing the labels.

By default, the negative class has the label of 0 in y. As a data preprocessing step, we will convert all the instances of 0 in y to -1 using NumPy's convenient conditional indexing syntax:

```
y[y == 0] = -1
```

We are also adding to X a third feature column that only contains instances of 1. This column is a constant and corresponds to the free coefficient w_0 in our model:

$$y = sign(w_0 + w_1x_1 + w_2x_2)$$

On the other hand, w_1 and w_2 are the coefficients for the first and second features in X.

We have now generated our toy example. If you now call Matplotlib to generate a scatter plot on X, for example, via the following code:

```
plt.scatter(X[:, 0], X[:, 1], c=y);
```

You will obtain the same plot as in *Figure 6.1*. And with that, we are ready to begin building our predictive model.

Building a linear model

Remember two core components of a machine learning pipeline: the model and the loss function. To build our model, we first need to write functions that correspond to these components. First, the model comes in the form of the `predict` function:

```
import jax.numpy as jnp


def predict(w, X):
    return jnp.dot(X, w)
```

This function takes in the model's parameters w, implicitly assumed to be in the form of a NumPy array, and the features of the training data points X, a NumPy two-dimensional matrix. Here we are using the `dot` function from the NumPy module of JAX, aliased `jnp` in the code, to take the dot product of w and X. If you are unfamiliar with the dot product, it is simply an algebraic operation that is a shorthand for the linear combination $w_0 + w_1x_1 + w_2x_2$ that corresponds to our model. Overall, this function encodes for our model that the prediction we make about the label of a data point is (the sign of) the dot product of the parameters and the data features.

While not a focus of our discussion, it is important at this point to note that the numpy module of JAX provides nearly identical APIs for mathematical operations as NumPy. The `dot` function is simply one example; others could be found on their documentation site: `https://jax.readthedocs.io/en/latest/jax.numpy.html`. This is to say that if you have accumulated a significant amount of code in NumPy but would like to convert it to JAX, replacing your import statement of `import numpy as np` with `import jax.numpy as np` would, in most cases, do the trick; no complicated, painstaking conversion is necessary.

So, we have implemented the prediction function of our model. Our next task is to write the loss function

$$L = \frac{1}{n} \sum_{i=1}^{n} \max(0, 1 - y_i \, \overline{y}_i)$$

The loss function can be written with the following code:

```
def loss(w):
    preds = predict(w, X)
    return jnp.mean(jnp.clip(1 - jnp.multiply(y, preds), \
      a_min=0))
```

Let's take a moment to break this code down. This `loss` function is a function of w, since, if w changes, the loss will change accordingly.

Now, let's focus on the term inside the summation symbol in the previous formula: it is the max between 0 and $1 - y_i \, \overline{y}_i$, where y_i is the true label of a data point and $\overline{y}_i$ is the corresponding prediction made by the model. As such, we compute this quantity with `jnp.clip(1 - jnp.multiply(y, preds), a_min=0)`, before which we call the `predict` function to obtain the values for $\overline{y}_i$, stored in the `preds` variable.

If you are familiar with the NumPy equivalent, you might have noticed that these functions that we are using, `clip` and `multiply`, have an identical interface in NumPy; again, JAX tries to make the transition for NumPy users as seamless as possible. Finally, we compute the mean of this max term across all training examples with the `mean` function.

Believe it or not, we have successfully implemented our linear model! With a specific value for w, we will be able to predict what the label of a data point is using the `predict` function and compute our loss with the `loss` function. At this point, we can try out different values for w; as a common practice, we will initialize w to be random numbers:

```
np.random.seed(0)
```

```
w = np.random.randn(3)
```

The last step of our training procedure is to find the best value for w that minimizes the loss, which we will implement next.

Gradient descent with automatic differentiation

Recall that in the gradient descent algorithm, we compute the gradient of the loss function for the current value of w and then adjust w by subtracting a fraction of the gradient (effectively moving in the opposite direction of the gradient).

Again, in the past, we would need to derive the gradient in closed form and implement it in our code. With automatic differentiation, we simply need the following:

```
from jax import grad
```

```
loss_grad = grad(loss)
```

loss is the function we implemented in the last subsection. Here we are using the grad function from JAX to obtain the *gradient function* of loss. This is to say that if we were to call loss_grad, the gradient function, on a given value of w using loss_grad(w), we would obtain the gradient of the loss function at w, in the same way loss(w) gives us the loss itself at w.

This is a so-called *function transformation*, which takes in a function in Python (loss in our case) and returns a related function (loss_grad) that could then be called on actual inputs to compute quantities that we are interested in. Function transformations are a powerful interface that makes it easy to work with functional logic and are the main way in which you use JAX. We will see that all other functionalities offered by JAX discussed in this chapter are function transformations.

With our gradient function in hand, we now implement gradient descent using a simple for loop:

```
n_iters = 200
lr = 0.01
loss_grad = grad(loss)

for i in range(n_iters):
    grads = loss_grad(w)
    w = w - lr * grads

    tmp_loss = loss(w)

    if tmp_loss == 0:
        break
```

If you are looking at the Google Colab notebook, you might see some other book-keeping code that is used to show a real-time progress bar, but the preceding code is the main logic of gradient descent.

At each iteration of the `for` loop, we compute the gradient of the loss function at the current value of w, and then use that gradient to adjust the value of w: `w = w - lr * grads`. How big of a step we will take in the opposite direction of the gradient is controlled by the `lr` variable, set to `0.01`. This variable is typically referred to as the **learning rate** in the language of machine learning.

After the adjustment, we will check to see whether this new value of w does, in fact, minimize our loss at 0, in which case we simply exit the `for` loop with the `break` statement. If not, we repeat this process until some termination condition is satisfied; in our case, we simply say that we only do this for at most 200 times (specified by the `n_iters` variable).

When we run the code, we will observe that as the `for` loop progresses, the value of the loss decreases for each adjustment. At the end of the loop, our loss decreases to a small number: roughly 0.013. Using Matplotlib, we could quickly sketch out the progression of this decrease with `plt.plot(losses)`, which produces the following plot:

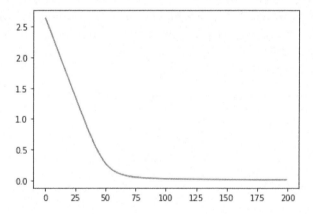

Figure 6.3 – The decrease in loss of the linear model

We see that with the random guess for the value of w at the beginning, we receive a loss of roughly 2.5, but using gradient descent, we have reduced it to almost zero. At this point, we can be confident that the value of w that we currently have after gradient descent fits our data well.

This concludes the training of our linear predictive model. A customary task that follows training a model is to examine the predictions made by the model across a whole feature space. This process helps ensure that our model is learning appropriately. When working in a low-dimensional space such as ours, we can even visualize this space.

Specifically, our decision boundary is a straight line that (hopefully) separates the two classes that we'd like to perform classification: $w_0 + w_1x_1 + w_2x_2 = 0$, where x_1 and x_2 are coordinates of points within our two-dimensional space. As such, we can draw this line by first generating a fine-grid array for the x coordinates (x_1):

```
xs = np.linspace(X[:, 0].min(), X[:, 0].max(), 100)
```

We can derive the y coordinates (x_2) using the equation for the line we had previously:

```
plt.plot(xs, (xs * w[0] + w[2]) / - w[1])
```

Plotting this line together with the scattered points corresponding to our training data, we obtain the following plot:

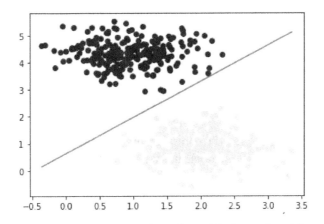

Figure 6.4 – The decision boundary of the learned model

We see that our decision boundary nicely separates the two classes that we have. Now, when we'd like to make a prediction regarding which class an unseen point belongs to, we simply put its features through our `predict` function and look at the sign of the output.

And that is all there is to it! Of course, when we work with more complicated models, other more specialized considerations need to be made. However, the high-level process remains unchanged: designing a model and its loss function and then using gradient descent (or some other loss minimization strategy) to find the optimal combination of parameters. We have seen that using the automatic differentiation module in JAX, we were able to do this easily with minimal code while avoiding the hairy math that is usually involved with deriving the gradient of a loss function.

With that said, the benefits that JAX offers don't stop there. In our next section, we will see how to make our current code more efficient by using JAX's internal **Just-In-Time** (**JIT**) **compiler**.

Just-In-Time compilation for improved efficiency

As we have learned from the last chapter, JIT compilation allows a piece of code that is expected to run many times to be executed more efficiently. This process is specifically useful in machine learning where functions such as the loss or the gradient of the loss of a model need to be computed many times during the loss minimization phase. We hence expect that by leveraging a JIT compiler, we can make our machine learning models train faster.

You might think that to do this, we would need to hook one of the JIT compilers we considered in the last chapter into JAX. However, JAX comes with its own JIT compiler, which requires minimal code to integrate in an existing program. We will see how to use it by modifying the training loop we made in the last section.

First, we reset the w_i parameters of our models:

```
np.random.seed(0)


w = np.random.randn(3)
```

Now, the way we will integrate the JIT compiler into our program is to point it to the gradient of our loss function. Remember that we can reap the benefits of JIT compilation by applying it to a piece of code that we expect to execute many times, which we have mentioned is exactly the case for the loss gradient. Recall that we were able to derive this gradient in the last section using the grad function transformation:

```
loss_grad = grad(loss)
```

To obtain the JIT-compiled version of this function, we can follow a very similar process, in which we transform this loss gradient function using jit:

```
from jax import jit


loss_grad = jit(grad(loss))
```

Amazingly, that is all we need to do. Now, if we run the same training loop we currently have, with this one line changed, we will obtain the same result, including the learning curve and the decision boundary we plotted earlier.

However, upon inspecting the running time of the training loop, we will notice that the training loop is now much more efficient: within our Google Colab notebook, the speed goes from roughly 77 iterations to 175 iterations per second! Note that although these numbers might vary across different runs of the code, the improvement should stay apparent. While this speedup might not be meaningful to us and our simple linear model, it will prove useful for more heavyweight models such as neural networks, with millions to billions of parameters, which take weeks and months to train.

Furthermore, this speedup was achieved with a single line of code changed using the function transformation, `jit`. This means that however complicated the functions you are working with are, if they are JAX-compatible, you can simply pass them through `jit` to enjoy the benefits of JIT compilation.

At this point, we have explored two powerful techniques to accelerate our machine learning pipeline: automatic differentiation and JIT compilation. In the next section, we will look at a final valuable feature of JAX – automatic vectorization.

Automatic vectorization for efficient kernels

You might remember from our discussions on NumPy that the library is efficient at applying numerical operations to all elements in an array or the elements along specific axes. By exploiting the fact that the same operation is to be applied to multiple elements, the library optimizes low-level code that performs the operation, making the computation much more efficient than doing the same thing via an iterative loop. This process is called **vectorization**.

When working with machine learning models, we would like to go through a procedure of vectorizing a specific function, rather than looping through an array or a matrix, to gain performance speedup. Vectorization is typically not easy to do and might involve clever tricks to rewrite the function that we'd like to vectorize into another form that admits vectorization easily.

JAX addresses this concern by providing a function transformation that automatically vectorizes a given function, even if the function is only designed to take in single-valued variables (which means traditionally, an iterative loop would be necessary). In this section, we will see how to use this feature by going through the process of kernelizing our predictive model. First, we need to briefly discuss what kernels are as well as their place in machine learning.

Data that is not linearly separable

Remember that the predictive model we currently have assumes that the target we'd like to predict for can be expressed as a linear combination of the data features; the model is thus a linear one. This assumption is quite restrictive in practice, as data can present highly nonlinear and still meaningful patterns.

For example, here we use the `make_moons` function from the same `datasets` module of scikit-learn to generate another toy dataset and visualize it, again using a scatter plot:

```
from sklearn.datasets import make_moons

X, y = make_moons(n_samples=200, noise=0.1, random_state=0)
X = np.hstack((X, np.ones_like(y).reshape(-1, 1)))
y[y == 0] = -1

plt.scatter(X[:, 0], X[:, 1], c=y);
```

This will generate the following plot:

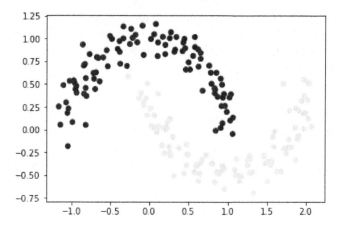

Figure 6.5 – A linearly non-separable dataset

Once again, this is a binary classification problem where we need to distinguish between the yellow and the dark blue points. As you can see, these data points are not linearly separable since, unlike our previous dataset, a straight line that perfectly separates the two classes here does not exist. In fact, if we were to try to fit a linear model to this data, we would obtain a model with a relatively high loss (roughly 0.7) and a decision boundary that is clearly unsuitable, as shown here:

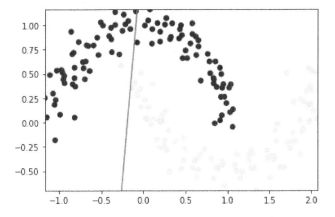

Figure 6.6 – Fitting a linear model on nonlinear data

How, then, could we modify our current model so that it can handle nonlinear data? A typical solution in these kinds of situations is the kernel method in machine learning, which we will briefly discuss next.

The kernel method in machine learning

Without going into much technical detail, the kernel method (sometimes referred to as the **kernel trick**) refers to the process of transforming a low-dimensional dataset, such as ours, that is nonlinear to higher dimensions, with the hope that in higher dimensions, linear hyperplanes that separate the data will exist.

To take a data point to higher dimensions, additional features are created from the features already included in the original data. In our running example, we are given the x and y coordinates of the data points; hence, our data is two-dimensional. A common way to compose more features in this case is to compute polynomials of these coordinates up to a degree, d. For instance, polynomials that are up to degree 2 for features x and y include xy and x^2. The larger d is, the more expressiveness we will gain from these new features we are creating, but we will also incur a higher computational cost.

Notice that these polynomial features are nonlinear, which motivates their use in helping us find a model that separates our nonlinear data. With these new, nonlinear features in hand, we will then fit our predictive model on this bigger, more expressive dataset we just engineered. Note that while the predictive model remains in the same form as the linear parameters w_i, the data features that the model learns from are nonlinear, so the resulting decision boundary will also be nonlinear.

I mentioned earlier that the more expressive we want the features we are synthetically creating to be, the more computational costs we will incur. Here, kernels are a way to manipulate the data points so that we can interact with them in higher dimensions without having to explicitly compute the high-dimensional features. In essence, a kernel is simply a function that takes in a pair of data points and returns the inner product of some transformation of the feature vectors. This is just to say that it returns a matrix that represents the two data points in higher dimensions.

In this chapter, we will use one of the most popular kernels in machine learning: the radial basis function, or RBF, kernel, which is defined as follows:

$$K(x, x') = e^{-(x-x')^2/l}$$

where x and x' are the low-dimensional feature vectors of the two data points, and l is commonly referred to as the length scale, a tunable parameter of the kernel. There are many benefits to using the RBF kernel that we won't be going into in much detail here, but on the highest level, RBF can be regarded as an infinite-dimensional kernel, which means that it will provide us with a high level of expressiveness in the features we are computing.

The new model using this kernel method, modified from our previous linear model, now makes the following assumption for each pair of feature vector x and label y:

$$y = \alpha_0 + \alpha_1 K(x, x_1) + \alpha_2 K(x, x_2) + \cdots + \alpha_n K(x, x_n)$$

where x_i is the i-th data point in the training set and α_i are the model parameters to be optimized. While this assumption is written to contrast the linear assumption that we had earlier:

$$y = w_0 + w_1 x_1 + w_2 x_2$$

x_i now refers to the entire feature vector of a data point, not the i-th feature of a data point. Further, we now have n terms of α_i, as opposed to 2 (or d) terms of w_i as before.

We see the role of the kernel here is to transform the feature of x by computing the inner product of its features and those of each of the data points in the training set. The output of the kernel is then used as the new features to be multiplied by the model parameters α_i, whose values will be optimized as part of the training process.

Let's now implement this kernel in our code:

```
lengthscale = 0.3


def rbf_kernel(x, z):
    return jnp.exp(- jnp.linalg.norm(x - z) ** 2 \
        / lengthscale)
```

Here we are setting the length scale at 0.3, but feel free to play around with this value and observe its effect on the learned model afterward. The rbf_kernel function takes in x and z, two given data points. The code inside the function is self-explanatory: we compute the squared norm of the difference between x and z (linalg.norm in JAX follows the same API as in NumPy), divide it by lengthscale, and use its negative as the input of the natural exponential function, exp.

Now, we need to implement the new version of the predict function for our kernelized model, which we will see how to do in the next subsection.

Automatic vectorization for kernelized models

You might remember that the job of the prediction function is to implement the assumption our model is making, which in this case is:

$$y = \alpha_0 + \alpha_1 K(x, x_1) + \alpha_2 K(x, x_2) + \cdots + \alpha_n K(x, x_n)$$

The challenge here is in the sum $\alpha_1 K(x, x_1) + \alpha_2 K(x, x_2) + \cdots + \alpha_n K(x, x_n)$, where $x_1, x_2, \ldots, x_n$ are the individual data points in our training set. In a naïve implementation, we would iterate through each data point x_i, compute $K(x, x_i)$, multiply it by α_i, and finally, add these terms together. Computing the inner product of two vectors is generally a computationally expensive operation, so repeating this computation n times would be prohibitively costly.

To make this kernelized model more practical, we'd like to *vectorize* this procedure. Normally, this would require reimplementing our kernel function using various tricks to enable vectorization. However, with JAX, we can effortlessly obtain the vectorized version of the rbf_kernel function using the vmap transformation:

```
from jax import vmap

kernel = rbf_kernel
vec_kernel = jit(vmap(vmap(kernel, (0, None)), (None, 0)))
```

Don't let the last line of code intimidate you. Here we are simply getting the vectorized form of our kernel function along the first axis (remember the kernel has two inputs) with vmap(kernel, (0, None), and then vectorizing that very vectorized-along-the-first-axis kernel along the second axis with vmap(vmap(kernel, (0, None)), (None, 0)). Finally, we derive the JIT-compiled version of the function with jit.

Aside from being a concise one-liner, this code perfectly illustrates why function transformation (JAX's design choice) is so useful: we can compose different function transformations in a nested way, repeatedly calling a transformation on the output of another transformation; in this case, we have the JIT-compiled function of a twice-vectorized function.

With this vectorized kernel function composed, we are now ready to implement the corresponding `predict` and `loss` functions:

```python
def predict(alphas, X_test):
    return jnp.dot(vec_kernel(X, X_test), alphas)


def loss(alphas):
    preds = predict(alphas, X)
    return jnp.mean(jnp.clip(1 - jnp.multiply(y, preds), \
      a_min=0))
```

Of note here is the `predict` function, where we are calling `vec_kernel(X, X_test)` to compute the vector of $[1, K(x, x_1), K(x, x_2), \ldots, K(x, x_n)]$ via vectorization. Remember that without `vmap`, we would need to either iterate through the individual data points (for example, using a `for` loop), which is specifically more inefficient, or rewrite our `rbf_kernel` function so that the function itself facilitates the vectorization. In the end, we simply compute the dot product between the returned output and the vector of the parameters we'd like to optimize, `alphas`.

Our loss function stays the same. We now can apply the same training procedure as we have before, this time on the `alphas` variable:

```python
np.random.seed(0)


alphas = np.random.randn(y.size)


for i in range(n_iters):
    grads = loss_grad(alphas)
    alphas = alphas - lr * grads


    tmp_loss = loss(alphas)


    if tmp_loss == 0:
        break
```

We can also plot out the progression of the loss throughout this training:

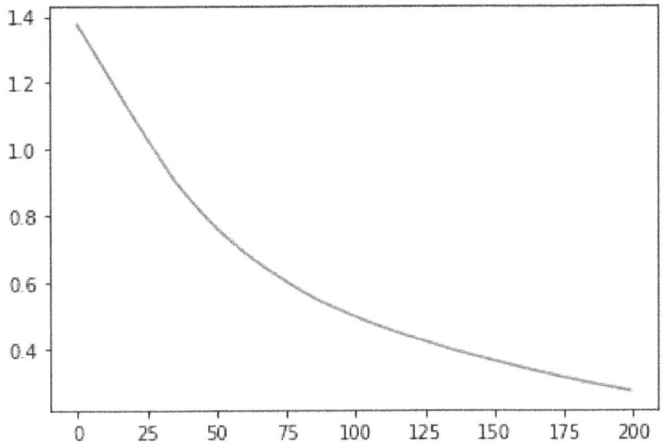

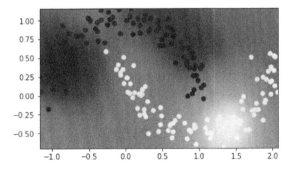

Figure 6.7 – The decrease in loss of the kernelized model

We see a steady decrease in loss, indicating that the model is fitting its parameters to the data. In the end, our loss is well below 0 . 7, which was the loss of the purely linear model we previously had.

Finally, we'd like to visualize what our model has learned. This is a bit more involved as we no longer have a nice linear equation that we can translate into a line as before. Instead, we visualize the predictions made by the model itself. In the following figure, we show these predictions made on a fine grid that spans across our training data points, where the colors show the predicted classes, and the hues show the confidence in the predictions:

Figure 6.8 – Predictions made by the learned kernelized model

We see that the model was able to identify the nonlinear pattern in our data, indicated by the yellow and dark blue blobs lying right in the center of the moons. As such, we have successfully modified our predictive model to learn from nonlinear data, which was done by using a kernel to create nonlinear features and JAX's automatic vectorization transformation to accelerate this computation.

Here, the speed we achieve is roughly 160 iterations per second. To once again see how big a speedup the JIT compiler offers our program, we remove the `jit()` function calls from the implementation of our model and rerun the code with the following changes:

```
kernel = rbf_kernel
vec_kernel = vmap(vmap(kernel, (0, None)), (None, 0))

loss_grad = grad(loss)
```

This time, the speedup is even more impressive: without JIT, the speed drops to 47 iterations per second.

This concludes our discussion on JAX and some of its main features. However, there are other more advanced tools included in JAX that we didn't cover but could prove useful in your machine learning applications such as asynchronous dispatch, parallelization, or computing convolutions. Information on these features may be found on the documentation page: `https://jax.readthedocs.io/en/latest/`.

Summary

JAX is a Python- and NumPy-friendly library that offers high-performance tools that are specific to machine learning tasks. JAX centers its API around function transformations, allowing users, in one line of code, to pass in generic Python functions and receive transformed versions of the functions that would otherwise either be expensive to compute or require more advanced implementations. The syntax of function transformations also enables flexible and complex compositions of functions, which are common in machine learning.

Throughout this chapter, we have seen how to utilize JAX to compute the gradient of machine learning loss functions using automatic differentiation, JIT-compile our code for further optimization, and vectorize kernel functions via a binary classification example. However, these tasks are present in most use cases, and you will be able to seamlessly apply what we have discussed here to your own machine learning needs.

At this point, we have reached the end of the first part of this book, in which we discuss Python-native and various other techniques to accelerate our Python applications. In the second part of the book, we examine parallel and concurrent programming, the techniques of which allow us to distribute computational loads across multiple threads and processes, making our applications more efficient on a linear scale.

Questions

1. What are the main components of a machine learning pipeline?

2. How is the loss function of a machine learning model typically minimized and how does JAX help with this process?

3. How can the predictive model used in this chapter handle nonlinear data and how does JAX help with this process?

Further reading

*   Linear models in machine learning: `https://blog.dataiku.com/top-machine-learning-algorithms-how-they-work-in-plain-english-1`

*   The JAX ecosystem: `https://moocaholic.medium.com/jax-a13e83f49897`

*   A brief tutorial that further explores JAX: `https://colinraffel.com/blog/you-don-t-know-jax.html`

Section 2: Concurrency and Parallelism

Advances in modern hardware allow parallel and concurrent processing of data, further increasing the performance of computer programs. The chapters in Section 2 discuss tools and libraries for implementing parallelism and concurrency, including hands-on examples that allow you to immediately apply the knowledge you learn.

This section contains the following chapters:

- *Chapter 7, Implementing Concurrency*
- *Chapter 8, Parallel Processing*
- *Chapter 9, Concurrent Web Requests*
- *Chapter 10, Concurrent Image Processing*
- *Chapter 11, Building Communication Channels with asyncio*
- *Chapter 12, Deadlocks*
- *Chapter 13, Starvation*
- *Chapter 14, Race Conditions*
- *Chapter 15, The Global Interpreter Lock*

7
Implementing Concurrency

So far, we have explored how to measure and improve the performance of programs by reducing the number of operations performed by the **central processing unit** (**CPU**) through clever algorithms and more efficient machine code. In this chapter, we will shift our focus to programs where most of the time is spent waiting for resources that are much slower than the CPU, such as persistent storage and network resources.

Asynchronous programming is a programming paradigm that helps to deal with slow and unpredictable resources (such as users) and is widely used to build responsive services and **user interfaces** (**UIs**). In this chapter, we will show you how to program asynchronously in Python using techniques such as coroutines and reactive programming. As we will see, the successful application of these techniques will allow us to speed up our programs without the use of specialized data structures or algorithms.

In this chapter, we will cover the following topics:

- Asynchronous programming
- The `asyncio` framework
- Reactive programming

Technical requirements

The code for this chapter can be found at `https://github.com/ PacktPublishing/Advanced-Python-Programming-Second-Edition/ tree/main/Chapter07`.

Asynchronous programming

Asynchronous programming is a way of dealing with slow and unpredictable resources. Rather than waiting idly for resources to become available, asynchronous programs can handle multiple resources concurrently and efficiently. Programming in an asynchronous way can be challenging because it is necessary to deal with external requests that can arrive in any order, may take a variable amount of time, or may fail unpredictably. In this section, we will introduce the topic by explaining the main concepts and terminology as well as by giving an idea of how asynchronous programs work.

Waiting for input/output

A modern computer employs different kinds of memory to store data and perform operations. In general, a computer possesses a combination of expensive memory that is capable of operating efficiently and cheaply and more abundant memory that is slower and is used to store a larger amount of data.

The memory hierarchy is shown in the following diagram:

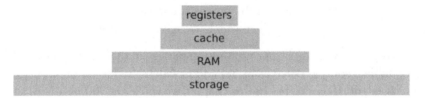

Figure 7.1 – Illustration of the memory hierarchy

At the top of the memory hierarchy, are the CPU **registers**. Those are integrated with the CPU and are used to store and execute machine instructions. Accessing data in a register generally takes one clock cycle. This means that if the CPU operates at 3 **gigahertz (GHz)**, the time it takes to access one element in a CPU register is in the order of 0.3 nanoseconds.

At the layer just below the registers, you can find the CPU **cache**, which comprise multiple levels and is integrated with the processor. The cache operates at a slightly slower speed than the registers but within the same **order of magnitude (OOM)**.

The next item in the hierarchy is the main memory (**random-access memory**, or **RAM**), which holds much more data but is slower than the cache. Fetching an item from memory can take a few hundred clock cycles.

At the bottom layer, you can find persistent **storage**, such as rotating disks (**hard disk drives (HDDs)**) and **solid-state drives** (**SSDs**). These devices hold the most data and are OOMs slower than the main memory. An HDD may take a few milliseconds to seek and retrieve an item, while an SSD is substantially faster and takes only a fraction of a millisecond.

To put the relative speed of each memory type into perspective, if you were to have the CPU with a clock speed of about 1 second, a register access would be equivalent to picking up a pen from a table. A cache access would be equivalent to picking up a book from a shelf. Moving higher up the hierarchy, a RAM access would be equivalent to loading up the laundry (about 20 times slower than the cache). When we move to persistent storage, things are quite different. Retrieving an element from an SSD will be equivalent to going on a 4-day road trip while retrieving an element from an HDD can take up to 6 months! The duration can stretch even further if we move on to access resources over the network.

Overall, accessing data from storage and other **input/output** (**I/O**) devices is much slower compared to the CPU; therefore, it is very important to handle those resources so that the CPU is never stuck waiting aimlessly. This can be accomplished by carefully designed software capable of managing multiple ongoing requests at the same time. This is the idea of concurrency or concurrent programming.

Concurrency

Concurrency is a way to implement a system that can deal with multiple requests at the same time. The idea is that we can move on and start handling other resources while we wait for a resource to become available. Concurrency works by splitting a task into smaller subtasks that can be executed out of order so that multiple tasks can be partially advanced without waiting for the previous tasks to finish.

As a first example, we will describe how to implement concurrent access to a slow network resource; the code for this example is included in `Chapter07/example1.py`. Let's say we have a web service that takes the square of a number, and the time between our request and the response will be approximately 1 second. We can implement the `network_request` function that takes a number and returns a dictionary that contains information about the success of the operation and the result. We can simulate such services using the `time.sleep` function, as follows:

```
import time

def network_request(number):
```

```
        time.sleep(1.0)
        return {"success": True, "result": number ** 2}
```

We will also write some additional code that performs the request, verifies that the request was successful, and prints the result. In the following code snippet, we define the `fetch_square` function and use it to calculate the square of the number 2 using a call to `network_request`:

```
def fetch_square(number):
    response = network_request(number)
    if response["success"]:
        print("Result is: \
            {}".format(response["result"]))


fetch_square(2)
# Output:
# Result is: 4
```

Fetching a number from the network will take 1 second because of the slow network. What if we want to calculate the square of multiple numbers? We can call `fetch_square`, which will start a network request as soon as the previous one is done. Its use is illustrated in the following code snippet:

```
fetch_square(2)
fetch_square(3)
fetch_square(4)
# Output:
# Result is: 4
# Result is: 9
# Result is: 16
```

This code as-is will take roughly 3 seconds to run, but it's not the best we can do. Notice that the calculation of the square of 2 is independent of that of the square of 3, and both are in turn independent of calculating the square of 4. As such, waiting for a previous result to finish before moving on to the next number is unnecessary, if we can technically submit multiple requests and wait for them at the same time.

In the following diagram, the three tasks are represented as boxes. The time spent by the CPU processing and submitting the request is in orange, while the waiting times are in blue. You can see how most of the time is spent waiting for the resources while our machine sits idle without doing anything else:

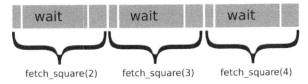

Figure 7.2 – Illustration of the execution time of independent calculations

Ideally, we would like to start another new task while we are waiting for the already submitted tasks to finish. In the following screenshot, you can see that as soon as we submit our request in `fetch_square(2)`, we can start preparing for `fetch_square(3)`, and so on. This allows us to reduce the CPU waiting time and to start processing the results as soon as they become available:

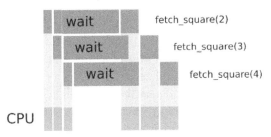

Figure 7.3 – A more efficient way of performing independent calculations

Again, this strategy is made possible by the fact that the three requests are completely independent, and we don't need to wait for the completion of a previous task to start the next one. Also, note how a single CPU can comfortably handle this scenario. While distributing the work on multiple CPUs can further speed up the execution, if the waiting time is large compared to the processing times, the speedup will be minimal.

To implement concurrency, it is necessary to think about our programs and their design differently; in the following sections, we'll demonstrate techniques and best practices to implement robust concurrent applications, starting with a new concept: callbacks.

Callbacks

The code we have seen so far blocks the execution of the program until the resource is available. The call responsible for the waiting is `time.sleep`. To make the code start working on other tasks, we need to find a way to avoid blocking the program flow so that the rest of the program can move on to these other tasks.

One of the simplest ways to accomplish this behavior is through callbacks. The strategy is quite similar to what we do when we request a cab. Imagine that you are at a restaurant and you've had a few drinks. It's raining outside, and you'd rather not take the bus; therefore, you request a taxi and ask them to call when they're outside so that you can come out and you don't have to wait in the rain. What you did, in this case, is request a taxi (that is, the slow resource), but instead of waiting outside until the taxi arrives, you provide your number and instructions (callback) so that you can come outside when they're ready and go home.

We will now show how this mechanism can work in code. We will compare the blocking code of `time.sleep` with the equivalent non-blocking code of `threading.Timer`.

For this example, which is implemented in `example2.py`, we will write a function, `wait_and_print`, that will block the program execution for 1 second and then print a message, as follows:

```
def wait_and_print(msg):
    time.sleep(1.0)
    print(msg)
```

If we want to write the same function in a non-blocking way, we can use the `threading.Timer` class. We can initialize a `threading.Timer` instance by passing the amount of time we want to wait and a **callback**. A callback is simply a function that will be called when the timer expires. Note in the following code snippet that we also must call the `Timer.start` method to activate the timer:

```
import threading

def wait_and_print_async(msg):
    def callback():
        print(msg)

    timer = threading.Timer(1.0, callback)
    timer.start()
```

An important feature of the `wait_and_print_async` function is that none of the statements is blocking the execution flow of the program.

> **How Is threading.Timer Capable of Waiting without Blocking?**
>
> The strategy used by `threading.Timer` involves starting a new thread that can execute code in parallel. If this is confusing, don't worry, as we will explore threading and parallel programming in detail in the following chapters.

This technique of registering callbacks for execution in response to certain events is commonly called the *Hollywood principle*. This is because, after auditioning for a movie or TV role at Hollywood, you may be told *Don't call us, we'll call you*, meaning that they won't tell you if they chose you for the role immediately, but they'll call you if they do.

To highlight the difference between the blocking and non-blocking versions of `wait_and_print`, we can test and compare the execution of the two versions. In the output comments, the waiting periods are indicated by `<wait...>`, as illustrated in the following code snippet:

```
# Synchronous
wait_and_print("First call")
wait_and_print("Second call")
print("After call")
# Output:
# <wait...>
# First call
# <wait...>
# Second call
# After call


# Asynchronous
wait_and_print_async("First call async")
wait_and_print_async("Second call async")
print("After submission")
# Output:
# After submission
# <wait...>
# First call
# Second call
```

The synchronous version behaves in a very familiar, expected way. The code waits for a second, prints `First call`, waits for another second, and then prints `Second call` and `After call` messages.

In the asynchronous version, `wait_and_print_async` *submits* (rather than *executes*) those calls and moves on *immediately*. You can see this mechanism in action by noticing that the `"After submission"` message is printed immediately.

With this in mind, we can explore a slightly more complex situation by rewriting our `network_request` function using callbacks. In `example3.py`, we define a `network_request_async` function, as follows:

```python
def network_request_async(number, on_done):

    def timer_done():
        on_done({"success": True, \
                 "result": number ** 2})

    timer = threading.Timer(1.0, timer_done)
    timer.start()
```

The biggest difference between `network_request_async` and its blocking counterpart is that `network_request_async` *doesn't return anything*. This is because we are merely submitting the request when `network_request_async` is called, but the value is available only when the request is completed.

If we can't return anything, how do we pass the result of the request? Rather than returning the value, we will pass the result as an argument to the `on_done` callback. The rest of the function consists of submitting a callback (called `timer_done`) to the `threading.Timer` class that will call `on_done` when it's ready.

The usage of `network_request_async` is quite similar to `threading.Timer`; all we have to do is pass the number we want to square and a callback that will receive the result *when it's ready*. This is demonstrated in the following code snippet:

```python
def on_done(result):
    print(result)

network_request_async(2, on_done)
```

Now, if we submit multiple network requests, we note that the calls get executed concurrently and do not block the code, as illustrated in the following code snippet:

```
network_request_async(2, on_done)
network_request_async(3, on_done)
network_request_async(4, on_done)
print("After submission")
```

In order to use network_request_async in fetch_square, we need to adapt the code to take advantage of asynchronous constructs. In the following code snippet, we modify fetch_square by defining and passing the on_done callback to network_request_async:

```
def fetch_square(number):
    def on_done(response):
        if response["success"]:
            print("Result is: \
                {}".format(response["result"]))

    network_request_async(number, on_done)
```

You may have noted that the asynchronous code is significantly more convoluted than its synchronous counterpart. This is due to the fact that we are required to write and pass a callback every time we need to retrieve a certain result, causing the code to become nested and hard to follow.

Fortunately, a concept that is essential to concurrent programming that we are examining next, futures, will help simplify matters.

Futures

Futures are a more convenient pattern that can be used to keep track of the results of asynchronous calls. In the preceding code snippet, we saw that rather than returning values, we accept callbacks and pass the results when they are ready. It is interesting to note that, so far, there is no easy way to track the status of the resource.

A **future** is an abstraction that helps us keep track of the requested resources that we are waiting to become available. In Python, you can find a future implementation in the `concurrent.futures.Future` class. A `Future` instance can be created by calling its constructor with no arguments, as in the following IPython snippet:

```
from concurrent.futures import Future
fut = Future()
# Result:
# <Future at 0x7f03e41599e8 state=pending>
```

A future represents a value that is not yet available. You can see that its string representation reports the current status of the result, which, in our case, is still pending. In order to make a result available, we can use the `fut.set_result` method, as follows:

```
fut.set_result("Hello")
# Result:
# <Future at 0x7f03e41599e8 state=finished returned
   str>

fut.result()
# Result:
# "Hello"
```

You can see that once we set the result, the `Future` instance will report that the task is finished and can be accessed using the `fut.result` method. It is also possible to subscribe a callback to a future so that, as soon as the result is available, the callback is executed. To attach a callback, it is sufficient to pass a function to the `fut.add_done_callback` method. When the task is completed, the function will be called with the `Future` instance as its first argument and the result can be retrieved using the `future.result()` method, as illustrated in the following code snippet:

```
fut = Future()
fut.add_done_callback(lambda future:
    print(future.result(), flush=True))
fut.set_result("Hello")
# Output:
# Hello
```

To understand how futures can be used in practice, we will adapt the `network_request_async` function to use futures in `example4.py`. The idea is that this time, instead of returning nothing, we return a `Future` instance that will keep track of the result for us. Note the following two things:

- We don't need to accept an `on_done callback` as callbacks can be connected later using the `fut.add_done_callback` method. Also, we pass the generic `fut.set_result` method as the callback for `threading.Timer`.

- This time, we are able to return a value, thus making the code a bit more similar to the blocking version we saw in the preceding section, as illustrated here:

```python
from concurrent.futures import Future


def network_request_async(number):
    future = Future()
    result = {"success": True, "result": number \
        ** 2}
    timer = threading.Timer(1.0, lambda: \
        future.set_result(result))
    timer.start()
    return future


fut = network_request_async(2)
```

> **Note**
> Even though we instantiate and manage futures directly in these examples, in practical applications, futures are handled by frameworks.

If you execute the preceding code, nothing will happen as the code only consists of preparing and returning a `Future` instance. To enable further operation of the future results, we need to use the `fut.add_done_callback` method. In the following code snippet, we adapt the `fetch_square` function to use futures:

```python
def fetch_square(number):
    fut = network_request_async(number)


    def on_done_future(future):
        response = future.result()
        if response["success"]:
```

```
        print("Result is: \
            {}".format(response["result"]))


    fut.add_done_callback(on_done_future)
```

As you can see, the code still looks quite similar to the callback version, but when `fetch_square` is called, the corresponding future will be processed, and the result string will be printed out.

Overall, futures are a different and slightly more convenient way of working with callbacks. Futures are also advantageous in the sense that they can keep track of the resource status, cancel (unschedule) scheduled tasks, and handle exceptions more naturally.

Event loops

So far, we have implemented parallelism using **operating system (OS)** threads. However, in many asynchronous frameworks, the coordination of concurrent tasks is managed by an **event loop**.

The idea behind an event loop is to continuously monitor the status of the various resources (for example, network connections and database queries) and trigger the execution of callbacks when specific events take place (for example, when a resource is ready or when a timer expires).

Why Not Just Stick to Threading?

Events loops are sometimes preferred as every unit of execution never runs at the same time as another, and this can simplify dealing with shared variables, data structures, and resources.

As the first example in `example5.py`, we will implement a thread-free version of `threading.Timer`. We can define a `Timer` class that will take a timeout and implement the `Timer.done` method, which returns `True` if the timer has expired. The code is illustrated in the following snippet:

```
class Timer:


    def __init__(self, timeout):
        self.timeout = timeout
        self.start = time.time()
```

```
        def done(self):
            return time.time() - self.start > self.timeout
```

To determine whether the timer has expired, we can write a loop that continuously checks the timer status by calling the `Timer.done` method. When the timer expires, we can print a message and exit the cycle. The code is illustrated in the following snippet:

```
timer = Timer(1.0)

while True:
    if timer.done():
        print("Timer is done!")
        break
```

By implementing the timer in this way, the flow of execution is never blocked, and we can, in principle, do other work inside the `while` loop.

Busy-Waiting

Waiting for events to happen by continuously polling using a loop is commonly termed **busy-waiting**.

Ideally, we would like to attach a custom function that executes when the timer goes off, just as we did in `threading.Timer`. To do this, we can implement a `Timer.on_timer_done` method that will accept a callback to be executed when the timer goes off in `example6.py`, as follows:

```
class Timer:
    # ... previous code
    def on_timer_done(self, callback):
        self.callback = callback
```

Note that `on_timer_done` merely stores a reference to the callback. The entity that monitors the event and executes the callback is the loop. This concept is demonstrated as follows. Rather than using the `print` function, the loop will call `timer.callback` when appropriate:

```
timer = Timer(1.0)
timer.on_timer_done(lambda: print("Timer is done!"))
```

```
while True:
    if timer.done():
        timer.callback()
        break
```

As you can see, an asynchronous framework is starting to take place. All we did outside the loop was define the timer and the callback, while the loop took care of monitoring the timer and executing the associated callback. We can further extend our code by implementing support for multiple timers.

A natural way to implement multiple timers is to add a few Timer instances to a list and modify our event loop to periodically check all the timers and dispatch the callbacks when required. In the following code snippet, we define two timers and attach a callback to each of them. Those timers are added to a list, timers, that is continuously monitored by our event loop. As soon as a timer is done, we execute the callback and remove the event from the list:

```
timers = []

timer1 = Timer(1.0)
timer1.on_timer_done(lambda: print("First timer is  \
    done!"))

timer2 = Timer(2.0)
timer2.on_timer_done(lambda: print("Second timer is  \
    done!"))

timers.append(timer1)
timers.append(timer2)

while True:
    for timer in timers:
        if timer.done():
            timer.callback()
            timers.remove(timer)
    # If no more timers are left, we exit the loop
    if len(timers) == 0:
        break
```

The main restriction of an event loop is, since the flow of execution is managed by a continuously running loop, that it **never uses blocking calls**. If we use any blocking statement (such as `time.sleep`) inside the loop, you can imagine how the event monitoring and callback dispatching will stop until the blocking call is done.

To avoid this, rather than using a blocking call such as `time.sleep`, we let the event loop detect and execute the callback when the resource is ready. By not blocking the execution flow, the event loop is free to monitor multiple resources in a concurrent way.

> **How Is the Event Loop Notified of Events?**
>
> Events notification is usually implemented through OS calls (such as the `select` Unix tool) that will resume the execution of the program whenever an event is ready (in contrast to busy-waiting).

The Python standard libraries include a very convenient event loop-based concurrency framework, `asyncio`, which will be the topic of the next section.

The asyncio framework

At this point, we have seen how concurrency works and how to use callbacks and futures. We can now move on and learn how to use the `asyncio` package, which has been present in the standard Python library since version 3.4. We will also explore the `async/await` syntax to deal with asynchronous programming in a very natural way.

As a first example, we will see how to retrieve and execute a simple callback using `asyncio`. The `asyncio` loop can be retrieved by calling the `asyncio.get_event_loop()` function. We can schedule a callback for execution using `loop.call_later`, which takes a delay in seconds and a callback. We can also use the `loop.stop` method to halt the loop and exit the program. To start processing the scheduled call, it is necessary to start the loop, which can be done using `loop.run_forever`. The following example in `example7.py` demonstrates the usage of these basic methods by scheduling a callback that will print a message and halt the loop:

```python
import asyncio

loop = asyncio.get_event_loop()

def callback():
    print("Hello, asyncio")
```

```
        loop.stop()


    loop.call_later(1.0, callback)
    loop.run_forever()
```

This code schedules a callback that will print out a message and then halt the loop. One of the main problems with callbacks is that they require you to break the program execution into small functions that will be invoked when a certain event takes place. As we saw in the earlier sections, callbacks can quickly become cumbersome. In the next section, we will see how to work with coroutines to, as with futures, simplify many aspects of concurrent programming.

Coroutines

Coroutines are another, perhaps more natural, way to break up the program execution into chunks. They allow the programmer to write code that resembles synchronous code but will execute asynchronously. You may think of a coroutine as a function that can be stopped and resumed. A basic example of coroutines is generators.

Generators can be defined in Python using the `yield` statement inside a function. In the following code example in `example8.py`, we implement the `range_generator` function, which produces and returns values from 0 to n. We also add a `print` statement to log the internal state of the generator:

```
def range_generator(n):
    i = 0
    while i < n:
        print("Generating value {}".format(i))
        yield i
        i += 1
```

When we call the `range_generator` function, the code is not executed immediately. Note that nothing is printed to output when the following snippet is executed. Instead, a `generator` object is returned:

```
generator = range_generator(3)
generator
# Result:
# <generator object range_generator at 0x7f03e418ba40>
```

In order to start pulling values from a generator, it is necessary to use the `next` function, as follows:

```
next(generator)
# Output:
# Generating value 0

next(generator)
# Output:
# Generating value 1
```

Note that every time we invoke `next`, the code runs until it encounters the next `yield` statement, and it is necessary to issue another `next` statement to resume the generator execution. You can think of a `yield` statement as a breakpoint where we can stop and resume execution (while also maintaining the internal state of the generator). This ability to stop and resume execution can be leveraged by the event loop to allow for and implement concurrency.

It is also possible to *inject* (rather than *extract*) values in the generator through the `yield` statement. In the following code example in `example9.py`, we declare a `parrot` function that will repeat each message that we send:

```
def parrot():
    while True:
        message = yield
        print("Parrot says: {}".format(message))

generator = parrot()
generator.send(None)
generator.send("Hello")
generator.send("World")
```

To allow a generator to receive a value, you can assign `yield` to a variable (in our case, it is `message = yield`). To insert values in the generator, we can use the `send` method. In the Python world, a generator that can also receive values is called a **generator-based coroutine**.

Note that we also need to issue a `generator.send(None)` request before we can start sending messages; this is to bootstrap the function execution and bring us to the first `yield` statement. Also, note that there is an infinite loop inside `parrot`; if we implement this without using generators, we will get stuck running the loop forever!

With this in mind, you can imagine how an event loop can partially progress several of these generators without blocking the execution of the whole program, as well as how a generator can be advanced only when some resource is ready, therefore eliminating the need for a callback.

It is possible to implement coroutines in `asyncio` using the `yield` statement. However, Python supports the definition of powerful coroutines using a more intuitive syntax. To define a coroutine with `asyncio`, you can use the `async def` statement, as follows:

```
async def hello():
    print("Hello, async!")


coro = hello()
coro
# Output:
# <coroutine object hello at 0x7f314846bd58>
```

As you can see, if we call the `hello` function, the function body is not executed immediately, but a `coroutine object` instance is returned. The `asyncio` coroutines do not support `next`, but they can be easily run in the `asyncio` event loop using the `run_until_complete` method, as follows:

```
import asyncio


loop = asyncio.get_event_loop()
loop.run_until_complete(coro)
```

> **Native Coroutines**
>
> Coroutines defined with the `async def` statement are also called *native coroutines.*

The `asyncio` module provides resources (called **awaitables**) that can be requested inside coroutines through the `await` syntax. For example, in `example10.py`, if we want to wait for a certain time and then execute a statement, we can use the `asyncio.sleep` function, as follows:

```
async def wait_and_print(msg):
    await asyncio.sleep(1)
    print("Message: ", msg)
```

```
loop = asyncio.get_event_loop()
loop.run_until_complete(wait_and_print("Hello"))
```

The result is beautiful, clean code. We are writing perfectly functional asynchronous code without all the ugliness of callbacks!

> **Breakpoints for Event Loops**
>
> You may have noted how `await` provides a breakpoint for the event loop so that, as it waits for the resource, the event loop can move on and concurrently manage other coroutines.

Even better, coroutines are also `awaitable`, and we can use the `await` statement to chain coroutines asynchronously. In the following example, we rewrite the `network_request` function, which we defined earlier, by replacing the call to `time.sleep` with `asyncio.sleep`:

```
async def network_request(number):
    await asyncio.sleep(1.0)
    return {"success": True, "result": number ** 2}
```

We can follow up by reimplementing `fetch_square`, as illustrated in the following code snippet. As you can see, we await `network_request` directly without needing additional futures or callbacks:

```
async def fetch_square(number):
    response = await network_request(number)
    if response["success"]:
        print("Result is: \
        {}".format(response["result"]))
```

The coroutines can be executed individually using `loop.run_until_complete`, as follows:

```
loop.run_until_complete(fetch_square(2))
loop.run_until_complete(fetch_square(3))
loop.run_until_complete(fetch_square(4))
```

Running tasks using `run_until_complete` serves as a demonstration for testing and debugging. However, our program will be started with `loop.run_forever` most of the time, and we will need to submit our tasks while the loop is already running.

`asyncio` provides the `ensure_future` function, which schedules coroutines (as well as futures) for execution. `ensure_future` can be used by simply passing the coroutine we want to schedule. The following code snippet in `example11.py` will schedule multiple calls to `fetch_square` that will be executed concurrently:

```
asyncio.ensure_future(fetch_square(2))
asyncio.ensure_future(fetch_square(3))
asyncio.ensure_future(fetch_square(4))


loop.run_forever()
# Hit Ctrl-C to stop the loop
```

As a bonus, when passing a coroutine, the `asyncio.ensure_future` function will return a `Task` instance (which is a subclass of `Future`) so that we can take advantage of the `await` syntax without having to give up the resource-tracking capabilities of regular futures.

Converting blocking code into non-blocking code

While `asyncio` supports connecting to resources in an asynchronous way, it is required to use blocking calls in certain cases. This happens, for example, when third-party **application programming interfaces (APIs)** exclusively expose blocking calls (which is the case for many database libraries), but also when executing long-running computations. In this subsection, we will learn how to deal with blocking APIs and make them compatible with `asyncio`. Here are the steps:

1. An effective strategy for dealing with blocking code is to run it in a separate thread. Threads are implemented at the OS level and allow parallel execution of blocking code. For this purpose, Python provides the `Executor` interface designed to run tasks in a separate thread and to monitor their progress using futures.

2. You can initialize a `ThreadPoolExecutor` instance by importing it from the `concurrent.futures` module. The executor will spawn a collection of threads (called workers) that will wait to execute whichever task we throw at them. Once a function is submitted, the executor will take care of dispatching its execution to an available worker thread and keep track of the result. The `max_workers` argument can be used to select the number of threads.

    Note that the executor will not destroy a thread once a task is completed. By doing so, it reduces the cost associated with the creation and destruction of threads.

3. In the following code example in example12.py, we create a
    ThreadPoolExecutor instance with three workers, and we submit a wait_and_
    return function that will block the program execution for 1 second and return a
    message string. We then use the submit method to schedule its execution:

```
import time
from concurrent.futures import ThreadPoolExecutor


executor = ThreadPoolExecutor(max_workers=3)


def wait_and_return(msg):
    time.sleep(1)
    return msg


print(executor.submit(wait_and_return, "Hello. \
    executor"))
# Result:
# <Future at 0x7ff616ff6748 state=running>
```

4. The executor.submit method immediately schedules the function and returns
    a future. It is possible to manage the execution of tasks in asyncio using the
    loop.run_in_executor method, which works quite similarly to executor.
    submit. The code is illustrated in the following snippet:

```
fut = loop.run_in_executor(executor, \
    wait_and_return, "Hello, asyncio executor")
# <Future pending ...more info...>
```

5. The run_in_executor method will also return an asyncio.Future instance
    that can be awaited from other code, the main difference being that the future
    will not be run until we start the loop. We can run and obtain the response using
    loop.run_until_complete, as illustrated in the following snippet:

```
loop.run_until_complete(fut)
# Result:
# 'Hello, executor'
```

6. As a practical example, we can use this technique to implement concurrent fetching of several web pages. To do this, we will import the popular (blocking) `requests` library and run the `requests.get` function in the executor in `example13.py`, as follows:

```python
import requests


async def fetch_urls(urls):
    responses = []
    for url in urls:
        responses.append(await \
            loop.run_in_executor(executor, \
                requests.get, url))
    return responses

responses = loop.run_until_complete(
  fetch_urls(
    [
    'http://www.google.com',
    'http://www.example.com',
    'http://www.facebook.com'
    ]
  )
)

print(response)
# Result
# [<Response [200]>, <Response [200]>, <Response
  [200]>]
```

7. This version of `fetch_url` will not block the execution and allow other coroutines in `asyncio` to run; however, it is not optimal as the function will not fetch a **Uniform Resource Locator (URL)** in parallel. To do this, we can use `asyncio.ensure_future` or employ the `asyncio.gather` convenience function that will submit all the coroutines at once and gather the results as they come. The usage of `asyncio.gather` is demonstrated in `example14.py`, as follows:

```python
def fetch_urls(urls):
    return asyncio.gather(
```

```
*[loop.run_in_executor(executor, \
    requests.get, url) for url in urls])
```

> **Upper Bound for the Number of Threads**
>
> The number of URLs you can fetch in parallel with this method will be dependent on the number of worker threads you have. To avoid this limitation, you should use a natively non-blocking library, such as `aiohttp`.

So far, we have seen how to work with concurrent programs in Python using core concepts such as callbacks, futures, and coroutines. For the remaining portion of this chapter, we will discuss a more streamlined programming paradigm for implementing concurrency.

Reactive programming

Reactive programming is a paradigm that aims at building better concurrent systems. Reactive applications are designed to comply with the following requirements exemplified by the reactive manifesto:

- **Responsive**: The system responds immediately to the user.
- **Elastic**: The system is capable of handling different levels of load and can adapt to accommodate increasing demands.
- **Resilient**: The system deals with failure gracefully. This is achieved by modularity and avoiding having a **single point of failure** (**SPOF**).
- **Message-driven**: The system should not block and take advantage of events and messages. A message-driven application helps achieve all the previous requirements.

The requirements for reactive systems are quite reasonable but abstract, which leads us to a natural question: how exactly does reactive programming work? In this section, we will learn about the principles of reactive programming using the **Reactive Extensions for Python** (**RxPY**) library.

> **Additional Information**
>
> The `RxPY` library is part of ReactiveX (`http://reactivex.io/`), which is a project that implements reactive programming tools for a large variety of languages.
>
> To install the library, simply run `pip install rx`.
>
> Note that the following code uses `RxPY` v3, the syntax of which is quite different from `RxPY` v1. If you are familiar with `RxPY` v1 and the discussion from this book's previous version, watch out for changes in syntax!

Observables

As the name implies, the main idea of reactive programming is to *react* to events. In the preceding section, we saw some examples of this idea with callbacks; you subscribe to them and the callback is executed as soon as the event takes place.

In reactive programming, this idea is expanded if we think of events as streams of data. This can be exemplified by showing examples of such streams in RxPY. A data stream can be created from an iterator using the `from_iterable` method in IPython, as follows:

```
from rx import from_iterable
obs = from_iterable(range(4))
```

In order to receive data from `obs`, we can use the `Observable.subscribe` method, which will execute the function we pass for each value that the data source emits. This method is shown in the following code snippet:

```
obs.subscribe(print)
# Output:
# 0
# 1
# 2
# 3
```

You may have noticed that observables are ordered collections of items just like lists or, more generally, iterators. This is not a coincidence.

The term *observable* comes from the combination of observer and iterable. An *observer* is an object that reacts to changes of the variable it observes, while an *iterable* is an object that can produce and keep track of an iterator.

In Python, iterators are objects that define the __next__ method, and whose elements can be extracted by calling `next`. An iterator can generally be obtained by a collection using `iter`; then, we can extract elements using `next` or a `for` loop. Once an element is consumed from the iterator, we can't go back. We can demonstrate its usage by creating an iterator from a list, as follows:

```
collection = list([1, 2, 3, 4, 5])
iterator = iter(collection)

print("Next")
print(next(iterator))
```

```
print(next(iterator))

print("For loop")
for i in iterator:
    print(i)

# Output:
# Next
# 1
# 2
# For loop
# 3
# 4
# 5
```

You can see how, every time we call next or we iterate, the iterator produces a value and advances. In a sense, we are *pulling* results from the iterator.

> **Iterators versus Generators**
>
> Iterators sound a lot like generators; however, they are more general. In Python, generators are returned by functions that use yield expressions. As we saw, generators support next; therefore, they are a special class of iterators.

Now, you can appreciate the contrast between an iterator and an observable. An observable *pushes* a stream of data to us whenever it's ready, but that's not everything. An observable can also tell us when there is an error and where there is no more data. In fact, it is possible to register further callbacks to the Observable.subscribe method.

In the following example in IPython, we create an observable and register callbacks to be called using on_next whenever the next item is available and using the on_completed argument when there is no more data:

```
obs = from_iterable(range(4))
obs.subscribe(on_next=lambda x: print("Next item:", x),
              on_completed=lambda: print("No more \
              data"))
# Output:
# Next element: 0
# Next element: 1
```

```
# Next element: 2
# Next element: 3
# No more data
```

With that said, the similarity between observables and iterators is more important, because we can use the same techniques that can be used with iterators to handle streams of events.

RxPy provides operators that can be used to create, transform, filter, and group observables. The power of reactive programming lies in the fact that those operations return other observables that can be conveniently chained and composed together. For a quick demonstration, we will examine the usage of the take operator next.

Given an observable, take will return a new observable that will stop after n items. Its usage is straightforward, as we can see here:

```
from rx.operators import take

op = take(4)
obs = from_iterable(range(1000))

op(obs).subscribe(print)
# Output:
# 0
# 1
# 2
# 3
```

The collection of operations implemented in RxPy is varied and rich and can be used to build complex applications using these operators as building blocks.

Useful operators

In this subsection, we will explore operators that transform the elements of a source observable in some way. The most prominent member of this family of operators is the familiar map operator, which emits the elements of the source observable after applying a function to them.

For example, we may use `map` to calculate the square of a sequence of numbers, as follows:

```
from rx.operators import map

map(lambda x: x**2)(from_iterable(range(4))). \
    subscribe(print)
# Output:
# 0
# 1
# 4
# 9
```

Operators can be represented with marble diagrams that help us better understand how the operator works, especially when taking into account the fact that elements can be emitted over a region of time. In a marble diagram, a data stream (in our case, an observable) is represented by a solid line. A circle (or another shape) identifies a value emitted by the observable, an *X* symbol represents an error, and a vertical line represents the end of the stream.

Here, we can see a marble diagram of `map`:

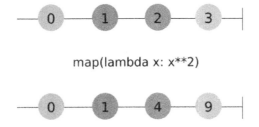

Figure 7.4 – Marble diagram illustrating the procedure of squaring numbers

The source observable is placed at the top of the diagram, the transformation is placed in the middle, and the resulting observable is placed at the bottom.

Another example of a transformation is `group_by`, which sorts items into groups based on a key. The `group_by` operator takes a function that extracts a key when given an element and produces an observable for each key with the elements associated with it.

The `group_by` operation can be expressed more clearly using a marble diagram. In the following diagram, you can see how `group_by` emits two observables. Additionally, the items are dynamically sorted into groups *as soon as they are emitted*:

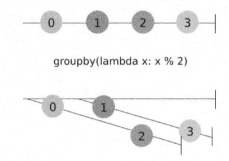

Figure 7.5 – Marble diagram illustrating grouping

We can further understand how `group_by` works with a simple example. Let's say that we want to group a number according to the fact that it's even or odd. We can implement this using `group_by` by passing the `lambda x: x % 2` expression as a key function, which will return `0` if the number is even and `1` if the number is odd, as follows:

```
from rx.operators import group_by


obs = group_by(lambda x: x % \
    2)(from_iterable(range(4)))
```

At this point, if we subscribe and print the content of `obs`, two observables are actually printed, as illustrated in the following code snippet:

```
obs.subscribe(print)
# <rx.linq.groupedobservable.GroupedObservable object
    at 0x7f0fba51f9e8>
# <rx.linq.groupedobservable.GroupedObservable object
    at 0x7f0fba51fa58>
```

You can determine the group key using the `key` attribute. To extract all the even numbers, we can take the first observable (corresponding to a key equal to 0) and subscribe to it. In the following code snippet, we show how this works:

```
obs.subscribe(lambda x: print("group key: ", x.key))
# Output:
# group key:   0
```

```
# group key:    1
take(1)(obs).subscribe(lambda x: x.subscribe(print))
# Output:
# 0
# 2
```

With `group_by`, we introduced an observable that emits other observables. This turns out to be quite a common pattern in reactive programming, and there are functions that allow you to combine different observables.

A useful tool for combining observables is `merge_all` which takes multiple observables and produces a single observable that contains the element of the two observables in the order they are emitted. This is better illustrated using a marble diagram, as follows:

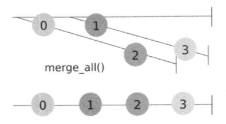

Figure 7.6 – Marble diagram illustrating merging

To demonstrate its usage, we can apply the operation to the observable of observables returned by `group_by`, as follows:

```
from rx.operators import merge_all


merge_all()(obs).subscribe(print)
# Output
# 0
# 1
# 2
# 3
```

With `merge_all`, the items are returned in the same order as they were initially (remember that `group_by` emits elements in the two groups as they come).

> **Tip**
> RxPy also provides the `merge` operation, which can be used to combine individual observables.

Hot and cold observables

In the preceding section, we learned how to create an observable using the from_ iterable method. RxPy provides many other tools to create more interesting event sources.

interval takes a time interval in seconds, period, and creates an observable that emits a value every time the period has passed. The following code can be used to define an observable, obs, that will emit a number, starting from zero, every second. We use the take operator to limit the timer to four events:

```python
from rx import interval
from rx.operators import take


take(4)(interval(1)).subscribe(print)
# Output:
# 0
# 1
# 2
# 3
```

A very important fact about interval is that the timer doesn't start until we subscribe. We can observe this by printing both the index and the delay from when the timer starts definition using time.time(), as follows:

```python
import time


start = time.time()
obs = map(lambda a: (a, time.time() - \
    start))(interval(1))


# Let's wait 2 seconds before starting the subscription
time.sleep(2)
take(4)(obs).subscribe(print)
# Output:
# (0, 3.003735303878784)
# (1, 4.004871129989624)
# (2, 5.005947589874268)
# (3, 6.00749135017395)
```

As you can see, the first element (corresponding to a 0 index) is produced after 3 seconds, which means that the timer started when we issue the subscribe(print) method.

Observables such as interval are called *lazy* because they start producing values only when requested (think of them as vending machines that won't dispense food unless we press the button). In Rx jargon, these kinds of observables are called **cold**. A property of cold observables is that, if we attach two subscribers, the interval timer will be started multiple times. This is quite evident from the following example. Here, we add a new subscription 0.5 seconds after the first, and you can see how the output of the two subscriptions comes at different times:

```
start = time.time()
obs = map(lambda a: (a, time.time() - \
   start))(interval(1))


# Let's wait 2 seconds before starting the subscription
time.sleep(2)
take(4)(obs).subscribe(lambda x: print("First \
   subscriber: {}".format(x)))
time.sleep(0.5)
take(4)(obs).subscribe(lambda x: print("Second  \
   subscriber: {}".format(x)))
# Output:
# First subscriber: (0, 3.0036110877990723)
# Second subscriber: (0, 3.5052847862243652)
# First subscriber: (1, 4.004414081573486)
# Second subscriber: (1, 4.506155252456665)
# First subscriber: (2, 5.005316972732544)
# Second subscriber: (2, 5.506817102432251)
# First subscriber: (3, 6.0062034130096436)
# Second subscriber: (3, 6.508296489715576)
```

Sometimes, we may not want this behavior as we may want multiple subscribers to subscribe to the same data source. To make the observable produce the same data, we can delay the data production and ensure that all the subscribers will get the same data using the publish method.

`publish` will transform our observable into `ConnectableObservable`, which won't start pushing data immediately, but only when we call the `connect` method. The usage of `publish` and `connect` is demonstrated in the following code snippet:

```python
from rx.operators import publish


start = time.time()
obs = publish()(map(lambda a: (a, time.time() - \
start))(interval(1)))
take(4)(obs).subscribe(lambda x: print("First \
    subscriber: {}".format(x)))
obs.connect() # Data production starts here


time.sleep(2)
take(4)(obs).subscribe(lambda x: print("Second \
    subscriber: {}".format(x)))
# Output:
# First subscriber: (0, 1.0016899108886719)
# First subscriber: (1, 2.0027990341186523)
# First subscriber: (2, 3.003532648086548)
# Second subscriber: (2, 3.003532648086548)
# First subscriber: (3, 4.004265308380127)
# Second subscriber: (3, 4.004265308380127)
# Second subscriber: (4, 5.005320310592651)
# Second subscriber: (5, 6.005795240402222)
```

In this example, you can see how we first issue `publish`, then we subscribe the first subscriber, and finally, we issue `connect`. When `connect` is issued, the timer will start producing data. The second subscriber joins the party late and, in fact, won't receive the first two messages but will start receiving data from the third, and so on. Note that, this time around, the subscribers share the exact same data. This kind of data source, where data is produced independently of the subscribers, is called **hot**.

Similar to `publish`, you can use the `replay` method that will produce the data *from the beginning* for each new subscriber. This is illustrated in the following example, which is identical to the preceding one except that we replaced `publish` with `replay`:

```python
from rx.operators import replay


start = time.time()
```

```
obs = replay()(map(lambda a: (a, time.time() - start) \
    ( interval(1)))
take(4)(obs).subscribe(lambda x: print("First    \
    subscriber: {}".format(x)))
obs.connect()

time.sleep(2)
take(4)(obs).subscribe(lambda x: print("Second    \
    subscriber: {}".format(x)))

First subscriber: (0, 1.0008857250213623)
First subscriber: (1, 2.0019824504852295)
Second subscriber: (0, 1.0008857250213623)
Second subscriber: (1, 2.0019824504852295)
First subscriber: (2, 3.0030810832977295)
Second subscriber: (2, 3.0030810832977295)
First subscriber: (3, 4.004604816436768)
Second subscriber: (3, 4.004604816436768)
```

Notice that even though the second subscriber arrives late to the party, it is still given all the items that have been given out so far.

Another way of creating hot observables is through the `Subject` class. `Subject` is interesting because it's capable of both receiving and pushing data, and thus it can be used to manually *push* items to an observable. Using `Subject` is very intuitive; in the following code snippet, we create a `Subject` instance and subscribe to it. Later, we push values to it using the `on_next` method; as soon as we do that, the subscriber is called:

```
from rx.subject import Subject

s = Subject()
s.subscribe(lambda x: print("Subject emitted value: \
    {}".format(x)))
s.on_next(1)
# Subject emitted value: 1
s.on_next(2)
# Subject emitted value: 2
```

Note that `Subject` is another example of a hot observable.

Building a CPU monitor

Now that we have a grasp of the main reactive programming concepts, we can implement an example application: a monitor that will give us real-time information about our CPU usage and that can detect spikes.

> **Note**
>
> The complete code for the CPU monitor can be found in the `cpu_monitor.py` file.

As a first step, let's implement a data source. We will use the `psutil` module that provides a function, `psutil.cpu_percent`, that returns the latest available CPU usage as a percentage (and doesn't block). The code is illustrated in the following snippet:

```
import psutil
psutil.cpu_percent()
# Result: 9.7
```

Since we are developing a monitor, we would like to sample this information over a few time intervals. To accomplish, this we can use the familiar `interval` observable, followed by `map`, just as we did in the previous section. Also, we would like to make this observable *hot* as, for this application, all subscribers should receive a single source of data; to make `interval` hot, we can use the `publish` and `connect` methods. The full code for the creation of a `cpu_data` observable is shown here:

```
cpu_data = publish()(map(lambda x: \
    psutil.cpu_percent())(interval(0.1)))
cpu_data.connect() # Start producing data
```

We can test our monitor by printing a sample of four items, as follows:

```
take(4)(cpu_data).subscribe(print)
# Output:
# 12.5
# 5.6
# 4.5
# 9.6
```

Now that our main data source is in place, we can implement a monitor visualization using `matplotlib`. The idea is to create a plot that contains a fixed number of measurements and, as new data arrives, we include the newest measurement and remove the oldest one. This is commonly referred to as a *moving window* and is better understood with an illustration. In the following diagram, our `cpu_data` stream is represented as a list of numbers. The first plot is produced as soon as we have the first four numbers and, each time a new number arrives, we shift the window by one position and update the plot:

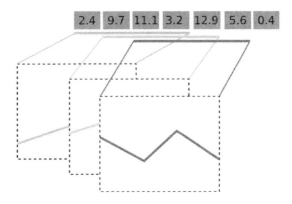

Figure 7.7 – Illustration of a moving window

To implement this algorithm, we can write a function called `monitor_cpu` that will create and update our plotting window. The function will do the following things:

- Initialize an empty plot and set up the correct plot limits.

- Transform our `cpu_data` observable to return a moving window over the data. This can be accomplished using the `buffer_with_count` operator, which will take the number of points in our window, `npoints`, as parameters and the shift as `1`.

- Subscribe to this new data stream and update the plot with the incoming data.

The complete code for the function is implemented in `cpu_monitor.py` and shown here and, as you can see, is extremely compact. Go ahead and install `matplotlib` if you don't have it in your environment already, using `pip install matplotlib`.

Take some time to run the function and play with the parameters. You can view the code here:

```
from rx.operators import buffer_with_count

import numpy as np
import pylab as plt
```

```
def monitor_cpu(npoints):
    lines, = plt.plot([], [])
    plt.xlim(0, npoints)
    plt.ylim(0, 100) # 0 to 100 percent

    cpu_data_window = buffer_with_count(npoints, \
        1)(cpu_data)

    def update_plot(cpu_readings):
        lines.set_xdata(np.arange(len(cpu_readings)))
        lines.set_ydata(np.array(cpu_readings))
        plt.draw()

    cpu_data_window.subscribe(update_plot)

    plt.show()
```

Another feature we may want to develop is an alert that triggers when the CPU has been high for a certain amount of time, as this may indicate that some of the processes in our machine are working very hard. This can be accomplished by combining buffer_with_count and map. We can take the CPU stream and a window, and test whether all items have a value higher than 20% usage (in a quad-core CPU, that corresponds to about one processor working at 100%) in the map function. If all the points in the window have a higher-than-20% usage, we display a warning in our plot window.

The implementation of the new observable can be written as follows and will produce an observable that emits True if the CPU has high usage, and False otherwise:

```
alertpoints = 4
high_cpu = map(lambda readings: all(r > 20 for r in \
    readings))(
        buffer_with_count(alertpoints, 1)(cpu_data)
)
```

Now that the high_cpu observable is ready, we can create a matplotlib label and subscribe to it for updates, as follows:

```
label = plt.text(1, 1, "normal")
def update_warning(is_high):
    if is_high:
```

```
                label.set_text("high")
        else:
                label.set_text("normal")
    high_cpu.subscribe(update_warning)
```

Run the program from your terminal, and an interactive window will open to display your CPU usage data in real time. Here is a screenshot showing the output of our program:

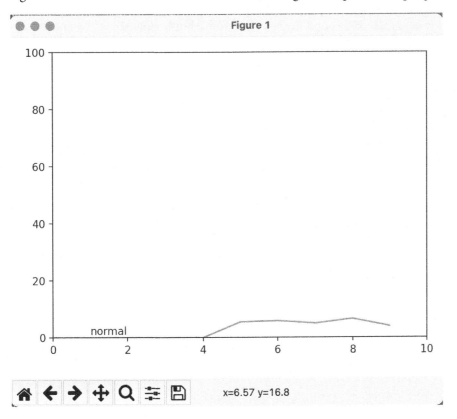

Figure 7.8 – Monitoring CPU usage

Here, the blue curve denotes the CPU usage, which stays below the normal threshold.

While this example is relatively simple, it possesses the core components of a reactive program, and more complex applications that fully utilize the power of RxPY may be built using this as a blueprint.

Summary

Asynchronous programming is useful when our code deals with slow and unpredictable resources, such as I/O devices and networks. In this chapter, we explored the fundamental concepts of concurrency and asynchronous programming and how to write concurrent code with the `asyncio` and `RxPy` libraries.

`asyncio` coroutines are an excellent choice when dealing with multiple, interconnected resources as they greatly simplify the code logic by cleverly avoiding callbacks. Reactive programming is also very good in these situations, but it truly shines when dealing with streams of data that are common in real-time applications and UIs.

Questions

1. How does asynchronous programming help programs run at higher speed?
2. What are the main differences between callbacks and futures in asynchronous programming?
3. What are the core characteristics/requirements of a reactive application?

Further reading

- Migrating to RxPY v3: `https://rxpy.readthedocs.io/en/latests/migration.html`

8
Parallel Processing

With parallel processing using multiple cores, you can increase the number of calculations your program can do in a given time frame without needing a faster processor. The main idea is to divide a problem into independent subunits and use multiple cores to solve those subunits in parallel.

Parallel processing is necessary to tackle large-scale problems. Every day, companies produce massive quantities of data that needs to be stored in multiple computers and analyzed. Scientists and engineers run parallel code on supercomputers to simulate massive systems.

Parallel processing allows you to take advantage of multicore **central processing units (CPUs)** as well as **graphics processing units (GPUs)** that work extremely well with highly parallel problems.

In this chapter, we will cover the following topics:

- Introduction to parallel programming
- Using multiple processes
- Parallel Cython with **Open Multi-Processing (OpenMP)**
- Automatic parallelism

Technical requirements

The code files for this chapter can be accessed through this link: `https://github.com/PacktPublishing/Advanced-Python-Programming-Second-Edition/tree/main/Chapter08`.

Introduction to parallel programming

To parallelize a program, it is necessary to divide the problem into subunits that can run independently (or almost independently) from each other.

A problem where the subunits are totally independent of each other is called *embarrassingly parallel*. An element-wise operation on an array is a typical example—the operation needs to only know the element it is handling now. Another example is our particle simulator. Since there are no interactions, each particle can evolve independently from the others. Embarrassingly parallel problems are very easy to implement and perform very well on parallel architectures.

Other problems may be divided into subunits but must share some data to perform their calculations. In those cases, the implementation is less straightforward and can lead to performance issues because of the communication costs.

We will illustrate the concept with an example. Imagine that you have a particle simulator, but this time, the particles attract other particles within a certain distance (as shown in the following figure):

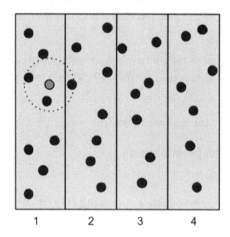

Figure 8.1 – Illustration of a neighboring region

To parallelize this problem, we divide the simulation box into regions and assign each region to a different processor. If we evolve the system one step at a time, some particles will interact with particles in a neighboring region. To perform the next iteration, communication with the new particle positions of the neighboring region is required.

Communication between processes is costly and can seriously hinder the performance of parallel programs. There exist two main ways to handle data communication in parallel programs: shared memory and distributed memory.

In **shared memory**, the subunits have access to the same memory space. An advantage of this approach is that you don't have to explicitly handle the communication as it is sufficient to write or read from the shared memory. However, problems arise when multiple processes try to access and change the same memory location at the same time. Care should be taken to avoid such conflicts using synchronization techniques.

In the **distributed memory** model, each process is completely separated from the others and possesses its own memory space. In this case, communication is handled explicitly between the processes. The communication overhead is typically costlier compared to shared memory as data can potentially travel through a network interface.

One common way to achieve parallelism with the shared memory model is through **threads**. Threads are independent subtasks that originate from a process and share resources, such as memory. This concept is further illustrated in the following diagram:

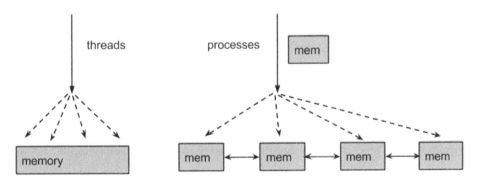

Figure 8.2 – Illustration of the difference between threads and processes

Threads produce multiple execution contexts and share the same memory space, while processes provide multiple execution contexts that possess their own memory space, and communication must be handled explicitly.

Python can spawn and handle threads, but they can't be used to increase performance; due to the Python interpreter design, only one Python instruction is allowed to run at a time—this mechanism is called the **Global Interpreter Lock (GIL)**. What happens is that each time a thread executes a Python statement, the thread acquires a lock and, when the execution is completed, the same lock is released. Since the lock can be acquired only by one thread at a time, other threads are prevented from executing Python statements while some other thread holds the lock.

Even though the GIL prevents parallel execution of Python instructions, threads can still be used to provide concurrency in situations where the lock can be released, such as in time-consuming **input/output (I/O)** operations or in C extensions.

Why Not Remove the GIL?

In past years, many attempts have been made, including the most recent *Gilectomy* experiment. First, removing the GIL is not an easy task and requires modification of most of the Python data structures. Additionally, such fine-grained locking can be costly and may introduce substantial performance loss in single-threaded programs. Despite this, some Python implementations (notable examples are Jython and IronPython) do not use the GIL.

The GIL can be completely sidestepped using processes instead of threads. Processes don't share the same memory area and are independent of each other—each process has its own interpreter. Processes have a few disadvantages: starting up a new process is generally slower than starting a new thread, they consume more memory, and **inter-process communication (IPC)** can be slow. On the other hand, processes are still very flexible, and they scale better as they can be distributed on multiple machines.

GPUs

GPUs are special processors designed for computer graphics applications. Those applications usually require processing the geometry of a **three-dimensional (3D)** scene and output an array of pixels to the screen. The operations performed by GPUs involve array and matrix operations on floating-point numbers.

GPUs are designed to run this graphics-related operation very efficiently, and they achieve this by adopting a highly parallel architecture. Compared to a CPU, a GPU has many more (thousands) of small processing units. GPUs are intended to produce data at about 60 **frames per second (FPS)**, which is much slower than the typical response time of a CPU, which possesses higher clock speeds.

GPUs possess a very different architecture from a standard CPU and are specialized for computing floating-point operations. Therefore, to compile programs for GPUs, it is necessary to utilize special programming platforms, such as **Compute Unified Device Architecture (CUDA)** and **Open Computing Language (OpenCL)**.

CUDA is a proprietary NVIDIA technology. It provides an **application programming interface (API)** that can be accessed from other languages. CUDA provides the **NVIDIA CUDA Compiler (NVCC)** tool that can be used to compile GPU programs written in a language such as C (CUDA C), as well as numerous libraries that implement highly optimized mathematical routines.

OpenCL is an open technology with an ability to write parallel programs that can be compiled for a variety of target devices (CPUs and GPUs of several vendors) and is a good option for non-NVIDIA devices.

GPU programming sounds wonderful on paper. However, don't throw away your CPU yet. GPU programming is tricky, and only specific use cases benefit from the GPU architecture. Programmers need to be aware of the costs incurred in memory transfers to and from the main memory and how to implement algorithms to take advantage of the GPU architecture.

Generally, GPUs are great at increasing the number of operations you can perform per unit of time (also called **throughput**); however, they require more time to prepare the data for processing. In contrast, CPUs are much faster at producing an individual result from scratch (also called **latency**).

For the right problem, GPUs provide extreme (10 to 100 times) speedup. For this reason, they often constitute a very inexpensive solution (the same speedup will require hundreds of CPUs) to improve the performance of numerically intensive applications. We will illustrate how to execute some algorithms on a GPU in the *Automatic parallelism* section.

Having said that, we will begin our discussion on multiprocessing using standard processes in the next section.

Using multiple processes

The standard `multiprocessing` module can be used to quickly parallelize simple tasks by spawning several processes while avoiding the GIL problem. Its interface is easy to use and includes several utilities to handle task submission and synchronization.

The Process and Pool classes

You can create a process that runs independently by subclassing `multiprocessing.Process`. You can extend the `__init__` method to initialize resources, and you can write a portion of the code that will be executed in a subprocess by implementing the `Process.run` method. In the following code snippet, we define a `Process` class that will wait for 1 second and print its assigned `id` value:

```python
import multiprocessing
import time


class Process(multiprocessing.Process):
    def __init__(self, id):
        super(Process, self).__init__()
        self.id = id

    def run(self):
        time.sleep(1)
        print("I'm the process with id:
            {}".format(self.id))
```

To spawn the process, we must instantiate the `Process` class and call the `Process.start` method. Note that you don't directly call `Process.run`; the call to `Process.start` will create a new process that, in turn, will call the `Process.run` method. We can add the following lines at the end of the preceding snippet to create and start the new process:

```python
if __name__ == '__main__':
    p = Process(0)
    p.start()
```

> **The special __name__ Variable**
>
> Note that we need to place any code that manages processes inside the `if __name__ == '__main__'` condition, as shown in the previous code snippet, to avoid many undesirable behaviors. All the code shown in this chapter will be assumed to follow this practice.

The instructions after `Process.start` will be executed immediately without waiting for the p process to finish. To wait for the task completion, you can use the `Process.join` method, as follows:

```
if __name__ == '__main__':
    p = Process(0)
    p.start()
    p.join()
```

We can launch four different processes that will run in parallel in the same way. In a serial program, the total required time will be 4 seconds. Since the execution is concurrent, the resulting wall clock time will be of 1 second. In the following code snippet, we create four processes that will execute concurrently:

```
if __name__ == '__main__':
    processes = Process(1), Process(2), Process(3),
        Process(4)
    [p.start() for p in processes]
```

Note that the order of the execution for parallel processes is unpredictable and ultimately depends on how the **operating system (OS)** schedules this. You can verify this behavior by executing the program multiple times; the order will likely be different between runs.

The `multiprocessing` module exposes a convenient interface that makes it easy to assign and distribute tasks to a set of processes that reside in the `multiprocessing.Pool` class.

The `multiprocessing.Pool` class spawns a set of processes—called *workers*—and lets us submit tasks through the `apply`/`apply_async` and `map`/`map_async` methods.

The `pool.map` method applies a function to each element of a list and returns a list of results. Its usage is equivalent to the built-in (serial) `map`.

To use a parallel map, you should first initialize a `multiprocessing.Pool` object that takes the number of workers as its first argument; if not provided, that number will be equal to the number of cores in the system. You can initialize a `multiprocessing.Pool` object in the following way:

```
pool = multiprocessing.Pool()
pool = multiprocessing.Pool(processes=4)
```

Let's see `pool.map` in action. If you have a function that computes the square of a number, you can map the function to the list by calling `pool.map` and passing the function and the list of inputs as arguments, as follows:

```
def square(x):
    return x * x


inputs = [0, 1, 2, 3, 4]
outputs = pool.map(square, inputs)
```

The `pool.map_async` function is just like `pool.map` but returns an `AsyncResult` object instead of the actual result. When we call `pool.map`, the execution of the main program is stopped until all the workers are finished processing the result. With `map_async`, the `AsyncResult` object is returned immediately without blocking the main program and the calculations are done in the background. We can then retrieve the result using the `AsyncResult.get` method at any time, as shown in the following lines of code:

```
outputs_async = pool.map_async(square, inputs)
outputs = outputs_async.get()
```

`pool.apply_async` assigns a task consisting of a single function to one of the workers. It takes the function and its arguments and returns an `AsyncResult` object. We can obtain an effect similar to `map` using `apply_async`, as shown here:

```
results_async = [pool.apply_async(square, i) for i in \
    range(100))]
results = [r.get() for r in results_async]
```

To use the results computed and returned by these processes, we can simply access the data stored in `results`.

The Executor interface

From version 3.2 onward, it is possible to execute Python code in parallel using the `Executor` interface provided in the `concurrent.futures` module. We already saw the `Executor` interface in action in the previous chapter, when we used `ThreadPoolExecutor` to perform multiple tasks concurrently. In this subsection, we'll demonstrate the usage of the `ProcessPoolExecutor` class.

`ProcessPoolExecutor` exposes a very lean interface, at least when compared to the more featureful `multiprocessing.Pool`. A `ProcessPoolExecutor` class can be instantiated, similar to `ThreadPoolExecutor`, by passing a number of worker threads using the `max_workers` argument (by default, `max_workers` will be the number of CPU cores available). The main methods available to the `ProcessPoolExecutor` class are `submit` and `map`.

The `submit` method will take a function and return a `Future` instance that will keep track of the execution of the submitted function. The `map` method works similarly to the `pool.map` function, except that it returns an iterator rather than a list. The code is illustrated in the following snippet:

```
from concurrent.futures import ProcessPoolExecutor

executor = ProcessPoolExecutor(max_workers=4)
fut = executor.submit(square, 2)
# Result:
# <Future at 0x7f5b5c030940 state=running>

result = executor.map(square, [0, 1, 2, 3, 4])
list(result)
# Result:
# [0, 1, 4, 9, 16]
```

To extract the result from one or more `Future` instances, you can use the `concurrent.futures.wait` and `concurrent.futures.as_completed` functions. The `wait` function accepts a list of `future` instances and will block the execution of the programs until all the futures have completed their execution. The result can then be extracted using the `Future.result` method. The `as_completed` function also accepts a function but will, instead, return an iterator over the results. The code is illustrated in the following snippet:

```
from concurrent.futures import wait, as_completed

fut1 = executor.submit(square, 2)
fut2 = executor.submit(square, 3)
wait([fut1, fut2])
# Then you can extract the results using fut1.result()
  and fut2.result()
```

```
results = as_completed([fut1, fut2])
list(results)
# Result:
# [4, 9]
```

Alternatively, you can generate futures using the `asyncio.run_in_executor` function and manipulate the results using all the tools and syntax provided by the `asyncio` libraries so that you can achieve concurrency and parallelism at the same time.

Monte Carlo approximation of pi

As an example, we will implement a canonical, embarrassingly parallel program—**the Monte Carlo approximation of pi**. Imagine that we have a square of size 2 units; its area will be 4 units. Now, we inscribe a circle of 1 unit radius in this square; the area of the circle will be $pi * r^2$. By substituting the value of r in the previous equation, we get that the numerical value for the area of the circle is $pi * (1)^2 = pi$. You can refer to the following screenshot for a graphical representation of this:

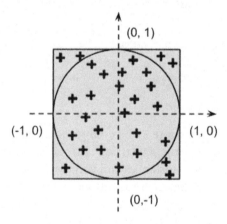

Figure 8.3 – Illustration of our strategy of approximation of pi

If we shoot a lot of random points on this, some points will fall into the circle, which we'll call *hits*, while the remaining points, *misses*, will be outside the circle. The area of the circle will be proportional to the number of hits, while the area of the square will be proportional to the total number of shots. To get the value of pi, it is sufficient to divide the area of the circle (equal to *pi*) by the area of the square (equal to 4), as illustrated in the following code snippet:

```
hits/total = area_circle/area_square = pi/4
pi = 4 * hits/total
```

The strategy we will employ in our program will be as follows:

- Generate a lot of uniformly random (x, y) numbers in the range $(-1, 1)$.

- Test whether those numbers lie inside the circle by checking whether $x^{**}2 + y^{**}2 <= 1$.

The first step when writing a parallel program is to write a serial version and verify that it works. In a real-world scenario, you also want to leave parallelization as the last step of your optimization process—first, because we need to identify the slow parts, and second, parallelization is time-consuming and *gives you at most a speedup equal to the number of processors*. The implementation of the serial program is shown here:

```
import random

samples = 1000000
hits = 0

for i in range(samples):
    x = random.uniform(-1.0, 1.0)
    y = random.uniform(-1.0, 1.0)

    if x**2 + y**2 <= 1:
        hits += 1

pi = 4.0 * hits/samples
```

The accuracy of our approximation will improve as we increase the number of samples. Note that each loop iteration is independent of the other—this problem is embarrassingly parallel.

To parallelize this code, we can write a function, called `sample`, that corresponds to a single hit-miss check. If the sample hits the circle, the function will return `1`; otherwise, it will return `0`. By running `sample` multiple times and summing the results, we'll get the total number of hits. We can run `sample` over multiple processors with `apply_async` and get the results in the following way:

```
def sample():
    x = random.uniform(-1.0, 1.0)
    y = random.uniform(-1.0, 1.0)
```

```
        if x**2 + y**2 <= 1:
            return 1
        else:
            return 0


    pool = multiprocessing.Pool()
    results_async = [pool.apply_async(sample) for i in \
        range(samples)]
    hits = sum(r.get() for r in results_async)
```

We can wrap the two versions in the pi_serial and pi_apply_async functions (you can find their implementation in the pi.py file) and benchmark the execution speed, as follows:

```
$ time python -c 'import pi; pi.pi_serial()'
real    0m0.734s
user    0m0.731s
sys     0m0.004s
$ time python -c 'import pi; pi.pi_apply_async()'
real    1m36.989s
user    1m55.984s
sys     0m50.386
```

As shown in the earlier benchmark, our first parallel version literally cripples our code, the reason being that the time spent doing the actual calculation is small compared to the overhead required to send and distribute the tasks to the workers.

To solve the issue, we have to make the overhead negligible compared to the calculation time. For example, we can ask each worker to handle more than one sample at a time, thus reducing the task communication overhead. We can write a sample_multiple function that processes more than one hit and modifies our parallel version by dividing our problem by 10; more intensive tasks are shown in the following code snippet:

```
    def sample_multiple(samples_partial):
        return sum(sample() for i inrange(samples_partial))


    n_tasks = 10
    chunk_size = samples/n_tasks
    pool = multiprocessing.Pool()
```

```
    results_async = [pool.apply_async(sample_multiple, \
        chunk_size) for i in range(n_tasks)]
    hits = sum(r.get() for r in results_async)
```

We can wrap this in a function called `pi_apply_async_chunked` and run it as follows:

```
$ time python -c 'import pi; pi.pi_apply_async_chunked()'
real    0m0.325s
user    0m0.816s
sys     0m0.008s
```

The results are much better; we more than doubled the speed of our program. You can also notice that the `user` metric is larger than `real`; the total CPU time is larger than the total time because more than one CPU worked at the same time. If you increase the number of samples, you will note that the ratio of communication to calculation decreases, giving even better speedups.

Everything is nice and simple when dealing with embarrassingly parallel problems. However, you sometimes have to share data between processes.

Synchronization and locks

Even if `multiprocessing` uses processes (with their own independent memory), it lets you define certain variables and arrays as shared memory. You can define a shared variable using `multiprocessing.Value`, passing its data type as a string (i for integer, d for double, f for float, and so on). You can update the content of the variable through the `value` attribute, as shown in the following code snippet:

```
    shared_variable = multiprocessing.Value('f')
    shared_variable.value = 0
```

When using shared memory, you should be aware of concurrent access. Imagine that you have a shared integer variable, and each process increments its value multiple times. You will define a `Process` class, as follows:

```
    class Process(multiprocessing.Process):

        def __init__(self, counter):
            super(Process, self).__init__()
            self.counter = counter
```

```
def run(self):
    for i in range(1000):
        self.counter.value += 1
```

You can initialize the shared variable in the main program and pass it to 4 processes, as shown in the following code snippet:

```
def main():
    counter = multiprocessing.Value('i', lock=True)
    counter.value = 0

    processes = [Process(counter) for i in range(4)]
    [p.start() for p in processes]
    [p.join() for p in processes] # processes are done
    print(counter.value)
```

If you run this program (shared.py in the code directory), you will note that the final value of counter is not 4000, but it has random values (on my machine, they are between 2000 and 2500). If we assume that the arithmetic is correct, we can conclude that there's a problem with the parallelization.

What happens is that multiple processes are trying to access the same shared variable at the same time. The situation is best explained by looking at the following diagram. In a serial execution, the first process reads the number (0), increments it, and writes the new value (1); the second process reads the new value (1), increments it, and writes it again (2).

In parallel execution, the two processes read the number (0), increment it, and write the value (1) at the same time, leading to a wrong answer:

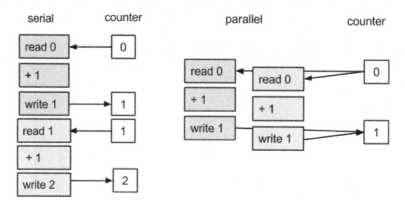

Figure 8.4 – Multiple processes accessing the same variable, leading to incorrect behavior

To solve this problem, we need to synchronize the access to this variable so that only one process at a time can access, increment, and write the value on the shared variable. This feature is provided by the multiprocessing.Lock class. A lock can be acquired and released through the acquire and release methods respectively or by using the lock as a context manager. Since the lock can be acquired by only one process at a time, this method prevents multiple processes from executing the protected section of code at the same time.

We can define a global lock and use it as a context manager to restrict access to the counter, as shown in the following code snippet:

```python
class Process(multiprocessing.Process):

    def __init__(self, counter):
        super(Process, self).__init__()
        self.counter = counter

    def run(self):
        for i in range(1000):
            with lock: # acquire the lock
                self.counter.value += 1
            # release the lock
```

Synchronization primitives, such as locks, are essential to solving many problems, but they should be kept to a minimum to improve the performance of your program.

> **Tip**
>
> The multiprocessing module includes other communication and synchronization tools; you can refer to the official documentation at http://docs.python.org/3/library/multiprocessing.html for a complete reference.

In *Chapter 4, C Performance with Cython*, we discussed Cython as a method of speeding up our programs. Cython itself also allows parallel processing via OpenMP, which we will examine next.

Parallel Cython with OpenMP

Cython provides a convenient interface to perform shared-memory parallel processing through *OpenMP*. This lets you write extremely efficient parallel code directly in Cython without having to create a C wrapper.

OpenMP is a specification and an API designed to write multithreaded, parallel programs. The OpenMP specification includes a series of C preprocessor directives to manage threads and provides communication patterns, load balancing, and other synchronization features. Several C/C++ and Fortran compilers (including the **GNU Compiler Collection (GCC)**) implement the OpenMP API.

We can introduce the Cython parallel features with a small example. Cython provides a simple API based on OpenMP in the `cython.parallel` module. The simplest way to achieve parallelism is through `prange`, which is a construct that automatically distributes loop operations in multiple threads.

First of all, we can write the serial version of a program that computes the square of each element of a NumPy array in the `hello_parallel.pyx` file. We define a function, `square_serial`, that takes a buffer as input and populates an output array with the squares of the input array elements; `square_serial` is shown in the following code snippet:

```
import numpy as np


def square_serial(double[:] inp):
    cdef int i, size
    cdef double[:] out
    size = inp.shape[0]
    out_np = np.empty(size, 'double')
    out = out_np

    for i in range(size):
        out[i] = inp[i]*inp[i]

    return out_np
```

Implementing a parallel version of the loop over the array elements involves substituting the `range` call with `prange`. There's a caveat—to use `prange`, the body of the loop must be interpreter-free. As already explained, we need to release the GIL and, since interpreter calls generally acquire the GIL, they need to be avoided to make use of threads.

In Cython, you can release the GIL using the `nogil` context, as follows:

```
with nogil:
    for i in prange(size):
        out[i] = inp[i]*inp[i]
```

Alternatively, you can use the `nogil=True` option of `prange` that will automatically wrap the loop body in a `nogil` block, as follows:

```
for i in prange(size, nogil=True):
    out[i] = inp[i]*inp[i]
```

Attempts to call Python code in a `prange` block will produce an error. Prohibited operations include function calls, object initialization, and so on. To enable such operations in a `prange` block (you may want to do so for debugging purposes), you have to re-enable the GIL using a `with gil` statement, as follows:

```
for i in prange(size, nogil=True):
    out[i] = inp[i]*inp[i]
    with gil:
        x = 0 # Python assignment
```

We can now test our code by compiling it as a Python extension module. To enable OpenMP support, it is necessary to change the `setup.py` file so that it includes the `-fopenmp` compilation option. This can be achieved by using the `distutils.extension.Extension` class in `distutils` and passing it to `cythonize`. The complete `setup.py` file looks like this:

```
from distutils.core import setup
from distutils.extension import Extension
from Cython.Build import cythonize

hello_parallel = Extension(
    'hello_parallel',
    ['hello_parallel.pyx'],
    extra_compile_args=['-fopenmp'],
    extra_link_args=['-fopenmp'])

setup(
    name='Hello',
```

```
    ext_modules = cythonize(['cevolve.pyx',
        hello_parallel]),
)
```

Using `prange`, we can easily parallelize the Cython version of our `ParticleSimulator` class. The following code snippet contains the `c_evolve` function of the `cevolve.pyx` Cython module that was written in *Chapter 4, C Performance with Cython*:

```
def c_evolve(double[:, :] r_i,double[:] ang_speed_i, \
                double timestep,int nsteps):

    # cdef declarations

    for i in range(nsteps):
        for j in range(nparticles):
            # loop body
```

First, we will invert the order of the loops so that the outermost loop will be executed in parallel (each iteration is independent of the other). Since the particles don't interact with each other, we can change the order of iteration safely, as shown in the following code snippet:

```
    for j in range(nparticles):
        for i in range(nsteps):

            # loop body
```

Next, we will replace the `range` call of the outer loop with `prange` and remove calls that acquire the GIL. Since our code was already enhanced with static types, the `nogil` option can be applied safely, as follows:

```
    for j in prange(nparticles, nogil=True)
```

We can now compare the functions by wrapping them in the `benchmark` function to assess any performance improvement, as follows:

```
In [3]: %timeit benchmark(10000, 'openmp') # Running on
    4 processors
1 loops, best of 3: 599 ms per loop
In [4]: %timeit benchmark(10000, 'cython')
1 loops, best of 3: 1.35 s per loop
```

Interestingly, we achieved a two-times speedup by writing a parallel version using `prange`.

As we mentioned earlier, normal Python programs have trouble achieving thread parallelism because of the GIL. So far, we worked around this problem using separate processes; starting a process, however, takes significantly more time and memory than starting a thread.

We also saw that sidestepping the Python environment allowed us to achieve a two-times speedup on already fast Cython code. This strategy allowed us to achieve lightweight parallelism but required a separate compilation step. In the next section, we will further explore this strategy using special libraries that are capable of automatically translating our code into a parallel version for efficient execution.

Automatic parallelism

Examples of packages that implement automatic parallelism are the (by now) familiar **just-in-time** (**JIT**) compilers `numexpr` and Numba. Other packages have been developed to automatically optimize and parallelize array and matrix-intensive expressions, which are crucial in specific numerical and **machine learning** (**ML**) applications.

Theano is a project that allows you to define a mathematical expression on arrays (more generally, *tensors*), and compile them to a fast language, such as C or C++. Many of the operations that Theano implements are parallelizable and can run on both the CPU and GPU.

TensorFlow is another library that, similar to Theano, is targeted toward array-intensive mathematical expressions but, rather than translating the expressions to specialized C code, executes the operations on an efficient C++ engine.

Both Theano and TensorFlow are ideal when the problem at hand can be expressed in a chain of matrix and element-wise operations (such as *neural networks*).

Getting started with Theano

Theano is somewhat similar to a compiler but with the added bonus of being able to express, manipulate, and optimize mathematical expressions as well as run code on the CPU and GPU. Since 2010, Theano has improved release after release and has been adopted by several other Python projects as a way to automatically generate efficient computational models on the fly.

The package may be installed using the following command:

```
$pip install Theano
```

In Theano, you first define the function you want to run by specifying variables and transformation using a pure Python API. This specification will then be compiled into machine code for execution.

As a first example, let's examine how to implement a function that computes the square of a number. The input will be represented by a scalar variable, a, and then we will transform it to obtain its square, indicated by a_sq. In the following code snippet, we will use the T.scalar function to define a variable and use the normal ** operator to obtain a new variable:

```
import theano.tensor as T
import theano as th
a = T.scalar('a')
a_sq = a ** 2
print(a_sq)
# Output:
# Elemwise{pow,no_inplace}.0
```

As you can see, no specific value is computed, and the transformation we apply is purely symbolic. In order to use this transformation, we need to generate a function. To compile a function, you can use the th.function utility that takes a list of the input variables as its first argument and the output transformation (in our case, a_sq) as its second argument, as illustrated in the following code snippet:

```
compute_square = th.function([a], a_sq)
```

Theano will take some time and translate the expression to efficient C code and compile it, all in the background! The return value of th.function will be a ready-to-use Python function, and its usage is demonstrated in the next line of code:

```
compute_square(2)
4.0
```

Unsurprisingly, compute_square correctly returns the input value squared. Note, however, that the return type is not an integer (like the input type) but a floating-point number. This is because the Theano default variable type is float64. You can verify that by inspecting the dtype attribute of the a variable, as follows:

```
a.dtype
# Result:
# float64
```

The Theano behavior is very different compared to what we saw with Numba. Theano doesn't compile generic Python code and, also, doesn't do any type of inference; defining Theano functions requires a more precise specification of the types involved.

The real power of Theano comes from its support for array expressions. Defining a **one-dimensional (1D)** vector can be done with the T.vector function; the returned variable supports broadcasting operations with the same semantics of NumPy arrays. For instance, we can take two vectors and compute the element-wise sum of their squares, as follows:

```
a = T.vector('a')
b = T.vector('b')
ab_sq = a**2 + b**2
compute_square = th.function([a, b], ab_sq)

compute_square([0, 1, 2], [3, 4, 5])
# Result:
# array([  9.,   17.,   29.])
```

The idea is, again, to use the Theano API as a mini-language to combine various NumPy array expressions that will be compiled as efficient machine code.

> **Note**
>
> One of the selling points of Theano is its ability to perform arithmetic simplifications and automatic gradient calculations. For more information, refer to the official documentation (https://theano-pymc.readthedocs.io/en/latest/).

To demonstrate Theano functionality on a familiar use case, we can implement our parallel calculation of pi again. Our function will take a collection of two random coordinates as input and return the pi estimate. The input random numbers will be defined as vectors named x and y, and we can test their position inside the circle using a standard element-wise operation that we will store in the hit_test variable, as illustrated in the following code snippet:

```
x = T.vector('x')
y = T.vector('y')

hit_test = x ** 2 + y ** 2 < 1
```

At this point, we need to count the number of `True` elements in `hit_test`, which can be done by taking its sum (it will be implicitly cast to integer). To obtain the `pi` estimate, we finally need to calculate the ratio of hits versus the total number of trials. The calculation is illustrated in the following code snippet:

```
hits = hit_test.sum()
total = x.shape[0]
pi_est = 4 * hits/total
```

We can benchmark the execution of the Theano implementation using `th.function` and the `timeit` module. In our test, we will pass two arrays of size `30000` and use the `timeit.timeit` utility to execute the `calculate_pi` function multiple times, as illustrated in the following code snippet:

```
calculate_pi = th.function([x, y], pi_est)

x_val = np.random.uniform(-1, 1, 30000)
y_val = np.random.uniform(-1, 1, 30000)

import timeit
res = timeit.timeit("calculate_pi(x_val, y_val)", \
"from __main__ import x_val, y_val, calculate_pi", \
  number=100000)
print(res)
# Output:
# 10.905971487998613
```

The serial execution of this function takes about 10 seconds. Theano is capable of automatically parallelizing the code by implementing element-wise and matrix operations using specialized packages, such as OpenMP and the **Basic Linear Algebra Subprograms** (**BLAS**) linear algebra routines. Parallel execution can be enabled using configuration options.

In Theano, you can set up configuration options by modifying variables in the `theano.config` object at import time. For example, you can issue the following commands to enable OpenMP support:

```
import theano
theano.config.openmp = True
theano.config.openmp_elemwise_minsize = 10
```

The parameters relevant to OpenMP are outlined here:

- `openmp_elemwise_minsize`: This is an integer number that represents the minimum size of the arrays where element-wise parallelization should be enabled (the overhead of the parallelization can harm performance for small arrays).

- `openmp`: This is a Boolean flag that controls the activation of OpenMP compilation (it should be activated by default).

Controlling the number of threads assigned for OpenMP execution can be done by setting the `OMP_NUM_THREADS` environmental variable before executing the code.

We can now write a simple benchmark to demonstrate OpenMP usage in practice. In a `test_theano.py` file, we will put the complete code for the `pi` estimation example, as follows:

```python
# File: test_theano.py
import numpy as np
import theano.tensor as T
import theano as th
th.config.openmp_elemwise_minsize = 1000
th.config.openmp = True


x = T.vector('x')
y = T.vector('y')


hit_test = x ** 2 + y ** 2 <= 1
hits = hit_test.sum()
misses = x.shape[0]
pi_est = 4 * hits/misses


calculate_pi = th.function([x, y], pi_est)


x_val = np.random.uniform(-1, 1, 30000)
y_val = np.random.uniform(-1, 1, 30000)


import timeit
res = timeit.timeit("calculate_pi(x_val, y_val)",
                    "from __main__ import x_val, y_val,
                    calculate_pi", number=100000)
print(res)
```

At this point, we can run the code from the command line and assess the scaling with an increasing number of threads by setting the OMP_NUM_THREADS environment variable, as follows:

```
$ OMP_NUM_THREADS=1 python test_theano.py
10.905971487998613
$ OMP_NUM_THREADS=2 python test_theano.py
7.538279129999864
$ OMP_NUM_THREADS=3 python test_theano.py
9.405846934998408
$ OMP_NUM_THREADS=4 python test_theano.py
14.634153957000308
```

Interestingly, there is a small speedup when using two threads, but the performance degrades quickly as we increase their number. This means that for this input size, it is not advantageous to use more than two threads as the price you pay to start new threads and synchronize their shared data is higher than the speedup that you can obtain from the parallel execution.

Achieving good parallel performance can be tricky as this will depend on the specific operations and how they access the underlying data. As a general rule, measuring the performance of a parallel program is crucial, and obtaining substantial speedups is a work of trial and error.

As an example, we can see that the parallel performance quickly degrades using slightly different code. In our hit test, we used the sum method directly and relied on the explicit casting of the hit_tests Boolean array. If we make the cast explicit, Theano will generate slightly different code that benefits less from multiple threads. We can modify the test_theano.py file to verify this effect, as follows:

```
# Older version
# hits = hit_test.sum()
hits = hit_test.astype('int32').sum()
```

If we rerun our benchmark, we see that the number of threads does not affect the running time significantly, as illustrated here:

```
$ OMP_NUM_THREADS=1 python test_theano.py
5.822126664999814
$ OMP_NUM_THREADS=2 python test_theano.py
5.697357518001809
```

```
$ OMP_NUM_THREADS=3 python test_theano.py
5.636914656002773
$ OMP_NUM_THREADS=4 python test_theano.py
5.764030176000233
```

Despite that, the timings improved considerably compared to the original version.

Profiling Theano

Given the importance of measuring and analyzing performance, Theano provides powerful and informative profiling tools. To generate profiling data, the only modification needed is the addition of the `profile=True` option to `th.function`, as illustrated in the following code snippet:

```
calculate_pi = th.function([x, y], pi_est,
    profile=True)
```

The profiler will collect data as the function is being run (for example, through `timeit` or direct invocation). The profiling summary can be printed to the output by issuing the `summary` command, as follows:

```
calculate_pi.profile.summary()
```

To generate profiling data, we can rerun our script after adding the `profile=True` option (for this experiment, we will set the `OMP_NUM_THREADS` environmental variable to `1`). Also, we will revert our script to the version that performed the casting of `hit_tests` implicitly.

> **Note**
>
> You can also set up profiling globally using the `config.profile` option.

The output printed by `calculate_pi.profile.summary()` is quite long and informative. A part of it is reported in the next block of code. The output is comprised of three sections that refer to timings sorted by `Class`, `Ops`, and `Apply`. In our example, we are concerned with `Ops`, which roughly maps to the functions used in the Theano compiled code. As you can see here, roughly 80% of the time is spent in taking the element-wise square and sum of the two numbers, while the rest of the time is spent calculating the sum:

```
Function profiling
==================
```

```
Message: test_theano.py:15


... other output
    Time in 100000 calls to Function.__call__ : 1.015549e+01s
... other output


Class
---
<% time> <sum %> <apply time> <time per call> <type>
<#call> <#apply> <Class name>
.... timing info by class


Ops
---
<% time> <sum %> <apply time> <time per call> <type> <#call>
<#apply> <Op name>
    80.0%    80.0%        6.722s        6.72e-
05s    C     100000         1    Elemwise{Composite{LT((sqr(
i0) + sqr(i1)), i2)}}
    19.4%    99.4%        1.634s        1.63e-
05s    C     100000         1    Sum{acc_dtype=int64}
     0.3%    99.8%        0.027s        2.66e-
07s    C     100000         1    Elemwise{Composite{((i0 *
i1) / i2)}}
     0.2%   100.0%        0.020s        2.03e-
07s    C     100000         1    Shape_i{0}
    ... (remaining 0 Ops account for    0.00%(0.00s) of the
    runtime)


Apply
------
<% time> <sum %> <apply time> <time per call> <#call> <id>
<Apply name>
... timing info by apply
```

This information is consistent with what was found in our first benchmark. The code went from about 11 seconds to roughly 8 seconds when two threads were used. From these numbers, we can analyze how the time was spent.

Out of these 11 seconds, 80% of the time (about 8.8 seconds) was spent doing element-wise operations. This means that, in perfectly parallel conditions, the increase in speed by adding two threads will be 4.4 seconds. In this scenario, the theoretical execution time would be 6.6 seconds. Considering that we obtained a timing of about 8 seconds, it looks like there is some extra overhead (1.4 seconds) for the thread usage.

TensorFlow

TensorFlow is another library designed for fast numerical calculations and automatic parallelism. It was released as an open source project by Google in 2015. TensorFlow works by building mathematical expressions similar to Theano, except that the computation is not compiled as machine code but is executed on an external engine written in C++. TensorFlow supports the execution and deployment of parallel code on one or more CPUs and GPUs.

We can install TensorFlow using the following command:

```
$pip install tensorflow
```

> **TensorFlow Version Compatibility**
>
> Note that as the default option, TensorFlow 2.x will be installed without further specifications. However, since the number of users of TensorFlow 1.x is still considerable, the code we use next will follow the syntax of TensorFlow 1.x. You can either install version 1 by specifying `pip install tensorflow==1.15` or disable version 2's behavior using `import tensorflow.compat.v1 as tf; tf.disable_v2_behavior()` when importing the library, as shown next.

The usage of TensorFlow is quite similar to that of Theano. To create a variable in TensorFlow, you can use the `tf.placeholder` function that takes a data type as input, as follows:

```
import tensorflow.compat.v1 as tf
tf.disable_v2_behavior()


a = tf.placeholder('float64')
```

TensorFlow mathematical expressions can be expressed quite similarly to Theano, except for a few different naming conventions as well as more restricted support for the NumPy semantics.

TensorFlow doesn't compile functions to C and then machine code like Theano does, but serializes the defined mathematical functions (the data structure containing variables and transformations is called a **computation graph**) and executes them on specific devices. The configuration of devices and context can be done using the tf.Session object.

Once the desired expression is defined, a tf.Session object needs to be initialized and can be used to execute computation graphs using the Session.run method. In the following example, we demonstrate the usage of the TensorFlow API to implement a simple element-wise sum of squares:

```
a = tf.placeholder('float64')
b = tf.placeholder('float64')
ab_sq = a**2 + b**2

with tf.Session() as session:
    result = session.run(ab_sq, feed_dict={a: [0, 1, \
        2], b: [3, 4, 5]})
    print(result)
# Output:
# array([ 9.,   17.,   29.])
```

Parallelism in TensorFlow is achieved automatically by its smart execution engine, and it generally works well without much fiddling. However, note that it is mostly suited for **deep learning** (**DL**) workloads that involve the definition of complex functions that use a lot of matrix multiplications and calculate their gradient.

We can now replicate the estimation of pi example using TensorFlow capabilities and benchmark its execution speed and parallelism against the Theano implementation. What we will do is this:

- Define our x and y variables and perform a hit test using broadcasted operations.

- Calculate the sum of hit_tests using the tf.reduce_sum function.

- Initialize a Session object with the inter_op_parallelism_threads and intra_op_parallelism_threads configuration options. These options control the number of threads used for different classes of parallel operations. Note that the first Session instance created with such options sets the number of threads for the whole script (even future Session instances).

We can now write a script name, `test_tensorflow.py`, containing the following code. Note that the number of threads is passed as the first argument of the script (`sys.argv[1]`):

```
import tensorflow.compat.v1 as tf
tf.disable_v2_behavior()
import numpy as np
import time
import sys

NUM_THREADS = int(sys.argv[1])
samples = 30000

print('Num threads', NUM_THREADS)
x_data = np.random.uniform(-1, 1, samples)
y_data = np.random.uniform(-1, 1, samples)

x = tf.placeholder('float64', name='x')
y = tf.placeholder('float64', name='y')

hit_tests = x ** 2 + y ** 2 <= 1.0
hits = tf.reduce_sum(tf.cast(hit_tests, 'int32'))

with tf.Session
    (config=tf.ConfigProto
        (inter_op_parallelism_threads=NUM_THREADS,
        intra_op_parallelism_threads=NUM_THREADS)) as \
            sess:
    start = time.time()
    for i in range(10000):
        sess.run(hits, {x: x_data, y: y_data})
    print(time.time() - start)
```

If we run the script multiple times with different values of NUM_THREADS, we see that the performance is quite similar to Theano and that the speedup increased by parallelization is quite modest, as illustrated here:

```
$ python test_tensorflow.py 1
13.059704780578613
$ python test_tensorflow.py 2
11.938535928726196
$ python test_tensorflow.py 3
12.783955574035645
$ python test_tensorflow.py 4
12.158143043518066
```

The main advantage of using software packages such as TensorFlow and Theano is the support for parallel matrix operations that are commonly used in ML algorithms. This is very effective because those operations can achieve impressive performance gains on GPU hardware that is designed to perform these operations with high throughput.

Running code on a GPU

In this subsection, we will demonstrate the usage of a GPU with Theano and TensorFlow. As an example, we will benchmark the execution of very simple matrix multiplication on the GPU and compare it to its running time on a CPU.

> **Note**
>
> The code in this subsection requires the possession of a GPU. For learning purposes, it is possible to use the Amazon **Elastic Compute Cloud** (**EC2**) service (https://aws.amazon.com/ec2) to request a GPU-enabled instance.

The following code performs a simple matrix multiplication using Theano. We use the T.matrix function to initialize a **two-dimensional** (**2D**) array, and then we use the T.dot method to perform the matrix multiplication:

```
from theano import function, config
import theano.tensor as T
import numpy as np
import time
```

```
N = 5000

A_data = np.random.rand(N, N).astype('float32')
B_data = np.random.rand(N, N).astype('float32')

A = T.matrix('A')
B = T.matrix('B')

f = function([A, B], T.dot(A, B))

start = time.time()
f(A_data, B_data)

print("Matrix multiply ({}) took {} seconds".format(N, \
    time.time() - start))
print('Device used:', config.device)
```

It is possible to ask Theano to execute this code on a GPU by setting the `config.device=gpu` option. For added convenience, we can set up the configuration value from the command line using the `THEANO_FLAGS` environmental variable, shown as follows. After copying the previous code into the `test_theano_matmul.py` file, we can benchmark the execution time by issuing the following command:

```
$ THEANO_FLAGS=device=gpu python test_theano_gpu.py
Matrix multiply (5000) took 0.4182612895965576 seconds
Device used: gpu
```

We can analogously run the same code on the CPU using the `device=cpu` configuration option, as follows:

```
$ THEANO_FLAGS=device=cpu python test_theano.py
Matrix multiply (5000) took 2.9623231887817383 seconds
Device used: cpu
```

As you can see, the *GPU is 7.2 times faster than the CPU* version for this example!

For comparison, we may benchmark equivalent code using TensorFlow. The implementation of a TensorFlow version is shown in the next code snippet. The main differences with the Theano version are outlined here:

- The usage of the `tf.device` config manager that serves to specify the target device (`/cpu:0` or `/gpu:0`).

- The matrix multiplication is performed using the `tf.matmul` operator.

This is illustrated in the following code snippet:

```python
import tensorflow as tf
import time
import numpy as np
N = 5000

A_data = np.random.rand(N, N)
B_data = np.random.rand(N, N)

# Creates a graph.

with tf.device('/gpu:0'):
    A = tf.placeholder('float32')
    B = tf.placeholder('float32')

    C = tf.matmul(A, B)

with tf.Session() as sess:
    start = time.time()
    sess.run(C, {A: A_data, B: B_data})
    print('Matrix multiply ({}) took: {}'.format(N, \
        time.time() - start))
```

If we run the `test_tensorflow_matmul.py` script with the appropriate `tf.device` option, we obtain the following timings:

```
# Ran with tf.device('/gpu:0')
Matrix multiply (5000) took: 1.417285680770874

# Ran with tf.device('/cpu:0')
Matrix multiply (5000) took: 2.9646761417388916
```

As you can see, the performance gain is substantial (but not as good as the Theano version) in this simple case.

Another way to achieve automatic GPU computation is the now-familiar Numba. With Numba, it is possible to compile Python code to programs that can be run on a GPU. This flexibility allows for advanced GPU programming as well as more simplified interfaces. In particular, Numba makes extremely easy-to-write, GPU-ready, generalized universal functions.

In the next example, we will demonstrate how to write a universal function that applies an exponential function on two numbers and sums the results. As we already saw in *Chapter 5*, *Exploring Compilers*, this can be accomplished using the nb.vectorize function (we'll also specify the cpu target explicitly). The code is shown here:

```
import numba as nb
import math
@nb.vectorize(target='cpu')
def expon_cpu(x, y):
    return math.exp(x) + math.exp(y)
```

The expon_cpu universal function can be compiled for the GPU device using the target='cuda' option. Also, note that it is necessary to specify the input types for CUDA universal functions. The implementation of expon_gpu is shown here:

```
@nb.vectorize(['float32(float32, float32)'],
   target='cuda')
def expon_gpu(x, y):
    return math.exp(x) + math.exp(y)
```

We can now benchmark the execution of the two functions by applying the functions on two arrays of size 1000000. Also, note in the following code snippet that we execute the function before measuring the timings to trigger the Numba JIT compilation:

```
import numpy as np
import time


N = 1000000
niter = 100


a = np.random.rand(N).astype('float32')
b = np.random.rand(N).astype('float32')
```

```
# Trigger compilation
expon_cpu(a, b)
expon_gpu(a, b)

# Timing
start = time.time()
for i in range(niter):
    expon_cpu(a, b)
print("CPU:", time.time() - start)

start = time.time()
for i in range(niter):
    expon_gpu(a, b)
print("GPU:", time.time() - start)
# Output:
# CPU: 2.4762887954711914
# GPU: 0.8668839931488037
```

Thanks to the GPU execution, we were able to achieve a three-times speedup over the CPU version. Note that transferring data on the GPU is quite expensive; therefore, GPU execution becomes advantageous only for very large arrays.

When To Use Which Package

To close out this chapter, we will include a brief discussion regarding the parallel processing tools that we have examined thus far. First, we have seen how to use multiprocessing to manage multiple processes natively in Python. If you are using Cython, you may appeal to OpenMP to implement parallelism while being able to avoid working with C wrappers.

Finally, we study Theano and TensorFlow as two packages that automatically compile array-centric code and parallelize the execution. While these two packages offer similar advantages when it comes to automatic parallelism, at the time of this writing, TensorFlow has gained significant popularity, especially within the DL community, where the parallelism of matrix multiplications is the norm.

On the other hand, the active development of Theano stopped in 2018. While the package may still be utilized for automatic parallelism and DL uses, no new versions will be released. For this reason, TensorFlow is often preferred by Python programmers nowadays.

Summary

Parallel processing is an effective way to improve performance on large datasets. Embarrassingly parallel problems are excellent candidates for parallel execution that can be easily implemented to achieve good performance scaling.

In this chapter, we illustrated the basics of parallel programming in Python. We learned how to circumvent Python threading limitations by spawning processes using the tools available in the Python standard library. We also explored how to implement a multithreaded program using Cython and OpenMP.

For more complex problems, we learned how to use the Theano, TensorFlow, and Numba packages to automatically compile array-intensive expressions for parallel execution on CPU and GPU devices.

In the next chapter, we will learn how to apply parallel programming techniques to build a hands-on application that makes and handles web requests concurrently.

Questions

1. Why doesn't running Python code across multiple threads offer any speedup? What is the alternative approach that we have discussed in this chapter?

2. In the `multiprocessing` module, what is the difference between the `Process` and the `Pool` interface in terms of implementing multiprocessing?

3. On a high level, how do libraries such as Theano and TensorFlow help in parallelizing Python code?

9
Concurrent Web Requests

This chapter will focus on concurrently making web requests. Intuitively, making requests to a web page to collect information about it is independent of applying the same task to another web page. This means that concurrency, specifically threading in this case, can be a powerful tool that provides a significant speedup in this process. In this chapter, we will learn about the fundamentals of web requests and how to interact with websites using Python. We will also learn how concurrency can help us make multiple requests efficiently. Finally, we will look at several good practices regarding web requests.

Overall, this chapter serves as a practical exercise for us to become more comfortable with concurrency in Python, which will help you tackle future concurrent programming projects with more confidence.

In this chapter, we will cover the following topics:

- The basics of web requests
- The requests module
- Concurrent web requests
- The problem with timeouts
- Good practices in making web requests

The basics of web requests

The worldwide capacity to generate data is estimated to double in size every 2 years. Even though there is an interdisciplinary field known as **data science** that is entirely dedicated to studying data, almost every programming task in software development also has something to do with collecting and analyzing data. A significant part of this is, of course, **data collection**. However, the data that we need for our applications is sometimes not stored nicely and cleanly in a database – sometimes, we need to collect the data we need from web pages.

For example, **web scraping** is a data extraction method that automatically makes requests to web pages and downloads specific information. Web scraping allows us to comb through numerous websites and collect any data we need systematically and consistently. The collected data can be analyzed later by our applications or simply saved on our computers in various formats. An example of this would be Google, which maintains and runs numerous web scrapers of its own to find and index web pages for its search engines.

The Python language itself provides several good options for applications of this kind. In this chapter, we will mainly work with the `requests` module to make client-side web requests from our Python programs. However, before we look into this module in more detail, we need to understand some web terminology to be able to effectively design our applications.

HTML

Hypertext Markup Language (**HTML**) is the standard and most common markup language for developing web pages and web applications. An HTML file is simply a plaintext file with the `.html` file extension. In an HTML document, text is surrounded and delimited by tags, written in angle brackets; that is, `<p>`, `<img>`, `<i>`, and so on. These tags typically consist of pairs – an opening tag and a closing tag – indicating the styling or the nature of the data included inside.

It is also possible to include other forms of media in HTML code, such as images or videos. Numerous other tags are used in common HTML documents. Some specify a group of elements that share some common characteristics, such as `<id></id>` and `<class></class>`.

The following is an example of HTML code:

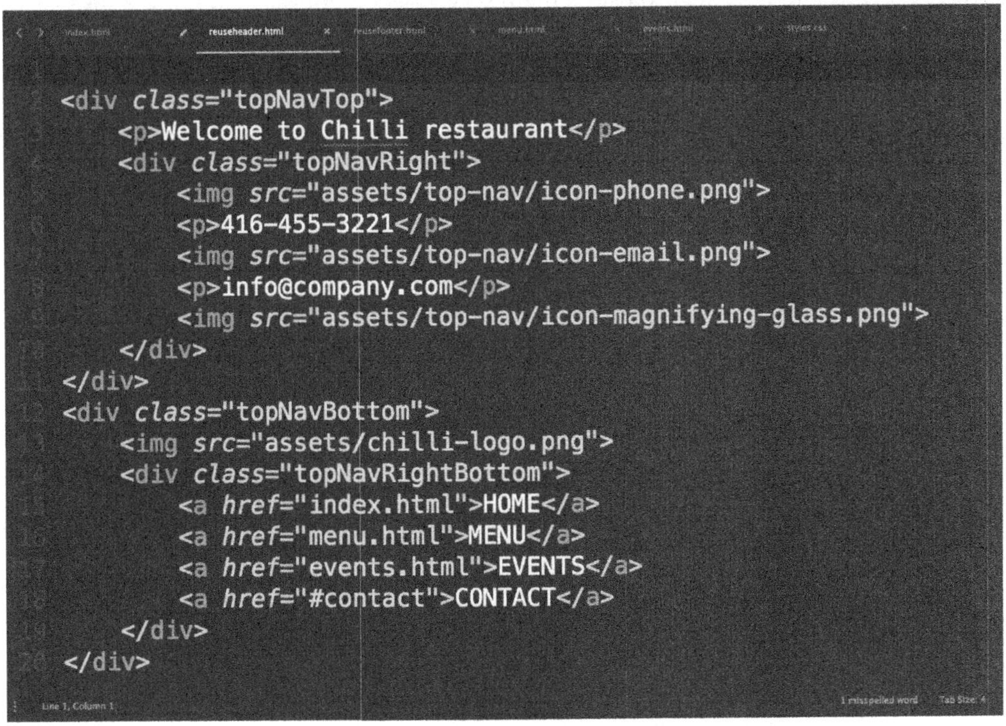

```
<div class="topNavTop">
    <p>Welcome to Chilli restaurant</p>
    <div class="topNavRight">
        <img src="assets/top-nav/icon-phone.png">
        <p>416-455-3221</p>
        <img src="assets/top-nav/icon-email.png">
        <p>info@company.com</p>
        <img src="assets/top-nav/icon-magnifying-glass.png">
    </div>
</div>
<div class="topNavBottom">
    <img src="assets/chilli-logo.png">
    <div class="topNavRightBottom">
        <a href="index.html">HOME</a>
        <a href="menu.html">MENU</a>
        <a href="events.html">EVENTS</a>
        <a href="#contact">CONTACT</a>
    </div>
</div>
```

Figure 9.1 – Sample HTML code

Fortunately, detailed knowledge of what each HTML tag accomplishes is not required for us to make effective web requests. As we will see later in this chapter, the more essential part of making web requests is the ability to interact with web pages efficiently.

HTTP requests

In a typical communication process on the web, HTML text is the data that is to be saved and/or further processed. This kind of data needs to be collected from web pages, but how can we go about doing that? Most of the communication is done via the internet – more specifically, the **World Wide Web** (**WWW**) – and this utilizes the **Hypertext Transfer Protocol** (**HTTP**). In HTTP, request methods are used to convey the information of what data is being requested and should be sent back from a server.

For example, when you type packtpub.com in your browser, the browser sends a request method via HTTP to the Packt website's main server, asking for data from the website. Now, if both your internet connection and Packt's server are working well, then your browser will receive a response from the server, as shown in the following diagram. This response will be in the form of an HTML document, which will be interpreted by your browser, and your browser will display the corresponding HTML output on the screen:

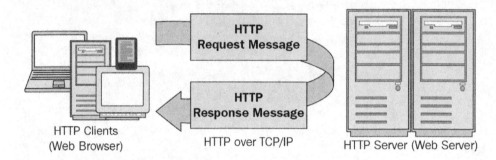

Figure 9.2 – Diagram of HTTP communication

Generally, request methods are defined as verbs that indicate the desired action to be performed while the HTTP client (web browsers) and the server communicate with each other: GET, HEAD, POST, PUT, DELETE, and so on. Of these methods, GET and POST are two of the most common request methods that are used in web scraping applications; their functionality is described here:

- The GET method requests specific data from the server. This method only retrieves data and has no other effect on the server and its databases.

- The POST method sends data in a specific form that is accepted by the server. This data could be, for example, a message to a bulletin board, mailing list, or newsgroup, information to be submitted to a web form, or an item to be added to a database.

All general-purpose HTTP servers that we commonly see on the internet are required to implement at least the GET (and HEAD) method, while the POST method is considered optional.

HTTP status code

It is not always the case that when a web request is made and sent to a web server, the server will process the request and return the requested data without fail. Sometimes, the server might be completely down or already busy interacting with other clients and therefore unresponsive to a new request; sometimes, the client itself makes bad requests to a server (for example, incorrectly formatted or malicious requests).

As a way to categorize these problems as well as provide the most information possible during the communication resulting from a web request, HTTP requires servers to respond to each request from its clients with an **HTTP response status code**. A status code is typically a three-digit number that indicates the specific characteristics of the response that the server sends back to a client.

In total, there are five large categories of HTTP response status codes, indicated by the first digit of the code. They are as follows:

- **1xx (informational status code)**: The request was received, and the server is processing it. For example, **100** means that the request header has been received and that the server is waiting for the request body; **102** indicates that the request is currently being processed (this is used for large requests and to prevent clients from timing out).

- **2xx (successful status code)**: The request was successfully received, understood, and processed by the server. For example, **200** means the request was successfully fulfilled; **202** indicates that the request has been accepted for processing, but the processing itself is not complete.

- **3xx (redirectional status code)**: Additional actions need to be taken so that the request can be successfully processed. For example, **300** means that there are multiple options regarding how the response from the server should be processed (for example, giving the client multiple video format options when a video file is to be downloaded); **301** indicates that the server has been moved permanently and all requests should be directed to another address (provided in the response from the server).

- **4xx (error status code for the client)**: The request was incorrectly formatted by the client and could not be processed. For example, **400** means that the client sent in a bad request (for example, a syntax error or the size of the request is too large); **404** (arguably the most well-known status code) indicates that the request method is not supported by the server.

- **5xx (error status code for the server)**: The request, although valid, could not be processed by the server. For example, **500** means that there is an internal server error in which an unexpected condition was encountered; **504** (Gateway Timeout) means that the server, which was acting as a gateway or a proxy, did not receive a response from the final server in time.

A lot more can be said about these status codes, but it is already sufficient for us to keep the big five categories previously mentioned in mind when making web requests from Python. If you would like to find more specific information about these or other status codes, the **Internet Assigned Numbers Authority (IANA)** maintains the official registry of HTTP status codes. Now, let's start learning about making web requests in Python.

The requests module

The `requests` module allows its users to make and send HTTP request methods. In the applications that we will be considering, it is mainly used to make contact with the server of the web pages we want to extract data from and obtain the response for the server.

Note

According to the official documentation of the module, the use of Python 3 is **highly recommended** over Python 2 for `requests`.

To install the module on your computer, run one of the following commands:

```
pip install requests
conda install requests
```

These commands should install `requests` and any other required dependencies (`idna`, `certifi`, `urllib3`, and so on) for you if your system does not have those already. After this, run `import requests` in a Python interpreter to confirm that the module has been installed successfully. Next, we will use `requests` to build the sequential, non-concurrent version of our program.

Making a request in Python

Let's look at an example usage of the module, as shown in the following code:

```python
import requests

url = 'http://www.google.com'

res = requests.get(url)

print(res.status_code)
print(res.headers)

with open('google.html', 'w') as f:
    f.write(res.text)

print('Done.')
```

In this example, we are using the `requests` module to download the HTML code of a web page; that is, `www.google.com`. The `requests.get()` method sends a GET request method to `url` and we store the response in the `res` variable. After checking the status and headers of the response by printing them out, we create a file called `google.html` and write the HTML code, which is stored in the response text, to the file.

After running the program (assuming that your internet is working and that the Google server is not down), you should get the following output:

```
200
{'Date': 'Sat, 17 Nov 2018 23:08:58 GMT', 'Expires': '-1',
'Cache-Control': 'private, max-age=0', 'Content-Type': 'text/
html; charset=ISO-8859-1', 'P3P': 'CP="This is not a P3P
policy! See g.co/p3phelp for more info."', 'X-XSS-Protection':
'1; mode=block', 'X-Frame-Options': 'SAMEORIGIN', 'Content-
Encoding': 'gzip', 'Server': 'gws', 'Content-Length': '4958',
'Set-Cookie': '1P_JAR=2018-11-17-23; expires=Mon, 17-Dec-2018
23:08:58 GMT; path=/; domain=.google.com, NID=146=NHT7fic3mjBO_
vdiFB3-gqnFPyGN1EGxyMkkNPnFMEVsqjGJ8S0EwrivDBWBgUS7hCPZGHbos
LE4uxz31shnr3X4adRpe7uICEiK8qh3Asu6LH_bIKSLWStAp8gMK1f9_GnQ0_
JKQoMvG-OLrT_fwV0hwTR5r2UVYsUJ6xHtX2s; expires=Sun, 19-May-2019
23:08:58 GMT; path=/; domain=.google.com; HttpOnly'}
Done.
```

The response had a `200` status code, which we know means that the request has been completed. The header of the response, which is stored in `res.headers`, also contains further specific information regarding the response. For example, we can see the date and time the request was made, that the content of the response is text and HTML, and that the total length of the content is `4958`.

The data that was sent from the server was also written to the `google.html` file. When you open this file in a text editor, you will be able to see the HTML code of the web page that we have downloaded using `requests`. On the other hand, if you use a web browser to open the file, you will see how **most** of the information from the original web page is now being displayed through a downloaded offline file.

For example, the following is how Google Chrome interprets the HTML file on my system:

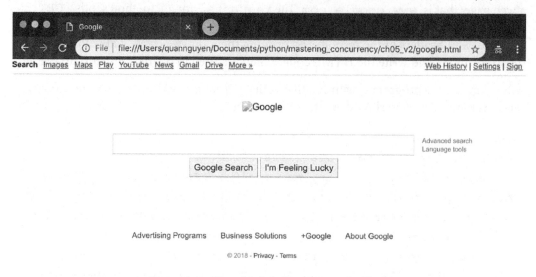

Figure 9.3 – Downloaded HTML opened offline

There is other information that is stored on the server that the web pages of that server refer to. This means that not all of the information that an online web page provides can be downloaded via a GET request, and this is why offline HTML code sometimes fails to contain all of the information available on the online web page that it was downloaded from. (For example, the downloaded HTML code in the preceding screenshot does not display the Google icon correctly.)

Running a ping test

With the basic knowledge of HTTP requests and the requests module in Python in hand, we will, for the remaining portion of this chapter, tackle the central problem of running a **ping test**. A ping test is a procedure in which you test the communication between your system and specific web servers, simply by requesting each of the servers in question. By considering the HTTP response status code (potentially) returned by the server, the test is used to evaluate either the internet connection of your system or the availability of the servers.

Ping tests are quite common among web administrators, who usually have to manage a large number of websites simultaneously. It is a good tool to quickly identify pages that are unexpectedly unresponsive or down. Many tools provide you with powerful options regarding ping tests and, in this chapter, we will be designing a ping test application that can concurrently send multiple web requests at the same time.

To simulate different HTTP response status codes to be sent back to our program, we will be using `httpstat.us`, a website that can generate various status codes and is commonly used to test how applications that make web requests can handle varying responses. Specifically, to use a request that will return a `200` status code in a program, we can simply send the request `httpstat.us/200`; the same applies to other status codes. In our ping test program, we will have a list of `httpstat.us` URLs with different status codes.

Let's take a look at the following code:

```
import requests

def ping(url):
    res = requests.get(url)
    print(f'{url}: {res.text}')

urls = [
    'http://httpstat.us/200',
    'http://httpstat.us/400',
    'http://httpstat.us/404',
    'http://httpstat.us/408',
    'http://httpstat.us/500',
    'http://httpstat.us/511'
]
for url in urls:
    ping(url)

print('Done.')
```

In this program, the `ping()` function takes in a URL and attempts to make a `GET` request to the site. Then, it prints out the content of the response returned by the server. In our main program, we have a list of different status codes that we mentioned earlier, each of which we will go through and call the `ping()` function on.

The final output, after running the preceding example, should be as follows:

```
http://httpstat.us/200: 200 OK
http://httpstat.us/400: 400 Bad Request
http://httpstat.us/404: 404 Not Found
http://httpstat.us/408: 408 Request Timeout
```

```
http://httpstat.us/500: 500 Internal Server Error
http://httpstat.us/511: 511 Network Authentication Required
Done.
```

Here, we can see that our ping test program was able to obtain the corresponding responses from the server. However, our current program is purely sequential, and we would like to implement a concurrent version of it. We will do this in the next section.

Concurrent web requests

In the context of concurrent programming, we can see that the process of making a request to a web server and obtaining the returned response is independent of the same procedure for a different web server. This is to say that we could apply concurrency and parallelism to our ping test application to speed up our execution.

In the concurrent ping test applications that we are designing, multiple HTTP requests will be made to the server simultaneously and the corresponding responses will be sent back to our program, as shown in the following diagram:

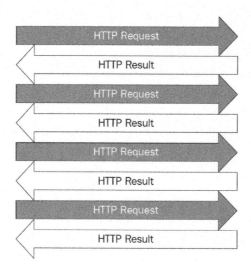

Figure 9.4 – Parallel HTTP requests

As we mentioned previously, concurrency and parallelism have significant applications in web development, and most servers nowadays can handle a large number of requests at the same time.

Now, let's see how we can make multiple web requests at the same time, with the help of threading.

Spawning multiple threads

To apply concurrency, we can simply use the `threading` module that we have been discussing to create separate threads to handle different web requests. Let's take a look at the following code:

```python
import threading
import requests
import time

def ping(url):
    res = requests.get(url)
    print(f'{url}: {res.text}')

urls = [
    'http://httpstat.us/200',
    'http://httpstat.us/400',
    'http://httpstat.us/404',
    'http://httpstat.us/408',
    'http://httpstat.us/500',
    'http://httpstat.us/524'
]

start = time.time()
for url in urls:
    ping(url)
print(f'Sequential: {time.time() - start : .2f} seconds')

print()

start = time.time()
threads = []
for url in urls:
    thread = threading.Thread(target=ping, args=(url,))
    threads.append(thread)
    thread.start()
```

```
for thread in threads:
    thread.join()


print(f'Threading: {time.time() - start : .2f} seconds')
```

In this example, we are including the sequential logic from the previous example to process our URL list so that we can compare the speed improvement when we apply threading to our ping test program. We are also creating a thread to ping each of the URLs in our URL list using the `threading` module; these threads will be executed independently from each other. The time it takes to process the URLs both sequentially and concurrently is also tracked using methods from the `time` module.

If you run the program, your output should be similar to the following:

```
http://httpstat.us/200: 200 OK
http://httpstat.us/400: 400 Bad Request
http://httpstat.us/404: 404 Not Found
http://httpstat.us/408: 408 Request Timeout
http://httpstat.us/500: 500 Internal Server Error
http://httpstat.us/524: 524 A timeout occurred
Sequential: 0.82 seconds


http://httpstat.us/404: 404 Not Found
http://httpstat.us/200: 200 OK
http://httpstat.us/400: 400 Bad Request
http://httpstat.us/500: 500 Internal Server Error
http://httpstat.us/524: 524 A timeout occurred
http://httpstat.us/408: 408 Request Timeout
Threading: 0.14 seconds
```

While the specific time that the sequential logic and threading logic takes to process all the URLs might be different from system to system, there should still be a clear distinction between the two. Specifically, here, we can see that the threading logic was almost six times faster than the sequential logic (which corresponds to the fact that we had six threads processing six URLs in parallel). There is no doubt, then, that concurrency can provide a significant speedup for our ping test application and for the process of making web requests in general.

Refactoring request logic

The current version of our ping test application works as intended, but we can improve its readability by refactoring the logic where we make web requests in a thread class. Consider the `MyThread` class:

```python
import threading
import requests

class MyThread(threading.Thread):
    def __init__(self, url):
        threading.Thread.__init__(self)
        self.url = url
        self.result = None

    def run(self):
        res = requests.get(self.url)
        self.result = f'{self.url}: {res.text}'
```

In this example, `MyThread` inherits from the `threading.Thread` class and contains two additional attributes: `url` and `result`. The `url` attribute holds the URL that the thread instance should process; the response that's returned from the web server to that thread will be written to the `result` attribute (in the `run()` function).

Outside of this class, we can simply loop through the URL list and create and manage the threads accordingly, while not having to worry about the request logic in the main program:

```python
urls = [
    'http://httpstat.us/200',
    'http://httpstat.us/400',
    'http://httpstat.us/404',
    'http://httpstat.us/408',
    'http://httpstat.us/500',
    'http://httpstat.us/524'
]

start = time.time()

threads = [MyThread(url) for url in urls]
for thread in threads:
```

```
        thread.start()
for thread in threads:
        thread.join()
for thread in threads:
        print(thread.result)


print(f'Took {time.time() - start : .2f} seconds')


print('Done.')
```

Note that we are now storing the responses in the `result` attribute of the `MyThread` class, instead of directly printing them out, as we did in the old `ping()` function from the previous examples. This means that, after making sure that all the threads have finished, we will need to loop through the threads one more time and print out those responses.

Refactoring the request logic should not greatly affect the performance of our current program; we are keeping track of the execution speed to see if this is the case. If you execute the program, you will obtain an output similar to the following:

```
http://httpstat.us/200: 200 OK
http://httpstat.us/400: 400 Bad Request
http://httpstat.us/404: 404 Not Found
http://httpstat.us/408: 408 Request Timeout
http://httpstat.us/500: 500 Internal Server Error
http://httpstat.us/524: 524 A timeout occurred
Took 0.14 seconds
Done.
```

Just as we expected, we are still achieving a significant speedup from the sequential version of the program with this refactored request logic. Again, our main program is now more readable, and further adjustments to the request logic (as we will see in the next section) can simply be directed to the `MyThread` class, without affecting the rest of the program.

Our program can now make concurrent web requests to specific sites and display the returned status code. However, there is a problem common in working with web requests that our program cannot handle yet: timeouts. We will learn how to address this in the next section.

The problem with timeouts

In this section, we will explore a potential improvement we can make to our ping test application: handling **timeouts**. Timeouts typically occur when the server takes an unusually long time to process a specific request, and the connection between the server and its client is terminated.

In the context of a ping test application, we will be implementing a customized threshold for the timeout. Recall that a ping test is used to determine whether specific servers are still responsive, so we can specify in our program that, if a request takes more than our timeout threshold for the server to respond, we will categorize that specific server with a timeout.

Support from httpstat.us and simulation in Python

In addition to different options for status codes, the `httpstat.us` website also provides us with a way to simulate a delay in its response when we send in requests. Specifically, we can customize the delay time (in milliseconds) with a query argument in our GET request. For example, `httpstat.us/200?sleep=5000` will return a response after a 5-second delay.

Now, let's see how a delay like this would affect the execution of our program. Consider the following program, which contains the current request logic of our ping test application but has a different URL list:

```python
import threading
import requests


class MyThread(threading.Thread):
    def __init__(self, url):
        threading.Thread.__init__(self)
        self.url = url
        self.result = None


    def run(self):
        res = requests.get(self.url)
        self.result = f'{self.url}: {res.text}'

urls = [
    'http://httpstat.us/200',
    'http://httpstat.us/200?sleep=20000',
    'http://httpstat.us/400'
```

```
]

threads = [MyThread(url) for url in urls]
for thread in threads:
    thread.start()
for thread in threads:
    thread.join()
for thread in threads:
    print(thread.result)

print('Done.')
```

Here, we have a URL that will take around 20 seconds to return a response. Considering that we will block the main program until all the threads finish their execution (with the `join()` method), our program will most likely appear to be hanging for 20 seconds before any response is printed out.

Run the program to experience this for yourself. A 20-second delay will occur (which will make the execution take significantly longer to finish) and we will obtain the following output:

```
http://httpstat.us/200: 200 OK
http://httpstat.us/200?sleep=20000: 200 OK
http://httpstat.us/400: 400 Bad Request
Took 22.60 seconds
Done.
```

Let's say that 20 seconds is too long of a response time, and we cannot afford to wait for a request that long. So, we would like to implement some logic that can handle long waiting times like this.

Timeout specifications

Overall, an efficient ping test application should not be waiting for responses from its websites for a long time; it should have a set threshold for a timeout that, if a server fails to return a response under that threshold, the application will deem that server non-responsive. So, we need to implement a way to keep track of how much time has passed since a request has been sent to a server. We will do this by counting down from the timeout threshold. Once that threshold has been passed, all the responses (whether they've returned yet or not) will be printed out.

Additionally, we will also be keeping track of how many requests are still pending and have not had their responses returned. We will be using the is_alive() method from the threading.Thread class to indirectly determine whether a response has been returned for a specific request. If, at one point, the thread that's processing a specific request is alive, we can conclude that that specific request is still pending.

Let's consider the following process_requests() function first:

```
import time


UPDATE_INTERVAL = 0.01


def process_requests(threads, timeout=5):
    def alive_count():
        alive = [1 if thread.is_alive() else 0 for thread \
            in threads]
        return sum(alive)

    while alive_count() > 0 and timeout > 0:
        timeout -= UPDATE_INTERVAL
        time.sleep(UPDATE_INTERVAL)
    for thread in threads:
        print(thread.result)
```

This function takes in a list of threads that we have been using to make web requests in the previous examples, as well as an optional argument specifying the timeout threshold. Inside this function, we have an inner function, alive_count(), which returns the count of the threads that are still alive at the time of the function call.

In the process_requests() function, so long as there are threads that are currently alive and processing requests, we will allow the threads to continue with their execution (this is done in the while loop with the double condition). The UPDATE_INTERVAL variable, as you can see, specifies how often we check for this condition. If either condition fails (if there are no alive threads left or if the threshold timeout is passed), then we will proceed with printing out the responses (even if some might have not been returned).

Let's turn our attention to the new `MyThread` class:

```python
import threading
import requests


class MyThread(threading.Thread):
    def __init__(self, url):
        threading.Thread.__init__(self)
        self.url = url
        self.result = f'{self.url}: Custom timeout'

    def run(self):
        res = requests.get(self.url)
        self.result = f'{self.url}: {res.text}'
```

This class is almost identical to the one we considered in the previous example, except that the initial value for the `result` attribute is a message indicating a timeout. In the case that we discussed earlier, where the timeout threshold specified in the `process_requests()` function is passed, this initial value will be used when the responses are printed out.

Finally, let's consider our main program in `example6.py`:

```python
urls = [
    'http://httpstat.us/200',
    'http://httpstat.us/200?sleep=4000',
    'http://httpstat.us/200?sleep=20000',
    'http://httpstat.us/400'
]

start = time.time()

threads = [MyThread(url) for url in urls]
for thread in threads:
    thread.setDaemon(True)
    thread.start()
process_requests(threads)

print(f'Took {time.time() - start : .2f} seconds')

print('Done.')
```

Here, in our URL list, we have a request that would take 4 seconds and another that would take 20 seconds, aside from the ones that would respond immediately. As the timeout threshold that we are using is 5 seconds, theoretically, we should be able to see that the 4-second-delay request will successfully obtain a response, while the 20-second-delay one will not.

There is another point to be made about this program: **daemon threads**. In the `process_requests()` function, if the timeout threshold is passed while there is still at least one thread being processed, then the function will proceed to print out the `result` attribute of each thread:

```
while alive_count() > 0 and timeout > 0:
    timeout -= UPDATE_INTERVAL
    time.sleep(UPDATE_INTERVAL)
for thread in threads:
    print(thread.result)
```

This means that we do not block our program until all of the threads have finished their execution by using the `join()` function, which means the program can simply move forward if the timeout threshold is reached. However, this also means that the threads themselves do not terminate at this point. The 20-second-delay request, specifically, will still most likely be running after our program exits out of the `process_requests()` function.

If the thread that's processing this request is not a daemon thread (as we know, daemon threads execute in the background and never terminate), it will block the main program from finishing until the thread itself finishes. By making this thread, and any other thread, a daemon thread, we allow the main program to finish as soon as it executes the last line of its instructions, even if there are threads still running.

Let's see this program in action. Execute this code; your output should be similar to the following:

```
http://httpstat.us/200: 200 OK
http://httpstat.us/200?sleep=4000: 200 OK
http://httpstat.us/200?sleep=20000: Custom timeout
http://httpstat.us/400: 400 Bad Request
Took 5.70 seconds
Done.
```

As you can see, it took around 5 seconds for our program to finish this time. This is because it spent 5 seconds waiting for the threads that were still running and, as soon as the 5-second threshold was passed, the program printed out the results. Here, we can see that the result from the 20-second-delay request was simply the default value of the `result` attribute of the `MyThread` class, while the rest of the requests were able to obtain the correct response from the server (including the 4-second-delay request since it had enough time to obtain the response).

If you would like to see the effect of non-daemon threads, which we discussed earlier, simply comment out the corresponding line of code in our main program, as follows:

```
threads = [MyThread(url) for url in urls]
for thread in threads:
    #thread.setDaemon(True)
    thread.start()
process_requests(threads)
```

You will see that the main program will hang for around 20 seconds as the non-daemon thread processing the 20-second-delay request is still running, before being able to finish its execution (even though the output that's produced will be identical).

Good practices in making web requests

There are a few aspects of making concurrent web requests that require careful consideration and implementation. In this section, we will be going over those aspects and some of the best practices that you should use when developing your applications.

Consider the terms of service and data-collecting policies

Unauthorized data collection has been the topic of discussion in the technology world for the past few years, and it will continue to be for a long time – and for good reasons too. So, it is extremely important for developers who are making automated web requests in their applications to look for websites' policies on data collecting. You can find these policies in their terms of service or similar documents. When in doubt, it is generally a good rule of thumb to contact the website directly to ask for more details.

Error handling

Errors are something that no one can easily avoid in the field of programming, and this is especially true when making web requests. Errors in these programs can include making bad requests (invalid requests or even bad internet connections), mishandling downloaded HTML code, or unsuccessfully parsing HTML code. So, it is important to make use of `try...except` blocks and other error-handling tools in Python to avoid crashing your application. Avoiding crashes is especially important if your code/applications are used in production and larger applications.

Specifically, in concurrent web scraping, it might be possible for some threads to collect data successfully, while others fail. By implementing error-handling functionalities in multithreaded parts of your program, you can make sure that a failed thread will not be able to crash the entirety of your program and ensure that successful threads can still return their results.

However, it is important to note that **blind error-catching** is still undesirable. This term indicates the practice where we have a large `try...except` block in our program that will catch all errors that occur in the program's execution, and no further information regarding the errors can be obtained; this practice is also known as error swallowing. It's highly recommended that you have some specific error handling code in a program so that not only can appropriate actions be taken with regards to that specific error, but other errors that have not been taken into account might also reveal themselves.

Update your program regularly

It is quite common for websites to change their request-handling logic, as well as their displayed data, regularly. If a program that makes requests to a website has considerably inflexible logic to interact with the server of the website (for example, structuring its requests in a specific format, only handling one kind of response, and so on), then if and when the website alters the way it handles its client requests, the program will most likely stop functioning correctly. This situation happens frequently with web scraping programs that look for data in specific HTML tags; when the HTML tags are changed, these programs will fail to find their data.

This practice is implemented to prevent automated data collecting programs from functioning. The only way to keep using a website that has recently changed its request-handling logic is to analyze the updated protocols and alter our programs accordingly.

Avoid making a large number of requests

Each time one of the programs that we have been discussing runs, it makes HTTP requests to a server that manages the site that you'd like to extract data from. This process happens significantly more frequently and over a shorter amount of time in a concurrent program, where multiple requests are being submitted to that server.

As we mentioned previously, servers nowadays can handle multiple requests simultaneously with ease. However, to avoid having to overwork and overconsume resources, servers are also designed to stop answering requests that come in too frequently. The websites of big tech companies, such as Amazon or Twitter, look for large amounts of automated requests that are made from the same IP address and implement different response protocols; some requests might be delayed, some might be refused a response, or the IP address might even be banned from making further requests for a specific amount of time.

Interestingly, making repeated, heavy-duty requests to servers is a form of hacking a website. In **Denial of Service (DoS)** and **Distributed Denial of Service (DDoS)** attacks, a very large number of requests are made at the same time to the server, flooding the bandwidth of the targeted server with traffic. As a result, normal, non-malicious requests from other clients are denied because the servers are busy processing the concurrent requests, as illustrated in the following diagram:

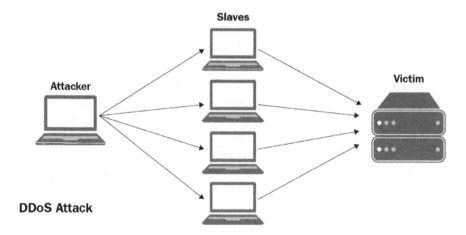

Figure 9.5 – Illustration of a DDoS attack

So, it is important to space out the concurrent requests that your application makes to a server so that the application will not be considered an attacker and be potentially banned or treated as a malicious client. This could be as simple as limiting the maximum number of threads/requests that can be implemented at a time in your program or pausing the threading for a specific amount of time (for example, using the `time.sleep()` function) before sending a request to the server.

Summary

In this chapter, we learned about the basics of HTML and web requests. The two most common web requests are `GET` and `POST` requests. There are five main categories of HTTP response status codes, each indicating a different concept regarding the communication between the server and its client. By considering the status codes that are received from different websites, we can write a ping test application that effectively checks the responsiveness of those websites.

Concurrency can be applied to the problem of making multiple web requests simultaneously via threading to provide a significant improvement in application speed. However, it is important to keep several considerations in mind when making concurrent web requests.

All in all, the exercise we just went through in this chapter will prove useful in helping us approach the general problem of converting a sequential program into its concurrent version. The simple ping test that we have built could also be extended to have more complex behaviors and functionalities. In the next chapter, we will consider a similar procedure for the application of image processing.

Questions

1. What is HTML?
2. What are HTTP requests?
3. What are HTTP response status codes?
4. How does the `requests` module help with making web requests?
5. What is a ping test and how is one typically designed?
6. Why is concurrency applicable in making web requests?
7. What are the considerations that need to be made while developing applications that make concurrent web requests?

Further reading

- *Automate the Boring Stuff with Python: Practical Programming for Total Beginners*, Al. Sweigart, No Starch Press, 2015

- *Web Scraping with Python*, Richard Lawson, Packt Publishing Ltd, 2015

- *Instant Web Scraping with Java*, Ryan Mitchell, Packt Publishing Ltd, 2013

10
Concurrent Image Processing

This chapter discusses the task of processing and manipulating images via concurrent programming, specifically multiprocessing. Since images are processed independently of one another, concurrent programming is an attractive option for achieving a significant speedup. This chapter lays out the basics behind image processing techniques, illustrates the improvements that concurrent programming provides, and goes over some of the best practices that are used in image processing applications. This discussion will consolidate our knowledge of how to leverage concurrent and parallel processing tools in Python.

The following topics will be covered in this chapter:

- Image processing fundamentals
- Applying concurrency to image processing
- Good concurrent image processing practices

Technical requirements

The following is a list of prerequisites for this chapter:

- You must have Python 3 installed on your computer.
- You must have OpenCV and NumPy installed for your Python 3 distribution.

The code for this chapter can be found in the following GitHub repository: `https://github.com/PacktPublishing/Advanced-Python-Programming-Second-Edition/tree/main/Chapter10`.

Image processing fundamentals

Digital/computational image processing (which we will refer to as **image processing** from this point forward) has become so popular in the modern era that it exists in numerous aspects of our everyday life. Image processing and manipulation are involved when you take a picture with your camera or phone using different filters, such as when advanced image editing software such as Adobe Photoshop is used, or even when you simply edit images using Microsoft Paint.

Many of the techniques and algorithms that are used in image processing were developed in the early 1960s for various purposes such as medical imaging, satellite image analysis, character recognition, and so on. However, these image processing techniques required significant computing power, and the fact that the available computer equipment at the time was unable to accommodate the need for fast number-crunching slowed down the use of image processing.

Fast-forwarding to the future, when powerful computers with fast, multicore processors were developed, image processing techniques became much more accessible, and research on image processing increased significantly. Nowadays, numerous image processing applications are being actively developed and studied, including pattern recognition, classification, feature extraction, and more. Some of the specific image processing techniques that take advantage of concurrent and parallel programming, and would otherwise be extremely computationally time-consuming, include **Hidden Markov models**, **independent component analysis**, and even **neural network models**.

The following is one of the simplest forms of image processing, where we convert a fully colored image into a grayscale one. This process is called **grayscaling**:

Figure 10.1 – An example use of image processing – grayscaling

Later in this chapter, we will see how grayscaling, along with other processing techniques, can be done using Python. To do this, we must install the necessary libraries and packages.

Python as an image processing tool

As we have stated multiple times throughout this book, the Python programming language is on its way to becoming the most popular programming language. This is especially true in the field of computational image processing, which, most of the time, requires fast prototyping and designing, as well as significant automation capabilities.

As we will find out in the following section, digital images are represented in two-dimensional and three-dimensional matrices so that computers can process them easily. Consequently, most of the time, digital image processing involves matrix calculation. Multiple Python libraries and modules not only provide efficient matrix calculation options but also interact seamlessly with other libraries that handle image reading/writing.

As we already know, automating tasks and making them concurrent is Python's strong suit. This makes Python the prime candidate to implement your image processing applications. For this chapter, we will be working with two main Python libraries: **OpenCV** (which stands for **Open Source Computer Vision**), which is a library that provides image processing and computer vision options in C++, Java, and Python, and NumPy, which, as we know, is one of the most popular Python modules and performs efficient and parallelizable number-crunching calculations. Let's see how we can install these libraries.

Installing OpenCV and NumPy

To install NumPy for your Python distribution using the `pip` package manager, run the following command:

```
pip install numpy
```

If you are using Anaconda/Miniconda to manage your packages, you must run the following command instead:

```
conda install numpy
```

Installing OpenCV might be more complicated, depending on your operating system. The easiest option is to have Anaconda handle the installation process by following the guide at `https://anaconda.org/conda-forge/opencv` after installing Anaconda (`https://www.anaconda.com/download/`) as your main Python package manager. If, however, you are not using Anaconda, the main option for installing OpenCV is to follow its official documentation guide, which can be found at `https://docs.opencv.org/master/df/d65/tutorial_table_of_content_introduction.html`. After successfully installing OpenCV, open a Python interpreter and try importing the library, as follows:

```
>>> import cv2
>>> print(cv2.__version__)
4.5.2
```

We will import OpenCV using the name `cv2`, which is the library alias of OpenCV in Python. The success message indicates the version of the OpenCV library that has been downloaded (4.5.2).

Computer image basics

Before we jump into processing and manipulating digital image files, we need to discuss the fundamentals of those files and how computers interpret data from them. Specifically, we need to understand how data regarding the colors and coordinates of individual pixels in an image file is represented, as well as how to extract it using Python.

RGB values

RGB values are the basics of how colors are represented digitally. Standing for **red**, **green**, and **blue** (**RGB**), these values are constructed from the fact that all colors can be generated from a specific combination of red, green, and blue. So, an RGB value is a tuple of three integer numbers, each of which ranges from 0 (which indicates no color at all) to 255 (which indicates the deepest shade of that specific color).

For example, red corresponds to the tuple (255, 0, 0); in this tuple, there is only the highest value for red and no values for the other colors, so the whole tuple represents the pure color red. Similarly, blue is represented by (0, 0, 255), while green is represented by (0, 255, 0). Yellow is the result of mixing equal amounts of red and green and is therefore represented by (255, 255, 0) (the maximum amount of red and green, with no blue). White, which is the combination of all three colors, is (255, 255, 255), while black, which is the opposite of white and therefore lacks all colors, is represented by (0, 0, 0).

This is illustrated by the following diagram:

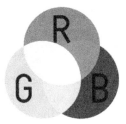

Figure 10.2 – Illustration of RGB values

Pixels and image files

So, an RGB value indicates a specific color, but how do we connect this to a computer image? If we were to view an image on our computer and try to zoom in as much as we could, we would observe that as we zoom in deeper and deeper, the image will start breaking apart into increasingly discernible colored squares. These squares are called pixels, which are the smallest units of color on a computer display or in a digital image:

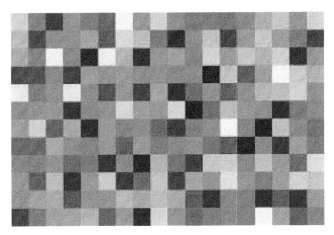

Figure 10.3 – Examples of pixels in digital images

A set of different pixels arranged in a tabular format (rows and columns of pixels) makes up a computer image. Each pixel, in turn, is an RGB value; in other words, a pixel is a tuple of three integers. This means that a computer image is simply a two-dimensional array of tuples, whose sides correspond to the size of the image. For example, a 128 x 128 image has 128 rows and 128 columns of RGB tuples for its data.

Coordinates inside an image

Like indexing two-dimensional arrays, the coordinate for a digital image pixel is a pair of two integers, representing the x- and y-coordinates of that pixel; the x-coordinate indicates the pixel's location along the horizontal axis starting from the left, while the y-coordinate indicates the pixel's location along the vertical axis starting from the top.

Here, we can see how heavy computational number-crunching processes are typically involved when it comes to image processing since each image is a matrix of integer tuples. This also suggests that, with the help of the NumPy library and concurrent programming, we can achieve significant improvements in execution time for Python image processing applications.

Following the convention of indexing two-dimensional arrays in NumPy, the location of a pixel is still a pair of integers, but the first number indicates the index of the row containing the pixel, which corresponds to the y-coordinate, and similarly, the second number indicates the x-coordinate of the pixel.

OpenCV API

There are a surprising number of methods for reading in, performing image processing, and displaying a digital image file in Python. However, OpenCV provides some of the easiest and most intuitive options to do this. One important thing to note regarding OpenCV is that it inverts RGB values as BGR values when interpreting its images. So, instead of red, green, and blue in order, the tuples in an image matrix will represent blue, green, and red, in that order.

Let's look at an example of interacting with OpenCV in Python:

```python
import cv2

im = cv2.imread('input/ship.jpg')
cv2.imshow('Test', im)
cv2.waitKey(0) # press any key to move forward here

print(im)
print('Type:', type(im))
print('Shape:', im.shape)
print('Top-left pixel:', im[0, 0])

print('Done.')
```

There are a few methods from OpenCV that have been used in this script that we need to discuss:

- `cv2.imread()`: This method takes in a path to an image file (compatible file extensions include `.jpeg`, `.jpg`, `.png`, and so on) and returns an image object, which, as we will see later, is represented by a NumPy array.

- `cv2.imshow()`: This method takes in a string and an image object and displays it in a separate window. The title of the window is specified by the passed-in string. The method should always be followed by the `cv2.waitKey()` method.

- `cv2.waitKey()`: This method takes in a number and blocks the program for a corresponding number of milliseconds unless the number 0 is passed in, in which case it will block indefinitely until the user presses a key on their keyboard. This method should always follow the `cv2.imshow()` method.

After calling `cv2.imshow()` on the `ship.jpg` file inside the input subfolder so that it's displayed from the Python interpreter, the program will stop until a key is pressed, at which point it will execute the rest of the program. If run successfully, the script will display the following output:

Figure 10.4 – Displaying an image using OpenCV

You should also obtain the following output for the rest of the main program after pressing any key to close the displayed picture:

```
> python example1.py
[[[199 136 86]
  [199 136 86]
  [199 136 86]
  ...,
  [198 140 81]
  [197 139 80]
  [201 143 84]]

[...Truncated for readability...]

 [[ 56 23 4]
  [ 59 26 7]
  [ 60 27 7]
  ...,
  [ 79 43 7]
  [ 80 44 8]
  [ 75 39 3]]]
Type: <class 'numpy.ndarray'>
Shape: (1118, 1577, 3)
Top-left pixel: [199 136 86]
Done.
```

The output confirms a few of the things that we discussed earlier:

- First, when printing out the image object that was returned by the cv2.imread() function, we obtained a matrix of numbers.

- Using the type() method from Python, we found that the class of this matrix is indeed a NumPy array: numpy.ndarray.

- Calling the shape attribute of the array, we can see that the image is a three-dimensional matrix of the shape (1118, 1577, 3), which corresponds to a table with 1118 rows and 1577 columns, each element of which is a pixel (three-number tuple). The numbers for the rows and columns also correspond to the size of the image.

- Focusing on the top-left pixel in the matrix (the first pixel in the first row; that is, `im[0, 0]`), we obtained the BGR value of (`199`,`136`,`86`) – `199` blue, `136` green, and `86` red. By looking up this BGR value through any online converter, we can see that this is a light blue that corresponds to the sky, which is the upper part of the image.

Image processing techniques

We have already seen some Python APIs that are provided by OpenCV to read data from image files. Before we can use OpenCV to perform various image processing tasks, let's discuss the theoretical foundation for several techniques that are commonly used in image processing.

Grayscaling

We saw an example of grayscaling earlier in this chapter. Arguably one of the most widely used image processing techniques, grayscaling is the process of reducing the dimensionality of the image pixel matrix by only considering the intensity information of each pixel, which is represented by the amount of light available.

As a result, the pixels of grayscale images no longer hold three-dimensional information (red, green, and blue), and only one-dimensional black-and-white data. These images are exclusively composed of shades of gray, with black indicating the weakest light intensity and white indicating the strongest.

Grayscaling serves many important purposes in image processing. Firstly, as we mentioned previously, it reduces the dimensionality of the image pixel matrix by mapping traditional three-dimensional color data to one-dimensional gray data. So, instead of having to analyze and process three layers of color data, image processing programs only have to do one-third of the job with grayscale images. Additionally, by only representing colors using one spectrum, important patterns in the image are more likely to be recognized with just black and white data.

There are multiple algorithms for converting color into grayscale: colorimetric conversion, luma coding, single-channel, and more. Luckily, we do not have to implement one ourselves, as the OpenCV library provides a one-line method to convert normal images into grayscale ones. Still using the image of a ship from the previous example, let's look at another example:

```
import cv2
```

```
im = cv2.imread('input/ship.jpg')
```

```
gray_im = cv2.cvtColor(im, cv2.COLOR_BGR2GRAY)


cv2.imshow('Grayscale', gray_im)
cv2.waitKey(0) # press any key to move forward here


print(gray_im)
print('Type:', type(gray_im))
print('Shape:', gray_im.shape)
cv2.imwrite('output/gray_ship.jpg', gray_im)


print('Done.')
```

In this example, we are using the cvtColor() method from OpenCV to convert our original image into a grayscale one. After running this script, the following output should be displayed on your computer:

Figure 10.5 – Output from grayscaling

By pressing any key to unblock your program, you should obtain the following output:

```
> python example2.py
[[128 128 128 ..., 129 128 132]
 [125 125 125 ..., 129 128 130]
 [124 125 125 ..., 129 129 130]
 ...,
 [ 20 21 20 ..., 38 39 37]
 [ 19 22 21 ..., 41 42 37]
 [ 21 24 25 ..., 36 37 32]]
Type: <class 'numpy.ndarray'>
Shape: (1118, 1577)
Done.
```

Here, we can see that the structure of our grayscale image object is different from what we saw with our original image object. Even though it is still represented by a NumPy array, it is now a two-dimensional array of integers, each of which ranges from 0 (for black) to 255 (for white). The table of pixels, however, still consists of 1118 rows and 1577 columns.

In this example, we also used the cv2.imwrite() method, which saves the image object to your local computer. This means that the grayscale image can be found in the output subfolder of this chapter's folder, as specified in our code.

Thresholding

Another important technique in image processing is **thresholding**. Intending to categorize each pixel in a digital image into different groups (also known as **image segmentation**), thresholding provides a quick and intuitive way to create binary images (with just black and white pixels).

The idea behind thresholding is to replace each pixel in an image with a white pixel if the pixel's intensity is greater than a previously specified threshold, and with a black pixel if the pixel's intensity is less than that threshold. Similar to the goal of grayscaling, thresholding amplifies the differences between high- and low-intensity pixels, and from that, important features and patterns in an image can be recognized and extracted.

Recall that grayscaling converts a fully colored image into a version that only has different shades of gray; in this case, each pixel has a value of an integer ranging from 0 to 255. From a grayscale image, thresholding can convert it into a fully black-and-white one, each pixel of which is now only either 0 (black) or 255 (white). So, after performing thresholding on an image, each pixel of that image can only hold two possible values, further reducing the complexity of our image data.

So, the key to an effective thresholding process is finding an appropriate threshold so that the pixels in an image are segmented in a way that allows separate regions in the image to become more obvious. The simplest form of thresholding is to use a constant threshold to process all the pixels throughout a whole image. Let's consider an example of this method:

```
import cv2


im = cv2.imread('input/ship.jpg')
gray_im = cv2.cvtColor(im, cv2.COLOR_BGR2GRAY)


ret, custom_thresh_im = cv2.threshold(gray_im, 127, 255, \
    cv2.THRESH_BINARY)
cv2.imwrite('output/custom_thresh_ship.jpg', \
    custom_thresh_im)


print('Done.')
```

In this example, after converting the image of a ship that we have been using to grayscale, we called the `threshold(src, thresh, maxval, type)` function from OpenCV, which takes in the following arguments:

- `src`: This argument takes in the input/source image.
- `thresh`: This is the constant threshold to be used throughout the image. Here, we are using `127`, as it is simply the middle point between 0 and 255.
- `maxval`: Pixels whose original values are greater than the constant threshold will take this value after the thresholding process. We pass in 255 to specify that those pixels should be completely white.
- `type`: This value indicates the thresholding type that's used by OpenCV. We are performing simple binary thresholding, so we pass in `cv2.THRESH_BINARY`.

After running the script, you should be able to find the following image in the output with the name `custom_thresh_ship.jpg`:

Figure 10.6 – Output from simple thresholding

Here, we can see that with a simple threshold (127), we have obtained an image that highlights separate regions of the image: the sky, the ship, and the sea. However, there are several problems that this simple thresholding method poses, the most common of which is finding the appropriate constant threshold. Since different images have different color tones, lighting conditions, and so on, it is undesirable to use a static value across different images as their thresholds.

This issue is addressed by adaptive thresholding methods, which use different thresholds whose values are dynamically determined for small regions of an image. This process allows the threshold to adjust according to the input image, and not depend solely on a static value. Let's consider two examples of these adaptive thresholding methods, namely **Adaptive Mean Thresholding** and **Adaptive Gaussian Thresholding**:

```
import cv2

im = cv2.imread('input/ship.jpg')
im = cv2.cvtColor(im, cv2.COLOR_BGR2GRAY)
```

```
mean_thresh_im = cv2.adaptiveThreshold(im, 255,
    cv2.ADAPTIVE_THRESH_MEAN_C, cv2.THRESH_BINARY, 11, 2)
cv2.imwrite('output/mean_thresh_ship.jpg', mean_thresh_im)

gauss_thresh_im = cv2.adaptiveThreshold(im, 255,
    cv2.ADAPTIVE_THRESH_GAUSSIAN_C, cv2.THRESH_BINARY, 11, 2)
cv2.imwrite('output/gauss_thresh_ship.jpg', \
    gauss_thresh_im)

print('Done.')
```

Similar to what we did with the `cv2.threshold()` method earlier, here, we are converting the original image into its grayscale version, and then we are passing it to the `adaptiveThreshold()` method from OpenCV. This method takes in similar arguments to the `cv2.threshold()` method, except that instead of taking in a constant to be the threshold, it takes in an argument for the adaptive method. We used `cv2.ADAPTIVE_THRESH_MEAN_C` and `cv2.ADAPTIVE_THRESH_GAUSSIAN_C`, respectively.

The second to last argument specifies the size of the window to perform thresholding on; this number has to be an odd positive integer. Specifically, we used 11 in our example, so for each pixel in the image, the algorithm will consider the neighboring pixels (in an 11 x 11 square surrounding the original pixel). The last argument specifies the adjustment to make for each pixel in the final output. These two arguments, again, help localize the threshold for different regions of the image, thus making the thresholding process more dynamic and, as its name suggests, adaptive.

After running the script, you should be able to find the following images as output with the names `mean_thresh_ship.jpg` and `gauss_thresh_ship.jpg`. The output for `mean_thresh_ship.jpg` is as follows:

Figure 10.7 – Output from mean thresholding

The output for gauss_thresh_ship.jpg is as follows:

Figure 10.8 – Output from Gaussian thresholding

Here, we can see that with adaptive thresholding, details in specific regions will be thresholded and highlighted in the final output image. These techniques are useful when we need to recognize small details in an image, while simple thresholding is useful when we only want to extract big regions of an image.

We have talked a lot about the basics of image processing and some common image processing techniques. We also know why image processing is a heavy number-crunching task, and that concurrent and parallel programming can be applied to speed up independent processing tasks. In the next section, we will look at a specific example of how to implement a concurrent image processing application that can handle a large number of input images.

Applying concurrency to image processing

First, head to the current folder for this chapter's code. Inside the input folder, there is a subfolder called large_input, which contains 400 images that we will be using for this example. These pictures are of different regions in our original ship image, and they have been cropped from it using the *array-indexing* and *-slicing* options that NumPy provides for slicing OpenCV image objects. If you are curious as to how these images were generated, check out the generate_input.py file.

Our goal in this section is to implement a program that can concurrently process these images using thresholding. To do this, let's look at the example5.py file:

```python
from multiprocessing import Pool
import cv2

import sys
from timeit import default_timer as timer


THRESH_METHOD = cv2.ADAPTIVE_THRESH_GAUSSIAN_C
INPUT_PATH = 'input/large_input/'
OUTPUT_PATH = 'output/large_output/'

n = 20
names = ['ship_%i_%i.jpg' % (i, j) for i in range(n) \
for j in range(n)]
```

```
def process_threshold(im, output_name, thresh_method):
    gray_im = cv2.cvtColor(im, cv2.COLOR_BGR2GRAY)
    thresh_im = cv2.adaptiveThreshold(
      gray_im, 255, thresh_method, \
        cv2.THRESH_BINARY, 11, 2
    )

    cv2.imwrite(OUTPUT_PATH + output_name, thresh_im)


if __name__ == '__main__':

    for n_processes in range(1, 7):
        start = timer()

        with Pool(n_processes) as p:
            p.starmap(
                process_threshold,
                [(
                    cv2.imread(INPUT_PATH + name), \
                    name, THRESH_METHOD)
                    for name in names
                ],
            )

        print('Took %.4f seconds with %i process(es). \
            ' % (timer() - start, n_processes))

    print('Done.')
```

In this example, we are using the Pool class from the multiprocessing module to manage our processes. As a refresher, a Pool object supplies convenient options to map a sequence of inputs to separate processes using the Pool.map() method. We are using the Pool.starmap() method in our example, however, to pass multiple arguments to the target function.

At the beginning of our program, we make several housekeeping assignments: the thresholding method to perform adaptive thresholding when processing the images, the paths for the input and output folders, and the names of the images to process. The `process_threshold()` function is what we use to process the images; it takes in an image object, the name for the processed version of the image, and which thresholding method to use. Again, this is why we need to use the `Pool.starmap()` method instead of the traditional `Pool.map()` method.

In the main program, to demonstrate the difference in performance between sequential and multiprocessing image processing, we want to run our program with different numbers of processes, specifically from one single process to six different processes. In each iteration of the `for` loop, we initialize a `Pool` object and map the necessary arguments of each image to the `process_threshold()` function, while keeping track of how much time it takes to process and save all of the images.

After running the script, the processed images can be found in the `output/large_output/` subfolder in our current chapter's folder. You should obtain an output similar to the following:

```
> python example5.py
Took 0.6590 seconds with 1 process(es).
Took 0.3190 seconds with 2 process(es).
Took 0.3227 seconds with 3 process(es).
Took 0.3360 seconds with 4 process(es).
Took 0.3338 seconds with 5 process(es).
Took 0.3319 seconds with 6 process(es).
Done.
```

We can see a big difference in execution time when we go from one single process to two separate processes. However, there is negligible or even negative speedup after going from two to higher numbers of processes. Generally, this is because of the heavy overhead, which is the product of implementing many separate processes, in comparison to a relatively low number of inputs.

So far, we have seen that concurrent programming could provide a significant speedup for image processing applications. However, if we take a look at our preceding program, we can see that there are additional adjustments that we can make to improve the execution time even further. Specifically, in the preceding program, we are sequentially reading in images by using list comprehension in the following line:

```
with Pool(n_processes) as p:
    p.starmap(process_threshold, [(
```

```
        cv2.imread(INPUT_PATH + name), \
        name,THRESH_METHOD)
    for name in names])
```

Theoretically, if we were to make the process of reading in different image files concurrent, we could also gain additional speedup with our program. This is especially true in an image processing application that deals with large input files, where significant time is spent waiting for input to be read. With that in mind, let's consider the following example, in which we will implement concurrent input/output processing:

```
from multiprocessing import Pool
import cv2

import sys
from functools import partial
from timeit import default_timer as timer


THRESH_METHOD = cv2.ADAPTIVE_THRESH_GAUSSIAN_C
INPUT_PATH = 'input/large_input/'
OUTPUT_PATH = 'output/large_output/'

n = 20
names = ['ship_%i_%i.jpg' % (i, j) for i in range(n) for \
    j in range(n)]


def process_threshold(name, thresh_method):
    im = cv2.imread(INPUT_PATH + name)
    gray_im = cv2.cvtColor(im, cv2.COLOR_BGR2GRAY)
    thresh_im = cv2.adaptiveThreshold( \
        gray_im, 255, thresh_method, cv2.THRESH_BINARY, 11, 2 \
    )

    cv2.imwrite(OUTPUT_PATH + name, thresh_im)
```

```
if __name__ == '__main__':

    for n_processes in range(1, 7):
        start = timer()

        with Pool(n_processes) as p:
            p.map(partial(process_threshold, \
                thresh_method=THRESH_METHOD), names)

        print('Took %.4f seconds with %i process(es).' % \
            (timer() - start, n_processes))

    print('Done.')
```

The structure of this program is similar to that of the previous one. However, instead of preparing the necessary images to be processed and other relevant input information, we implement them inside the `process_threshold()` function, which now only takes the name of the input image and handles reading the image itself.

As a side note, we are using Python's built-in `functools.partial()` method in our main program to pass in a partial argument (hence the name), specifically `thresh_method`, to the `process_threshold()` function, as this argument is fixed across all images and processes. More information about this tool can be found at `https://docs.python.org/3/library/functools.html`.

After running the script, you should obtain an output similar to the following:

```
> python example6.py
Took 0.5300 seconds with 1 process(es).
Took 0.4133 seconds with 2 process(es).
Took 0.2154 seconds with 3 process(es).
Took 0.2147 seconds with 4 process(es).
Took 0.2213 seconds with 5 process(es).
Took 0.2329 seconds with 6 process(es).
Done.
```

Compared to our previous output, this implementation of the application gives us a significantly better execution time!

Good concurrent image processing practices

So far, you have most likely realized that image processing is quite an involved process and that implementing concurrent and parallel programming in an image processing application can add more complexity to our work. There are, however, good practices that will guide us in the right direction while developing our image processing applications. The following sections discuss some of the most common practices that we should keep in mind.

Choosing the correct way (out of many)

We have hinted at this practice briefly when we learned about thresholding. How an image processing application handles and processes its image data heavily depends on the problems it is supposed to solve, and what kind of data will be fed to it. Therefore, there is significant variability when it comes to choosing specific parameters when processing your image.

For example, as we saw earlier, there are various ways to threshold an image, and each will result in a very different output: if you want to focus on only the large, distinct regions of an image, **simple constant thresholding** will prove to be more beneficial than **adaptive thresholding**; if, however, you want to highlight small changes in the details of an image, adaptive thresholding will be significantly better.

Let's consider another example, in which we will see how tuning a specific parameter for an image processing function results in better output. In this example, we are using a simple **Haar Cascade model** to detect faces in images. We will not go too deeply into how the model handles and processes its data since it is already built into OpenCV; again, we are only using this model at a high level, changing its parameters to obtain different results.

Navigate to the example7.py file in this chapter's folder. The script is designed to detect the faces in the obama1.jpeg and obama2.jpg images in our input folder:

```
import cv2

face_cascade = cv2.CascadeClassifier \
  ('input/haarcascade_frontalface_default.xml')

for filename in ['obama1.jpeg', 'obama2.jpg']:
    im = cv2.imread('input/' + filename)
    gray_im = cv2.cvtColor(im, cv2.COLOR_BGR2GRAY)
    faces = face_cascade.detectMultiScale(im)
```

```
    for (x, y, w, h) in faces:
        cv2.rectangle(im, (x, y), (x + w, y + h), \
        (0, 255, 0), 2)

    cv2.imshow('%i face(s) found' % len(faces), im)
    cv2.waitKey(0)

print('Done.')
```

First, the program loads the pre-trained Haar Cascade model from the input folder using the cv2.CascadeClassifier class. For each input image, the script converts it into grayscale and feeds it to the pre-trained model. The script then draws a green rectangle around each face it found in the image and displays it in a separate window.

Run the program; you will see the following image with the title 5 face(s) found:

Figure 10.9 – Correct face detection

It looks like our program is working well so far. Press any key to continue. You should see the following image with the title 7 face(s) found:

Figure 10.10 – Incorrect face detection

Now, our program is mistaking some other objects as actual faces, resulting in two false positives. The reason behind this involves how the pre-trained model was created. Specifically, the Haar Cascade model used a training dataset with images of specific (pixel) sizes, and when an input image contains faces of different sizes – which is common when it is a group picture with some people being close to the camera, while others being far away – is fed into this model, it will cause false positives in the output.

The scaleFactor parameter in the detectMultiScale method of the cv2.CascadeClassifier class addresses this issue. This parameter will scale down different areas of the input image before trying to predict whether those areas contain a face or not – doing this negates the potential difference in face sizes. To implement this, change the line where we pass the input images to the model to the following to specify the scaleFactor parameter as 1.2:

```
faces = face_cascade.detectMultiScale(im, scaleFactor=1.2)
```

Run the program; you will see that this time, our application can correctly detect all of the faces in our input images without making any false positives.

From this example, we can see that it is important to know about the potential challenges that the input images will pose to your image processing application in execution, as well as to try different methods or parameters within one method of processing to achieve the best results.

Spawning an appropriate number of processes

One point we noticed in our example of concurrent image processing is that the task of spawning processes takes a considerable amount of time. Due to this, if the number of processes available to analyze the data is too high in comparison to the amount of input, the improvement in execution time that's obtained from increasing the number of working processes will diminish and sometimes even become negative.

However, there is no concrete way to tell whether a specific number of separate processes is appropriate for a program unless we also take into account its input images. For example, if the input images are relatively large files, and it takes a significant amount of time for the program to load them from storage, having a larger number of processes might be beneficial; when some processes are waiting for their images to load, others can proceed to perform processing on theirs. In other words, having a larger number of processes will allow for some overlapping between loading and processing time, which will result in better speedup.

In short, it is important to test out different processes that are available for your image processing application to see what the optimal number for scalability is.

Processing input/output concurrently

We saw that loading input images in a sequential way might harm the execution time of an image processing application, as opposed to allowing separate processes to load their inputs. This is specifically true if the image files are significantly large, as the loading time in separate processes might overlap with the loading/processing time in other processes. The same is applicable for writing output images to files.

Summary

Image processing is the task of analyzing and manipulating digital image files to create new versions of the images or to extract important data from them. These digital images are represented by tables of pixels, which are RGB values or, in essence, tuples of numbers. Therefore, digital images are simply multi-dimensional matrices of numbers, which results in the fact that image processing tasks typically come down to heavy number-crunching.

Since images can be analyzed and processed independently from each other in an image processing application, concurrent and parallel programming – specifically, multiprocessing – provides a way for us to make significant improvements to the execution time of the application. Additionally, there are several good practices to follow while implementing a concurrent image processing program.

We have seen how we can apply parallel programming to accelerate the task of image processing. The exercises in this chapter allowed us to examine various aspects of the workflow and how each of them could be parallelized, thus allowing us to build up more confidence in implementing concurrent applications in Python.

In the next chapter, we will go through a similar exercise, where we aim to use asynchronous programming to build communication channels.

Questions

1. What is an image processing task?

2. What is the smallest unit of digital imaging? How is it represented in computers?

3. What is grayscaling? What purpose does this technique serve?

4. What is thresholding? What purpose does this technique serve?

5. Why should image processing be made concurrent?

6. What are some good practices for concurrent image processing?

Further reading

- *Automate the Boring Stuff with Python: Practical Programming for Total Beginners*, Al Sweigart, No Starch Press, 2015.

- *Learning Image Processing with OpenCV*, Garcia, Gloria Bueno, et al, Packt Publishing Ltd, 2015.

- *A Computational Introduction to Digital Image Processing*, Alasdair McAndrew, Chapman and Hall/CRC, 2015.

- Howse, J., P. Joshi, and M. Beyeler. OpenCV: *Computer Vision Projects with Python*. Packt Publishing Ltd, 2016.

11
Building Communication Channels with asyncio

Communication channels are a big part of applied concurrency in the field of computer science. In this chapter, we will cover the fundamental theories of transports, which are classes provided by the `asyncio` module to abstract various forms of communication channels. We will also cover an implementation of a simple echoing server-client logic in Python, to further illustrate the use of `asyncio` and concurrency in communication systems. This chapter will help us frame what we have learned so far about asynchronous programming in the practical context of communication channels, and the code we work with will serve as a base for more complex applications.

The following topics will be covered in this chapter:

- The ecosystem of communication channels
- Getting started with Python and Telnet
- Client-side communication with `aiohttp`

Technical requirements

The code files for this chapter can be accessed through this link:

`https://github.com/PacktPublishing/Advanced-Python-Programming-Second-Edition/tree/main/Chapter11`

The ecosystem of communication channels

The term *communication channel* is used to denote both the physical wiring connection between different systems and the logical communication of data that facilitates computer networks. In this chapter, we will only be concerned with the latter, as it is a problem that is related to computing and is more germane to the idea of asynchronous programming.

First, in this section, we will be discussing the general structure of a communication channel, and two specific elements in that structure that are particularly relevant to asynchronous programming. The first element is communication protocol layers.

Communication protocol layers

Most data transmission processes that are done through communication channels are facilitated in the form of the **Open Systems Interconnection** (**OSI**) model protocol layers. The OSI model lays out the major layers and topics in an intersystem communication process.

The following diagram shows the general structure of the OSI model:

7 Layers of the OSI Model

Application	• End User layer • HTTP, FTP, IRC, SSH, DNS
Presentation	• Syntax layer • SSL, SSH, IMAP, FTP, MPEG, JPEG
Session	• Synch & send to port • API's, Sockets, WinSock
Transport	• End-to-end connections • TCP, UDP
Network	• Packets • IP, ICMP, IPSec, IGMP
Data Link	• Frames • Ethernet, PPP, Switch, Bridge
Physical	• Physical structure • Coax, Fiber, Wireless, Hubs, Repeaters

Figure 11.1 – OSI model structure

As indicated, there are seven main layers of communication in a data transmission process, with varying degrees of computing level and specificity. We will not be going into the details of the purposes and specific functions of each layer, but it is still important that you understand the general ideas behind the media and host layers.

The three bottom layers contain low-level operations that interact with the underlying process of the communication channel. The operations in the physical and data link layers include coding schemes, access schemes, low-level error detection and correction, bit synchronization, and so on. These operations are used to implement and specify the logic of processing and preparing data before transferring it. The network layer, on the other hand, handles forwarding packets of data from one system (for example, the server) to another (for example, the client) in a computer network, by determining the address of the recipient and which path of data transfer to take.

On the other hand, the top layers deal with high-level data communication and manipulation. Among these layers, we will be focusing on the transport layer, as it is directly utilized by the `asyncio` module in the implementation of communication channels. This layer is often viewed as the conceptual transition between the media layers and the host layers (for example, the client and the server), responsible for sending data along with **end-to-end** (**E2E**) connections between different systems. Additionally, because packets of data (prepared by the network layer) might be lost or corrupted during transmission processes due to network errors, the transport layer is also in charge of detecting these errors via methods in error detection code.

The other host layers implement mechanisms for handling, interpreting, and providing the data sent from another system. After receiving data from the transport layer, the session layer handles the authentication, authorization, and session restoration processes. The presentation layer then translates the same data and reorganizes it into an interpretable representation. Finally, the application layer displays that data in a user-friendly format. With that in mind, let's see how we can apply the framework of asynchronous programming to communication channels.

Asynchronous programming for communication channels

The asynchronous programming model nicely complements the process of facilitating communication channels. For instance, in **HyperText Transfer Protocol** (**HTTP**) communication, the server can asynchronously handle multiple clients at the same time: while it is waiting for a specific client to make an HTTP request, it can switch to another client and process that client's request. Similarly, if a client needs to make HTTP requests to multiple servers and must wait for large responses from some servers, it can consider the more lightweight responses, which have already been processed and were sent back to the client first. The following diagram shows an example of how servers and clients interact with each other asynchronously in HTTP requests:

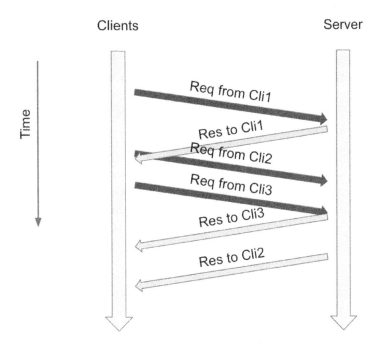

Figure 11.2 – Asynchronous, interleaved HTTP requests

Overall, asynchronous programming is an attractive framework for building communication channels. As such, we will see how this can be done with the `asyncio` module.

Transports and protocols in asyncio

The `asyncio` module provides several different transport classes. In essence, these classes are implementations of the functionalities of the transport layer that were discussed in the preceding section. As the transport layer plays an integral role in communication channels, the transport classes give `asyncio` (and, consequently, developers) more control over the process of implementing our own communication channels.

The `asyncio` module combines the abstract of transports with the implementation of an asynchronous program. Specifically, even though transports are the central elements of communication channels, in order to utilize the transport classes and other relevant communication channel tools, we need to initiate and call an event loop, which is an instance of the `asyncio.AbstractEventLoop` class. The event loop itself will then create transports and manage the low-level communication procedures.

It is important to note that a `transport` object in an established communication channel in `asyncio` is always associated with an instance of the `asyncio.Protocol` class. As the name suggests, the `Protocol` class specifies the underlying protocols that the communication channels use; for each connection made with another system, a new protocol object from this class will be created. While working closely with a `transport` object, a protocol object can call various methods from the `transport` object; this is where we can implement the specific inner workings of a communication channel.

For this reason, we generally need to focus on the implementation of an `asyncio.Protocol` subclass and its methods while building a connection channel. In other words, we use `asyncio.Protocol` as a parent class to derive a subclass that meets the needs of our communication channel. To do this, we overwrite the following methods from the `asyncio.Protocol` base class in our own custom protocol subclass:

- `Protocol.connection_made(transport)`: This method is automatically called whenever a connection from another system is made. The `transport` argument holds the `transport` object that is associated with the connection. Again, each `transport` object needs to be paired with a protocol; we generally store this `transport` object as an attribute of this specific protocol object in the `connection_made()` method.

- `Protocol.data_received(data)`: This method is automatically called whenever the one system that we are connected to sends its data. Note that the `data` argument, which holds the sent information, is usually represented in bytes, so the `encode()` function of Python should be used before `data` is processed further.

Next, let's consider other important methods from the transport classes from `asyncio`. All transport classes inherit from a parent transport class, called `asyncio.BaseTransport`, for which we have the following common methods:

- `BaseTransport.get_extra_info()`: This method returns, as the name suggests, additional channel-specific information for the calling `transport` object. The result can include information regarding the socket, the pipe, and the subprocess associated with that transport. Later in this chapter, we will be calling `BaseTransport.get_extra_info('peername')` to obtain the remote address from which the transport traveled.

- `BaseTransport.close()`: This method is used to close the calling `transport` object, after which the connections between different systems will be stopped. The corresponding protocol of the transport will automatically call its `connection_lost()` method.

Out of the many implementations of transport classes, we will focus on the `asyncio.`
`WriteTransport` class, which again inherits the methods from the `BaseTransport`
class and additionally implements other methods that are used to facilitate write-only
transport functionalities. Here, we will be using the `WriteTransport.write()`
method, which will write the data that we would like to send to the other system that we
communicate with via the `transport` object. As a part of the `asyncio` module, this
method is not a blocking function; instead, it buffers and sends out the written data in an
asynchronous way.

Before we dive into a working example in Python, let's briefly discuss the big picture of
what we are trying to accomplish—or, in other words, the general structure of our program.

The big picture of asyncio's server client

As mentioned earlier, we need to implement a subclass of `asyncio.Protocol` to
specify the underlying organization of our communication channel. There is an event loop
at the heart of each asynchronous program, so we also need to create a server outside of
the context of the protocol class and initiate that server inside of the event loop of our
program. This process will set up the asynchronous architecture of our entire server and
can be done via the `asyncio.create_server()` method, which we will look at in
our upcoming example.

Finally, we will run the event loop of our asynchronous program forever by using the
`AbstractEventLoop.run_forever()` method. Similar to an actual, real-life server,
we would like to keep our server running until it encounters a problem, in which case we
will close the server gracefully. The following diagram illustrates this whole process:

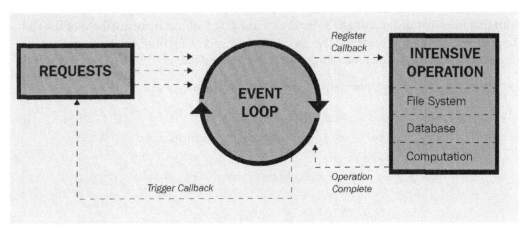

Figure 11.3 – Asynchronous program structure in communication channels

And with that, we are ready to start building our application, starting from the next section.

Getting started with Python and Telnet

Let's look at a specific Python example that implements a server that facilitates asynchronous communication.

Starting a server

Let's look at the `EchoServerClientProtocol` class, as follows:

```python
import asyncio


class EchoServerClientProtocol(asyncio.Protocol):
    def connection_made(self, transport):
        peername = transport.get_extra_info('peername')
        print('Connection from {}'.format(peername))
        self.transport = transport


    def data_received(self, data):
        message = data.decode()
        print('Data received: {!r}'.format(message))
```

Here, our `EchoServerClientProtocol` class is a subclass of `asyncio.Protocol`. As we discussed earlier, inside of this class, we need to implement the `connection_made(transport)` and `data_received(data)` methods. In the `connection_made()` method, we simply obtain the address of the connected system via the `get_extra_info()` method (with the `'peername'` argument), print a message out with that information, and finally store the `transport` object in an attribute of the class. To print out a similar message in the `data_received()` method, we again use the `decode()` method to obtain a string object from byte data.

Let's move on to the main program of our script, as follows:

```python
loop = asyncio.get_event_loop()
coro = loop.create_server(EchoServerClientProtocol, \
    '127.0.0.1', 8888)
server = loop.run_until_complete(coro)

# Serve requests until Ctrl+C is pressed
print('Serving on {}'.format(server.sockets[0] \
    .getsockname()))
try:
```

```
    loop.run_forever()
except KeyboardInterrupt:
    pass

# Close the server
server.close()
loop.run_until_complete(server.wait_closed())
loop.close()
```

We are using the familiar `asyncio.get_event_loop()` function to create an event loop for our asynchronous program. Then, we create a server for our communication by having that event loop call the `create_server()` method; this method takes in a subclass from the `asyncio.Protocol` class, an address for our server (in this case, it is our localhost: `127.0.0.1`), and finally, a port for that address (typically, `8888`).

Note that this method does not create a server itself; it only initiates the process of creating a server asynchronously and returns a coroutine that will finish the process. For this reason, we need to store the returned coroutine from the method in a variable (`coro`, in our case) and have our event loop run that coroutine. After printing out a message using the `sockets` attribute of our server object, we will run the event loop forever, to keep the server running, except for the case of a `KeyboardInterrupt` exception being invoked.

Finally, at the end of our program, we will handle the house-cleaning portion of the script, which is closing the server gracefully. This is typically done by having the server object call the `close()` method (to initiate the closing process of the server) and using the event loop to run the `wait_closed()` method on the server object, to make sure that the server is properly closed. Finally, we close the event loop.

Installing Telnet

Before we can run our sample Python program, we have to install the Telnet program to correctly simulate a connection channel between a client and a server. Telnet is a program that provides Terminal commands that facilitate protocols for bidirectional, interactive, text-oriented communication. If you already have Telnet working on your computer, simply skip to the next section; otherwise, find the information appropriate to your system in this section.

In Windows systems, Telnet is already installed, but might not be enabled. To enable it, you can either utilize the **Turn Windows features on or off** window and make sure that the **Telnet Client** box is checked, or run the following command:

```
dism /online /Enable-Feature /FeatureName:TelnetClient
```

Linux systems typically come with Telnet preinstalled, so if you own a Linux system, simply move on to the next section.

In macOS systems, it is possible that Telnet has already been installed on your computer. If not, you will need to do it via the Homebrew package management software, as follows:

```
brew install telnet
```

Note that macOS systems do have a preinstalled alternative to Telnet, called Netcat. If you do not want Telnet installed on your macOS computer, simply use the `nc` command instead of `telnet` in the following examples, and you will achieve the same effect.

Simulating a connection channel

There are multiple steps to running the following server example. First, we need to run the script to start the server, from which you will obtain the following output:

```
> python example1.py
Serving on ('127.0.0.1', 8888)
```

Notice that the program will run until you invoke the *Ctrl* + *C* key combination. With the program still running in one Terminal (this is our server Terminal), open another Terminal and connect to the server (127.0.0.1) at the specified port (8888), as illustrated here; this will serve as our client Terminal:

```
telnet 127.0.0.1 8888
```

Now, you will see some changes in both the server and the client Terminals. Most likely, your client Terminal will have the following output:

```
> telnet 127.0.0.1 8888
Trying 127.0.0.1...
Connected to localhost.
```

This is from the interface of the Telnet program, which indicates that we have successfully connected to our local server. The more interesting output is on our server Terminal, which will be similar to the following:

```
> python example1.py
Serving on ('127.0.0.1', 8888)
Connection from ('127.0.0.1', 60332)
```

Recall that this is an information message that we implemented in our
`EchoServerClientProtocol` class—specifically, in the `connection_made()`
method. Again, as a connection between the server and a new client is made, this method
will be called automatically to initiate the communication. From the output message, we
know that the client is making their requests from port `60332` of server `127.0.0.1`
(which is the same as the running server, since they are both local).

Another feature that we implemented in the `EchoServerClientProtocol` class
was in the `data_received()` method. Specifically, we print the decoded data that is
sent from the client. To simulate this type of communication, simply type a message in
your client Terminal and press the *Return* (*Enter*, for Windows) key. You will not see any
changes in the client Terminal output, but the server Terminal should print out a message,
as specified in the `data_received()` method of our protocol class.

For example, this is my server Terminal output when I send the message `Hello,`
`World!` from my client Terminal:

```
> python example1.py
Serving on ('127.0.0.1', 8888)
Connection from ('127.0.0.1', 60332)
Data received: 'Hello, World!\r\n'
```

The `\r` and `\n` characters are simply the return characters included in the message string.
With our current protocol, you can send multiple messages to the server and can even
have multiple clients send messages to the server. To implement this, simply open another
Terminal and connect to the local server again. You will see from your server Terminal that a
different client (from a different port) has made a connection to the server, while the original
communication of our server with the old client is still being maintained. This is another
result achieved from asynchronous programming, allowing multiple clients to communicate
with the same server seamlessly, without using threading or multiprocessing.

Sending messages back to clients

So, in our current example, we can have our asynchronous server receive, read, and
process messages from clients. However, for our communication channel to be useful,
we would also like to send messages from the server to the clients. In this section, we will
update our server to an echo server, which, by definition, will send all data that it receives
from a specific client back to the client.

To do this, we will be using the write() method from the asyncio. WriteTransport class. Consider the data_received() method of the EchoServerClientProtocol class, as follows:

```python
import asyncio

class EchoServerClientProtocol(asyncio.Protocol):
    def connection_made(self, transport):
        peername = transport.get_extra_info('peername')
        print('Connection from {}'.format(peername))
        self.transport = transport

    def data_received(self, data):
        message = data.decode()
        print('Data received: {!r}'.format(message))

        self.transport.write(('Echoed back: {}'.format \
            (message)).encode())

loop = asyncio.get_event_loop()
coro = loop.create_server(EchoServerClientProtocol, \
    '127.0.0.1', 8888)
server = loop.run_until_complete(coro)

# Serve requests until Ctrl+C is pressed
print('Serving on {}'.format(server.sockets[0] \
    .getsockname()))
try:
    loop.run_forever()
except KeyboardInterrupt:
    pass

# Close the server
server.close()
loop.run_until_complete(server.wait_closed())
loop.close()
```

After receiving the data from the `transport` object and printing it out, we write a corresponding message to the `transport` object, which will go back to the original client. By running this script and simulating the same communication that we implemented in the last example with Telnet or Netcat, you will see that after typing a message in the client Terminal, the client receives an echoed message from the server. This is my output after initiating the communication channel and typing in the `Hello, World!` message:

```
> telnet 127.0.0.1 8888
Trying 127.0.0.1...
Connected to localhost.
Hello, World!
Echoed back: Hello, World!
```

In essence, this example illustrates the capability of a bidirectional communication channel that we can implement through a custom `asyncio.Protocol` class. While running a server, we can obtain data sent from various clients connected to the server, process the data, and finally send the desired result back to the appropriate clients.

Closing transports

Occasionally, we will want to forcefully close a transport in a communication channel. For example, even with asynchronous programming and other forms of concurrency, it is possible for your server to be overwhelmed with constant communications from multiple clients. On the other hand, it is undesirable to have the server completely handle some of the sent requests and plainly reject the rest of the requests as soon as the server is at its maximum capacity.

So, instead of keeping the communication open for each client connected to the server, we can specify in our protocol that each connection should be closed after a successful communication. We will do this by using the `BaseTransport.close()` method to forcefully close the calling `transport` object, which will stop the connection between the server and that specific client. Again, we are modifying the `data_received()` method of the `EchoServerClientProtocol` class, as follows:

```python
import asyncio


class EchoServerClientProtocol(asyncio.Protocol):
    def connection_made(self, transport):
        peername = transport.get_extra_info('peername')
        print('Connection from {}'.format(peername))
```

```
        self.transport = transport

    def data_received(self, data):
        message = data.decode()
        print('Data received: {!r}'.format(message))

        self.transport.write(('Echoed back: \
            {}'.format(message)).encode())

        print('Close the client socket')
        self.transport.close()

loop = asyncio.get_event_loop()
coro = loop.create_server(EchoServerClientProtocol, \
    '127.0.0.1', 8888)
server = loop.run_until_complete(coro)

# Serve requests until Ctrl+C is pressed
print('Serving on {}'.format(server.sockets[0].getsockname()))
try:
    loop.run_forever()
except KeyboardInterrupt:
    pass

# Close the server
server.close()
loop.run_until_complete(server.wait_closed())
loop.close()
```

Run the script, connect to the specified server, and type in some messages to see the changes that we implemented. With our current setup, after a client connects and sends a message to the server, it will receive an echoed message back, and its connection with the server will be closed. This is the output (again, from the interface of the Telnet program) that I obtained after simulating this process with our current implementation of the protocol:

```
> telnet 127.0.0.1 8888
Trying 127.0.0.1...
Connected to localhost.
```

```
Hello, World!
Echoed back: Hello, World!
Connection closed by foreign host.
```

So far, we have covered examples of implementing asynchronous communication channels with the `asyncio` module, mostly from the perspective of the server side of the communication process; in other words, we have been handling and processing requests sent from external systems. This, however, is only one side of the equation, and we also have the client side of communication to explore. In the next section, we will discuss applying asynchronous programming to make requests to servers.

Client-side communication with aiohttp

As you have most likely guessed, the end goal of this process is to efficiently collect data from external systems by asynchronously making requests to those systems. We will be revisiting the concept of web scraping, which is the process of automating HTTP requests to various websites and extracting specific information from their **HyperText Markup Language** (**HTML**) source code. If you have not read *Chapter 9, Concurrent Web Requests*, I highly recommend going through it before proceeding with this section, as that chapter covers the fundamental ideas of web scraping and other relevant, important concepts.

In this section, you will also be introduced to another module that supports asynchronous programming options: `aiohttp` (which stands for **asynchronous input/output (I/O) HTTP**). This module provides high-level functionalities that streamline HTTP communication procedures, and it also works seamlessly with the `asyncio` module, to facilitate asynchronous programming.

Installing aiohttp and aiofiles

The `aiohttp` module does not come preinstalled with your Python distribution; however, similarly to other packages, you can easily install the module by using the `pip` or `conda` commands. We will also be installing another module, `aiofiles`, which facilitates asynchronous file writing. If you use `pip` as your package manager, simply run the following commands:

```
pip install aiohttp
pip install aiofiles
```

If you'd like to use Anaconda, run the following commands:

```
conda install aiohttp
conda install aiofiles
```

As always, to confirm that you have successfully installed a package, open your Python interpreter and try to import the module. In this case, run the following code:

```
>>> import aiohttp
>>> import aiofiles
```

There will be no error messages if the package has been successfully installed.

Fetching a website's HTML code

First, let's look at how to make a request and obtain the HTML source code from a single website with `aiohttp`. Note that even with only one task (a website), our application remains asynchronous, and the structure of an asynchronous program still needs to be implemented as follows:

```
import aiohttp
import asyncio

async def get_html(session, url):
    async with session.get(url, ssl=False) as res:
        return await res.text()

async def main():
    async with aiohttp.ClientSession() as session:
        html = await get_html(session, ' \
            http://packtpub.com')
        print(html)

loop = asyncio.get_event_loop()
loop.run_until_complete(main())
```

Let's consider the `main()` coroutine first. We are initiating an instance from the `aiohttp.ClientSession` class within a context manager; note that we are also placing the `async` keyword in front of this declaration since the whole context block itself will also be treated as a coroutine. Inside of this block, we are calling and waiting for the `get_html()` coroutine to process and return.

Turning our attention to the `get_html()` coroutine, we can see that it takes in a session object and a **Uniform Resource Locator** (**URL**) for the website that we want to extract the HTML source code from. Inside of this function, we make another context manager asynchronous, which is used to make a `GET` request and store the response from the server to the `res` variable. Finally, we return the HTML source code stored in the response. Since the response is an object returned from the `aiohttp.ClientSession` class, its methods are asynchronous functions, and therefore we need to specify the `await` keyword when we call the `text()` function.

As you run the program, the entire HTML source code of Packt's website will be printed out. For example, here is a portion of my output:

```
<!doctype html>
<html lang="en">
<head>
<script>
    var BASE_URL = 'https://www.packtpub.com/';
    var require = {
        "baseUrl": "https://www.packtpub.com/static
            /version1611744644/frontend/Packt/default/en_GB"
    };
</script>
<meta charset="utf-8" />
<meta name="title" content="Packt | Programming Books, eBooks
&amp; Videos for Developers" />
<meta name="description" content="Packt is the online
library and learning platform for professional developers.
Learn Python, JavaScript, Angular and more with eBooks,
videos and courses" />
<meta name="robots" content="INDEX,FOLLOW" />
<meta name="viewport" content="width=device-width, initial-
scale=1, maximum-scale=1, user-scalable=1, shrink-to-
fit=no" />
<meta name="" content="charset=utf-8" />
<title>Packt | Programming Books, eBooks &amp
...
```

At this point, we can collect data by making requests to multiple websites asynchronously and print out the response HTML. Most of the time, simply printing out the HTML is inappropriate; instead, we'd like to write the returned HTML code to output files. In essence, this process is asynchronous downloading, which is also implemented in the underlying architecture of popular download managers. To do this, we will use the `aiofiles` module, in combination with `aiohttp` and `asyncio`.

Writing files asynchronously

First, we will write a `download_html()` coroutine, as follows:

```
async def download_html(session, url):
    async with session.get(url, ssl=False) as res:
        filename = f'output/{os.path.basename(url)}.html'

        async with aiofiles.open(filename, 'wb') as f:
            while True:
                chunk = await res.content.read(1024)
                if not chunk:
                    break
                await f.write(chunk)

        return await res.release()
```

This is an updated version of the `get_html()` coroutine from the last example. Instead of using an `aiohttp.ClientSession` instance to make a GET request and print out the returned HTML code, we now write the HTML code to the file using the `aiofiles` module. For example, to facilitate asynchronous file writing, we use the asynchronous `open()` function from `aiofiles` to read in a file in a context manager. Furthermore, we read the returned HTML in chunks, asynchronously, using the `read()` function for the `content` attribute of the response object; this means that after reading `1024` bytes of the current response, the execution flow will be released back to the event loop, and the task-switching event will take place.

The `main()` coroutine and the main program of this example remain relatively the same as those in our last example, as we can see here:

```
async def main(url):
    async with aiohttp.ClientSession() as session:
        await download_html(session, url)
```

```
urls = [
    'http://packtpub.com',
    'http://python.org',
    'http://docs.python.org/3/library/asyncio',
    'http://aiohttp.readthedocs.io',
    'http://google.com'
]

loop = asyncio.get_event_loop()
loop.run_until_complete(
    asyncio.gather(*(main(url) for url in urls))
)
```

The `main()` coroutine takes in a URL and passes it to the `download_html()` coroutine, along with an `aiohttp.ClientSession` instance. Finally, in our main program, we create an event loop and pass each item in a specified list of URLs to the `main()` coroutine. After running the program, your output should look like this, although the time it takes to run the program might vary:

```
> python3 example5.py
Took 0.72 seconds.
```

Additionally, a subfolder named `output` (inside of the `Chapter18` folder) will be filled with the downloaded HTML code from each website in our list of URLs. Again, these files were created and written asynchronously, via the functionalities of the `aiofiles` module, which we discussed earlier. As you can see, to compare the speed of this program and its corresponding synchronous version, we are also keeping track of the time it takes to run the entire program.

Now, head to the `Chapter11/example6.py` file. This script contains the code of the synchronous version of our current program. Specifically, it makes HTTP `GET` requests to individual websites in order, and the process of file writing is also implemented sequentially. This script produced the following output:

```
> python3 example6.py
Took 1.47 seconds.
```

While it achieved the same results (downloading the HTML code and writing it to files), our sequential program took significantly more time than its asynchronous counterpart.

Summary

Asynchronous programming can provide functionalities that complement the process of efficiently facilitating communication channels. Together with the `aiohttp` module, `asyncio` offers efficiency and flexibility regarding client-side communication processes. The `aiofiles` module, which can work in conjunction with the other two asynchronous programming modules, can also help to facilitate asynchronous file reading and writing.

We have now explored three of the biggest, most important topics in concurrent programming: threading, multiprocessing, and asynchronous programming. We have shown how each of them can be applied to various programming problems and provide significant improvements in speed. The code we developed in this chapter serves as a base that may be easily modified to build more complex applications.

In the next chapter of this book, we will start to discuss problems that concurrent programming commonly poses to developers and programmers, starting with deadlocks.

Questions

1. What is a communication channel? What is its connection to asynchronous programming?

2. What are the two main parts of the OSI model protocol layers? What purpose does each of them serve?

3. What is the transport layer? Why is it crucial to communication channels?

4. How does `asyncio` facilitate the implementation of server-side communication channels?

5. How does `asyncio` facilitate the implementation of client-side communication channels?

6. What is `aiofiles`?

Further reading

For more information, you can refer to the following links:

- *IoT Systems and Communication Channels* (`bridgera.com/iot-communication-channels/`), by *Bridgera*

- *Automate the Boring Stuff with Python: Practical Programming for Total Beginners*, *Al Sweigart, No Starch Press*

- *Transports and protocols* (`docs.python.org/3/library/asyncio-protocol`), Python documentation

12
Deadlocks

Deadlocks, one of the most common concurrency problems, will be the first problem that we will analyze in this book. In this chapter, we will discuss the theoretical causes of deadlocks in concurrent programming. We will cover a classical synchronization problem in concurrency, called the **dining philosophers problem**, as a real-life example of a deadlock. We will also illustrate an actual implementation of a deadlock in Python and discuss several methods to address this problem. This chapter will also cover the concept of livelocks, which are relevant to deadlocks and are also a common problem in concurrent programming.

The following topics will be covered in this chapter:

- The concept of deadlocks
- Approaches to deadlock situations
- The concept of livelocks

By the end of this chapter, we will have gained a deep understanding of the problem, its place in concurrent programming, and the practical approaches to solving it.

Technical requirements

The code files for this chapter can be accessed through this link: `https://github.com/PacktPublishing/Advanced-Python-Programming-Second-Edition/tree/main/Chapter12`.

The concept of deadlocks

In concurrent programming, a deadlock refers to a specific situation in which no progress can be made, and the program becomes locked in its current state. In most cases, this phenomenon is caused by a lack of, or mishandled, coordination between different lock objects (for thread synchronization purposes). In this section, we will discuss a thought experiment, commonly known as the dining philosophers problem, to illustrate the concept of a deadlock and its causes; from there, you will learn how to simulate the problem in a Python concurrent program.

The dining philosophers problem

The dining philosophers problem was first introduced by Edgar Dijkstra, a leading pioneer in concurrent programming, in 1965. This problem was first demonstrated using different technical terms (resource contention in computer systems) and was later rephrased by Tony Hoare, a British computer scientist and the inventor of the quicksort sorting algorithm. The problem statement is as follows.

Five philosophers sit around a table, and each has a bowl of food in front of them. Placed between these five bowls of food are five forks, so each philosopher has one fork to their left and one fork to their right. This setup is shown in the following diagram:

Figure 12.1 – An illustration of the dining philosophers problem

Each silent philosopher is to alternate between thinking and eating. Each is required to have both of the forks around them to be able to pick up the food from their bowl, and no fork can be shared between two or more different philosophers. When a philosopher finishes eating a specific amount of food, they are to place both of the forks back in their respective, original locations. At this point, the philosophers around that philosopher will be able to use those forks.

Since the philosophers are silent and cannot communicate with each other, they have no way to let each other know they need the forks to eat. In other words, the only way for a philosopher to eat is to have both of the forks already available to them. For this problem, a set of instructions must be designed for the philosophers to efficiently switch between eating and thinking so that each philosopher is provided with enough food.

Now, a potential approach to this problem would be the following set of instructions:

1. A philosopher must think until the fork on their left becomes available. When that happens, the philosopher is to pick it up.

2. A philosopher must think until the fork on their right becomes available. When that happens, the philosopher is to pick it up.

3. If a philosopher is holding two forks, they will eat a specific amount of food from the bowl in front of them, and then the following will apply:

    - Afterward, the philosopher has to put the right fork down in its original place.

    - Afterward, the philosopher has to put the left fork down in its original place.

4. The process repeats from the first step.

It is clear to see how this set of instructions can lead to a situation where no progress can be made; namely, if, in the beginning, all of the philosophers start to execute their instructions at the same time. Since all of the forks are on the table at the beginning and are therefore available to be picked up by nearby philosophers, each philosopher will be able to execute the first instruction (picking up the fork on their left).

Now, after this step, each philosopher will be holding a fork with their left hand, and no forks will be left on the table. Since no philosopher has both forks in their hands, they cannot eat their food. Furthermore, the set of instructions that they were given specifies that only after a philosopher has eaten a specific amount of food can they put their forks down on the table. This means that so long as a philosopher has not eaten, they will not release the fork that they are holding.

So, as each philosopher is holding only one fork with their left hand, this means they cannot eat or put down the fork they are holding. The only time a philosopher gets to eat their food is when their neighboring philosopher puts their fork down, which is only possible if they can eat their food; this creates a never-ending circle of conditions that can never be satisfied. This situation is, in essence, the nature of a deadlock, in which all of the elements of a system are stuck in place, and no progress can be made.

It is not difficult to imagine real-world situations that involve shared resources and are modeled by this dining philosophers problem. For example, the original problems that inspired Dijkstra to construct this formulation involved working with external devices such as tape drives.

Another example is in terms of banks: to execute transactions between two bank accounts, you must ensure that both accounts are locked from other transactions for the correct amount of money to be transferred. Here, the analogy does not exactly hold – a philosopher corresponds to a transaction that locks accounts (the forks) – but the same technical difficulties could arise. Other examples include making online reservations and allowing a database to be modified by multiple clients at the same time.

With that said, we will be exclusively focusing on the formal dining philosophers problem as it provides a clean, abstract setting that could easily be analyzed and taken apart. With that in mind, let's consider the formal concept of a deadlock and the relevant theories around it.

A deadlock in a concurrent system

Given a concurrent program with multiple threads or processes, the execution flow enters a deadlock if a process (or thread) is waiting on a resource that is being held and utilized by another process, which is, in turn, waiting for another resource that is held by a different process. In other words, processes cannot proceed with their execution instructions while waiting for resources that can only be released after the execution is completed; therefore, these processes are unable to change their execution states.

A deadlock is also defined by the conditions that a concurrent program needs to have at the same time for a deadlock to occur. These conditions were first proposed by the computer scientist Edward G. Coffman, Jr., and are therefore known as the **Coffman conditions**. These conditions are as follows:

- At least one resource has to be in a non-shareable state. This means that that resource is being held by an individual process (or thread) and cannot be accessed by others; the resource can only be accessed and held by a single process (or thread) at any given time. This condition is also known as **mutual exclusion**.

- One process (or thread) exists that is simultaneously accessing a resource and waiting for another held by other processes (or threads). In other words, this process (or thread) needs access to two resources to execute its instructions, one of which it is already holding, the other of which it is waiting for from other processes (or threads). This condition is called **hold and wait**.

- Resources can only be released by a process (or a thread) holding them if there are specific instructions for the process (or thread) to do so. This is to say that unless the process (or thread) voluntarily and actively releases the resource, that resource remains in a non-shareable state. This is the **no preemption condition**.

- The final condition is called **circular wait**. As its name suggests, this condition specifies that a set of processes (or threads) exist so that the first process (or thread) in the set is waiting for a resource to be released by the second process (or thread), which, in turn, needs to be waiting for the third process (or thread); finally, the last process (or thread) in the set is waiting for the first one.

Let's quickly take a look at a basic example of a deadlock. Consider a concurrent program in which there are two different processes (process **A** and process **B**) and two different resources (resource **R1** and resource **R2**), as follows:

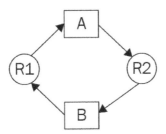

Figure 12.2 – Sample deadlock diagram

Neither of the resources can be shared across separate processes, and each process needs to access both resources to execute its instructions. Take process **A**, for example. It is already holding resource **R1**, but it also needs **R2** to proceed with its execution. However, **R2** cannot be acquired by process **A**, as it is being held by process **B**. So, process **A** cannot proceed. The same goes for process **B**, which is holding **R2** and needs **R1** to proceed. **R1** is, in turn, held by process **A**.

Python simulation

In this section, we will implement the preceding situation in an actual Python program. Specifically, we will have two locks (we will call them **lock A** and **lock B**) and two separate threads interacting with the locks (**thread A** and **thread B**). In our program, we will set up a situation in which thread A has acquired lock A and is waiting to acquire lock B, which has already been acquired by thread B, which is, in turn, waiting for lock A to be released.

If you have already downloaded the code for this book from the relevant GitHub page, then go ahead and navigate to the `Chapter12` folder. Let's consider the `Chapter12/example1.py` file, as follows:

```python
import threading
import time


def thread_a():
    print('Thread A is starting...')

    print('Thread A waiting to acquire lock A.')
    lock_a.acquire()
    print('Thread A has acquired lock A, performing some \
        calculation...')
    time.sleep(2)

    print('Thread A waiting to acquire lock B.')
    lock_b.acquire()
    print('Thread A has acquired lock B, performing some \
        calculation...')
    time.sleep(2)

    print('Thread A releasing both locks.')
    lock_a.release()
    lock_b.release()
```

```
def thread_b():
    print('Thread B is starting...')


    print('Thread B waiting to acquire lock B.')
    lock_b.acquire()
    print('Thread B has acquired lock B, performing some \
      calculation...')
    time.sleep(5)


    print('Thread B waiting to acquire lock A.')
    lock_a.acquire()
    print('Thread B has acquired lock A, performing some \
      calculation...')
    time.sleep(5)


    print('Thread B releasing both locks.')
    lock_b.release()
    lock_a.release()

lock_a = threading.Lock()
lock_b = threading.Lock()

thread1 = threading.Thread(target=thread_a)
thread2 = threading.Thread(target=thread_b)

thread1.start()
thread2.start()

thread1.join()
thread2.join()

print('Finished.')
```

In this script, the `thread_a()` and `thread_b()` functions specify thread A and thread B, respectively. In our main program, we also have two `threading.Lock` objects: lock A and lock B. The general structure of the thread instructions is as follows:

1. Start the thread.

2. Try to acquire the lock with the same name as the thread (thread A will try to acquire lock A, while thread B will try to acquire lock B).

3. Perform some calculations.

4. Try to acquire the other lock (thread A will try to acquire lock B, while thread B will try to acquire lock A).

5. Perform some other calculations.

6. Release both locks.

7. End the thread.

> **Note**
>
> Note that we are using the `time.sleep()` function to simulate the action of some calculations being processed.

First of all, we are starting both threads A and B almost simultaneously, within the main program. With the structure of the thread instruction set in mind, we can see that at this point, both threads will be initiated; thread A will try to acquire lock A and will succeed in doing so since lock A is still available at this point. The same goes for thread B and lock B. The two threads will then go on to perform some calculations on their own.

Let's consider the current state of our program: lock A has been acquired by thread A, and lock B has been acquired by thread B. After their respective calculation processes are complete, thread A will then try to acquire lock B, and thread B will try to acquire lock A. We can easily see that this is the beginning of our deadlock situation: since lock B is already being held by thread B and cannot be acquired by thread A, thread B, for the same reason, cannot acquire lock A.

Both of the threads will now wait infinitely to acquire their respective second lock. However, the only way a lock can be released is for a thread to continue its execution instructions and release all of the locks it has at the end. So, our program will be stuck in its execution at this point, and no further progress will be made.

The following diagram further illustrates the process of how the deadlock unfolds, in sequence:

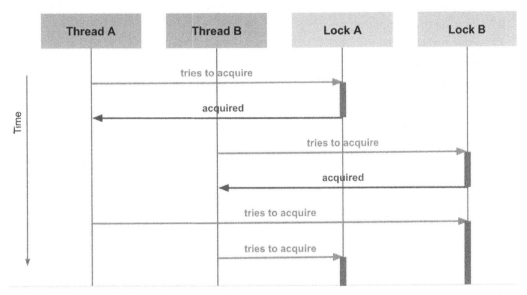

Figure 12.3 – Deadlock sequence diagram

Now, let's look at the deadlock that we have created in action. By running the script, you should obtain the following output:

```
> python example1.py
Thread A is starting...
Thread A waiting to acquire lock A.
Thread B is starting...
Thread A has acquired lock A, performing some calculation...
Thread B waiting to acquire lock B.
Thread B has acquired lock B, performing some calculation...
Thread A waiting to acquire lock B.
Thread B waiting to acquire lock A.
```

As we discussed previously, since each thread is trying to acquire a lock that is currently held by the other thread, the only way for a lock to be released is for a thread to continue its execution. This is a deadlock, and your program will hang infinitely, never reaching the final print statement in the last line of the program.

This behavior is undesirable in every way. In the next section, we will be discussing potential approaches to prevent deadlocks from occurring.

Approaches to deadlock situations

Intuitively, each of the following approaches looks to eliminate one of the four Coffman conditions from our program to prevent deadlocks. Our first solution is to implement ranking among the competing resources.

Implementing ranking among resources

From both the dining philosophers problem and our Python example, we can see that the last condition of the four Coffman conditions, circular wait, is at the heart of the deadlock problem. It specifies that the different processes (or threads) in our concurrent program wait for resources held by other processes (or threads) circularly. By taking a closer look, we can see that the root cause for this condition is the order (or lack thereof) in which the processes (or threads) access the resources.

In the dining philosophers problem, each philosopher is instructed to pick up the fork on their left first, while in our Python example, the threads always try to acquire the locks with the same name before performing any calculations. As you have seen, when the philosophers want to start eating at the same time, they will pick up their respective left forks and will be stuck in an infinite waiting loop. Similarly, when the two threads start their execution at the same time, they will acquire their locks and, again, wait for the other locks infinitely.

The conclusion that we can infer from this is that if, instead of accessing the resources arbitrarily, the processes (or threads) were to access them in a predetermined, static order, the circular nature of the way that they acquire and wait for the resources will be eliminated. So, for our two-lock Python example, instead of having thread A try to acquire lock A and thread B try to acquire lock B in their respective execution instructions, we will want both threads to try and acquire the locks in the same order. For example, both threads will now try to acquire lock A first, perform some calculations, try to acquire lock B, perform further calculations, and, finally, release both threads.

This change is implemented in the `Chapter12/example2.py` file, as follows:

```python
import threading
import time


def thread_a():
    print('Thread A is starting...')

    print('Thread A waiting to acquire lock A.')
    lock_a.acquire()
```

```
    print('Thread A has acquired lock A, performing some \
        calculation...')
    time.sleep(2)

    print('Thread A waiting to acquire lock B.')
    lock_b.acquire()
    print('Thread A has acquired lock B, performing some \
        calculation...')
    time.sleep(2)

    print('Thread A releasing both locks.')
    lock_a.release()
    lock_b.release()

def thread_b():
    print('Thread B is starting...')

    print('Thread B waiting to acquire lock A.')
    lock_a.acquire()
    print('Thread B has acquired lock A, performing some \
        calculation...')
    time.sleep(5)

    print('Thread B waiting to acquire lock B.')
    lock_b.acquire()
    print('Thread B has acquired lock B, performing some \
        calculation...')
    time.sleep(5)

    print('Thread B releasing both locks.')
    lock_b.release()
    lock_a.release()

lock_a = threading.Lock()
lock_b = threading.Lock()
```

```
thread1 = threading.Thread(target=thread_a)
thread2 = threading.Thread(target=thread_b)


thread1.start()
thread2.start()


thread1.join()
thread2.join()


print('Finished.')
```

This version of the script is now able to finish its execution and should produce the following output:

```
> python3 example2.py
Thread A is starting...
Thread A waiting to acquire lock A.
Thread A has acquired lock A, performing some calculation...
Thread B is starting...
Thread B waiting to acquire lock A.
Thread A waiting to acquire lock B.
Thread A has acquired lock B, performing some calculation...
Thread A releasing both locks.
Thread B has acquired lock A, performing some calculation...
Thread B waiting to acquire lock B.
Thread B has acquired lock B, performing some calculation...
Thread B releasing both locks.
Finished.
```

This approach efficiently eliminates the deadlock problem in our two-lock example, but how well does it hold up for the dining philosophers problem? To answer this question, let's try to simulate the problem and the solution in Python by ourselves. The Chapter12/example3.py file contains the implementation of the dining philosophers problem in Python, as follows:

```
import threading


# The philosopher thread
```

```
def philosopher(left, right):
    while True:
        with left:
            with right:
                print(f'Philosopher at \
                    {threading.currentThread()} is eating.')

# The chopsticks
N_FORKS = 5
forks = [threading.Lock() for n in range(N_FORKS)]

# Create all of the philosophers
phils = [ \
    threading.Thread(target=philosopher,args=(forks[n], forks \
        [(n + 1) % N_FORKS])) for n in range(N_FORKS)]

# Run all of the philosophers
for p in phils:
    p.start()
```

Here, we have the `philosopher()` function as the underlying logic for our separate threads. It takes in two `Threading.Lock` objects and simulates the previously discussed eating procedure, with two context managers. In our main program, we create a list of five lock objects, named `forks`, and a list of five threads, named `phils`, with the specification that the first thread will take in the first and second locks, the second thread will take in the second and third locks, and so on; and the fifth thread will take in the fifth and first locks (in order). Finally, we start all five threads simultaneously.

If we run the script, we will see that deadlock occurs almost immediately. The following is my output, up until the program hangs infinitely:

```
> python3 example3.py
Philosopher at <Thread(Thread-1, started 123145445048320)> is
eating.
Philosopher at <Thread(Thread-1, started 123145445048320)> is
eating.
Philosopher at <Thread(Thread-1, started 123145445048320)> is
eating.
```

```
Philosopher at <Thread(Thread-1, started 123145445048320)> is
eating.
Philosopher at <Thread(Thread-1, started 123145445048320)> is
eating.
Philosopher at <Thread(Thread-1, started 123145445048320)> is
eating.
Philosopher at <Thread(Thread-3, started 123145455558656)> is
eating.
Philosopher at <Thread(Thread-1, started 123145445048320)> is
eating.
Philosopher at <Thread(Thread-3, started 123145455558656)> is
eating.
Philosopher at <Thread(Thread-3, started 123145455558656)> is
eating.
Philosopher at <Thread(Thread-3, started 123145455558656)> is
eating.
Philosopher at <Thread(Thread-3, started 123145455558656)> is
eating.
Philosopher at <Thread(Thread-5, started 123145466068992)> is
eating.
Philosopher at <Thread(Thread-3, started 123145455558656)> is
eating.
Philosopher at <Thread(Thread-3, started 123145455558656)> is
eating.
```

The question that naturally follows is: how can we implement an order in which the locks are acquired in the philosopher() function? We will be using the built-in id() function in Python here, which returns the unique, constant identity of the parameter, as the keys to sort the lock objects. We will also implement a custom context manager to factor out this sorting logic in a separate class. Navigate to Chapter12/example4.py for this specific implementation, which looks as follows:

```
class acquire(object):
    def __init__(self, *locks):
        self.locks = sorted(locks, key=lambda x: id(x))

    def __enter__(self):
        for lock in self.locks:
```

```
            lock.acquire()


    def __exit__(self, ty, val, tb):
        for lock in reversed(self.locks):
            lock.release()
        return False


# The philosopher thread
def philosopher(left, right):
    while True:
        with acquire(left,right):
            print(f'Philosopher at \
                {threading.currentThread()} is eating.')
```

With the main program remaining the same, this script will produce an output showing that this solution of ranking can effectively address the dining philosophers problem.

However, there is a problem with this approach when it is applied to some particular cases. Keeping the high-level idea of concurrency in mind, we know that one of our main goals when applying concurrency to our programs is to improve the speed. Let's go back to our two-lock example and examine the execution time of our program with resource ranking implemented. Take a look at the Chapter12/example5.py file; it is simply the two-lock program with ranked (or ordered) locking implemented, combined with a timer that has been added to keep track of how much time it takes for the two threads to finish executing.

After running the script, your output should look similar to the following:

```
> python3 example5.py
Thread A is starting...
Thread A waiting to acquire lock A.
Thread B is starting...
Thread A has acquired lock A, performing some calculation...
Thread B waiting to acquire lock A.
Thread A waiting to acquire lock B.
Thread A has acquired lock B, performing some calculation...
Thread A releasing both locks.
Thread B has acquired lock A, performing some calculation...
Thread B waiting to acquire lock B.
```

```
Thread B has acquired lock B, performing some calculation...
Thread B releasing both locks.
Took 14.01 seconds.
Finished.
```

Here, you can see that the combined execution of both threads took around 14 seconds. However, if we take a closer look at the specific instructions in the two threads, we will see that aside from interacting with the locks, thread A would take around 4 seconds to do its calculations (simulated by two time.sleep(2) commands), while thread B would take around 10 seconds (two time.sleep(5) commands).

Does this mean that our program is taking as long as it would if we were to execute the two threads sequentially? We will test this theory with our Chapter12/example6.py file, in which we specify that each thread should execute its instructions one at a time with the same thread_a() and thread_b() functions:

```
lock_a = threading.Lock()
lock_b = threading.Lock()

thread1 = threading.Thread(target=thread_a)
thread2 = threading.Thread(target=thread_b)

start = timer()

thread1.start()
thread1.join()

thread2.start()
thread2.join()

print('Took %.2f seconds.' % (timer() - start))
print('Finished.')
```

If you run this script, you will see that this sequential version of our two-lock program will take the same amount of time as its concurrent counterpart:

```
> python3 example6.py
Thread A is starting...
Thread A waiting to acquire lock A.
Thread A has acquired lock A, performing some calculation...
```

```
Thread A waiting to acquire lock B.
Thread A has acquired lock B, performing some calculation...
Thread A releasing both locks.
Thread B is starting...
Thread B waiting to acquire lock A.
Thread B has acquired lock A, performing some calculation...
Thread B waiting to acquire lock B.
Thread B has acquired lock B, performing some calculation...
Thread B releasing both locks.
Took 14.01 seconds.
Finished.
```

This interesting phenomenon is a direct result of the heavy requirements that we have placed on the locks in the program. In other words, since each thread has to acquire both locks to complete its execution, each lock cannot be acquired by more than one thread at any given time. The locks must be acquired in a specific order, and the execution of individual threads cannot happen simultaneously. If we were to go back and examine the output produced by the Chapter12/example5.py file, it would be apparent that thread B could not start its calculations after thread A released both locks at the end of its execution.

It is quite intuitive, then, to conclude that if you placed enough locks on the resources of your concurrent program, it would become entirely sequential in its execution, and, combined with the overhead of concurrent programming functionalities, it would have an even worse speed than the purely sequential version of the program. However, we did not see this sequentiality that's created by locks in the dining philosophers problem (simulated in Python). This is because, in the two-thread problem, two locks were enough to sequentialize the program execution, while five were not enough to do the same for the dining philosophers problem.

We will explore another instance of this phenomenon in *Chapter 13, Starvation*.

Ignoring locks and sharing resources

Locks are undoubtedly an important tool in synchronization tasks, and in concurrent programming in general. However, if using locks leads to an undesirable situation, such as a deadlock, then it is natural for us to explore the option of simply not using locks in our concurrent programs. By ignoring locks, our program's resources effectively become shareable among different processes/threads in a concurrent program, thus eliminating the first of the four Coffman conditions: **mutual exclusion**.

This approach to the problem of a deadlock is straightforward to implement; let's try this with the two preceding examples. In the two-lock example, we simply remove the code that specifies any interaction with the lock objects both inside the thread functions and in the main program. In other words, we are not utilizing a locking mechanism anymore. The Chapter12/example7.py file contains the implementation of this approach, as follows:

```python
import threading
import time
from timeit import default_timer as timer

def thread_a():
    print('Thread A is starting...')

    print('Thread A is performing some calculation...')
    time.sleep(2)

    print('Thread A is performing some calculation...')
    time.sleep(2)

def thread_b():
    print('Thread B is starting...')

    print('Thread B is performing some calculation...')
    time.sleep(5)

    print('Thread B is performing some calculation...')
    time.sleep(5)

thread1 = threading.Thread(target=thread_a)
thread2 = threading.Thread(target=thread_b)

start = timer()

thread1.start()
thread2.start()
```

```
thread1.join()
thread2.join()

print('Took %.2f seconds.' % (timer() - start))

print('Finished.')
```

If you run the script, your output should look similar to the following:

```
> python3 example7.py
Thread A is starting...
Thread A is performing some calculation...
Thread B is starting...
Thread B is performing some calculation...
Thread A is performing some calculation...
Thread B is performing some calculation...
Took 10.00 seconds.
Finished.
```

It is clear that since we are not using locks to restrict access to any calculation processes, the executions of the two threads have become entirely independent of one another, so the threads were run completely in parallel. For this reason, we also obtained a better speed: since the threads ran in parallel, the total time that the whole program took was the same as the time that the longer of the two threads took (in other words, thread B, with 10 seconds).

What about the dining philosophers problem? It seems that we can also conclude that without locks (the forks), the problem can be solved easily. Since the resources (food) are unique to each philosopher (in other words, no philosopher should eat another philosopher's food), it should be the case that each philosopher can proceed with their execution without worrying about the others. By ignoring the locks, each can be executed in parallel, similar to what we saw in our two-lock example.

Doing this, however, means that we are completely misunderstanding the problem. We know that locks are utilized so that processes and threads can access the shared resources in a program in a systematic, coordinated way, to avoid mishandling the data. Therefore, removing any locking mechanisms in a concurrent program means that the likelihood of the shared resources, which are now free from access limitations, being manipulated in an uncoordinated way (and therefore, becoming corrupted) increases significantly.

So, by ignoring locks, it is relatively likely that we will need to completely redesign and restructure our concurrent program. If the shared resources still need to be accessed and manipulated in an organized way, other synchronization methods will need to be implemented. The logic of our processes and threads might need to be altered to interact with this new synchronization method appropriately, the execution time might be negatively affected by this change in the structure of the program, and other potential synchronization problems might also arise.

An additional note about locks

While the approach of dismissing locking mechanisms in our program to eliminate deadlocks might raise some questions and concerns, it does effectively reveal a new point for us about lock objects in Python: it is possible for an element of a concurrent program to completely bypass the locks when accessing a given resource. In other words, lock objects only prevent different processes/threads from accessing and manipulating a shared resource if those processes or threads acquire the lock objects.

Locks, then, do not lock anything. They are simply flags that help indicate whether a resource should be accessed at a given time; if a poorly instructed, or even malicious, process/thread attempts to access that resource without checking that the lock object exists, it will most likely be able to do that without difficulty. In other words, locks are not connected to the resources that they are supposed to lock, and they most certainly do not block processes/threads from accessing those resources.

So, simply using locks is inefficient for designing and implementing a secure, dynamic, concurrent data structure. To achieve that, we would need to either add more concrete links between the locks and their corresponding resources or utilize a different synchronization tool altogether (for example, atomic message queues).

Concluding note on deadlock solutions

In this chapter, you have seen two of the most common approaches to the deadlock problem. Each addresses one of the four Coffman conditions, and while both (somewhat) successfully prevent deadlocks from occurring in our examples, each raises different, additional problems and concerns. So, it is important to truly understand the nature of your concurrent programs to know which of the two is applicable, if either of them is.

It is also possible that some programs, through deadlocks, are revealed to us as unsuitable to be made concurrent; some programs are better left sequential and will be made worse with forced concurrency. As we have discussed, while concurrency provides significant improvements in many areas of our applications, some are inherently inappropriate for concurrent programming. In deadlock situations, developers should be ready to consider different approaches to designing a concurrent program and should not be reluctant to implement another method when one concurrent approach does not work.

The concept of livelocks

The concept of a livelock is connected to a deadlock; some even consider it an alternate version of a deadlock. In a livelock situation, the processes (or threads) in the concurrent program can switch their states; in fact, they switch states constantly. Yet, they simply switch back and forth infinitely, and no progress is made. We will now consider an actual scenario of a livelock.

Suppose that a pair of spouses are eating dinner together at a table. They only have one fork to share, so only one of them can eat at any given point. Additionally, the spouses are polite to each other, so even if one spouse is hungry and wants to eat their food, they will leave the fork on the table if their partner is also hungry. This specification is at the heart of creating a livelock for this problem: when both spouses are hungry, each will wait for the other to eat first, creating an infinite loop in which each spouse switches between wanting to eat and waiting for the other spouse to eat.

Let's simulate this problem in Python. Navigate to `Chapter12/example8.py` and take a look at the `Spouse` class:

```
class Spouse(threading.Thread):

    def __init__(self, name, partner):
        threading.Thread.__init__(self)
        self.name = name
        self.partner = partner
        self.hungry = True

    def run(self):
        while self.hungry:
            print('%s is hungry and wants to eat.' % self.name)
```

```
        if self.partner.hungry:
            print('%s is waiting for their partner to eat \
                first...' % self.name)
    else:
        with fork:
            print('%s has stared eating.' % self.name)
            time.sleep(5)

            print('%s is now full.' % self.name)
            self.hungry = False
```

This class inherits from the threading.Thread class and implements the logic that we discussed previously. It takes in a name for the Spouse instance and another Spouse object as its partner; when initialized, a Spouse object is also always hungry (the hungry attribute is always set to True). The run() function in the class specifies the logic when the thread is started: so long as the Spouse object's hungry attribute is set to True, the object will attempt to use the fork, which is a lock object, to eat. However, it always checks whether its partner also has its hungry attribute set to True, in which case it will not proceed to acquire the lock, and will instead wait for its partner to do it.

In our main program, we create the fork as a lock object first; then, we create two Spouse thread objects, which are each other's partner attributes. Finally, we start both threads and run the program until both threads finish executing:

```
fork = threading.Lock()

partner1 = Spouse('Wife', None)
partner2 = Spouse('Husband', partner1)
partner1.partner = partner2

partner1.start()
partner2.start()

partner1.join()
partner2.join()

print('Finished.')
```

If you run the script, you will see that, as we discussed, each thread will go into an infinite loop, switching between wanting to eat and waiting for its partner to eat; the program will run forever until Python is interrupted. The following code shows the first few lines of output that I obtained:

```
> python3 example8.py
Wife is hungry and wants to eat.
Wife is waiting for their partner to eat first...
Husband is hungry and wants to eat.
Wife is hungry and wants to eat.
Husband is waiting for their partner to eat first...
Wife is waiting for their partner to eat first...
Husband is hungry and wants to eat.
Wife is hungry and wants to eat.
Husband is waiting for their partner to eat first...
Wife is waiting for their partner to eat first...
Husband is hungry and wants to eat.
Wife is hungry and wants to eat.
Husband is waiting for their partner to eat first...
...
```

And with that, we can conclude our discussion on deadlocks and livelocks.

Summary

In this chapter, we covered the causes of deadlocks in concurrent applications and implemented approaches to prevent them from occurring. Our examples have shown that concurrency cannot always be achieved straightforwardly and that some situations may require special handling. These discussions have prepared us for deadlocks in the real world and pointed us toward potential solutions.

In the next chapter, we will discuss another common problem in concurrent programming: starvation.

Questions

1. What can lead to a deadlock situation, and why is it undesirable?

2. How is the dining philosophers problem related to the problem of a deadlock?

3. What are the four Coffman conditions?

4. How can resource ranking solve the problem of a deadlock? What other problems can occur when this is implemented?

5. How can ignoring locks solve the problem of a deadlock? What other problems can occur when this is implemented?

6. How is a livelock related to a deadlock?

Further reading

- *Parallel Programming with Python*, by Jan. Palach, Packt Publishing Ltd, 2014

- *Python Parallel Programming Cookbook*, by Giancarlo Zaccone, Packt Publishing Ltd, 2015

- *Python Thread Deadlock Avoidance* (`dabeaz.blogspot.com/2009/11/python-thread-deadlock-avoidance_20`)

13
Starvation

In this chapter, we will discuss the concept of **starvation** and its potential causes in concurrent programming. We will cover a number of variations of the **readers-writers problems**, which are prime examples of starvation, and we will simulate them in example Python code. This chapter will also cover the relationship between *deadlock* and *starvation*, as well as some potential solutions for starvation.

The following topics will be covered in this chapter:

- Understanding starvation
- Approaching the readers-writers problem
- Solutions to starvation

By the end of the chapter, you will have a deep understanding of starvation, what causes it, and what practical solutions can be implemented to address the problem.

Technical requirements

The code files for this chapter can be accessed through this link: `https://github.com/PacktPublishing/Advanced-Python-Programming-Second-Edition/tree/main/Chapter13`.

Understanding starvation

Starvation is a problem in concurrent systems, in which a process (or a thread) cannot gain access to the necessary resources in order to proceed with its execution and, therefore, cannot make any progress. In this section, we will look into the characteristics of a starvation situation, analyze its most common causes, and finally, consider a sample program that exemplifies starvation.

What is starvation?

It is quite common for a concurrent program to implement some sort of ordering between the different processes in its execution. For example, consider a program that has three separate processes, as follows:

- One is responsible for handling extremely pressing instructions that need to be run as soon as the necessary resources become available.

- Another process is responsible for other important executions, which are not as essential as the tasks in the first process.

- The last one handles miscellaneous, very infrequent tasks.

Furthermore, these three processes need to utilize the same resources in order to execute their respective instructions.

Intuitively, we have every reason to implement a specification that allows the first process to have the highest priority of execution and access to resources, then the second process, and then the last process, with the lowest priority. However, imagine situations in which the first two processes (with higher priorities) run so often that the third process cannot execute its instructions; anytime the third process needs to run, it checks to see whether the resources are available to be used and finds out that one of the other higher-priority processes is using them.

This is a situation of starvation – the third process is given no opportunity to execute and, therefore, no progress can be made with that process. In a typical concurrent program, it is quite common to have more than three processes at different priority levels, yet the situation is fundamentally similar – some processes are given more opportunities to run and, therefore, they are constantly executing. Others have lower priorities and cannot access the necessary resources to execute.

Scheduling

In the next few subsections, we will be discussing the potential candidates that cause starvation situations. Most of the time, a poorly coordinated set of *scheduling instructions* is the main cause of starvation. For example, a considerably naive algorithm that deals with three separate tasks might implement constant communication and interaction between the first two tasks.

This setup leads to the fact that the execution flow of the algorithm switches solely between the first and second tasks, while the third finds itself idle and unable to make any progress with its execution – in this case, because it is starved of CPU execution flow. Intuitively, we can identify the root of the problem as the fact that the algorithm allows the first two tasks to always dominate the CPU and, hence, effectively prevents any other task from also utilizing the CPU. A characteristic of a good scheduling algorithm is the ability to distribute the execution flow and allocate the resources equally and appropriately.

As mentioned previously, many concurrent systems and programs implement a specific order of priority, in terms of process and thread execution. This implementation of ordered scheduling may very likely lead to the starvation of processes and threads of lower priorities and can result in a condition called **priority inversion**.

Suppose that, in your concurrent program, you have process A of the highest priority, process B of a medium priority, and finally, process C of the lowest priority; process C would most likely be put in the situation of starvation. Additionally, if the execution of process A, the prioritized process, is dependent on the completion of process C, which is already in starvation, then process A might never be able to complete its execution either, even though it is given the highest priority in the concurrent program.

The following diagram further illustrates the concept of priority inversion – a high-priority task running from the time **t2** to **t3** needs to access some resources, which are being utilized by a low-priority task:

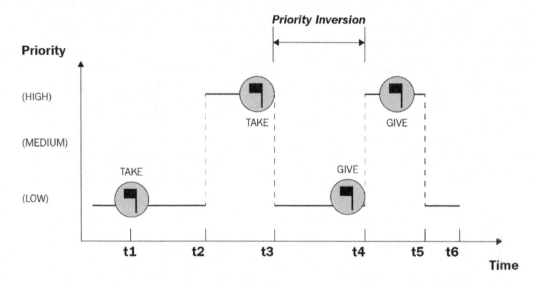

Figure 13.1 – A diagram of priority inversion

To reiterate, combining starvation and priority inversion can lead to a situation where even the high-priority tasks are unable to execute their instructions.

Causes of starvation

With the complexity of designing a scheduling algorithm in mind, let's discuss the specific causes of starvation. The situations that we described in the preceding section indicate some potential causes of a starvation situation. However, starvation can arise from a number of sources, as follows:

- Processes (or threads) with high priorities dominate the execution flow in the CPU and, hence, low-priority processes (or threads) are not given the opportunity to execute their own instructions.

- Processes (or threads) with high priorities dominate the usage of non-shareable resources and, hence, low-priority processes (or threads) are not given the opportunity to execute their own instructions. This situation is similar to the first one but addresses the priority of accessing resources, instead of the priority of the execution itself.

- Processes (or threads) with low priorities are waiting for resources to execute their instructions, but as soon as the resources become available, other processes (or threads) with higher priorities are immediately given access to them, so the low-priority processes (or threads) wait indefinitely.

There are other causes of starvation as well, but the preceding are the most common root causes.

Starvation's relationship to deadlock

Interestingly, deadlock situations can also lead to starvation, as the definition of starvation states that if there is a process (or a thread) that is unable to make any progress because it cannot gain access to the necessary process, the process (or thread) is experiencing starvation.

Recall our example of deadlock, the Dining Philosophers problem, illustrated as follows:

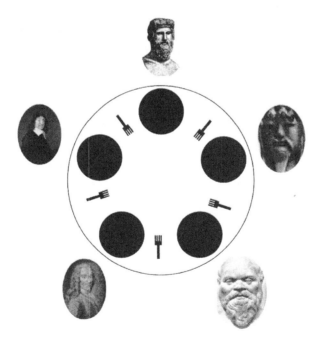

Figure 13.2 – An illustration of the Dining Philosophers problem

When deadlock occurs in this situation, no philosopher can obtain the necessary resources to execute their instructions (each philosopher is required to have two forks to start eating). Each philosopher that is in deadlock is therefore also in a state of starvation.

The readers-writers problem describes in detail the various types of starvation, which we will consider next.

Approaching the readers-writers problem

The readers-writers problem is one of the classic use cases in concurrent programming, illustrating problems that might occur in a concurrent program. Throughout the analysis of the different variations of the readers-writers problem, we will reveal more about starvation, as well as its common causes. We will also simulate the problem in Python so that a deeper understanding of the problem can be gained.

Problem statement

In a readers-writers problem, first and foremost, we have a shared resource, which, in most cases, is a text file. Different threads interact with that text file; each is either a reader or a writer. A **reader** is a thread that simply accesses the shared resource (the text file) and reads in the data included in that file, while a **writer** is a thread that accesses, and possibly mutates, the contents of the text file.

We know that writers and readers cannot access the shared resources simultaneously since if a thread is writing data to the file, no other thread should be accessing the file to read any data from it. The goal of the readers-writers problem is therefore to find a correct and efficient way to design and coordinate the scheduling of these reader and writer threads. Successful implementation of that goal is not only that the program as a whole executes in the most optimized way but also that all threads are given sufficient opportunity to execute their instructions and no starvation can occur. Additionally, the shared resource (the text file) needs to be handled appropriately so that no data will be corrupted.

The following diagram further illustrates the setup of the readers-writers problem:

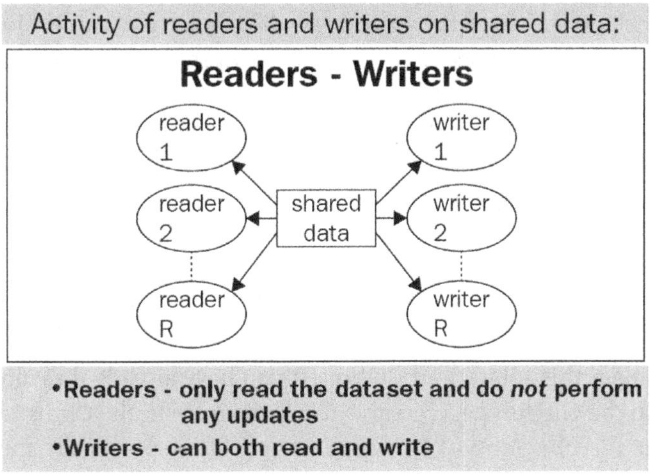

Figure 13.3 – A diagram of the readers-writers problem

In the following subsections, we will be exploring different variations of the problem with increasing levels of complexity. From there, we will also implement sample solutions to these problems, thus gaining hands-on experience in preventing starvation in concurrent applications.

The first readers-writers problem

As we mentioned, the problem asks us to come up with a scheduling algorithm so that readers and writers can access the text file appropriately and efficiently, without mishandling or corrupting the data that is included. A naive solution to this problem is to impose a lock on the text file so that it becomes a non-shareable resource; this means that only one thread (either a reader or a writer) can access (and potentially manipulate) the text file at any given time.

Yet, this approach simply equates to a sequential program – if the shared resource can be utilized by only one thread at a given time, none of the processing time between different threads can be overlapped and, effectively, the execution becomes sequential. Therefore, this is not an optimal solution, as it is taking advantage of concurrent programming.

One insight regarding the reader threads can lead to a more optimal solution to this problem – since readers simply read in the text file and do not alter the data in it, multiple readers can be allowed to access the text file simultaneously. Indeed, even if more than one reader is fetching data from the text file at the same time, the data is not being changed in any way, and the consistency and accuracy of the data are therefore maintained.

Following this approach, we will implement a specification in which no reader will be kept waiting if the shared resource is being opened for reading by another reader. Specifically, in addition to a lock on the shared resource, we will also have a counter for the number of readers currently accessing the resource. If at any point in the program that counter goes from zero to one (in other words, at least one reader is starting to access the resource), we will lock the resource from the writers; similarly, whenever the counter decreases to zero (in other words, no reader is asking for access to the resource), we will release the lock on the resource so that writers can access it.

This specification is efficient for the readers in the sense that once the first reader has accessed the resource and placed a lock on it, no writers can access it, and the subsequent readers will not have to re-lock it until the last reader finishes reading the resource.

Let's try to implement this solution in Python. If you have already downloaded the code for this book from the GitHub page, go ahead and navigate to the `Chapter13` folder. Let's take a look at the `Chapter13/example1.py` file – specifically, the `writer()` and `reader()` functions, as follows:

```python
def writer():
    global text

    while True:
        with resource:
            print(f'Writing being done by \
                    {threading.current_thread().name}.')
            text += f'Writing was done by \
                    {threading.current_thread().name}. '

def reader():
    global rcount

    while True:
        with rcounter:
            rcount += 1
            if rcount == 1:
                resource.acquire()

        print(f'Reading being done by \
                {threading.current_thread().name}:')
```

```
        print(text)

    with rcounter:
        rcount -= 1
        if rcount == 0:
            resource.release()
```

In the preceding script, the `writer()` function, which is to be called by a `threading.Thread` instance (in other words, a separate thread), specifies the logic of the writer threads that we discussed previously – accessing the shared resource (in this case, the global variable, `text`, which is simply a Python string) and writing some data to the resource. Note that we are putting all of its instructions inside a `while` loop to simulate the constant nature of the application (writers and readers constantly trying to access the shared resource).

We can also see the reader logic in the `reader()` function. Before asking for access to the shared resource, each reader will increment a counter for the number of readers that are currently active and trying to access the resource. Similarly, after reading data off the file, each reader needs to decrement the number of readers. During this process, if a reader is the first reader to access the file (in other words, when the counter is one), it will put a lock on the file so that no writers can access it; conversely, when a reader is the last reader to read the file, it has to release that lock.

One note about the handling of that counter of readers – you might have noticed that we are using a lock object named `rcounter` when incrementing/decrementing the counter variable (`rcount`). This is a method that is used to avoid a race condition, which is another common concurrency-related problem, for the counter variable; specifically, without the lock, multiple threads can be accessing and altering the counter variable at the same time, but the only way to ensure the integrity of the data is for this counter variable to be handled sequentially. We will discuss race conditions (and the practice that is used to avoid them) in more detail in the next chapter.

Going back to our current script – in the main program, we will set up the `text` variable, the counter for readers, and two lock objects (for the reader counter and the shared resource respectively). We are also initializing and starting three reader threads and two writer threads, as follows:

```
text = 'This is some text. '
rcount = 0


rcounter = threading.Lock()
```

```
resource = threading.Lock()


threads = [threading.Thread(target=reader) for i in \
    range(3)] + [ \
        threading.Thread(target=writer) for i in \
            range(2)]


for thread in threads:
    thread.start()
```

It is important to note that, since the instructions of the reader and writer threads are both wrapped in `while` loops, the script, when started, will run infinitely. You should cancel the Python execution after around 3–4 seconds, when enough output has been produced so that the general behavior of the program can be observed.

The following code shows the first few lines of output that I obtained after running the script:

```
> python3 example1.py
Reading being done by Thread-1:
This is some text.
Reading being done by Thread-2:
Reading being done by Thread-1:
This is some text.
This is some text.
Reading being done by Thread-2:
Reading being done by Thread-1:
This is some text.
This is some text.
Reading being done by Thread-3:
Reading being done by Thread-1:
This is some text.
This is some text.
...
```

As you can see, there is a specific pattern in the preceding output – all of the threads that were accessing the shared resource were readers. In fact, throughout my entire output, no writer was able to access the file and, therefore, the `text` variable only contains the initial string, `This is some text.`, and was not altered in any way. The output that you obtain should also have the same pattern (the shared resource not being altered).

In this case, the writers are experiencing starvation, as none of them are able to access and use the resource. This is a direct result of our scheduling algorithm; since multiple readers are allowed to access the text file simultaneously, if there are multiple readers accessing the text file frequently enough, it will create a continuous stream of readers going through the text file, leaving no room for a writer to attempt to access the file.

This scheduling algorithm inadvertently gives priority to the readers over the writers and is therefore called **reader preference**. So, this design is undesirable.

The second readers-writers problem

The problem with the first approach is that when a reader is accessing the text file and a writer is waiting for the file to be unlocked, if another reader starts its execution and wants to access the file, it will be given priority over the writer that has already been waiting. Additionally, if more and more readers keep requesting access to the file, the writer will be waiting indefinitely, and that was what we observed in our first code example.

To address this problem, we will implement the specification that once a writer makes a request to access the file, no reader should be able to jump in line and access the file before that writer. To do this, we will have an additional lock object in our program to specify whether a writer is waiting for the file and, consequently, whether a reader thread can attempt to read the file; we will call this lock read_try.

Similar to how the first of the readers accessing the text file always locks it from the writers, we will now have the first of the multiple writers that are waiting to access the read_try file lock, so that no reader can, again, jump in line before those writers that requested access before it. As we discussed in reference to the readers, since we are keeping track of the number of writers waiting for the text file, we will need to implement a counter for the number of writers, and its corresponding lock, in our program.

The Chapter13/example2.py file contains the code for this implementation, as follows (note that the reader() function is being omitted in the text):

```python
import threading


def writer():
    global text
    global wcount

    while True:
        with wcounter:
            wcount += 1
```

```
                if wcount == 1:
                    read_try.acquire()

            with resource:
                print(f'Writing being done by \
                    {threading.current_thread().name}.')
                text += f'Writing was done by \
                    {threading.current_thread().name}. '

            with wcounter:
                wcount -= 1
                if wcount == 0:
                    read_try.release()

def reader():
    ...

text = 'This is some text. '
wcount = 0
rcount = 0

wcounter = threading.Lock()
rcounter = threading.Lock()
resource = threading.Lock()
read_try = threading.Lock()

threads = [threading.Thread(target=reader) for i in \
  range(3)] +
    [threading.Thread(target=writer) for i in \
      range(2)]

for thread in threads:
    thread.start()
```

Compared to our first solution to the problem, the main program remains relatively the same (except for the initialization of the `read_try` lock, the `wcount` counter, and its lock, `wcounter`), but in our `writer()` function, we are locking `read_try` as soon as there is at least one writer waiting to access the file; when the last writer finishes its execution, it will release the lock so that any reader waiting for the file can now access it.

Again, to see the output produced by the program, we will have it run for 3–4 seconds and then cancel the execution, as the program would otherwise run forever. The following is the output that I obtained via this script:

```
> python3 example2.py
Reading being done by Thread-1:
This is some text.
Reading being done by Thread-1:
This is some text.
Writing being done by Thread-4.
Writing being done by Thread-5.
Writing being done by Thread-4.
Writing being done by Thread-4.
Writing being done by Thread-4.
Writing being done by Thread-5.
Writing being done by Thread-4.
...
```

It can be observed that while some readers were able to access the text file (indicated by the first four lines of my output), once a writer gained access to the shared resource, no reader was able to access it anymore. The rest of my output included messages about writing instructions – `Writing being done by`, and so on. As opposed to what we saw in the first solution of the readers-writers problem, this solution is giving priority to writers, and, as a consequence, the readers are starved. This is therefore called **writer preference**.

The priority that writers were given over readers resulted from the fact that while only the first and the last writers have to acquire and release the `read_try` lock respectively, each reader wanting to access the text file has to interact with that lock object individually. Once `read_try` is locked by a writer, no reader can even attempt to execute its instructions, let alone try to access the text file.

There are cases in which some readers are able to gain access to the text file if the readers are initialized and executed before the writers (for example, in our program, the readers were the first three elements, and the writers were the last two, in our list of threads). However, once a writer is able to access the file and acquire the read_try lock during its execution, starvation will most likely occur for the readers.

This solution is also not desirable, as it gives higher priority to the writer threads in our program.

The third readers-writers problem

You have seen that both of the solutions that we tried to implement can result in starvation by not giving equal priorities to the separate threads; one can starve the writers, and the other can starve the readers. A balance between these two approaches might give us an implementation with equal priorities among the readers and writers, and, hence, solve the problem of starvation.

Recall that – in our second approach, we placed a lock on a reader's attempt to access the text file, requiring that no writer would be starved once it started waiting for the file. In this solution, we will implement a lock that also utilizes this logic but is then applied to both readers and writers. All of the threads will then be subjected to the constraints of the lock, and equal priority will hence be achieved among the separate threads.

Specifically, this is a lock that specifies whether a thread will be given access to the text file at a given moment; we will call this the **service lock**. Each writer or reader has to try to acquire this service lock before executing any of its instructions. A writer, having obtained this service lock, will also attempt to obtain the resource lock and release the service lock immediately thereafter. The writer will then execute its writing logic and finally release the resource lock at the end of its execution.

Let's take a look at the writer() function in the Chapter13/example3.py file for our implementation in Python, as follows:

```python
def writer():
    global text

    while True:
        with service:
            resource.acquire()

        print(f'Writing being done by \
            {threading.current_thread().name}.')
```

```
        text += f'Writing was done by \
            {threading.current_thread().name}. '

    resource.release()
```

On the other hand, a reader will also need to acquire the service lock first. Since we are still allowing multiple readers to access the resource at the same time, we are implementing the reader counter and its corresponding lock.

The reader will acquire the service lock and the counter lock, increment the reader counter (and, potentially, lock the resource), and then release the service lock and counter lock sequentially. Now, it will actually read data off the text file, and finally, it will decrement the reader counter and potentially release the resource lock if it is the last reader to access the file at that time.

The reader() function contains the following specification:

```
def reader():
    global rcount

    while True:
        with service:
            rcounter.acquire()
            rcount += 1
            if rcount == 1:
                resource.acquire()
        rcounter.release()

        print(f'Reading being done by \
            {threading.current_thread().name}:')
        #print(text)

        with rcounter:
            rcount -= 1
            if rcount == 0:
                resource.release()
```

Finally, in our main program, we initialize the text string, the reader counter, all of the necessary locks, and the reader and writer threads, as follows:

```
text = 'This is some text. '
rcount = 0

rcounter = threading.Lock()
resource = threading.Lock()
service = threading.Lock()

threads = [threading.Thread(target=reader) for i in \
    range(3)] + [
        threading.Thread(target=writer) for i in range(2)]

for thread in threads:
    thread.start()
```

Note that we are commenting the code that prints out the current content of the text file in the reader() function for readability for our output later on. Run the program for 3–4 seconds and then cancel it. The following output is what I obtained on my personal computer:

```
> python3 example3.py
Reading being done by Thread-3:
Writing being done by Thread-4.
Reading being done by Thread-1:
Writing being done by Thread-5.
Reading being done by Thread-2:
Reading being done by Thread-3:
Writing being done by Thread-4.
...
```

The pattern that we have with this current output is that the readers and writers are able to access the shared resource cooperatively and efficiently; all of the readers and writers are executing their instructions, and no thread is being starved by this scheduling algorithm.

Note that as you work with a readers-writers problem in your concurrent program, you do not have to reinvent the wheel regarding the approaches that we just discussed. PyPI actually has an external library called `readerwriterlock` that contains the implementation of the three approaches in Python, as well as support for timeouts. Go to `https://pypi.org/project/readerwriterlock/` to find out more about the library and its documentation.

Solutions to starvation

Through an analysis of different approaches to the readers-writers problem, you have seen the key to solving starvation – since some threads will be starved if they are not given a high priority in accessing the shared resources, implementing fairness in the execution of all of the threads will prevent starvation from occurring. Fairness, in this case, does not require a program to forgo any order or priority that it has imposed on the different threads; but to implement fairness, a program needs to ensure that all threads are given sufficient opportunities to execute their instructions.

Keeping this idea in mind, we can potentially address the problem of starvation by implementing one (or a combination) of the following approaches:

- **Increasing the priority of low-priority threads**: As we did with the writer threads in the second approach and the reader threads in the third approach to the readers-writers problem, prioritizing the threads that would otherwise not have any opportunity to access the shared resource can successfully eliminate starvation.

- **First-in-first-out thread queue**: To ensure that a thread that started waiting for the shared resource before another thread will be able to acquire the resource before the other thread, we can keep track of the threads requesting access in a first-in-first-out queue.

- **Other methods**: Several methods can also be implemented to balance the selection frequency of different threads – for example, a priority queue that also gives gradually increasing priority to threads that have been waiting in the queue for a long time, or if a thread has been able to access the shared resource many times, it will be given less priority.

Solving starvation in your concurrent program can be a rather complex and involved process, and a deep understanding of its scheduling algorithm, combined with an understanding of how processes and threads interact with the shared resources, is necessary during the process. As you saw in the example of the readers-writers problem, it can also take several implementations and revisions of different approaches to arrive at a good solution to starvation.

Summary

In this chapter, we have covered starvation and the specific situations in which it could occur by analyzing different instances of the readers-writers problem. We have gained insight into how starvation can be solved with different scheduling algorithms – by making sure that the priority is distributed appropriately among different processes and threads, starvation can be eliminated. These discussions will serve as a guide to solutions to real-life instances of starvation.

In the next chapter, we will discuss the last of the three common problems of concurrent programming – **race conditions**. We will cover the basic foundation and causes of race conditions, relevant concepts, and the connection of race conditions to other concurrency-related problems.

Questions

1. What is starvation and why is it undesirable in a concurrent program?

2. What are the underlying causes of starvation? What are the common high-level causes of starvation that can manifest from the underlying causes?

3. What is the connection between deadlock and starvation?

4. What is the readers-writers problem?

5. What is the first approach to the readers-writers problem? Why does starvation arise in that situation?

6. What is the second approach to the readers-writers problem? Why does starvation arise in that situation?

7. What is the third approach to the readers-writers problem? Why does it successfully address starvation?

8. What are some common solutions to starvation?

Further reading

- *Parallel Programming with Python, Jan Palach, Packt Publishing Ltd, 2014*

- *Python Parallel Programming Cookbook, Giancarlo Zaccone, Packt Publishing Ltd, 2015*

- *Starvation and Fairness, Jakob Jenkov* (`tutorials.jenkov.com/java-concurrency/starvation-and-fairness`)

- *Faster Fair Solution for the Reader-Writer Problem, V. Popov and O. Mazonka*

14
Race Conditions

In this chapter, we will discuss the concept of **race conditions** and their potential causes in the context of concurrency. The definition of a critical section, which is a concept highly relevant to race conditions and concurrent programming, will also be covered. We will use some example code in Python to simulate race conditions and the solutions that are commonly used to address them. Finally, real-life applications that commonly deal with race conditions will also be discussed.

In this chapter, we will cover the following topics:

- The concept of race conditions
- Simulating race conditions in Python
- Locks as a solution to race conditions
- Race conditions in real life

This chapter, similar to the previous two chapters, offers a closer look at what could go wrong in concurrent programming and exposes us to a wide range of approaches in terms of how to avoid and prevent that. In this chapter, our focus will be on race conditions.

Technical requirements

The code for this chapter can be found in the following GitHub repository: `https://github.com/PacktPublishing/Advanced-Python-Programming-Second-Edition/tree/main/Chapter14`.

The concept of race conditions

Typically, a **race condition** is defined as a phenomenon during which the output of a system is both indeterminate and dependent on the scheduling algorithm and the order in which tasks are scheduled and executed. When data becomes mishandled or corrupted during this process, a race condition becomes a bug in the system. Given the nature of this problem, it is quite common for a race condition to occur in concurrent systems, which emphasizes the importance of scheduling and coordinating independent tasks.

A race condition can occur in both an electronic hardware system and a software application; in this chapter, we will only discuss race conditions in the context of software development – specifically, **concurrent software applications**. This section will cover the theoretical foundations of race conditions and their root causes along with the concept of *critical sections*.

Critical sections

Critical sections indicate shared resources that are accessed by multiple processes or threads in a concurrent application, These can lead to unexpected, and even erroneous, behavior. We have learned that there are multiple methods to protect the integrity of the data contained in these resources, and we call these protected sections *critical sections*.

As you can imagine, the data in these critical sections, when interacted with and altered concurrently or in parallel, can become mishandled or corrupted. This is especially true when the threads and processes interacting with it are poorly coordinated and scheduled. Therefore, the logical conclusion is to not allow multiple agents to go into a critical section at the same time. We call this concept **mutual exclusion**.

In the next subsection, we will discuss the relationship between critical sections and the causes of race conditions.

How race conditions occur

Let's consider a simple concurrent program in order to understand what can give rise to a race condition:

1. Suppose that the program has a shared resource and two separate threads (*thread 1* and *thread 2*) that will access and interact with that resource. Specifically, the shared resource is a number and, as per their respective execution instructions, each thread is to read in that number, increment it by 1, and finally, update the value of the shared resource with the incremented number.

2. Next, suppose that the shared number is originally 2, and then thread 1 accesses and interacts with the number; the shared resource will become 3.

3. After thread 1 successfully alters and exits the resource, thread 2 begins to execute its instructions, and the shared resource that is a number is updated to 4. Throughout this process, the number that was originally 2 was incremented twice (each time by a separate thread) and held a value of 4 at the end. In this case, the shared number was not mishandled or corrupted.

4. Then, imagine a scenario in which the shared number is still 2 at the beginning, yet both of the threads access the number at the same time. Now, each of the threads reads in the number 2 from the shared resource; they each increment the number 2 to 3 individually, and then write the number 3 back to the shared resource. Even though the shared resource was accessed and interacted with twice by a thread, it only held a value of 3 at the end of the process.

This is an example of a race condition occurring in a concurrent program: since the second thread to access a shared resource does it before the first thread finishes its execution (in other words, before writing the new value to the shared resource), the second thread fails to take in the updated resource value. This leads to the fact that when the second thread writes to the resource, the value that is processed and updated by the first thread is overwritten. At the end of the execution of the two threads, the shared resource has, technically, only been updated by the second thread.

The following diagram further illustrates the contrast between a correct data handling process and a situation involving a race condition:

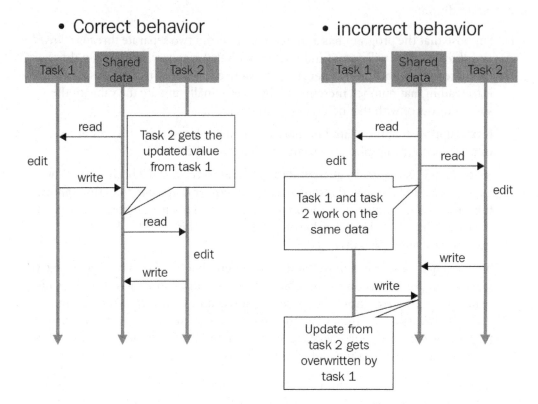

Figure 14.1 – Mishandling shared data

Intuitively, we can see that a race condition results in the mishandling and corruption of data. In the preceding example, we can see that a race condition only occurs with two separate threads accessing a common resource, causing the shared resource to be updated incorrectly and hold an incorrect value at the end of the program. We understand that most real-life concurrent applications contain significantly more threads and processes along with additional shared resources, and the more threads/processes that interact with the shared resource, the more likely it is that a race condition will occur.

Before we discuss a solution that we can implement to solve the problem of race conditions, let's try to simulate the problem in Python.

Simulating race conditions in Python

If you have already downloaded the code for this book from the GitHub page, go ahead and navigate to the `Chapter14` folder.

To simulate a race condition, first, we need a common resource. In this case, it's a counter variable along with multiple threads that can access it simultaneously. Let's take a look at the `Chapter14/example1.py` file—specifically, the `update()` function, as follows:

```python
import random
import time

def update():
    global counter

    current_counter = counter # reading in shared resource
    time.sleep(random.randint(0, 1)) # simulating heavy
    calculations
    counter = current_counter + 1 # updating shared
    resource
```

The goal of the preceding `update()` function is to increment a global variable called `counter`, and it is to be called by a separate thread in our script. Inside the function, we are interacting with a shared resource—in this case, `counter`. Then, we assign the value of `counter` to another local variable, called `current_counter` (this is to simulate the process of reading data from more complex data structures for the shared resources).

Next, we will pause the execution of the function by using the `time.sleep()` method. The length of the period during which the program will be paused is pseudo-randomly chosen between `0` and `1`, generated by the function call, `random.randint(0, 1)`. So, the program will either pause for one second or not at all. Finally, we assign the newly computed value of `current_counter` (which is its one-increment) to the originally shared resource (the `counter` variable).

Now, we can move on to our main program:

```python
import threading

counter = 0

threads = [threading.Thread(target=update) for i in \
    range(20)]
```

```
for thread in threads:
    thread.start()
for thread in threads:
    thread.join()


print(f'Final counter: {counter}.')
print('Finished.')
```

Here, we are initializing the `counter` global variable with a set of `threading.Thread` objects in order to execute the `update()` function concurrently; we are initializing 20 `thread` objects to increment our shared counter 20 times. After starting and joining all of the threads that we have, we can finally print out the end value of our shared `counter` variable.

Theoretically, a well-designed concurrent program will successfully increment the shared counter 20 times in total, and since its original value is 0, the end value of the counter should be 20 at the end of the program. However, as you run this script, the `counter` variable that you obtain will most likely not hold an end value of 20. The following is my output, obtained from running the script:

```
> python3 example1.py
Final counter: 9.
Finished.
```

The preceding output indicates that the counter was only successfully incremented nine times. This is a direct result of the race condition that our concurrent program has. This race condition occurs when a specific thread spends time reading in and processing the data from the shared resource (specifically, for one second using the `time.sleep()` method), and another thread reads in the current value of the `counter` variable, which, at this point, has not been updated by the first thread since it has not completed its execution.

Interestingly, if a thread does not spend any time processing the data (in other words, when 0 is chosen by the pseudo-random `random.randint()` method), the value of the shared resource can potentially be updated just in time for the next thread to read and process it. This phenomenon is illustrated by the fact that the end value of the counter varies within different runs of the program. For example, the following is the output that I obtained after running the script three times. The output from the first run is as follows:

```
> python3 example1.py
Final counter: 9.
Finished.
```

The output from the second run is as follows:

```
> python3 example1.py
Final counter: 12.
Finished.
```

The output from the third run is as follows:

```
> python3 example1.py
Final counter: 5.
Finished.
```

Again, the final value of the counter is dependent on the number of threads that spend one second pausing and the number of threads not pausing at all. Since these two numbers are, in turn, dependent on the `random.randint()` method, the final value of the counter changes between different runs of the program. We will still have a race condition in our program, except for when we can ensure that the final value of the counter is always 20 (that is, the counter is being successfully incremented 20 times in total).

In the next section, we will discuss the most common solution to race conditions: locks.

Locks as a solution to race conditions

Intuitively, since the race conditions that we observed arose when multiple threads or processes accessed and wrote to a shared resource simultaneously, the key idea behind solving race conditions is isolating the executions of different threads/processes, especially when interacting with a shared resource. Specifically, we need to make sure that a thread/process can only access the shared resource after any other threads/processes interacting with the resource have finished their interactions with that resource.

With locks, we can turn a shared resource inside a concurrent program into a critical section, whose integrity of data is guaranteed to be protected. We will see this in action next.

The effectiveness of locks

A critical section guarantees the mutual exclusion of a shared resource and cannot be accessed concurrently by multiple processes or threads; this will prevent any protected data from being updated or altered with conflicting information, resulting from race conditions.

In the following diagram, **Thread B** is blocked from accessing the shared resource—the critical section named var—by a **mutex (mutual exclusion)** lock. This is because **Thread A** is already accessing the resource:

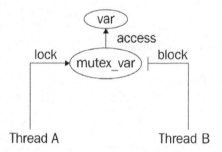

Figure 14.2 – Locks prevent simultaneous access to a critical section

Now, we will specify that, in order to gain access to a critical section in a concurrent program, a thread or process needs to acquire a lock object that is associated with the critical section; similarly, that thread or process also needs to release that lock upon leaving the critical section. This setup will effectively prevent multiple accesses to the critical section and will, therefore, prevent race conditions. The following diagram illustrates the execution flow of multiple threads interacting with multiple critical sections, with the implementation of locks in place:

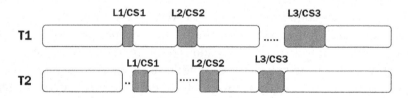

Figure 14.3 – Locks and critical sections in multiple threads

As you can see in the preceding diagram, threads **T1** and **T2** both interact with three critical sections in their respective execution instructions: **CS1**, **CS2**, and **CS3**. Here, **T1** and **T2** attempt to access **CS1** at almost the same time. Additionally, since **CS1** is protected with lock **L1**, only **T1** can acquire lock **L1** and, hence, access/interact with the critical section. In contrast, **T2** has to spend time waiting for **T1** to exit out of the critical section and release the lock before accessing the section itself. Similarly, for the critical sections, **CS2** and **CS3**, although both threads require access to a critical section at the same time, only one can process it, while the other has to wait to acquire the lock associated with the critical section.

Now, let's implement this solution using *Python*.

Implementation in Python

Navigate to the `Chapter14/example2.py` file and consider our corrected `update()` function, as follows:

```
import random
import time


def update():
    global counter

    with count_lock:
        current_counter = counter # reading in shared
        resource
        time.sleep(random.randint(0, 1)) # simulating heavy
        calculations
        counter = current_counter + 1
```

Here, you can see that all of the execution instructions of a thread specified in the `update()` function are under the context manager of a lock object named `count_lock`. So, every time a thread is called to run the function, it will first have to acquire the lock object before any instructions can be executed. In our main program, we simply create the lock object in addition to what we already have, as follows:

```
import threading


counter = 0
count_lock = threading.Lock()


threads = [threading.Thread(target=update) for i in \
    range(20)]


for thread in threads:
    thread.start()
for thread in threads:
    thread.join()


print(f'Final counter: {counter}.')
print('Finished.')
```

Run the program. Your output should look similar to the following:

```
> python3 example2.py
Final counter: 20.
Finished.
```

Here, you can see that the counter was successfully incremented 20 times and held the correct value at the end of the program. Furthermore, no matter how many times the script is executed, the final value of the counter will always be **20**. This is the advantage of using locks to implement critical sections in your concurrent programs.

The downside of locks

In *Chapter 12, Deadlocks*, we covered an interesting phenomenon in which the use of locks can lead to undesirable results. Specifically, we discovered that with enough locks implemented in a concurrent program, the whole program can become sequential. Let's analyze this concept with our current program. Consider the Chapter14/example3.py file, as follows:

```python
import threading
import random; random.seed(0)
import time


def update(pause_period):
    global counter

    with count_lock:
        current_counter = counter # reading in shared
        resource
        time.sleep(pause_period) # simulating heavy
        calculations
        counter = current_counter + 1 # updating shared
        resource

pause_periods = [random.randint(0, 1) for i in range(20)]


###################################################################
```

```python
counter = 0
count_lock = threading.Lock()


start = time.perf_counter()
for i in range(20):
    update(pause_periods[i])


print('--Sequential version--')
print(f'Final counter: {counter}.')
print(f'Took {time.perf_counter() - start : .2f} seconds.')


###############################################################


counter = 0

threads = [threading.Thread(target=update, \
    args=(pause_periods[i],)) for i in range(20)]


start = time.perf_counter()
for thread in threads:
    thread.start()
for thread in threads:
    thread.join()


print('--Concurrent version--')
print(f'Final counter: {counter}.')
print(f'Took {time.perf_counter() - start : .2f} seconds.')


###############################################################


print('Finished.')
```

The goal of this script is to compare the speed of our current concurrent program with its sequential version. Here, we are still using the same update() function, with locks, and we are running it 20 times, both sequentially and concurrently, as we did earlier. Additionally, we are creating a list of determined periods for pausing:

```
pause_periods = [random.randint(0, 1) for i in range(20)]
```

This is so that these periods are consistent between when we simulate the sequential version and when we simulate the concurrent version (for this reason, the update() function now takes in a parameter that specifies the period of pausing each time it is called).

This is the setup we need to simulate the *sequentiality* of a program with many locks, which we will see firsthand in the next subsection.

Turning a concurrent program into a sequential program

Here, we simply call the update() function inside a for loop, with 20 iterations, keeping track of the time it takes for the loop to finish. Note that, even though this is to simulate the sequential version of the program, the update() function still needs the lock object to be created beforehand, so we are initializing it here:

```
counter = 0
count_lock = threading.Lock()

start = time.perf_counter()
for i in range(20):
    update(pause_periods[i])

print('--Sequential version--')
print(f'Final counter: {counter}.')
print(f'Took {time.perf_counter() - start : .2f} seconds.')
```

The last step is to reset the counter and run the concurrent version of the program that we already implemented. Again, we need to pass in the corresponding pause period while initializing each of the threads that run the update() function. Additionally, we are keeping track of the time it takes for this concurrent version of the program to run:

```
counter = 0

threads = [threading.Thread(target=update, \
args=(pause_periods[i],)) for i in range(20)]
```

```
start = time.perf_counter()
for thread in threads:
    thread.start()
for thread in threads:
    thread.join()

print('--Concurrent version--')
print(f'Final counter: {counter}.')
print(f'Took {time.perf_counter() - start : .2f} seconds.')
```

Now, after you have run the script, you will observe that both the sequential version and the concurrent version of our program took the same amount of time to run. Specifically, the following is the output that I obtained; in this case, they both took approximately 12 seconds. The actual time that your program takes might be different, but the speed of the two versions should still be equal:

```
> python3 example3.py
--Sequential version--
Final counter: 20.
Took 12.03 seconds.
--Concurrent version--
Final counter: 20.
Took 12.03 seconds.
Finished.
```

So, our concurrent program is taking just as much time as its sequential version, which negates one of the biggest purposes of implementing concurrency in a program: *improving speed*. But why would concurrent and traditional sequential applications with the same sets of instructions and elements also have the same speed? Should the concurrent program always produce a faster speed than the sequential one?

Recall that, in our program, the critical section is being protected by a lock object, and no multiple threads can access it at the same time. Since the execution of the program (incrementing the counter 20 times) depends on a thread accessing the critical section, the placement of the lock object in the critical section means that only one thread can be executing at any given time. With this specification, the executions of any two threads cannot overlap with each other, and no additional speed can be gained from this implementation of concurrency.

This is the phenomenon that we encountered when analyzing the problem of deadlock: if enough locks are placed in a concurrent program, that program will become entirely sequential. This is the reason why locks are sometimes undesirable solutions to problems in concurrent programming. However, this situation only happens if all of the executions of the concurrent program are dependent upon interacting with the critical section. Most of the time, reading and manipulating the data of a shared resource is only a portion of the entire program; therefore, concurrency still provides the intended additional speed for our program.

An additional aspect of locks is the fact that they do not actually lock anything. We will discuss this point in more detail next.

Locks do not lock anything

The only way that a lock object is utilized, with respect to a specific shared resource, is for the threads and processes interacting with that resource to also interact with the lock. In other words, if those threads and processes choose to not check with the lock before accessing and altering the shared resource, the lock object itself cannot stop them from doing so.

In our examples, you have discovered that to implement the acquiring/releasing process of a lock object, the instructions of a thread or process need to be wrapped around by a lock context manager; this specification is dependent on the implementation of *the thread/ process execution logic* and not the resource. That is because the lock objects that we have seen are not in any way connected to the resources that they are supposed to protect. So, if the thread/process execution logic does not require any interaction with the lock object associated with the shared resource, that thread or process can simply gain access to the resource without difficulty, potentially resulting in the *mismanipulation* and corruption of data.

This is not only true in the scope of having multiple threads and processes in a single concurrent program. Let's suppose that we have a concurrent system consisting of multiple components that all interact and manipulate the data of a resource shared across the system, and this resource is associated with a lock object; it follows that, if any of these components fail to interact with that lock, it can simply bypass the protection implemented by the lock and access the shared resource. More importantly, this characteristic of locks also has implications regarding the security of a concurrent program. If an outside, malicious agent is connected to the system (for instance, a malicious client interacting with a server) and intends to corrupt the data shared across the system, that agent can be instructed to simply ignore the lock object and access that data in an intrusive way.

The view that locks don't lock anything was popularized by Raymond Hettinger, a Python core developer who worked on the implementation of various elements in Python concurrent programming. It is argued that using lock objects alone does not guarantee a secure implementation of concurrent data structures and systems. Locks need to be concretely linked to the resources that they are supposed to protect, and nothing should be able to access a resource without first acquiring the lock that is associated with it. Alternatively, other concurrent synchronization tools, such as atomic message queues can provide a solution to this problem.

You have now learned about the concept of race conditions, how they are caused in concurrent systems, and how to effectively prevent them. In the next section, we will provide an overarching view of how race conditions can occur in real-life examples, within the various subfields of computer science.

Race conditions in real life

In particular, we will discuss the topics of security, file management, and networking. Race conditions don't simply exist in simple, minimal code examples about global counters. They are present in many important tasks such as security, file management, and networking. In this section, we will briefly discuss what some of these examples might look like from a theoretical perspective.

Security

Concurrent programming can have significant implications in terms of the security of the system in question. Recall that a race condition arises between the process of reading and altering the data of a resource; a race condition in an authenticating system can cause the corruption of data between the **time of check** (when the credentials of an agent are checked) and the **time of use** (when the agent can utilize the resource). This problem is also known as a **Time-Of-Check-To-Time-Of-Use** (**TOCTTOU**) bug, which is undoubtedly detrimental to security systems.

The careless protection of shared resources when handling race conditions, as we briefly touched upon in the last section, can provide external agents with access to those supposedly protected resources. Those agents can then change the data of the resources to create **privilege escalation** (simply put, to give themselves illegal access to more shared resources), or they can simply corrupt the data, causing the whole system to malfunction.

Interestingly, race conditions can also be used to implement computer security. As race conditions result from the uncoordinated access of multiple threads/processes to a shared resource, the specification in which a race condition occurs is significantly random. For example, in our Python example, you learned that, when simulating a race condition, the final value of the counter varies between different executions of the program; this is (partly) because of the unpredictable nature of the situation in which multiple threads are running and accessing the shared resources. (I say partly since the randomness also results from the random pausing periods that we generate in each execution of the program.) So, race conditions are sometimes intentionally provoked, and the information obtained when the race condition occurs can be used to generate digital fingerprints for security processes—again, this information is significantly random and is, therefore, valuable for security purposes.

Operating systems

Race conditions can occur in the context of file and memory management in an operating system, when two separate programs attempt to access the same resource, such as memory space. Imagine a situation where two processes from different programs have been running for a significant amount of time, and even though they were originally initialized apart from each other in terms of memory space, enough data has been accumulated and the stack of execution of one process now collides with that of the other process. This can lead to the two processes sharing the same portion of memory space and, ultimately, can result in unpredictable consequences.

Another aspect of the complexity of race conditions is illustrated by version 7 of Unix's operating system — specifically, in the `mkdir` command. Typically, the `mkdir` command is used to create a new directory in the Unix operating system; this is done by calling the `mknod` command to create the actual directory and the `chown` command to specify the owner of that directory. Because there are two separate commands to be run and a definite gap exists between when the first command is finished and the second is called, this can cause a race condition.

During the gap between the two commands, if someone deletes the new directory created by the `mknod` command and links the reference to another file, when the `chown` command is run, the ownership of that file will change. The following diagram further illustrates this exploitation:

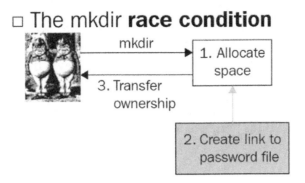

Figure 14.4 – The mkdir race condition

By exploiting this vulnerability, someone can, theoretically, change the ownership of any file in an operating system so that someone can create a new directory.

Networking

In networking, race conditions can take the form of giving multiple users unique privileges in a network. Specifically, let's say a given server should only have exactly one user with admin privileges. If two users, who are both eligible to become the server admin, request access to those privileges at the same time, then it is possible for both of them to gain that access. This is because, at the point when both of the user requests are received by the server, neither of the users have been granted admin privileges yet, and the server thinks that admin privileges can still be given out.

This form of a race condition is quite common when a network is highly optimized for parallel processing (for example, non-blocking sockets), without any careful consideration of the resources shared across the network.

Overall, race conditions can manifest themselves in many important tasks in computer science and engineering, such as security, operating systems, and as we just saw, networking. This requires the concurrency engineer to be extra vigilant about the correctness of their programs.

Summary

A race condition occurs when two or more threads/processes access and alter a shared resource simultaneously, resulting in mishandled and corrupted data. Race conditions also have significant implications in real-life applications, such as security, operating systems, and networking.

In this chapter, we learned how to isolate the execution of different threads/processes to tackle many forms of race conditions. We have examined how to use locks to turn a shared resource into a critical section to protect the integrity of its data. Additionally, we have discussed a number of practical disadvantages when it comes to using locks.

In the next chapter, we will consider one of the biggest problems in Python concurrent programming: the infamous **Global Interpreter Lock (GIL)**. You will learn about the basic idea behind the GIL, its purposes, and how to effectively work with it in concurrent Python applications.

Questions

1. What is a critical section?
2. What is a race condition, and why is it undesirable in a concurrent program?
3. What is the underlying cause of a race condition?
4. How can locks solve the problem of race conditions?
5. Why are locks sometimes undesirable in a concurrent program?
6. What is the significance of race conditions in real-life systems and applications?

Further reading

For more information, please refer to the following resources:

- *Parallel Programming with Python*, by Jan Palach, Packt Publishing Ltd, 2014.
- *Python Parallel Programming Cookbook*, by Giancarlo Zaccone, Packt Publishing Ltd, 2015.
- *Race Conditions and Critical Sections* (`tutorials.jenkov.com/java-concurrency/race-conditions-and-critical-sections`), by Jakob Jenkov.
- *Race conditions, files, and security flaws; or the tortoise and the hare redux*, by Matt Bishop, Technical Report CSE-95-98 (1995).
- *Computer and Information Security, Chapter 11, Software Flaws and Malware 1 Illustration* (`slideplayer.com/slide/10319860/`).

15
The Global Interpreter Lock

One of the major players in Python concurrent programming is the **Global Interpreter Lock (GIL)**. In this chapter, we will cover a definition and the purposes of the GIL and how it affects concurrent Python applications. The problems that the GIL poses for Python concurrent systems and the controversy around its implementation will also be discussed. Finally, we will mention some thoughts on how Python programmers and developers should think about, and interact with, the GIL.

The following topics will be covered in this chapter:

- Introducing the GIL
- The potential removal of the GIL from Python
- Working with the GIL

While our discussions in this chapter will mostly be theoretical, we will be able to gain a deep insight into the ecosystem of concurrent programming in Python.

Technical requirements

The code for this chapter can be found in the following GitHub repository:

```
https://github.com/PacktPublishing/Advanced-Python-
Programming-Second-Edition/tree/main/Chapter15
```

Introducing the GIL

The GIL is quite popular in the Python concurrent programming community. Designed as a lock that will only allow one thread to access and control the Python interpreter at any given time, the GIL in Python is often known as *the infamous GIL* that prevents multithreaded programs from reaching their fully optimized speed.

In this section, we will discuss the concept behind the GIL, as well as its purpose: why it was designed and implemented and how it affects multithreaded programming in Python.

Analyzing memory management in Python

Before we jump into the specifics of the GIL and its effects, let's consider the problems that Python core developers encountered during the early days of Python that gave rise to a need for the GIL. Specifically, there is a significant difference between Python programming and programming in other popular languages, in terms of managing objects in the memory space.

For example, in the programming language C++, a variable is actually a location in the memory space where a value will be written. This setup leads to the fact that, when a non-pointer variable is assigned with a specific value, the programming language will effectively copy that specific value to the memory location (that is, the **variable**). Additionally, when a variable is assigned with another variable (that is not a pointer), the memory location of the latter will be copied to that of the former; no further connection between these two variables will be maintained after the assignment.

On the other hand, Python considers a variable as simply a name, while the actual values of its variables are isolated in another region in the memory space. When a value is assigned to a variable, the variable is effectively given a reference to the location in the memory space of the value (even though the term *referencing* is not used in the same sense as C++ referencing). Memory management in Python is, therefore, fundamentally different from the model of putting a value into a memory space that we see in C++.

This means that when an assignment instruction is executed, Python simply interacts with references and switches them around—not the actual values themselves. Also, for this reason, multiple variables can be referenced by the same value, and the changes made by one variable will be reflected throughout all of the other associated variables.

Let's analyze this feature in Python. If you have already downloaded the code for this book from the GitHub page, go ahead and navigate to the Chapter15 folder. Let's take a look at the Chapter15/example1.py file here:

```python
import sys

print(f'Reference count when direct-referencing:  \
    {sys.getrefcount([7])}.')

a = [7]
print(f'Reference count when referenced once:  \
    {sys.getrefcount(a)}.')

b = a
print(f'Reference count when referenced twice:  \
    {sys.getrefcount(a)}.')

################################################################

a[0] = 8
print(f'Variable a after a is changed: {a}.')
print(f'Variable b after a is changed: {b}.')

print('Finished.')
```

In this example, we are looking at the management of the value [7] (a list of one element: the integer 7). We mentioned that values in Python are stored independently of variables, and value management in Python simply references variables to the appropriate values. The sys.getrefcount() method in Python takes in an object and returns the counter of all references that the value associated with that object has. Here, we are calling sys.getrefcount() three times: on the actual value, [7]; the variable a that is assigned the value; and finally, the variable b that is assigned with the variable a.

Additionally, we are exploring the process of mutating the value by using a variable referenced with it and the resulting values of all of the variables associated with that value. Specifically, we are mutating the first element of the list via variable a, and printing out the values of both a and b. Run the script, and your output should be similar to this:

```
> python3 example1.py
Reference count when direct-referencing: 1.
Reference count when referenced once: 2.
Reference count when referenced twice: 3.
Variable a after a is changed: [8].
Variable b after a is changed: [8].
Finished.
```

As you can see, this output is consistent with what we discussed as the following ways:

1. For the first sys.getrefcount() function call, there is only one reference count for the value [7], which is created when we directly reference it.

2. When we assign the list to variable a, the value has two references, since a is now associated with the value.

3. Finally, when a is assigned to b, [7] is additionally referenced by b, and the reference count is now 3.

4. In the output of the second part of the program, we can see that when we changed the value of the variable that a references, [7] was mutated instead of variable a. As a result, variable b, which was referencing the same value as a, also had its value changed.

The following diagram illustrates this process:

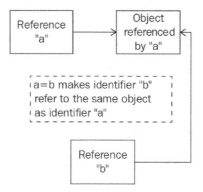

Figure 15.1 – Diagram of Python's referencing scheme

Overall, in Python programs, variables simply make references to the actual values (objects), and an assignment statement between two variables makes the two variables reference the same object, as opposed to copying the actual value to another memory location, as in C++.

The problem that the GIL addresses

Keeping Python's implementation of memory and variable management in mind, we can see references to a given value in Python are constantly changing in a program, and keeping track of the reference count for a value is therefore highly important.

Now, applying what you learned in *Chapter 14, Race Conditions*, you should know that in a Python concurrent program, this reference count is a shared resource that needs protection from race conditions. In other words, this reference count is a critical section that, if handled carelessly, will result in an incorrect interpretation of how many variables are referencing a particular value. This will cause memory leaks that will make Python programs significantly inefficient and may even release a memory that is actually being referenced by some variables, losing that value forever.

As you learned in the previous chapter, a solution to making sure that race conditions will not occur with regard to a particular shared resource is to place a lock on that resource, effectively allowing one thread, at the most, to access the resource at any given time within a concurrent program. We also discussed that if enough locks are placed in a concurrent program, that program will become entirely sequential, and no additional speed will be gained by implementing concurrency.

The GIL is a solution to the combination of the two preceding problems, being one single lock on the entire execution of Python. The GIL must first be acquired by any Python instruction that wants to be executed (**central processing unit** (**CPU**)-bound tasks), preventing a race condition from occurring for any reference count.

In the early days of the development of the Python language, other solutions to the problem described here were also proposed, but the GIL was the most efficient and simple to implement, by far. Since the GIL is a lightweight, overarching lock for the entire execution of Python, no other lock needs to be implemented to guarantee the integrity of other critical sections, keeping the performance overhead of Python programs at a minimum.

Problems raised by the GIL

Intuitively, with a lock guarding all CPU-bound tasks in Python, a concurrent program will not be able to become fully multithreading. The GIL effectively prevents CPU-bound tasks from being executed in parallel across multiple threads. To understand the effect of this feature of the GIL, let's consider an example in Python. Navigate to `Chapter15/example2.py`, which has the following content:

```python
import time
import threading

COUNT = 50000000

def countdown(n):
    while n > 0:
        n -= 1

###################################################################

start = time.time()
countdown(COUNT)

print('Sequential program finished.')
print(f'Took {time.time() - start : .2f} seconds.')

###################################################################

thread1 = threading.Thread(target=countdown, args=( \
    COUNT // 2,))
thread2 = threading.Thread(target=countdown, args=( \
    COUNT // 2,))

start = time.time()
thread1.start()
thread2.start()
thread1.join()
```

```
thread2.join()


print('Concurrent program finished.')
print(f'Took {time.time() - start : .2f} seconds.')
```

In this example, we are comparing the speed of executing a particular program in Python sequentially and concurrently, via multithreading. Specifically, we have a function named countdown() that simulates a heavy CPU-bound task, which takes in a number, n, and decrements it until it becomes zero or negative. We then call countdown() on 50,000,000 once, as a sequential program. Finally, we call the function twice, each in a separate thread, on 25,000,000, which is exactly half of 50,000,000; this is the multithreading version of the program. We are also keeping track of the time it takes for Python to run both the sequential program and the multithreading program.

Theoretically, the multithreading version of the program should take half as long as the sequential version, as the task is effectively being split in half and run in parallel, via the two threads that we created. However, the output produced by the program would suggest otherwise. The following output is what I obtained through running the script:

```
> python3 example2.py
Sequential program finished.
Took 2.80 seconds.
Concurrent program finished.
Took 2.74 seconds.
```

Contrary to what we predicted, the concurrent version of the countdown took almost as long as the sequential version; multithreading did not offer any considerable speedup for our program. This is a direct effect of having the GIL guarding CPU-bound tasks, as multiple threads are not allowed to run simultaneously. Sometimes, a multithreading program can take even longer to complete its execution than its sequential counterpart, since there is also the overhead of acquiring and releasing the GIL.

This is undoubtedly a significant problem for multithreading, and for concurrent programming in Python in general, because as long as a program contains CPU-bound instructions, those instructions will, in fact, be sequential in the execution of the program. However, instructions that are not CPU-bound happen outside the GIL, and thus they are not affected by the GIL (for example, **input/output (I/O)**-bound instructions).

With these problems identified, let's next see what the infamous GIL is.

The potential removal of the GIL from Python

You have learned that the GIL sets a significant constraint on our multithreading programs in Python, especially those with CPU-bound tasks. For this reason, many Python developers have come to view the GIL in a negative light, and the term *the infamous GIL* has started to become popular. It is not surprising, then, that some have even advocated the complete removal of the GIL from the Python language.

In fact, multiple attempts to remove the GIL have been made by prominent Python users. However, the GIL is so deeply implanted in the implementation of the language, and the execution of most libraries and packages that are not thread-safe is so significantly dependent on the GIL, that the removal of the GIL will actually engender bugs as well as backward-incompatibility issues for your Python programs. A number of Python developers and researchers tried to completely omit the GIL from Python execution, and most existing C extensions, which depend heavily on the functionalities of the GIL, stopped working.

Now, there are other viable solutions to address the problems that we have discussed; in other words, the GIL is in every way replaceable. However, most of these solutions contain so many complex instructions that they actually decrease the performance of sequential and I/O-bound programs, which are not affected by the GIL. So, these solutions will slow down single-threaded or multithreaded I/O programs, which actually make up a large percentage of existing Python applications. Interestingly, the creator of Python, Guido van Rossum, also commented on this topic in his article *It isn't Easy to Remove the GIL*, as follows:

> *"I'd welcome a set of patches into Py3k only if the performance for a single-threaded program (and for a multi-threaded but I/O-bound program) does not decrease."*

Unfortunately, this request has not been achieved by any of the proposed alternatives to the GIL. The GIL remains an integral part of the Python language.

With this covered, let's now see how to work with the GIL.

Working with the GIL

There are a few ways to deal with the GIL in your Python applications, and these will be addressed in the following sections.

Implementing multiprocessing, rather than multithreading

This is perhaps the most popular and easiest method to circumvent the GIL and achieve optimal speed in a concurrent program. As the GIL only prevents multiple threads from executing CPU-bound tasks simultaneously, processes executing over multiple cores of a system, each having its own memory space, are completely immune to the GIL.

Specifically, considering the preceding countdown example, let's compare the performance of that CPU-bound program when it is sequential, multithreading, and multiprocessing. Navigate to the Chapter15/example3.py file. The first part of the program is identical to what we saw earlier, but at the end, we add in an implementation of a multiprocessing solution for the problem of counting down from 50,000,000, using two separate processes, as follows:

```python
COUNT = 50000000

def countdown(n):
    while n > 0:
        n -= 1

if __name__ == '__main__':

    ###################################################
    # Sequential

    start = time.time()
    countdown(COUNT)

    ###################################################
    # Multithreading

    thread1 = threading.Thread(target=countdown, \
        args=(COUNT // 2,))
    thread2 = threading.Thread(target=countdown, \
        args=(COUNT // 2,))
```

```
start = time.time()
thread1.start()
thread2.start()
thread1.join()
thread2.join()


##########################################################

# Multiprocessing

pool = Pool(processes=2)
start = time.time()
pool.apply_async(countdown, args=(COUNT//2,))
pool.apply_async(countdown, args=(COUNT//2,))
pool.close()
pool.join()
```

After running the program, this was my output:

```
> python3 example3.py
Sequential program finished.
Took 2.95 seconds.

Multithreading program finished.
Took 2.69 seconds.

Multiprocessing program finished.
Took 1.54 seconds.
```

There is still a minimal difference in speed between the sequential and multithreading versions of the program. However, the multiprocessing version was able to cut that speed by almost half in its execution. As discussed in earlier chapters, since processes are fairly heavyweight, multiprocessing instructions contain significant overhead, which is the reason why the speed of the multiprocessing program was not exactly half of the sequential program.

Getting around the GIL with native extensions

There are Python-native extensions that are written in C/C++ and are therefore able to avoid the limitations that the GIL sets out; one example is the most popular Python scientific computing package, NumPy. Within these extensions, manual releases of the GIL can be made so that the execution can simply bypass the lock. However, these releases need to be implemented carefully and accompanied by the reassertion of the GIL before the execution goes back to the main Python execution.

Utilizing a different Python interpreter

The GIL only exists in CPython, which is the most common interpreter for the language by far and is built in C. However, there are other interpreters for Python, such as Jython (written in Java) and IronPython (written in C++), that can be used to avoid the GIL and its effects on multithreading programs. Keep in mind that these interpreters are not as widely used as CPython, and some packages and libraries might not be compatible with one or both of what? please clarify.

Summary

While the GIL in Python offers a simple and intuitive solution to one of the more difficult problems in the language, it also raises a number of problems of its own, concerning the ability to run multiple threads in a Python program to process CPU-bound tasks. Multiple attempts have been made to remove the GIL from the main implementation of Python, but none has been able to achieve it while maintaining the effectiveness of processing non-CPU-bound tasks, which are affected by the GIL.

Overall, we have discussed practical methods that make working with the GIL easier. We have also learned that while it possesses considerable notoriety among the Python community, the GIL only affects a certain portion of the ecosystem. This should better inform our opinion about the GIL.

In the last four chapters, we discussed some of the most well-known and common problems in concurrent programming in Python. For the remainder of the book, we will be looking at a different topic—advanced design patterns in Python. In the next chapter, we will start with the *factory* pattern.

Questions

1. What are the differences in memory management between Python and C++?

2. Which problem does the GIL solve for Python?

3. Which problem does the GIL create for Python?

4. What are some of the approaches to circumventing the GIL in Python programs?

Further reading

For more information, you can refer to the following sources:

- *What Is the Python Global Interpreter Lock (GIL)?* (realpython.com/python-gil/), *Abhinav Ajitsaria*

- *The Python GIL Visualized* (dabeaz.blogspot.com/2010/01/python-gil-visualized), *Dave Beazley*

- *Copy Operations in Python* (pythontic.com/modules/copy/introduction)

- *It isn't Easy to Remove the GIL* (www.artima.com/weblogs/viewpost.jsp?thread=214235), *Guido van Rossum*

- *Parallel Programming with Python*, by *Jan Palach, Packt Publishing Ltd* (2014)

- *Learning Concurrency in Python: Build highly efficient, robust, and concurrent applications, Elliot Forbes* (2017)

Section 3: Design Patterns in Python

Design patterns offer specialized design solutions to various software engineering problems, making software resilient, scalable, and robust. The chapters in Section 3 iterate through a wide-ranging collection of design patterns, preparing you for most software engineering use cases in the real world.

This section contains the following chapters:

- *Chapter 16, The Factory Pattern*
- *Chapter 17, The Builder Pattern*
- *Chapter 18, Other Creational Patterns*
- *Chapter 19, The Adapter Pattern*
- *Chapter 20, The Decorator Pattern*
- *Chapter 21, The Bridge Pattern*
- *Chapter 22, The Façade Pattern*
- *Chapter 23, Other Structural Patterns*
- *Chapter 24, The Chain of Responsibility Pattern*
- *Chapter 25, The Command Pattern*
- *Chapter 26, The Observer Pattern*

16
The Factory Pattern

Design patterns are reusable programming solutions that have been used in various real-world contexts and have proved to produce the expected results. In this chapter, we will learn about one of the most common design patterns: the factory design pattern. As we will see later, this pattern makes it easier to track which objects are created within a program, thus separating the code that creates an object from the code that uses it. We will study the factory design pattern's two forms: the **factory method** and the **abstract method**.

In this chapter, we will cover the following topics:

- Understanding design patterns
- Implementing the factory method
- Applying the abstract factory

By the end of this chapter, we will have gained a deep understanding of the factory design pattern and its benefits via a hands-on example.

Technical requirements

The code files for this chapter can be found at `https://github.com/PacktPublishing/Advanced-Python-Programming-Second-Edition/tree/main/Chapter16`.

Understanding design patterns

Design patterns are shared among programmers and continue to be improved over time. This topic is popular thanks to the book by Erich Gamma, Richard Helm, Ralph Johnson, and John Vlissides, titled *Design Patterns: Elements of Reusable Object-Oriented Software*.

> **Gang of Four**
>
> The book by Erich Gamma, Richard Helm, Ralph Johnson, and John Vlissides is also called the *Gang of Four* book for short (or the *GOF* book for an even shorter name).

Generally, a design pattern helps the programmer create a commonly used implementation pattern, especially in **object-oriented programming (OOP)**. The benefits of viewing applications from the design pattern's perspective are plenty. First, it narrows down the most effective ways of building a given application and the necessary steps to do it. Second, you could consult existing examples of the same design pattern to improve your application. Overall, design patterns are highly useful guidelines in software engineering.

There are several categories of design patterns that are used in OOP, depending on the type of problem they address and/or the types of solutions they help us build. In their book, the *Gang of Four* presents 23 design patterns, split into three categories: **creational**, **structural**, and **behavioral**.

Creational design patterns are the first category we will cover in this chapter; *Chapter 17, The Builder Pattern*, and *Chapter 18, Other Creational Patterns*, will cover the latter. These patterns deal with different aspects of object creation. Their goal is to provide better alternatives for situations where direct object creation, which in Python happens within the `__init__()` function, is not convenient.

> **Important Note**
>
> See `https://docs.python.org/3/tutorial/classes.html` for a quick overview of object classes and the special `__init__()` method that Python uses to initialize a new class instance.

We will start with the first creational design pattern from the *Gang of Four* book: the **factory design pattern**. In the factory design pattern, a **client** (meaning client code) asks for an object without knowing where the object is coming from (that is, which class is used to generate it). The idea behind a factory is to simplify the object creation process. It is easier to track which objects are created if this is done through a central function, compared to letting a client create objects using a direct class instantiation. A factory reduces the complexity of maintaining an application by decoupling the code that creates an object from the code that uses it.

Factories typically come in two forms: the **factory method**, which is a method (or simply a function for a Python developer) that returns a different object per input parameter, and the **abstract factory**, which is a group of factory methods that are used to create a family of related objects.

That is all the theory we need to get started. In the next section, we will discuss the factory method.

Implementing the factory method

The factory method is based on a single function that's written to handle our object creation task. We execute it, passing a parameter that provides information about what we want. As a result, the object we wanted is created.

Interestingly, when we use the factory method, we don't need to know any details about how the resulting object is implemented and where it is coming from. First, we will discuss some real-life applications that use the factory method and then implement an example application that processes XML and JSON files.

Real-world examples

An example of the factory method pattern that's used in real life is in the context of a plastic toy construction kit. The molding material that's used to construct plastic toys is the same, but different toys (different figures or shapes) can be produced using the right plastic molds. This is like having a factory method in which the input is the name of the toy that we want (for example, `duck` or `car`) and the output (after the molding) is the plastic toy that was requested.

In the software world, the *Django* web framework uses the factory method pattern to create the fields of a web form. The `forms` module, which is included in Django, supports the ability to create different kinds of fields (for example, `CharField`, `EmailField`, and so on). Parts of their behavior can be customized using attributes such as `max_length` or `required` (`j.mp/djangofac`).

Consider the following example:

```
from django import forms

class PersonForm(forms.Form):
    name = forms.CharField(max_length=100)
    birth_date = forms.DateField(required=False)
```

The preceding code could be written by a developer for a form (the `PersonForm` form, which contains the `name` and `birth_date` fields) as part of a Django application's UI code.

Use cases

If you realize that you cannot track the objects that are created by your application because the code that creates them is in many different places instead of in a single function/method, you should consider using the factory method pattern. The factory method centralizes object creation and tracking your objects becomes much easier. Note that it is absolutely fine to create more than one factory method, and this is how it is typically done in practice. Each factory method logically groups objects that have similarities. For example, one factory method might be responsible for connecting you to different databases (MySQL and SQLite), another factory method might be responsible for creating the geometrical object that you've requested (circle and triangle), and so on.

The factory method is also useful when you want to decouple object creation from object usage. We are not coupled/bound to a specific class when creating an object; we just provide partial information about what we want by calling a function. This means that introducing changes to the function is easy and does not require any changes to be made to the code that uses it.

Another use case worth mentioning is related to improving the performance and memory usage of an application. A factory method can improve performance and memory usage by creating new objects only if it is necessary. When we create objects using a direct class instantiation, extra memory is allocated every time a new object is created (unless the class uses caching internally, which is usually not the case). We can see that, in practice, in the following code (in the `id.py` file), it creates two instances of the same class, A, and uses the `id()` function to compare their **memory addresses**. These addresses are also printed in the output so that we can inspect them. The fact that the memory addresses are different means that two distinct objects are created, as follows:

```python
class A:
    pass


if __name__ == '__main__':
    a = A()
    b = A()
    print(id(a) == id(b))
    print(a, b)
```

Executing the `python id.py` command on my computer results in the following output:

```
False
<__main__.A object at 0x7f5771de8f60> <__main__.A object at
0x7f5771df2208>
```

Note that the addresses that you see if you execute the file are not the same as the ones I can see because they depend on the current memory layout and allocation. But the result must be the same: the two addresses should be different. There's one exception that happens if you write and execute the code in the Python **Read-Eval-Print Loop** (REPL) – or, simply put, the interactive prompt – but that's a REPL-specific optimization that does not happen normally.

Implementing the factory method

Data comes in many forms. There are two main file categories for storing/retrieving data: human-readable files and binary files. Examples of human-readable files include XML, RSS/Atom, YAML, and JSON. Examples of binary files include the `.sq3` file format that's used by SQLite and the `.mp3` audio file format, which is used to listen to music.

In this example, we will focus on two popular human-readable formats: **XML** and **JSON**. Although human-readable files are generally slower to parse than binary files, they make data exchange, inspection, and modification much easier. For this reason, it is advised that you work with human-readable files unless other restrictions do not allow it (mainly unacceptable performance and proprietary binary formats).

In this case, we have some input data stored in an XML file and a JSON file, and we want to parse them and retrieve some information. At the same time, we want to centralize the client's connection to those (and all future) external services. We will use the factory method to solve this problem. This example focuses only on XML and JSON but adding support for more services should be straightforward.

First, let's take a look at the data files.

The JSON file, `movies.json`, which can be found in the `data` subfolder of this chapter's code folder, is an example of a dataset containing information about American movies (title, year, director name, genre, and so on). This is a big file but here is a portion of its content to illustrate how its content is organized:

```
[
  {"title":"After Dark in Central Park",
   "year":1900,
   "director":null, "cast":null, "genre":null},
```

```
{"title":"Boarding School Girls' Pajama Parade",
 "year":1900,
 "director":null, "cast":null, "genre":null},
{"title":"Buffalo Bill's Wild West Parad",
 "year":1900,
 "director":null, "cast":null, "genre":null},
{"title":"Caught",
 "year":1900,
 "director":null, "cast":null, "genre":null},
{"title":"Clowns Spinning Hats",
 "year":1900,
 "director":null, "cast":null, "genre":null},
 ...
 ]
```

The XML file, person.xml, is based on a Wikipedia example (j.mp/wikijson) and contains information about individuals (firstName, lastName, gender, and so on), as follows:

1. We start with the enclosing tag of the persons XML container:

```
<persons>
```

2. Then, an XML element representing a person's data code is presented, as follows:

```
<person>
  <firstName>John</firstName>
  <lastName>Smith</lastName>
  <age>25</age>
  <address>
    <streetAddress>21 2nd Street</streetAddress>
    <city>New York</city>
    <state>NY</state>
    <postalCode>10021</postalCode>
  </address>
  <phoneNumbers>
    <phoneNumber type="home">
      212 555-1234</phoneNumber>
    <phoneNumber type="fax">646 555-4567</phoneNumber>
```

```
    </phoneNumbers>
    <gender>
      <type>male</type>
    </gender>
  </person>
```

3. An XML element representing another person's data must then be provided:

```
  <person>
    <firstName>Jimy</firstName>
    <lastName>Liar</lastName>
    <age>19</age>
    <address>
      <streetAddress>18 2nd Street</streetAddress>
      <city>New York</city>
      <state>NY</state>
      <postalCode>10021</postalCode>
    </address>
    <phoneNumbers>
    <phoneNumber type="home">212 555-1234</phoneNumber>
    </phoneNumbers>
    <gender>
      <type>male</type>
    </gender>
  </person>
```

4. An XML element representing a third person's data is then shown:

```
  <person>
    <firstName>Patty</firstName>
    <lastName>Liar</lastName>
    <age>20</age>
    <address>
      <streetAddress>18 2nd Street</streetAddress>
      <city>New York</city>
      <state>NY</state>
      <postalCode>10021</postalCode>
    </address>
```

```
<phoneNumbers>
  <phoneNumber type="home">
    212 555-1234</phoneNumber>
  <phoneNumber type="mobile">
    001 452-8819</phoneNumber>
</phoneNumbers>
<gender>
  <type>female</type>
</gender>
</person>
```

5. Finally, we must close the XML container:

```
</persons>
```

6. We will use two libraries that are part of the Python distribution for working with JSON and XML, json and xml.etree.ElementTree, as follows:

```
import json
import xml.etree.ElementTree as etree
```

7. The JSONDataExtractor class parses the JSON file and has a parsed_data() method that returns all the data as a dictionary (dict). The property decorator is used to make parsed_data() appear as a normal attribute instead of a method, as follows:

```
class JSONDataExtractor:
  def __init__(self, filepath):
    self.data = dict()
    with open(filepath, mode='r', encoding='utf-8') as
    f:self.data = json.load(f)
  @property
  def parsed_data(self):
      return self.data
```

8. The XMLDataExtractor class parses the XML file and has a parsed_data() method that returns all the data as a list of xml.etree.Element, as follows:

```
class XMLDataExtractor:
  def __init__(self, filepath):
    self.tree =  etree.parse(filepath)
```

```
@property
def parsed_data(self):
    return self.tree
```

9. The `dataextraction_factory()` function is a factory method. It returns an instance of `JSONDataExtractor` or `XMLDataExtractor`, depending on the extension of the input file path, as follows:

```
def dataextraction_factory(filepath):
    if filepath.endswith('json'):
        extractor = JSONDataExtractor
    elif filepath.endswith('xml'):
        extractor = XMLDataExtractor
    else:
        raise ValueError('Cannot extract data from
            {}'.format(filepath))
    return extractor(filepath)
```

10. The `extract_data_from()` function is a wrapper of `dataextraction_factory()`. It adds exception handling, as follows:

```
def extract_data_from(filepath):
    factory_obj = None
    try:
        factory_obj = dataextraction_factory(filepath)
    except ValueError as e:
        print(e)
    return factory_obj
```

11. The `main()` function demonstrates how the factory method design pattern can be used. The first part makes sure that exception handling is effective, as follows:

```
def main():
    sqlite_factory =
      extract_data_from('data/person.sq3')
    print()
```

12. The next part shows how to work with the JSON files using the factory method. Based on the parsing, the title, year, director name, and genre of the movie can be shown (when the value is not empty), as follows:

```
json_factory = extract_data_from('data/movies.json')
json_data = json_factory.parsed_data
print(f'Found: {len(json_data)} movies')
for movie in json_data:
    print(f"Title: {movie['title']}")
    year = movie['year']
    if year:
    print(f"Year: {year}")
    director = movie['director']
    if director:
    print(f"Director: {director}")
    genre = movie['genre']
    if genre:
    print(f"Genre: {genre}")
    print()
```

13. The final part shows you how to work with the XML files using the factory method. XPath is used to find all the person elements that have Liar as the last name (using liars = xml_data.findall(f".//person[lastName='Liar']")). For each matched person, their basic name and phone number information is shown, as follows:

```
xml_factory = extract_data_from('data/person.xml')
xml_data = xml_factory.parsed_data
liars =
    xml_data.findall(f".//person[lastName='Liar']")
print(f'found: {len(liars)} persons')
for liar in liars:
    firstname = liar.find('firstName').text
    print(f'first name: {firstname}')
    lastname = liar.find('lastName').text
    print(f'last name: {lastname}')
    [print(f"phone number ({p.attrib['type']}):",
        p.text)
```

```
        for p in liar.find('phoneNumbers')]
    print()
```

Here is the summary of the implementation (you can find the code in the `factory_method.py` file):

1. We start by importing the modules we need (`json` and `ElementTree`).

2. We define the JSON data extractor class (`JSONDataExtractor`).

3. We define the XML data extractor class (`XMLDataExtractor`).

4. We add the factory function, `dataextraction_factory()`, to get the right data extractor class.

5. We also add our wrapper for handling exceptions – the `extract_data_from()` function.

6. Finally, we have the `main()` function, followed by Python's conventional trick for calling it when invoking this file from the command line. The following are the aspects of the `main` function:

   - We try to extract data from a SQL file (`data/person.sq3`) to show how the exception is handled.

   - We extract data from a JSON file and parse the result.

   - We extract data from an XML file and parse the result.

The following is the type of output (for the different cases) you will get by calling the `python factory_method.py` command.

First, there is an exception message that you'll see when you try to access a SQLite (`.sq3`) file:

```
Cannot extract data from data/person.sq3
```

Then, we get the following result from processing the `movies` file (JSON):

```
Found: 9 movies
Title: After Dark in Central Park
Year: 1900

Title: Boarding School Girls' Pajama Parade
Year: 1900
```

```
Title: Buffalo Bill's Wild West Parad
Year: 1900


Title: Caught
Year: 1900


Title: Clowns Spinning Hats
Year: 1900


Title: Capture of Boer Battery by British
Year: 1900
Director: James H. White
Genre: Short documentary


Title: The Enchanted Drawing
Year: 1900
Director: J. Stuart Blackton


Title: Family Troubles
Year: 1900


Title: Feeding Sea Lions
Year: 1900
```

Finally, we get this result from processing the person XML file to find the people whose last name is Liar:

```
found: 2 persons
first name: Jimy
last name: Liar
phone number (home): 212 555-1234


first name: Patty
last name: Liar
phone number (home): 212 555-1234
phone number (mobile): 001 452-8819
```

Notice that although `JSONDataExtractor` and `XMLDataExtractor` have the same interfaces, what is returned by `parsed_data()` is not handled uniformly. Different Python code must be used to work with each **data extractor**. Although it would be nice to be able to use the same code for all extractors, this is not realistic for the most part, unless we use some kind of common mapping for the data, which is often provided by external data providers. A useful exercise would be to assume that you can use the same code to handle the XML and JSON files and see what changes are required to support a third format, such as SQLite. Find a SQLite file or create your own and try it.

At this point, we have learned about the factory method, which, again, is the first form of the factory design pattern. In the next section, we will talk about the second: the abstract factory design pattern.

Applying the abstract factory

The abstract factory design pattern is a generalization of the factory method. An abstract factory is a (logical) group of factory methods, where each factory method is responsible for generating a different kind of object.

In this section, we are going to discuss some examples, use cases, and a possible implementation of this pattern.

Real-world examples

The abstract factory is used in car manufacturing. The same machinery is used for stamping the parts (doors, panels, hoods, fenders, and mirrors) of different car models. The model that is assembled by the machinery is configurable and easy to change at any time.

In the software category, the `factory_boy` (https://github.com/FactoryBoy/factory_boy) package provides an abstract factory implementation for creating Django models in tests. It is used to create instances of models that support **test-specific attributes**. This is important because, this way, your tests become readable, and you avoid sharing unnecessary code.

> **Important Note**
> Django models are special classes that are used by the framework to help store and interact with data in the database (tables). See the Django documentation (`https://docs.djangoproject.com`) for more details.

Use cases

Since the abstract factory pattern is a generalization of the factory method pattern, it offers the same benefits, it makes tracking an object creation easier, it decouples object creation from object usage, and it gives us the potential to improve the memory usage and performance of our application.

But a question is raised: *How do we know when to use the factory method versus using an abstract factory?* The answer is that we usually start with the factory method, which is simpler. If we find out that our application requires many factory methods, which it makes sense to combine to create a family of objects, we end up with an abstract factory.

A benefit of the abstract factory that is usually not very visible from a user's point of view when they're using the factory method is that we can modify the behavior of our application dynamically (at runtime) by changing the active factory method. The classic example is the ability to change the look and feel of an application (for example, Apple-like, Windows-like, and so on) for the user while the application is in use, without the need to terminate it and start it again.

Implementing the abstract factory pattern

To demonstrate the abstract factory pattern, I will reuse one of my favorite examples, which is included in the book *Python 3 Patterns, Recipes, and Idioms*, by Bruce Eckel. Imagine that we are creating a game, or we want to include a mini-game as part of our application to entertain our users. We want to include at least two games – one for children and one for adults. We will decide which game to create and launch at runtime, based on user input. An abstract factory takes care of the game creation part.

Let's start with the kid's game. It is called *FrogWorld*. The main hero is a frog who enjoys eating bugs. Every hero needs a good name, and in our case, the name is given by the user at runtime. The `interact_with()` method is used to describe how the frog interacts with an obstacle (for example, a bug, a puzzle, and other frogs), as follows:

```python
class Frog:
    def __init__(self, name):
        self.name = name

    def __str__(self):
        return self.name

    def interact_with(self, obstacle):
        act = obstacle.action()
```

```
                msg = f'{self} the Frog encounters {obstacle}
            and {act}!'
        print(msg)
```

There can be many different kinds of obstacles but for our example, an obstacle can only be a bug. When the frog encounters a bug, only one action is supported. It eats it:

```
class Bug:
    def __str__(self):
        return 'a bug'

    def action(self):
        return 'eats it'
```

The `FrogWorld` class is an abstract factory. Its main responsibilities are creating the main character and the obstacle(s) in the game. Keeping the creation methods separate and their names generic (for example, `make_character()` and `make_obstacle()`) allows us to change the active factory (and therefore the active game) dynamically without making any code changes. In a statically typed language, the abstract factory would be an abstract class/interface with empty methods, but in Python, this is not required because the types are checked at runtime (`j.mp/ginstromdp`). The code is as follows:

```
class FrogWorld:
    def __init__(self, name):
        print(self)
        self.player_name = name

    def __str__(self):
        return '\n\n\t------ Frog World -------'

    def make_character(self):
        return Frog(self.player_name)

    def make_obstacle(self):
        return Bug()
```

The *WizardWorld* game is similar. The only difference is that the wizard battles against monsters such as orcs instead of eating bugs!

Here is the definition of the `Wizard` class, which is similar to the `Frog` one:

```python
class Wizard:
    def __init__(self, name):
        self.name = name

    def __str__(self):
        return self.name

    def interact_with(self, obstacle):
        act = obstacle.action()
        msg = f'{self} the Wizard battles against
          {obstacle} and {act}!'
        print(msg)
```

Then, the definition of the `Ork` class is as follows:

```python
class Ork:
    def __str__(self):
        return 'an evil ork'

    def action(self):
        return 'kills it'
```

We also need to define the `WizardWorld` class, similar to the `FrogWorld` one that we have discussed; the obstacle, in this case, is an `Ork` instance:

```python
class WizardWorld:
    def __init__(self, name):
        print(self)
        self.player_name = name

    def __str__(self):
        return '\n\n\t------ Wizard World -------'

    def make_character(self):
        return Wizard(self.player_name)
```

```
    def make_obstacle(self):
        return Ork()
```

The `GameEnvironment` class is the main entry point of our game. It accepts the factory as input and uses it to create the world of the game. The `play()` method initiates the interaction between the created hero and the obstacle, as follows:

```
class GameEnvironment:
    def __init__(self, factory):
        self.hero = factory.make_character()
        self.obstacle = factory.make_obstacle()

    def play(self):
        self.hero.interact_with(self.obstacle)
```

The `validate_age()` function prompts the user to give a valid age. If the age is not valid, it returns a tuple with the first element set to `False`. If the age is fine, the first element of the tuple is set to `True`. This is where we care about the second element of the tuple, which is the age given by the user, as follows:

```
def validate_age(name):
    try:
        age = input(f'Welcome {name}. How old are you? ')
        age = int(age)
    except ValueError as err:
        print(f"Age {age} is invalid, please try again...")
        return (False, age)
    return (True, age)
```

Last but not least comes the `main()` function. It asks for the user's name and age, and decides which game should be played, given the age of the user, as follows:

```
def main():
    name = input("Hello. What's your name? ")
    valid_input = False
    while not valid_input:
        valid_input, age = validate_age(name)
    game = FrogWorld if age < 18 else WizardWorld
    environment = GameEnvironment(game(name))
    environment.play()
```

The following is a summary of the implementation we just discussed (see the complete code in the `abstract_factory.py` file):

1. First, we define the `Frog` and `Bug` classes for the FrogWorld game.
2. We add the `FrogWorld` class, where we use our `Frog` and `Bug` classes.
3. We define the `Wizard` and `Ork` classes for the WizardWorld game.
4. We add the `WizardWorld` class, where we use our `Wizard` and `Ork` classes.
5. We define the `GameEnvironment` class.
6. We add the `validate_age()` function.
7. Finally, we have the `main()` function, followed by the conventional trick for calling it. The following are the aspects of this function:

   - We get the user's input for their name and age.
   - We decide which game class to use based on the user's age.
   - We instantiate the right game class, and then the `GameEnvironment` class.
   - We call `play()` on the environment object to play the game.

Let's call this program using the `python abstract_factory.py` command and see some sample output.

The sample output for a teenager is as follows:

```
Hello. What's your name? Billy
Welcome Billy. How old are you? 12


        ------ Frog World -------
Billy the Frog encounters a bug and eats it!
```

The sample output for an adult is as follows:

```
Hello. What's your name? Charles
Welcome Charles. How old are you? 25


        ------ Wizard World -------
Charles the Wizard battles against an evil ork and kills
it!
```

Try extending the game to make it more complete. You can go as far as you want; create many obstacles, many enemies, and whatever else you like.

Summary

In this chapter, we learned how to use the factory method and the abstract factory design patterns. Both patterns are used when we want to track object creation, decouple object creation from object usage, or even improve the performance and resource usage of an application. Improving performance was not demonstrated in this chapter. You may consider trying it as a good exercise.

The factory method design pattern is implemented as a single function that doesn't belong to any class and is responsible for creating a single kind of object (a shape, a connection point, and so on). We saw how the factory method relates to toy construction, mentioned how it is used by Django to create different form fields, and discussed other possible use cases for it. As an example, we implemented a factory method that provided access to XML and JSON files.

The abstract factory design pattern is implemented as several factory methods that belong to a single class and are used to create a family of related objects (the parts of a car, the environment of a game, and so forth). We mentioned how the abstract factory is related to car manufacturing, how the `django_factory` package for Django makes use of it to create clean tests, and then we covered its common use cases. Our implementation example of the abstract factory was a mini-game that shows how we can use many related factories in a single class.

In the next chapter, we will discuss the builder pattern, which is another creational pattern that can be used for fine-tuning the creation of complex objects.

Questions

1. What are the high-level benefits of using the factory pattern?

2. What are the two forms of the factory pattern and their main differences?

3. How should we decide which form of the factory pattern we should use when building an application?

17
The Builder Pattern

In the previous chapter, we covered the first two creational patterns—the factory method and abstract factory, both of which offer approaches to improve the way we create objects in nontrivial cases. The builder design pattern, on the other hand, as we'll discuss in this chapter, is useful for managing objects that consist of multiple parts that need to be implemented sequentially. By decoupling the construction of an object and its representation, the builder pattern allows us to reuse a construction multiple times.

Just as with the previous chapter, we will discuss real-life applications that use this design pattern as well as implementing a hands-on example ourselves.

In this chapter, we will discuss the following topics:

- Understanding the builder pattern
- Real-world examples
- Use cases
- Implementing an ordering application

By the end of the chapter, we will understand how to use the builder pattern and its practical benefits.

Technical requirements

The code files for this chapter can be accessed through this link:

```
https://github.com/PacktPublishing/Advanced-Python-
Programming-Second-Edition/tree/main/Chapter17
```

Understanding the builder pattern

Imagine that we want to create an object that is composed of multiple parts and the composition needs to be done step by step. The object is not complete unless all its parts are fully created. That's where the **builder-design pattern** can help us. The builder pattern separates the construction of a complex object from its representation. By keeping the construction separate from the representation, the same construction can be used to create several different representations (`j.mp/builderpat`).

A practical example can help us understand what the purpose of the builder pattern is. Suppose that we want to create a **HyperText Markup Language** (**HTML**) page generator. The basic structure (construction part) of an HTML page is always the same: it begins with `<html>` and finishes with `</html>`; inside the HTML section are the `<head>` and `</head>` elements; inside the head section are the `<title>` and `</title>` elements; and so forth. But the representation of the page can differ. Each page has its own title, its own headings, and different `<body>` contents. Moreover, the page is usually built in steps: one function adds the title, another adds the main heading, another the footer, and so on. Only after the whole structure of a page is complete can it be shown to the client using a final render function. We can take it even further and extend the HTML generator so that it can generate totally different HTML pages. One page might contain tables, another page might contain image galleries, yet another page contains the contact form, and so on.

The HTML page-generation problem can be solved using the builder pattern. In this pattern, there are two main participants, outlined as follows:

- **The builder**: The component responsible for creating the various parts of a complex object. In this example, these parts are the title, heading, body, and the footer of the page.

- **The director**: The component that controls the building process using a `builder` instance. It calls the builder's functions for setting the title, the heading, and so on, and using a different `builder` instance allows us to create a different HTML page without touching any of the code of the director.

First, let's discuss in the next section some real-life examples where this pattern applies.

Real-world examples

In our everyday life, the *builder design pattern* is used in fast-food restaurants. The same procedure is always used to prepare a burger and the packaging (box and paper bag), even if there are many different kinds of burgers (classic, cheeseburger, and more) and different packages (small-sized box, medium-sized box, and so forth). The difference between a classic burger and a cheeseburger is in the representation, and not in the construction procedure. In this case, the **director** is the cashier who gives the crew instructions about what needs to be prepared, and the **builder** is the person from the crew that takes care of a specific order.

We can also find software examples, as follows:

- The HTML example that was mentioned at the beginning of the chapter is actually used by `django-widgy` (`https://wid.gy/`), a third-party tree editor for Django that can be used as a **content management system** (**CMS**). The `django-widgy` editor contains a page builder that can be used for creating HTML pages with different layouts.

- The `django-query-builder` library (`https://github.com/ambitioninc/django-query-builder`) is another third-party Django library that relies on the builder pattern. This library can be used for building **Structured Query Language** (**SQL**) queries dynamically, allowing you to control all aspects of a query and create a different range of queries, from simple to very complex ones.

In the next section, we will see how this design pattern actually works.

Use cases

We use the builder pattern when we know that an object must be created in multiple steps, and different representations of the same construction are required. These requirements exist in many applications, such as page generators (for example, the HTML page generator mentioned in this chapter), document converters, and **user interface** (**UI**) form creators (`j.mp/pipbuild`).

Some online resources mention that the builder pattern can also be used as a solution to the telescopic constructor problem. The telescopic constructor problem occurs when we are forced to create a new constructor for supporting different ways of creating an object. The problem is that we end up with many constructors and long parameter lists that are hard to manage. An example of the telescopic constructor is listed on the Stack Overflow website (j.mp/sobuilder). Fortunately, this problem does not exist in Python, because it can be solved in at least two ways, as outlined here:

- With named parameters that define different behaviors in the constructor of the class (j.mp/sobuipython)

- With argument list unpacking, which is similar in spirit to named parameters (j.mp/arglistpy)

These features that are specific to Python help us control the behavior of its code easily, thus avoiding the problem we described previously.

At this point, the distinction between the builder pattern and the factory pattern might not be very clear. The main difference is that the factory pattern creates an object in a single step, whereas the builder pattern creates an object in multiple steps, and almost always through the use of a director. Some targeted implementations of the builder pattern, such as Java's `StringBuilder`, bypass the use of a director, but that's the exception to the rule.

Another difference is that while the factory pattern returns a created object immediately, in the builder pattern the client code explicitly asks the director to return the final object when it needs it (j.mp/builderpat).

The new computer analogy might help you to distinguish between the builder pattern and the factory pattern. Assume that you want to buy a new computer. If you decide to buy a specific, preconfigured computer model—for example, the latest Apple 1.4 **gigahertz** (**GHz**) Mac mini—you use the factory pattern. All the hardware specifications are already predefined by the manufacturer, who knows what to do without consulting you. The manufacturer typically receives just a single instruction. Code-wise, this is how it would look (`apple_factory.py`):

```python
MINI14 = '1.4GHz Mac mini'
class AppleFactory:
    class MacMini14:
        def __init__(self):
            self.memory = 4 # in gigabytes
            self.hdd = 500 # in gigabytes
```

```
        self.gpu = 'Intel HD Graphics 5000'

    def __str__(self):
        info = (f'Model: {MINI14}',
                f'Memory: {self.memory}GB',
                f'Hard Disk: {self.hdd}GB',
                f'Graphics Card: {self.gpu}')
        return '\n'.join(info)

def build_computer(self, model):
    if model == MINI14:
        return self.MacMini14()
    else:
        msg = f"I don't know how to build {model}"
        print(msg)
```

Now, we add the main part of the program—the snippet that uses the `AppleFactory` class. The code is illustrated here:

```
if __name__ == '__main__':
    afac = AppleFactory()
    mac_mini = afac.build_computer(MINI14)
    print(mac_mini)
```

> **Note**
>
> Notice the nested `MacMini14` class. This is a neat way of forbidding the direct instantiation of a class.

Another option would be to buy a custom PC. In this case, you use the builder pattern. You are the director who gives orders to the manufacturer (`builder`) about your ideal computer specifications. Code-wise, this is how it looks (`computer_builder.py`):

1. We define a `Computer` class, as follows:

    ```
    class Computer:
        def __init__(self, serial_number):
            self.serial = serial_number
            self.memory = None # in gigabytes
    ```

```
        self.hdd = None # in gigabytes
        self.gpu = None

    def __str__(self):
        info = (f'Memory: {self.memory}GB',
                f'Hard Disk: {self.hdd}GB',
                f'Graphics Card: {self.gpu}')
        return '\n'.join(info)
```

2. We define a `ComputerBuilder` class, as follows:

```
class ComputerBuilder:
    def __init__(self):
        self.computer = Computer('AG23385193')

    def configure_memory(self, amount):
        self.computer.memory = amount

    def configure_hdd(self, amount):
        self.computer.hdd = amount

    def configure_gpu(self, gpu_model):
        self.computer.gpu = gpu_model
```

3. We define a `HardwareEngineer` class, as follows:

```
class HardwareEngineer:
    def __init__(self):
        self.builder = None

    def construct_computer(self, memory, hdd, gpu):
        self.builder = ComputerBuilder()
        steps = (self.builder.configure_memory(memory),
                 self.builder.configure_hdd(hdd),
                 self.builder.configure_gpu(gpu))
        [step for step in steps]
```

```
        @property
        def computer(self):
            return self.builder.computer
```

4. We end our code with the `main()` function, followed by a trick to call it when the file is called from the command line, as illustrated in the following code snippet:

```
def main():
    engineer = HardwareEngineer()
    engineer.construct_computer(hdd=500,
                                memory=8,
                                gpu='GeForce GTX 650 Ti')
    computer = engineer.computer
    print(computer)


if __name__ == '__main__':
    main()
```

The basic changes are the introduction of a builder (`ComputerBuilder`), a director (`HardwareEngineer`), and the step-by-step construction of a computer, which now supports different configurations (notice that `memory`, `hdd`, and `gpu` are parameters and are not preconfigured). What do we need to do if we want to support the construction of tablets? Implement this as an exercise.

You might also want to change the computer's `serial_number` value into something different for each computer because as it is now, this means that all computers will have the same serial number (which is impractical).

Implementing an ordering application

Let's see how we can use the builder design pattern to make a pizza-ordering application. The pizza example is particularly interesting because a pizza is prepared in steps that should follow a specific order. To add the sauce, you first need to prepare the dough. To add the topping, you first need to add the sauce. And you can't start baking the pizza unless both the sauce and the topping are placed on the dough. Moreover, each pizza usually requires a different baking time, depending on the thickness of its dough and the topping used.

We start by importing the required modules and declaring a few Enum parameters (j.mp/pytenum) plus a constant that is used many times in the application. The STEP_DELAY constant is used to add a time delay between the different steps of preparing a pizza (prepare the dough, add the sauce, and so on), as follows:

```python
from enum import Enum
import time
PizzaProgress = Enum('PizzaProgress', 'queued preparation \
    baking ready')
PizzaDough = Enum('PizzaDough', 'thin thick')
PizzaSauce = Enum('PizzaSauce', 'tomato creme_fraiche')
PizzaTopping = Enum('PizzaTopping', 'mozzarella \
    double_mozzarella bacon ham mushrooms red_onion oregano')
STEP_DELAY = 3 # in seconds for the sake of the example
```

Our end product is a pizza, which is described by the Pizza class. When using the builder pattern, the end product does not have many responsibilities since it is not supposed to be instantiated directly. A builder creates an instance of the end product and makes sure that it is properly prepared. That's why the Pizza class is so minimal. It basically initializes all data to sane default values. An exception is the prepare_dough() method.

The prepare_dough() method is defined in the Pizza class instead of a builder for two reasons—first, to clarify the fact that the end product is typically minimal, which does not mean that you should never assign it any responsibilities; second, to promote code reuse through composition.

So, we define our Pizza class as follows:

```python
class Pizza:
    def __init__(self, name):
        self.name = name
        self.dough = None
        self.sauce = None
        self.topping = []

    def __str__(self):
        return self.name
```

```
        def prepare_dough(self, dough):
            self.dough = dough
            print(f'preparing the {self.dough.name} dough of your \
                {self}...')
            time.sleep(STEP_DELAY)
            print(f'done with the {self.dough.name} dough')
```

There are two builders: one for creating a margarita pizza (MargaritaBuilder) and another for creating a creamy bacon pizza (CreamyBaconBuilder). Each builder creates a Pizza instance and contains methods that follow the pizza-making procedure: prepare_dough(), add_sauce(), add_topping(), and bake(). To be precise, prepare_dough() is just a wrapper to the prepare_dough() method of the Pizza class.

Notice how each builder takes care of all the pizza-specific details. For example, the topping of the margarita pizza is double mozzarella and oregano, while the topping of the creamy bacon pizza is mozzarella, bacon, ham, mushrooms, red onion, and oregano.

This part of our code is laid out as follows:

1.   We define a MargaritaBuilder class, as follows:

```
    class MargaritaBuilder:
        def __init__(self):
            self.pizza = Pizza('margarita')
            self.progress = PizzaProgress.queued
            self.baking_time = 5 # in seconds for the sake of
            the example

        def prepare_dough(self):
            self.progress = PizzaProgress.preparation
            self.pizza.prepare_dough(PizzaDough.thin)

        def add_sauce(self):
            print('adding the tomato sauce to your \
                margarita...')
            self.pizza.sauce = PizzaSauce.tomato
            time.sleep(STEP_DELAY)
            print('done with the tomato sauce')
```

```python
    def add_topping(self):
        topping_desc = 'double mozzarella, oregano'
        topping_items = (PizzaTopping.double_mozzarella,
        PizzaTopping.oregano)
        print(f'adding the topping ({topping_desc}) to \
            your margarita')
        self.pizza.topping.append([t for t in \
            topping_items])
        time.sleep(STEP_DELAY)
        print(f'done with the topping ({topping_desc})')

    def bake(self):
        self.progress = PizzaProgress.baking
        print(f'baking your margarita for \
            {self.baking_time} seconds')
        time.sleep(self.baking_time)
        self.progress = PizzaProgress.ready
        print('your margarita is ready')
```

2. We define a `CreamyBaconBuilder` class, as follows:

```python
class CreamyBaconBuilder:
    def __init__(self):
        self.pizza = Pizza('creamy bacon')
        self.progress = PizzaProgress.queued
        self.baking_time = 7 # in seconds for the sake of
        the example

    def prepare_dough(self):
        self.progress = PizzaProgress.preparation
        self.pizza.prepare_dough(PizzaDough.thick)

    def add_sauce(self):
        print('adding the crème fraîche sauce to your \
            creamy bacon')
        self.pizza.sauce = PizzaSauce.creme_fraiche
        time.sleep(STEP_DELAY)
```

```
                    print('done with the crème fraîche sauce')


        def add_topping(self):
            topping_desc = 'mozzarella, bacon, ham, \
                mushrooms, red onion, oregano'
            topping_items =   (PizzaTopping.mozzarella,
                               PizzaTopping.bacon,
                               PizzaTopping.ham,
                               PizzaTopping.mushrooms,
                               PizzaTopping.red_onion,
                               PizzaTopping.oregano)
            print(f'adding the topping ({topping_desc}) to \
                your creamy bacon')
            self.pizza.topping.append([t for t in \
                topping_items])
            time.sleep(STEP_DELAY)
            print(f'done with the topping ({topping_desc})')


        def bake(self):
            self.progress = PizzaProgress.baking
            print(f'baking your creamy bacon for \
                {self.baking_time} seconds')
            time.sleep(self.baking_time)
            self.progress = PizzaProgress.ready
            print('your creamy bacon is ready')
```

The director in this example is the waiter. The core of the `Waiter` class is the `construct_pizza()` method, which accepts a `builder` as a parameter and executes all the pizza-preparation steps in the right order. Choosing the appropriate builder, which can even be done at runtime, gives us the ability to create different pizza styles without modifying any of the code of the director (`Waiter`). The `Waiter` class also contains the `pizza()` method, which returns the end product (prepared pizza) as a variable to the caller, as follows:

```
class Waiter:
    def __init__(self):
        self.builder = None
```

```
def construct_pizza(self, builder):
    self.builder = builder
    steps = (builder.prepare_dough,
             builder.add_sauce,
             builder.add_topping,
             builder.bake)
    [step() for step in steps]


@property
def pizza(self):
    return self.builder.pizza
```

The validate_style() function is similar to the validate_age() function, as described in *Chapter 16, The Factory Pattern*. It is used to make sure that the user gives valid input, which in this case is a character that is mapped to a pizza builder. The m character uses the MargaritaBuilder class, and the c character uses the CreamyBaconBuilder class. These mappings are in the builder parameter. A tuple is returned, with the first element set to True if the input is valid or False if it is invalid, as follows:

```
def validate_style(builders):
    try:
        input_msg = 'What pizza would you like, [m]argarita or \
        [c]reamy bacon? '
        pizza_style = input(input_msg)
        builder = builders[pizza_style]()
        valid_input = True
    except KeyError:
        error_msg = 'Sorry, only margarita (key m) and creamy \
        bacon (key c) are available'
        print(error_msg)
        return (False, None)
    return (True, builder)
```

The last part is the main() function. The main() function contains code for instantiating a pizza builder. The pizza builder is then used by the Waiter director for preparing the pizza. The created pizza can be delivered to the client at any later point. The code is illustrated in the following snippet:

```
def main():
    builders = dict(m=MargaritaBuilder, c=CreamyBaconBuilder)
    valid_input = False
    while not valid_input:
        valid_input, builder = validate_style(builders)
    print()
    waiter = Waiter()
    waiter.construct_pizza(builder)
    pizza = waiter.pizza
    print()
    print(f'Enjoy your {pizza}!')
```

Here is a summary of the implementation (see the complete code in the builder.py file):

1. We start with a couple of imports we need, for the standard Enum class and the time module.

2. We declare variables for a few constants: PizzaProgress, PizzaDough, PizzaSauce, PizzaTopping, and STEP_DELAY.

3. We define our Pizza class.

4. We define classes for two builders, MargaritaBuilder and CreamyBaconBuilder.

5. We define our Waiter class.

6. We add the validate_style() function to improve things regarding exception handling.

7. Finally, we have the main() function, followed by the snippet for calling it when the program is run. In the main function, the following happens:

   - We make it possible to choose the pizza builder based on the user's input, after validation via the validate_style() function.

   - The pizza builder is used by the waiter for preparing the pizza.

   - The created pizza is then delivered.

Here is the output produced by calling the `python builder.py` command to execute this example program:

```
What pizza would you like, [m]argarita or [c]reamy bacon? r
Sorry, only margarita (key m) and creamy bacon (key c) are
available
What pizza would you like, [m]argarita or [c]reamy bacon? m

preparing the thin dough of your margarita...
done with the thin dough
adding the tomato sauce to your margarita...
done with the tomato sauce
adding the topping (double mozzarella, oregano) to your
margarita
done with the topping (double mozzarella, oregano)
baking your margarita for 5 seconds
your margarita is ready

Enjoy your margarita!
```

But…supporting only two pizza types is a shame. Feel like getting a Hawaiian pizza builder? Consider using inheritance after thinking about the advantages and disadvantages. Check the ingredients of a typical Hawaiian pizza and decide which class you need to extend: `MargaritaBuilder` or `CreamyBaconBuilder`? Perhaps both (`j.mp/pymulti`)?

In his book, *Effective Java (Second Edition)*, Joshua Bloch describes an interesting variation of the builder pattern where calls to builder methods are chained. This is accomplished by defining the builder itself as an inner class and returning itself from each of the setter-like methods on it. The `build()` method returns the final object. This pattern is called the **fluent builder**. Here's a Python implementation, which was kindly provided by a reviewer of the book:

```python
class Pizza:
    def __init__(self, builder):
        self.garlic = builder.garlic
        self.extra_cheese = builder.extra_cheese
```

```python
    def __str__(self):
        garlic = 'yes' if self.garlic else 'no'
        cheese = 'yes' if self.extra_cheese else 'no'
        info = (f'Garlic: {garlic}', f'Extra cheese: {cheese}')
        return '\n'.join(info)

    class PizzaBuilder:
        def __init__(self):
            self.extra_cheese = False
            self.garlic = False

        def add_garlic(self):
            self.garlic = True
            return self

        def add_extra_cheese(self):
            self.extra_cheese = True
            return self

        def build(self):
            return Pizza(self)

if __name__ == '__main__':
    pizza = Pizza.PizzaBuilder().add_garlic().add_extra_ \
        cheese().build()
    print(pizza)
```

With this fluent builder pattern, we see that we could quickly build the final `Pizza` object by chaining the `add_garlic()`, `add_extra_cheese()`, and `build()` methods on one line of code, which could come in handy in many situations.

Summary

In this chapter, we have seen how to use the builder design pattern. We use the builder pattern for creating an object in situations where using the factory pattern (either a factory method or an abstract factory) is not a good option. The builder pattern is usually a better candidate than the factory pattern when we want to create a complex object, when different representations of an object are required, or when we want to create an object at one point in time but access it at a later point.

We saw how the builder pattern is used in fast-food restaurants for preparing meals, and how two third-party Django packages, django-widgy and django-query-builder, use it for generating HTML pages and dynamic SQL queries, respectively. We focused on the differences between the builder pattern and the factory pattern and provided a preconfigured (factory) and customer (builder) computer order analogy to clarify them. We also looked at how to create a pizza-ordering application with preparation dependencies. Throughout these examples, we have clearly seen the benefits and flexibility of the builder pattern, which will help you better approach future applications that require the design pattern.

In the next chapter, you will learn about other useful creational patterns.

Questions

1.   What are the high-level applications of the builder pattern?

2.   What are some common computer applications that require or benefit from the builder pattern?

3.   How does the builder pattern create an object and how is that process different from what the factory pattern does?

18

Other Creational Patterns

In the previous chapter, we covered a third creational pattern, builder, which offers a nice way of creating the various parts of a complex object. Apart from the factory method, the abstract factory, and the builder patterns covered so far, other creational patterns are interesting to discuss, such as the **prototype** pattern and the **singleton** pattern.

In this chapter, we will discuss the following topics:

- Implementing the prototype pattern
- Implementing the singleton pattern

These topics will complete our discussions on creational patterns and help cover the use cases where the design patterns we have seen so far are not appropriate. By the end of the chapter, we will have an overall understanding of creational patterns and the use cases of each one.

Technical requirements

The code files for this chapter can be accessed through this link: `https://github.com/PacktPublishing/Advanced-Python-Programming-Second-Edition/tree/main/Chapter18`.

Implementing the prototype pattern

The prototype pattern is useful when you need to create objects based on an existing object using the **cloning** technique. As you may have guessed, the idea is to use a copy of that object's complete structure to produce the new object. We will see that this is almost natural in Python because we have a **copy** feature that helps greatly in using this technique. In the general case of creating a copy of an object, what happens is that you make a new reference to the same object, a method called a **shallow copy**. But if you need to duplicate the object, which is the case with a prototype, you make a **deep copy**.

Sometimes, we need to create an exact copy of an object. For instance, assume that you want to create an application for storing, sharing, and editing presentation and marketing content for products promoted by a group of salespeople. Think of the popular distribution model called **direct selling** or **network marketing**, the home-based activity where individuals partner with a company to distribute products within their social network using promotional tools (brochures, PowerPoint presentations, videos, and so on).

Let's say a user, *Bob*, leads a team of distributors within a network marketing organization. They use a presentation video daily to introduce the product to their prospects. At some point, Bob gets his friend, Alice, to join him and she also uses the same video (one of the governing principles is to follow the system or, as they say, *Duplicate what already works*). But Alice soon finds prospects that could join her team and help her business grow, if only the video was in French, or at least subtitled. *What should they do?* The original presentation video cannot be used for the different custom needs that may arise.

To help everyone, the system could allow distributors with certain rank or trust levels, such as *Bob*, to create independent copies of the original presentation video, as long as the new version is validated by the compliance team of the backing company before public use. Each copy is called a **clone**; it is an exact copy of the original object at a specific point in time.

So, Bob, with the validation of the compliance team, makes a copy of the presentation video to address the new need and hands it over to Alice. She could then adapt that version by adding French subtitles.

With cloning, Bob and Alice can have their own copy of a video, and as such, changes by each one of them will not affect the other person's version of the material. In the alternative situation, which is what actually happens by default, each person would hold a reference to the same (reference) object; changes made by Bob would impact Alice, and vice versa.

The prototype design pattern helps us with creating object clones. In its simplest version, this pattern is just a `clone()` function that accepts an object as an input parameter and returns a clone of it. In Python, this can be done using the `deepcopy()` function from the `copy` module.

The structure of our discussions will be the same as in previous chapters. First, we will briefly discuss real-life applications and use cases, and then implement a hands-on example in Python.

Real-world examples

A famous non-technical example is the sheep named Dolly, which was created by researchers in Scotland by cloning a cell from a mammary gland.

Many Python applications make use of the prototype pattern (`j.mp/pythonprot`), but it is seldom referred to as *prototype* since cloning objects is a built-in feature of the language.

Use cases

The prototype pattern is useful when we have an existing object that needs to stay untouched, and we want to create an exact copy of it, allowing changes in some parts of the copy.

There is also the frequent need for duplicating an object that is populated from a database and has references to other database-based objects. It is costly (multiple queries to a database) to clone such a complex object, so a prototype is a convenient way to solve the problem.

Implementation

Nowadays, some organizations, even of small size, deal with many websites and apps via their infrastructure/DevOps teams, hosting providers, or cloud service providers.

When you have to manage multiple websites, there is a point where it becomes difficult to manage everything. You need to access information quickly, such as IP addresses that are involved, domain names and their expiration dates, and maybe details about the DNS parameters. So, you need a kind of inventory tool.

Let's imagine how these teams deal with this type of data for daily activities and touch on the implementation of a piece of software that helps consolidate and maintain the data (other than in Excel spreadsheets):

1. First, we need to import Python's standard `copy` module, as follows:

   ```
   import copy
   ```

2. At the heart of this system, we will have a `Website` class for holding all the useful information such as the name, the domain name, the description, and the author of a website we are managing.

   In the `__init__()` method of the class, only some parameters are fixed, `name`, `domain`, `description`, and `author`, which correspond to the information we listed previously. But we also want flexibility, and client code can pass more parameters in the form of keywords (`name=value`) using the `kwargs` variable-length collection (a Python dictionary).

   Note that there is a Python idiom to set an arbitrary attribute named `attr` with a value, `val`, on an object, `obj`, using the `setattr()` built-in function: `setattr(obj, attr, val)`.

   So, we are using this technique for the optional attributes of our class, at the end of the initialization method, as follows:

   ```
   for key in kwargs:
       setattr(self, key, kwargs[key])
   ```

   So, our `Website` class is defined as follows:

   ```
   class Website:
       def __init__(self, name, domain, description, \
           author, **kwargs):
           '''Examples of optional attributes (kwargs):
               category, creation_date, technologies, \
               keywords.
           '''
           self.name = name
           self.domain = domain
           self.description = description
           self.author = author
   ```

```
        for key in kwargs:
            setattr(self, key, kwargs[key])

    def __str__(self):
        summary = [f'Website "{self.name}"\n',]

        infos = vars(self).items()
        ordered_infos = sorted(infos)
        for attr, val in ordered_infos:
            if attr == 'name':
                continue
            summary.append(f'{attr}: {val}\n')

        return ''.join(summary)
```

3. Next, the `Prototype` class implements the prototype design pattern.

    At the heart of the `Prototype` class is the `clone()` method, which is in charge of cloning the object using the `copy.deepcopy()` function. Since cloning means we allow values to be set for optional attributes, notice how we use the `setattr()` technique here with the `attrs` dictionary.

    Also, for more convenience, the `Prototype` class contains the `register()` and `unregister()` methods, which can be used to keep track of the cloned objects in a dictionary:

```
class Prototype:
    def __init__(self):
        self.objects = dict()

    def register(self, identifier, obj):
        self.objects[identifier] = obj

    def unregister(self, identifier):
        del self.objects[identifier]

    def clone(self, identifier, **attrs):
        found = self.objects.get(identifier)
        if not found:
```

```
            raise ValueError(f'Incorrect object \
                identifier:{identifier}')
        obj = copy.deepcopy(found)
        for key in attrs:
            setattr(obj, key, attrs[key])


        return obj
```

4. In the main() function, as shown in the following code, we can clone a first Website instance, site1, to get a second object, site2. Basically, we instantiate the Prototype class and we use its .clone() method. That is what the following code shows:

```
def main():
    keywords = ('python', 'data', 'apis', \
        'automation')
    site1 = Website('ContentGardening',
            domain='contentgardening.com',
            description='Automation and data-driven \
                apps',
            author='Kamon Ayeva',
            category='Blog',
            keywords=keywords)

    prototype = Prototype()
    identifier = 'ka-cg-1'
    prototype.register(identifier, site1)

    site2 = prototype.clone(identifier,
            name='ContentGardeningPlayground',
            domain='play.contentgardening.com',
            description='Experimentation for \
                techniques featured on the blog',
            category='Membership site',
            creation_date='2018-08-01')
```

5. To end that function, we can use the id() function, which returns the memory address of an object, for comparing both objects' addresses, as follows. When we clone an object using a deep copy, the memory addresses of the clone must be different from the memory addresses of the original object:

```
for site in (site1, site2):
    print(site)
print(f'ID site1 : {id(site1)} != ID site2 : \
    {id(site2)}')
```

You will find the program's full code in the prototype.py file. Here is a summary of what we do in the code:

1. We start by importing the copy module.

2. We define the Website class, with its initialization method, (__init__()), and its string representation method (__str__()), as shown earlier.

3. We define our Prototype class as shown earlier.

4. Then, we have the main() function, where we do the following:

   - We define the keywords list we need.

   - We create the instance of the Website class, called site1 (we use the keywords list here).

   - We create the Prototype object and we use its register() method to register site1 with its identifier (this helps us keep track of the cloned objects in a dictionary).

   - We clone the site1 object to get site2.

   - We display the result (both Website objects)

Following is the sample output when I execute the python prototype.py command on my machine:

```
Website "ContentGardening"
author: Kamon Ayeva
category: Blog
description: Automation and data-driven apps
domain: contentgardening.com
keywords: ('python', 'data', 'apis', 'automation')
```

```
Website "ContentGardeningPlayground"
author: Kamon Ayeva
category: Membership site
creation_date: 2018-08-01
description: Experimentation for techniques featured on the
blog
domain: play.contentgardening.com
keywords: ('python', 'data', 'apis', 'automation')


ID site1 : 140263689073376 != ID site2 : 140263689058816
```

Indeed, `Prototype` works as expected. We can see the information about the original `Website` object and its clone. Looking at the output of the `id()` function, we can see that the two addresses are different.

With this program, we mark the end of our discussion on the prototype pattern. In the next section, we will cover the singleton pattern.

Implementing the singleton pattern

The singleton pattern offers a way to implement a class from which you can only create one object, hence the name singleton. As you will understand with our exploration of this pattern, or while doing your own research, there have always been discussions about this pattern, and some even consider it an **anti-pattern**.

Besides that, what is interesting is that it is useful when we need to create one and only one object, for example, to store and maintain a global state for our program. In Python, this pattern can be implemented using some special built-in features.

The singleton pattern restricts the instantiation of a class to *one* object, which is useful when you need one object to coordinate actions for the system.

The basic idea is that only one instance of a particular class is created for the needs of the program. To ensure that this works, we need mechanisms that prevent the instantiation of the class more than once and also prevent cloning.

First, let's discuss some real-life examples of the singleton pattern.

Real-world examples

We can think of a captain of a ship or a boat as a real-life example of the singleton pattern. On the ship, he is the one in charge. He is responsible for important decisions, and several requests are directed to him because of this responsibility.

In software, the Plone CMS has, at its core, an implementation of the singleton. There are actually several singleton objects available at the root of a Plone site, called **tools**, each in charge of providing a specific set of features for the site. For example, the **Catalog tool** deals with content indexation and search features (built-in search engines for small sites where you don't need to integrate products such as ElasticSearch), the **Membership tool** deals with things related to user profiles, and the **Registry tool** provides a configuration registry to store and maintain different kinds of configuration properties for the Plone site. Each tool is global to the site, created from a specific `singleton` class, and you can't create another instance of that `singleton` class in the context of the site.

Use cases

As stated previously, one use case of the singleton pattern is to create a single object that maintains the global state of your program. Other possible use cases are as follows:

- Controlling concurrent access to a shared resource; for example, an object class that manages the connection to a database

- A service or resource that is transversal in the sense that it can be accessed from different parts of the application or by different users and does its work; for example, the class at the core of the logging system or utility

Implementation

Let's implement a program to fetch content from web pages, inspired by the tutorial from Michael Ford (`https://docs.python.org/3/howto/urllib2.html`). We have only taken the simple part since the focus is to illustrate our pattern more than it is to build a special web-scraping tool.

We will use the `urllib` module to connect to web pages using their URLs; the core of the program would be the `URLFetcher` class, which takes care of doing the work via a `fetch()` method.

We want to be able to track the list of web pages that were tracked, hence the use of the singleton pattern. We need a single object to maintain that global state:

1. First, our naive version, inspired by the tutorial but modified to help us track the list of URLs that were fetched, would be as follows:

```python
import urllib.parse
import urllib.request


class URLFetcher:

    def __init__(self):
        self.urls = []

    def fetch(self, url):
        req = urllib.request.Request(url)
        with urllib.request.urlopen(req) as response:
            if response.code == 200:
                the_page = response.read()
                print(the_page)

                urls = self.urls
                urls.append(url)
                self.urls = urls
```

2. As an exercise, add the usual if __name__ == '__main__' block with a few lines of code to call the .fetch() method on an instance of URLFetcher.

But then, does our class implement a singleton? Here is a clue. To create a singleton, we need to make sure you can only create one instance of it. So, to see whether our class implements a singleton, we could use a trick that consists of comparing two instances using the is operator.

You may have guessed the second exercise. Put the following code in your if __name__ == '__main__' block instead of what you had previously:

```python
f1 = URLFetcher()
f2 = URLFetcher()
print(f1 is f2)
```

As an alternative, use this concise, but still elegant, form:

```
print(URLFetcher() is URLFetcher())
```

With this change, when executing the program, you should get False as the output.

3. Okay! This means that the first try does not yet give us a singleton. Remember, we want to manage a global state, using one, and only one, instance of the class for the program. The current version of the class does not yet implement a singleton.

   After checking the literature and the forums on the web, you will find that there are several techniques, each with pros and cons, and some are probably outdated.

   Since many people use Python 3 nowadays, the recommended technique we will choose is the **metaclass** technique. We first implement a metaclass for the singleton. This class implements the singleton pattern as follows:

```
class SingletonType(type):
    _instances = {}
    def __call__(cls, *args, **kwargs):
        if cls not in cls._instances:
            cls._instances[cls] = super \
                (SingletonType,cls).__call__(*args, \
                **kwargs)
        return cls._instances[cls]
```

4. Now, we will rewrite our URLFetcher class to use that metaclass. We also add a dump_url_registry() method, which is useful for getting the current list of URLs tracked:

```
class URLFetcher(metaclass=SingletonType):

    def fetch(self, url):
        req = urllib.request.Request(url)
        with urllib.request.urlopen(req) as response:
            if response.code == 200:
                the_page = response.read()
                print(the_page)

        urls = self.urls
        urls.append(url)
        self.urls = urls
```

```
        def dump_url_registry(self):
                return ', '.join(self.urls)


if __name__ == '__main__':
        print(URLFetcher() is URLFetcher())
```

This time, you get `True` by executing the program.

5. Let's complete the program to do what we wanted, using a `main()` function that we will call as follows:

```
def main():

        MY_URLS = ['http://google.com',
                        'http://python.org',
                        'https://www.python.org/error',
                        ]

        print(URLFetcher() is URLFetcher())

        fetcher = URLFetcher()
        for url in MY_URLS:
                try:
                        fetcher.fetch(url)
                except Exception as e:
                        print(e)

        print('-------')
        done_urls = fetcher.dump_url_registry()
        print(f'Done URLs: {done_urls}')
```

You will find the program's full code in the `singleton.py` file. Here is a summary of what we do:

1. We start with our required module imports (`urllib.parse` and `urllib.request`).

2. As shown earlier, we define the `SingletonType` class, with its special `__call__()` method.

3. As shown earlier, we define URLFetcher, the class implementing the fetcher for the web pages, initializing it with the urls attribute. As discussed, we add its fetch() and dump_url_registry() methods.

4. Then, we add our main() function.

5. Lastly, we add Python's conventional snippet used to call the main function.

The following is the output when executing the python singleton.py command:

```
[output truncated]
</script>\n    <script>window.jQuery ||
document.write(\'<script src="/static/js/libs/jquery-
1.8.2.min.js"><\\/script>\')</script>\n    <script
src="//ajax.googleapis.com/ajax/libs/jqueryui/1.12.1/jquery
-ui.min.js"></script>\n    <script>window.jQuery ||
document.write(\'<script src="/static/js/libs/jquery-ui-
1.12.1.min.js"><\\/script>\')</script>\n\n    <script
src="/static/js/libs/masonry.pkgd.min.js"></script>\n
<script src="/static/js/libs/html-
includes.js"></script>\n\n    <script
type="text/javascript" src="/static/js/main-
min.dd72c1659644.js" charset="utf-8"></script>\n    \n\n
<!--[if lte IE 7]>\n    <script type="text/javascript"
src="/static/js/plugins/IE8-min.8af6e26c7a3b.js"
charset="utf-8"></script>\n    \n    \n    <![endif]--
>\n\n
<!--[if lte IE 8]>\n    <script type="text/javascript"
src="/static/js/plugins/getComputedStyle-
min.d41d8cd98f00.js" charset="utf-8"></script>\n    \n
\n    <![endif]-->\n\n    \n\n    \n
\n\n</body>\n</html>\n'
HTTP Error 404: Not Found
-------
Done URLs: http://google.com, http://python.org
```

We can see that we get the expected result: both the content of the pages that the program was able to connect to and the list of URLs the operation was successful for.

We see that the URL, `https://www.python.org/error`, does not come in the list returned by `fetcher.dump_url_registry()`; indeed, it is an erroneous URL and the `urlllib` request to it gets a `404` response code.

> **Note**
> The link to the preceding URL is not supposed to work; that's exactly the point.

Summary

In this chapter, we have seen how to use two other creational design patterns: the prototype and the singleton.

A prototype is used to create exact copies of objects. As seen in the implementation example we discussed, using a prototype in Python is natural and based on built-in features, so it is not something even mentioned. The singleton pattern can be implemented by making the `singleton` class use a metaclass, its type, having previously defined said metaclass. As required, the metaclass's `__call__()` method holds the code that ensures that only one instance of the class can be created.

Overall, these two design patterns help us implement the use cases that other creational patterns do not support; in effect, we have grown our design pattern toolbox to cover more use cases.

The next chapter is about the adapter pattern, a structural design pattern that can be used to make two incompatible software interfaces compatible.

Questions

1. What are the high-level benefits of using the prototype pattern?
2. How is the prototype pattern useful in the specific case of database management?
3. What are the high-level benefits of using the singleton pattern?
4. In the context of concurrency, in which situation should the singleton pattern be used?

Further reading

Design Patterns by Gamma Enrich, Helm Richard, Johnson Ralph, and Vlissides John available at `https://www.amazon.com/Design-Patterns-Object-Oriented-Addison-Wesley-Professional-ebook/dp/B000SEIBB8`

19

The Adapter Pattern

In previous chapters, we covered creational patterns, which are **Object-Oriented Programming (OOP)** patterns that help us with object creation procedures. The next category of patterns we want to present is **structural design patterns**.

A structural design pattern proposes a way of composing objects to create new functionality. The first of these patterns we will cover is the **adapter** pattern.

In this chapter, we will discuss the following topics:

- Understanding the adapter pattern
- Real-world examples
- Use cases
- Implementation

By the end of the chapter, you will know how to use this design pattern to create interfaces that could help application layers that otherwise could not communicate.

Technical requirements

The code files for this chapter can be accessed through this link: `https://github.com/PacktPublishing/Advanced-Python-Programming-Second-Edition/tree/main/Chapter19`.

Understanding the adapter pattern

The adapter pattern is a structural design pattern that helps us make two incompatible interfaces compatible. *What does that really mean?* If we have an old component and we want to use it in a new system, or a new component that we want to use in an old system, the two can rarely communicate without requiring code changes. But changing the code is not always possible, either because we don't have access to it or because it is impractical. In such cases, we can write an extra layer that makes all the required modifications for enabling communication between the two interfaces. This layer is called an *adapter*.

To further understand this design pattern, let's consider some real-life examples.

Real-world examples

When you are traveling from most European countries to the UK or US, or the other way around, you need to use a plug adapter for charging your laptop. Another kind of adapter is needed for connecting some devices to your computer: a USB adapter.

In the software category, the Zope application server (`http://www.zope.org`) is known for its **Zope Component Architecture (ZCA)**, which contributed to the implementation of interfaces and adapters used by several big Python web projects. *Pyramid*, built by former Zope developers, is a Python web framework that took good ideas from Zope to provide a more modular approach for developing web apps. Pyramid uses adapters to make it possible for existing objects to conform to specific APIs without the need to modify them. Another project from the Zope ecosystem, *Plone CMS*, uses adapters under the hood.

Use cases

Usually, one of the two incompatible interfaces is either foreign or old/legacy. If the interface is foreign, it means that we have no access to the source code. If it is old, it is usually impractical to refactor it.

Using an adapter to make things work after they have been implemented is a good approach because it does not require access to the source code of the foreign interface. It is also often a pragmatic solution if we have to reuse some legacy code.

With that, let's start implementing a hands-on application in Python.

Implementation

Let's look at a relatively simple application to illustrate the concept of adaptation. Consider an example of a club's activities. It mainly needs to organize performances and events for the entertainment of its clients, by hiring talented artists.

At the core, we have a `Club` class that represents the club where hired artists perform some evenings. The `organize_performance()` method is the main action that the club can perform. The code is as follows:

```
class Club:
    def __init__(self, name):
        self.name = name

    def __str__(self):
        return f'the club {self.name}'

    def organize_event(self):
        return 'hires an artist to perform for the people'
```

Most of the time, our club hires a DJ to perform, but our application addresses the need to organize a diverse range of performances by a musician or music band, a dancer, a one-man or one-woman show, and so on.

Through our research to try and reuse existing code, we find an open source contributed library that brings us two interesting classes: `Musician` and `Dancer`. In the `Musician` class, the main action is performed by the `play()` method. In the `Dancer` class, it is performed by the `dance()` method.

In our example, to indicate that these two classes are external, we place them in a separate module. The code for the `Musician` class is as follows:

```
class Musician:
    def __init__(self, name):
    self.name = name

    def __str__(self):
    return f'the musician {self.name}'

    def play(self):
    return 'plays music'
```

Then, the `Dancer` class is defined as follows:

```
class Dancer:
    def __init__(self, name):
        self.name = name

    def __str__(self):
        return f'the dancer {self.name}'

    def dance(self):
        return 'does a dance performance'
```

The client code, using these classes, only knows how to call the `organize_performance()` method (on the `Club` class); it has no idea about `play()` or `dance()` (on the respective classes from the external library).

How can we make the code work without changing the `Musician` *and* `Dancer` *classes?*

Adapters to the rescue! We create a generic `Adapter` class that allows us to adapt several objects with different interfaces into one unified interface. The `obj` argument of the `__init__()` method is the object that we want to adapt, and `adapted_methods` is a dictionary containing key/value pairs matching the method the client calls and the method that should be called.

The code for the `Adapter` class is as follows:

```
class Adapter:
    def __init__(self, obj, adapted_methods):
        self.obj = obj
        self.__dict__.update(adapted_methods)

    def __str__(self):
        return str(self.obj)
```

When dealing with different instances of the classes, we have two cases:

- The compatible object that belongs to the `Club` class needs no adaptation. We can treat it as it is.
- The incompatible objects need to be adapted first, using the `Adapter` class.

The result is that the client code can continue using the known `organize_ performance()` method on all objects without the need to be aware of any interface differences between the used classes. Consider the following code:

```python
def main():
    objects = [Club('Jazz Cafe'), Musician('Roy Ayers'), \
      Dancer('Shane Sparks')]

    for obj in objects:
        if hasattr(obj, 'play') or hasattr(obj, 'dance'):
            if hasattr(obj, 'play'):
                adapted_methods = \
                    dict(organize_event=obj.play)
            elif hasattr(obj, 'dance'):
                adapted_methods = \
                    dict(organize_event=obj.dance)

            # referencing the adapted object here
            obj = Adapter(obj, adapted_methods)

        print(f'{obj} {obj.organize_event()}')
```

Let's recapitulate the complete code of our adapter pattern implementation:

1. We define the `Musician` and `Dancer` classes (in `external.py`).
2. Then, we need to import those classes from the external module (in `adapter.py`):

    ```python
    from external import Musician, Dance
    ```

3. We then define the `Adapter` class (in `adapter.py`).
4. We add the `main()` function, as shown earlier, and the usual trick to call it (in `adapter.py`).

Here is the output when executing the `python adapter.py` command, as usual:

```
the club Jazz Cafe hires an artist to perform for the
people
the musician Roy Ayers plays music
the dancer Shane Sparks does a dance performance
```

As you can see, we managed to make the `Musician` and `Dancer` classes compatible with the interface expected by the client, without changing their source code.

Summary

This chapter covered the adapter design pattern. The adapter makes things work after they have been implemented. The Pyramid web framework, the Plone CMS, and other Zope-based or related frameworks use the adapter pattern to achieve interface compatibility. In the *Implementation* section, we saw how to achieve interface conformance using the adapter pattern without modifying the source code of the incompatible model. This is achieved through a generic `Adapter` class that does the work for us.

Overall, we could use the adapter pattern to make two (or more) incompatible interfaces compatible, which has a lot of usage in software engineering.

In the next chapter, we will cover the decorator pattern.

20
The Decorator Pattern

As we saw in the previous chapter, using an **adapter**, the first structural design pattern, you can adapt an object implementing a given interface to implement another interface. This is called **interface adaptation** and includes the kinds of patterns that encourage composition over inheritance, and it could bring benefits when you have to maintain a large codebase.

A second interesting structural pattern to learn about is the **decorator** pattern, which allows us to add responsibilities to an object dynamically and transparently (without affecting other objects); this will be the topic of this chapter. Throughout our discussions, we will learn more about a specific usage of this design pattern: **memoization**.

We will discuss the following topics:

- Introducing the decorator pattern
- Real-world examples
- Use cases
- Implementation

Technical requirements

The code files for this chapter can be accessed through this link: `https://github.com/PacktPublishing/Advanced-Python-Programming-Second-Edition/tree/main/Chapter20`.

Introducing the decorator pattern

As Python developers, we can write decorators in a **Pythonic** way (meaning using the language's features), thanks to the built-in decorator feature (`https://docs.python.org/3/reference/compound_stmts.html#function`). What exactly is this feature? A Python decorator is a **callable** (function, method, or class) that gets a function object, `func_in`, as input and returns another function object, `func_out`. It is a commonly used technique for extending the behavior of a function, method, or class.

But this feature should not be completely new to you. We have already seen how to use the built-in `property` decorator, which makes a method appear as a variable in both *Chapter 16, The Factory Pattern*, and *Chapter 17, The Builder Pattern*. There are also several other useful built-in decorators in Python. In the *Implementation* section of this chapter, we will learn how to implement and use our own decorators.

Note that there is no one-to-one relationship between the decorator pattern and Python's decorator feature. Python decorators can actually do much more than the decorator pattern. One of the things they can be used for is to implement the decorator pattern (`j.mp/moinpydec`).

Now, let's discuss some examples where the decorator pattern applies.

Real-world examples

The decorator pattern is generally used for extending the functionality of an object. In everyday life, examples of functionality extensions are adding a holder stand to a phone or using different camera lenses.

In the Django framework, which uses decorators a lot, we have the `View` decorators, which can be used for the following (`j.mp/djangodec`):

- Restricting access to views based on the HTTP request

- Controlling the caching behavior on specific views

- Controlling compression on a per-view basis

- Controlling caching based on specific HTTP request headers

Both the Pyramid framework and the Zope application server also use decorators to achieve various goals, such as the following:

- Registering a function as an event subscriber

- Protecting a method with a specific permission

- Implementing the adapter pattern

To be more concrete, we will iterate the specific use cases of the design pattern in the next section.

Use cases

The decorator pattern shines when used for implementing cross-cutting concerns (j.mp/wikicrosscut). Examples of cross-cutting concerns are as follows:

- Data validation

- Caching

- Logging

- Monitoring

- Debugging

- Business rules

- Encryption

In general, all parts of an application that are generic and can be applied to many different parts of it are considered to be cross-cutting concerns.

Another popular example of using the decorator pattern is **graphical user interface (GUI)** toolkits. In a GUI toolkit, we want to be able to add features such as borders, shadows, colors, and scrolling to individual components/widgets.

Now, let's move on to the implementation part of the chapter, in which we will see how the decorator pattern helps with memoization.

Implementation

Python decorators are generic and very powerful. You can find many examples of how they can be used in the decorator library of python.org (j.mp/pydeclib). In this section, we will see how we can implement a memoization decorator (j.mp/memoi). All recursive functions can benefit from memoization, so let's try a function, number_sum(), that returns the sum of the first n numbers. Note that this function is already available in the math module as fsum(), but let's pretend it is not.

First, let's look at the naive implementation (the number_sum_naive.py file):

```
def number_sum(n):
    '''Returns the sum of the first n numbers'''
    assert(n >= 0), 'n must be >= 0'

    if n == 0:
        return 0
    else:
        return n + number_sum(n-1)

if __name__ == '__main__':
    from timeit import Timer
    t = Timer('number_sum(30)', 'from __main__ import \
        number_sum')
    print('Time: ', t.timeit())
```

A sample execution of this example shows how slow this implementation is. It takes roughly 3 seconds to calculate the sum of the first 30 numbers on a MacBook, which can be seen when executing the python number_sum_naive.py command:

```
Time:   3.023907012
```

Let's see whether using memoization can help us improve the performance number. In the following code, we use dict for caching the already computed sums. We also change the parameter passed to the number_sum() function. We want to calculate the sum of the first 300 numbers instead of only the first 30.

Here is the new version of the code, using memoization:

```python
sum_cache = {0:0}


def number_sum(n):
    '''Returns the sum of the first n numbers'''
    assert(n >= 0), 'n must be >= 0'

    if n in sum_cache:
        return sum_cache[n]
    res = n + number_sum(n-1)
    # Add the value to the cache
    sum_cache[n] = res
    return res

if __name__ == '__main__':
    from timeit import Timer
    t = Timer('number_sum(300)', 'from __main__ import \
        number_sum')
    print('Time: ', t.timeit())
```

Executing the memoization-based code shows that performance improves dramatically and is acceptable even for computing large values.

A sample execution, using python number_sum.py, is as follows:

```
Time:   0.12304591899999999
```

But there are already a few problems with this approach. While the performance is not an issue any longer, the code is not as clean as it is when not using memoization. And what happens if we decide to extend the code with more math functions and turn it into a module? We can think of several functions that would be useful for our module, for problems such as Pascal's triangle or the Fibonacci numbers suite algorithm.

So, if we wanted a function in the same module as `number_sum()`, for the Fibonacci numbers suite, using the same memoization technique, we would add code that looks as follows:

```
cache_fib = {0:0, 1:1}


def fibonacci(n):
    '''Returns the suite of Fibonacci numbers'''
    assert(n >= 0), 'n must be >= 0'


    if n in cache_fib:
        return cache_fib[n]
    res = fibonacci(n-1) + fibonacci(n-2)
    cache_fib[n] = res
    return res
```

Do you notice the problem already? We ended up with a new `dict` called `cache_fib`, which acts as our cache for the `fibonacci()` function, and a function that is more complex than it would be without using memoization. Our module is becoming unnecessarily complex. Is it possible to write these functions keeping them as simple as the naive versions, but achieving performance similar to the performance of the functions that use memoization?

Fortunately, it is, and the solution is to use the decorator pattern.

First, we create a `memoize()` decorator, as shown in the following example. Our decorator accepts the `fn` function, which needs to be memoized, as an input. It uses `dict` named `cache` as the cached data container. The `functools.wraps()` function is used for convenience when creating decorators. It is not mandatory but a good practice to use it since it makes sure that the documentation, and the signature of the function that is decorated, is preserved (j.mp/funcwraps). The `*args` argument list is required in this case because the functions that we want to decorate accept input arguments (such as the n argument for our two functions):

```
import functools


def memoize(fn):
    cache = dict()
```

```
    @functools.wraps(fn)
    def memoizer(*args):
        if args not in cache:
            cache[args] = fn(*args)
        return cache[args]


    return memoizer
```

Now, we can use our `memoize()` decorator with the naive version of our functions. This has the benefit of readable code without performance impact. We apply a decorator using what is known as decoration (or a decoration line). A decoration uses the `@name` syntax, where `name` is the name of the decorator that we want to use. It is nothing more than syntactic sugar for simplifying the usage of decorators. We can even bypass this syntax and execute our decorator manually, but that is left as an exercise for you.

So, the `memoize()` decorator can be used with our recursive functions as follows:

```
@memoize
def number_sum(n):
    '''Returns the sum of the first n numbers'''
    assert(n >= 0), 'n must be >= 0'
    if n == 0:
        return 0
    else:
        return n + number_sum(n-1)


@memoize
def fibonacci(n):
    '''Returns the suite of Fibonacci numbers'''
    assert(n >= 0), 'n must be >= 0'
    if n in (0, 1):
        return n
    else:
        return fibonacci(n-1) + fibonacci(n-2)
```

In the last part of the code, via the `main()` function, we show how to use the decorated functions and measure their performance. The `to_execute` variable is used to hold a list of tuples containing the reference to each function and the corresponding `timeit.Timer()` call (to execute it while measuring the time spent), thus avoiding code repetition. Note how the `__name__` and `__doc__` method attributes show the proper function names and documentation values, respectively. Try removing the `@functools.wraps(fn)` decoration from `memoize()`, and see whether this is still the case.

Here is the last part of the code:

```python
def main():
    from timeit import Timer

    to_execute = [
        (number_sum,
            Timer('number_sum(300)', 'from __main__ import \
                number_sum')),
        (fibonacci,
            Timer('fibonacci(100)', 'from __main__ import \
                fibonacci'))
    ]

    for item in to_execute:
        fn = item[0]
        print(f'Function "{fn.__name__}": {fn.__doc__}')
        t = item[1]
        print(f'Time: {t.timeit()}')
        print()

if __name__ == '__main__':
    main()
```

Let's recapitulate how we write the complete code of our math module (the `mymath.py` file):

1. After the import of Python's `functools` module that we will be using, we define the `memoize()` decorator function.

2. Then, we define the `number_sum()` function, decorated using `memoize()`.

3. We also define the `fibonacci()` function, as decorated.

4. Finally, we add the `main()` function, as shown earlier, and use the usual trick to call it.

Here is a sample output when executing the `python mymath.py` command:

```
Function "number_sum": Returns the sum of the first n
numbers
Time: 0.152614356

Function "fibonacci": Returns the suite of Fibonacci
numbers
Time: 0.142395913
```

(The execution times might differ in your case.)

At this point, we end up with readable code and acceptable performance. Now, you might argue that this is not the decorator pattern, since we don't apply it at runtime. The truth is that a decorated function cannot be undecorated, but you can still decide at runtime whether the decorator will be executed or not. That's an interesting exercise left for you.

> **Note**
> Use a decorator that acts as a wrapper, which decides whether or not the real decorator is executed based on some condition.

Another interesting property of decorators not covered in this chapter is that you can decorate a function with more than one decorator. So, here's another exercise: create a decorator that helps you to debug recursive functions, apply it to `number_sum()` and `fibonacci()`, and finally, determine the order in which the multiple decorators are executed.

Summary

This chapter covered the decorator pattern and its relationship to the Python programming language. We used the decorator pattern conveniently to extend the behavior of an object without using inheritance. Python, with its built-in decorator feature, extends the decorator concept even more, by allowing us to extend the behavior of any callable (function, method, or class) without using inheritance or composition.

We have seen a few examples of real-world objects that are decorated, such as cameras. From a software point of view, both Django and Pyramid use decorators to achieve different goals, such as controlling HTTP compression and caching.

The decorator pattern is a great solution for implementing cross-cutting concerns because they are generic and do not fit well into the OOP paradigm. We mentioned several categories of cross-cutting concerns in the *Use cases* section. In fact, in the *Implementation* section, a cross-cutting concern was demonstrated: memoization. We saw how decorators can help us to keep our functions clean, without sacrificing performance.

The next chapter covers the bridge pattern.

Questions

1. What is the main motivation for the decorator pattern?
2. Why is the decorator pattern particularly relevant in Python?
3. How does the decorator pattern help with memoization?

21

The Bridge Pattern

In the previous two chapters, we covered our first structural pattern, **adapter**, which is used to make two incompatible interfaces compatible, and **decorator**, which allows us to add responsibilities to an object in a dynamic way. There are more similar patterns. Let's continue with the series!

A third structural pattern to look at is the **bridge** pattern. We can actually compare the *bridge* and the *adapter* patterns by looking at the way they work. While the adapter is used to make unrelated classes work together (as we saw in the implementation example discussed in *Chapter 19, The Adapter Pattern*), the bridge pattern is designed upfront to decouple an implementation from its abstraction, as we are going to see in this chapter.

Specifically, we will discuss the following topics:

- Real-world examples
- Use cases
- Implementation

By the end of this chapter, we will know how to implement this design pattern and understand better the aforementioned difference with the adapter pattern.

Technical requirements

The code files for this chapter can be accessed through this link: `https://github.com/PacktPublishing/Advanced-Python-Programming-Second-Edition/tree/main/Chapter21`.

Real-world examples

In our modern, everyday lives, one example of the bridge pattern that I can think of is **information products** from the *digital economy*. Nowadays, the information product, or **infoproduct** is part of the resources you can find online for training, self-improvement, or your ideas and business development. The purpose of an information product found on certain marketplaces, or the website of the provider, is to deliver information on a given topic in such a way that it is easy to access and consume. The material provided can be a PDF document or ebook, an ebook series, a video, a video series, an online course, a subscription-based newsletter, or a combination of all those formats.

In the software realm, **device drivers** are often cited as an example of the bridge pattern, when the developer of an **operating system (OS)** defines the interface for device vendors to implement it.

Next, let's discuss when this design pattern should be employed.

Use cases

Using the bridge pattern is a good idea when you want to share an implementation among multiple objects. Basically, instead of implementing several specialized classes, defining all that is required within each class, you can define the following special components:

- An abstraction that applies to all the classes
- A separate interface for the different objects involved

Next, we will see an implementation example that illustrates this approach.

Implementation

Let's assume we are building an application where the user is going to manage and deliver content after fetching it from diverse sources, which could be the following:

- A web page (based on its URL)
- A resource accessed on an FTP server

- A file on the local filesystem

- A database server

So, here is the idea: instead of implementing several content classes, each holding the methods responsible for getting the content pieces, assembling them, and showing them inside the application, we can define an abstraction for the Resource Content and a separate interface for the objects that are responsible for fetching the content. Let's try it!

We begin with the class for our Resource Content abstraction, called ResourceContent. Then, we will need to define the interface for implementation classes that help fetch content, that is, the ResourceContentFetcher class. This concept is called the **Implementor**.

The first trick we use here is to use the _imp attribute on the ResourceContent class to maintain a reference to the object, which represents the *Implementor*:

```python
class ResourceContent:
    """

    Define the abstraction's interface.
    Maintain a reference to an object which represents \
      the Implementor.
    """

    def __init__(self, imp):
        self._imp = imp

    def show_content(self, path):
        self._imp.fetch(path)
```

As you may know by now, we define the equivalent of an interface in the Python language using two features: the metaclass feature (which helps define the *type of a type*), and **abstract base classes (ABC)**, as shown here:

```python
class ResourceContentFetcher(metaclass=abc.ABCMeta):
    """

    Define the interface for implementation classes that \
      fetch content.
    """
```

```
@abc.abstractmethod
def fetch(path):
    pass
```

Now, we can add an implementation class called URLFetcher to fetch content from a web page or resource:

```
class URLFetcher(ResourceContentFetcher):
    """
    Implement the Implementor interface and define its \
      concrete
    implementation.
    """

    def fetch(self, path):
        # path is an URL
        req = urllib.request.Request(path)
        with urllib.request.urlopen(req) as response:
            if response.code == 200:
                the_page = response.read()
                print(the_page)
```

We can also add an implementation class called LocalFileFecher to fetch content from a file on the local filesystem:

```
class LocalFileFetcher(ResourceContentFetcher):
    """
    Implement the Implementor interface and define its \
      concrete
    implementation.
    """

    def fetch(self, path):
        # path is the filepath to a text file
        with open(path) as f:
            print(r.read())
```

Based on that, our `main` function for showing content using both *content fetchers* could look like the following:

```
def main():
    url_fetcher = URLFetcher()
    iface = ResourceContent(url_fetcher)
    iface.show_content('http://python.org')

    print('====================')

    localfs_fetcher = LocalFileFetcher()
    iface = ResourceContent(localfs_fetcher)
    iface.show_content('file.txt')
```

Overall, our process could be summarized in the following UML diagram, where `LocalFileFetcher` and `URLFetcher` both inherit from `ResrouceContentFetcher`, and `ResourceContent` stores a `Fetcher` object in its `_imp` field:

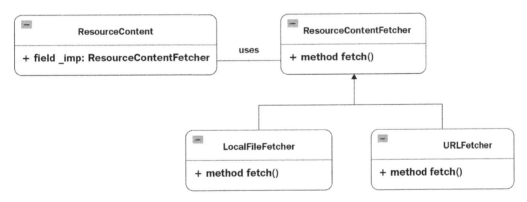

Figure 21.1 — UML diagram of the content-fetching application

Let's see a summary for the complete code of our example (the `bridge.py` file):

1. We import the three modules we need for the program (`abc`, `urllib.parse`, and `urllib.request`).
2. We define the `ResourceContent` class for the interface of the abstraction.
3. We define the `ResourceContentFetcher` class for the implementator.

4. We define two `implementation` classes:

- `URLFetcher` for fetching content from a URL

- `LocalFileFetcher` for fetching content from the local filesystem

5. Finally, we add the `main()` function, as shown previously, and the usual trick
    to call it.

Here is some sample output when executing the `python bridge.py` command:

```
[output truncated]
des.js"></script>\n\n     <script type="text/javascript"
src="/static/js/main-min.dd72c1659644.js" charset="utf-
8"></script>\n     \n\n     <!--[if lte IE 7]>\n     <script
type="text/javascript" src="/static/js/plugins/IE8-
min.8af6e26c7a3b.js" charset="utf-8"></script>\n     \n
\n     <![endif]-->\n\n     <!--[if lte IE 8]>\n     <script
type="text/javascript"
src="/static/js/plugins/getComputedStyle-
min.d41d8cd98f00.js" charset="utf-8"></script>\n     \n
\n     <![endif]-->\n\n     \n\n     \n
\n\n</body>\n</html>\n'
====================
Lorem ipsum dolor sit amet, consectetur adipiscing elit.
Proin in nibh in enim euismod mattis placerat in velit.
Donec malesuada risus sed venenatis pharetra. Proin
tincidunt porttitor euismod. Etiam non odio sodales,
tincidunt elit ac, sodales nisi. Donec massa felis,
pharetra ut libero nec, consectetur venenatis dui.
Phasellus nec sem non erat ultricies finibus. Donec sed
blandit arcu. Aliquam erat volutpat. Donec aliquam ipsum
risus, et accumsan nibh faucibus non. Aenean faucibus
feugiat diam vitae rutrum. Sed ullamcorper leo sed orci
efficitur rhoncus.

Duis vitae dolor vestibulum nibh semper faucibus. Vivamus
libero quam, ultrices quis sapien vel, blandit ultricies
purus. Nunc nisl lorem, rutrum id aliquam nec, dictum non
```

```
ligula. Duis ullamcorper, nulla quis luctus commodo, massa
lorem tristique orci, quis aliquam diam est semper nisi.
Maecenas tempor odio auctor nulla efficitur, non convallis
tellus iaculis. Fusce quis purus nibh. Nulla tempor est vel
metus sodales, in dapibus risus molestie. Donec tristique
tellus in pretium pulvinar. Pellentesque ut vehicula
mauris. Vivamus pellentesque, tellus in dictum vehicula,
justo ex volutpat sem, at cursus nisl elit non ex. Sed sed
leo eget eros lobortis laoreet. Sed ornare vitae mi a
vestibulum. Suspendisse potenti. Donec sed ligula ac enim
mattis posuere.
```

This is a basic illustration of how, using the bridge pattern in your design, you can extract content from different sources and integrate the results in the same data manipulation system or user interface.

Summary

In this chapter, we discussed the bridge pattern. Sharing similarities with the adapter pattern, the bridge pattern differs in the sense that it is used upfront to define an abstraction and its implementation in a decoupled way so that both can vary independently.

The bridge pattern is useful when writing software for problem domains such as OSs, device drivers, GUIs, and website builders where we have multiple themes, and we need to change the theme of a website based on certain properties.

To help you understand this pattern, we discussed an example in the domain of content extraction and management, where we defined an interface for the abstraction, an interface for the Implementor, and two implementations.

In the next chapter, we are going to cover the façade pattern.

Questions

1. What is the main motivation for the bridge pattern?
2. How does the bridge pattern differ from the adapter pattern?
3. How is the bridge pattern implemented in the Python example of content extraction we considered?

22
The Façade Pattern

In the previous chapter, we covered a third structural pattern, the bridge pattern, which helps to define an abstraction and its implementation in a decoupled way, so that both can vary independently. Now, we will learn about another structural pattern, the **façade** pattern, which achieves an important goal in many software use cases: hiding the inner workings of an application and only giving access to what is necessary.

In the chapter, we will discuss the following topics:

- Understanding the façade pattern
- Real-world examples
- Use cases
- Implementation

Throughout this chapter, we will see why façade is a good pattern to employ and what its benefits are, and as always, implement a hands-on example in Python.

Technical requirements

The code files for this chapter can be accessed through this link: https://github.com/PacktPublishing/Advanced-Python-Programming-Second-Edition/tree/main/Chapter22.

Understanding the façade pattern

As systems evolve, they can get very complex. It is not unusual to end up with a very large (and sometimes confusing) collection of classes and interactions. In many cases, we don't want to expose this complexity to the client. This is where façade comes to our rescue.

The façade design pattern helps us to hide the internal complexity of our systems and expose only what is necessary to the client through a simplified interface. In essence, a façade is an abstraction layer implemented over an existing complex system.

Let's take the example of a computer to illustrate things. A computer is a complex machine that depends on several parts to be fully functional. To keep things simple, the word *computer*, in this case, refers to an IBM derivative that uses a von Neumann architecture. Booting a computer is a particularly complex procedure. The CPU, main memory, and hard disk need to be up and running, the boot loader must be loaded from the hard disk to the main memory, the CPU must boot the **operating system** (**OS**) kernel, and so forth. Instead of exposing all this complexity to the client, we create a façade that encapsulates the whole procedure, making sure that all steps are executed in the right order.

In terms of object design and programming, we should have several classes, but only the `Computer` class needs to be exposed to the client code. The client will only have to execute the `start()` method of the `Computer` class, for example, and all the other complex parts are taken care of by the façade `Computer` class.

Let's discuss more real-life examples of the façade pattern in the next section.

Real-world examples

The façade pattern is quite common in life. When you call a bank or a company, you are usually first connected to the customer service department. The customer service employee acts as a façade between you and the actual department (billing, technical support, general assistance, and so on), and the employee that will help you with your specific problem.

Another example is the key used to turn on a car or motorcycle, which can also be considered a façade. It is a simple way of activating a system that is very complex internally. And, of course, the same is true for other complex electronic devices that we can activate with a single button, such as computers.

In software, the `django-oscar-datacash` module is a Django third-party module that integrates with the **DataCash** payment gateway. The module has a gateway class that provides fine-grained access to the various DataCash APIs. On top of that, it also offers a façade class that provides a less granular API (for those who don't want to mess with the details), and the ability to save transactions for auditing purposes.

In the next section, we will see why the façade pattern is important in software.

Use cases

The most common reason to use the façade pattern is to provide a single, simple entry point to a complex system. By introducing a façade, the client code can use a system by simply calling a single method/function. At the same time, the internal system does not lose any functionality; it just encapsulates it.

Not exposing the internal functionality of a system to the client code gives us an extra benefit: we can introduce changes to the system, but the client code remains unaware of and unaffected by the changes. No modifications are required to the client code.

The façade is also useful if you have more than one layer in your system. You can introduce one façade entry point per layer, and let all layers communicate with each other through their façades. This, in turn, promotes **loose coupling** and keeps the layers as independent as possible.

With that, we are now ready to try our hand at an actual implementation example in the next section.

Implementation

Assume that we want to create an OS using a multiserver approach, similar to how it is done in **MINIX 3** (j.mp/minix3) or **GNU Hurd** (j.mp/gnuhurd). A multiserver OS has a minimal kernel, called the **microkernel**, which runs in privileged mode. All the other services of the system are following a server architecture (driver server, process server, file server, and so forth). Each server belongs to a different memory address space and runs on top of the microkernel in user mode. The pros of this approach are that the OS can become more fault-tolerant, reliable, and secure. For example, since all drivers are running in user mode on a driver server, a bug in a driver cannot crash the whole system, nor can it affect the other servers. The cons of this approach are the performance overhead and the complexity of system programming. These are a result of the communication happening between a server and the microkernel, as well as between the independent servers, using message passing. Message passing is more complex than the shared memory model used in monolithic kernels, such as Linux (j.mp/helenosm).

We begin with a `Server` interface. An `Enum` parameter describes the different possible states of a server. We use the **Abstract Base Class (ABC)** module to forbid direct instantiation of the `Server` interface and make the fundamental `boot()` and `kill()` methods mandatory, assuming that different actions are needed to be taken for booting, killing, and restarting each server. If you have not used the ABC module before, note the following important things:

- We need to subclass `ABCMeta` using the `metaclass` keyword.

- We use the `@abstractmethod` decorator for stating which methods should be implemented (mandatory) by all subclasses of the server.

Try removing the `boot()` or `kill()` method of a subclass and see what happens. Do the same after removing the `@abstractmethod` decorator as well. Do things work as you expected?

Let's consider the following code:

```python
State = Enum('State', 'new running sleeping restart \
   zombie')


class Server(metaclass=ABCMeta):
    @abstractmethod
    def __init__(self):
        pass

    def __str__(self):
        return self.name

    @abstractmethod
    def boot(self):
        pass

    @abstractmethod
    def kill(self, restart=True):
        pass
```

A modular OS can have a great number of interesting servers: a file server, a process server, an authentication server, a network server, a graphical/window server, and so forth. The following example includes two stub servers: `FileServer` and `ProcessServer`. Apart from the methods required to be implemented by the `Server` interface, each server can have its own specific methods. For instance, `FileServer` has a `create_file()` method for creating files, and `ProcessServer` has a `create_process()` method for creating processes.

The `FileServer` class is as follows:

```python
class FileServer(Server):
    def __init__(self):
        '''actions required for initializing the file \
            server'''
        self.name = 'FileServer'
        self.state = State.new

    def boot(self):
        print(f'booting the {self}')
        '''actions required for booting the file server'''
        self.state = State.running

    def kill(self, restart=True):
        print(f'Killing {self}')
        '''actions required for killing the file server'''
        self.state = State.restart if restart else \
            State.zombie

    def create_file(self, user, name, permissions):
        '''check validity of permissions, user rights, \
            etc.'''
        print(f"trying to create the file '{name}' for \
            user '{user}' with permissions {permissions}")
```

The `ProcessServer` class is as follows:

```python
class ProcessServer(Server):
    def __init__(self):
        '''actions required for initializing the process \
            server'''
        self.name = 'ProcessServer'
        self.state = State.new


    def boot(self):
        print(f'booting the {self}')
        '''actions required for booting the process \
            server'''
        self.state = State.running


    def kill(self, restart=True):
        print(f'Killing {self}')
        '''actions required for killing the process \
            server'''
        self.state = State.restart if restart else \
            State.zombie


    def create_process(self, user, name):
        '''check user rights, generate PID, etc.'''
        print(f"trying to create the process '{name}' for \
            user '{user}'")
```

The `OperatingSystem` class is a façade. In its `__init__()` method, all the necessary server instances are created. The `start()` method, used by the client code, is the entry point to the system. More wrapper methods can be added, if necessary, as access points to the services of the servers, such as the `create_file()`, and `create_process()` wrappers. From the client's point of view, all those services are provided by the `OperatingSystem` class. The client should not be confused by unnecessary details such as the existence of servers and the responsibility of each server.

The code for the `OperatingSystem` class is as follows:

```python
class OperatingSystem:
    '''The Facade'''
    def __init__(self):
        self.fs = FileServer()
        self.ps = ProcessServer()

    def start(self):
        [i.boot() for i in (self.fs, self.ps)]

    def create_file(self, user, name, permissions):
        return self.fs.create_file(user, name, permissions)

    def create_process(self, user, name):
        return self.ps.create_process(user, name)
```

As you are going to see in a minute, when we present a summary of the example, there are many dummy classes and servers. They are there to give you an idea about the required abstractions (`User`, `Process`, `File`, and so forth) and servers (`WindowServer`, `NetworkServer`, and so forth) for making the system functional. A recommended exercise is to implement at least one service of the system (for example, file creation). Feel free to change the interface and the signature of the methods to fit your needs. Make sure that after your changes, the client code does not need to know anything other than the façade `OperatingSystem` class.

This application could be summarized in the following UML diagram, where
`OperatingSystem` interacts with both `FileServer` and `ProcessServer`,
hiding their methods away from the client code:

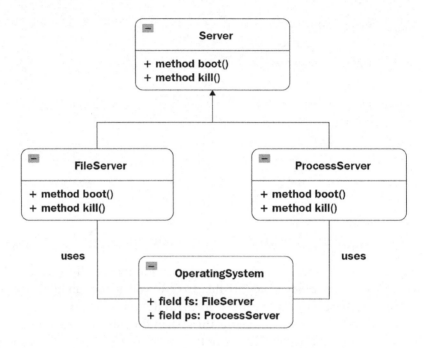

Figure 22.1 — UML diagram for the OS example

We are going to recapitulate the details of our implementation example; the full code is in
the `facade.py` file:

1. We start with the imports we need:

    ```
    from enum import Enum
    from abc import ABCMeta, abstractmethod
    ```

2. We define the `State` constant using `Enum`, as shown earlier.

3. We then add the `User`, `Process`, and `File` classes, which do nothing in this
    minimal but functional example:

    ```
    class User:
        pass


    class Process:
    ```

```
        pass

    class File:
        pass
```

4. We define the base `Server` class, as shown earlier.

5. We then define the `FileServer` class and the `ProcessServer` class, which are both subclasses of `Server`.

6. We add two other dummy classes, `WindowServer` and `NetworkServer`:

```
    class WindowServer:
        pass

    class NetworkServer:
        pass
```

7. Then, we define our façade class, `OperatingSystem`, as shown earlier.

8. Finally, here is the main part of the code, where we use the façade we have defined:

```
    def main():
        os = OperatingSystem()
        os.start()
        os.create_file('foo', 'hello', '-rw-r-r')
        os.create_process('bar', 'ls /tmp')

    if __name__ == '__main__':
        main()
```

As you can see, executing the `python facade.py` command shows the starting message of our two stub servers:

```
booting the FileServer
booting the ProcessServer
trying to create the file 'hello' for user 'foo' with
permissions -rw-r-r
trying to create the process 'ls /tmp' for user 'bar'
```

The façade `OperatingSystem` class does a good job. The client code can create files and processes without needing to know internal details about the OS, such as the existence of multiple servers. To be precise, the client code can call the methods for creating files and processes, but they are currently dummies. As an interesting exercise, you can implement one of the two methods, or even both.

Summary

In this chapter, we have learned how to use the façade pattern. This pattern is ideal for providing a simple interface to client code that wants to use a complex system but does not need to be aware of the system's complexity. We discussed a Django third-party module that uses façade: `django-oscar-datacash`. It uses the façade pattern to provide a simple DataCash API and the ability to save transactions.

We also learned how to implement the interface used by a multiserver OS. Overall, we learned that a façade is an elegant way of hiding the complexity of a system because, in most cases, the client code should not be aware of such details.

In the next chapter, we will cover other structural design patterns.

Questions

1. What are the high-level benefits of using the façade pattern?
2. How does using the façade pattern help when it comes to making changes to an application?
3. How is the façade pattern implemented in the Python example of the OS we considered?

Further reading

Design Patterns by Gamma Enrich, Helm Richard, Johnson Ralph, and Vlissides John available at `https://www.amazon.com/Design-Patterns-Object-Oriented-Addison-Wesley-Professional-ebook/dp/B000SEIBB8`

23
Other Structural Patterns

Besides the patterns we covered in the previous chapters, there are other structural patterns we can cover: **flyweight**, **model-view-controller** (**MVC**), and **proxy**. These patterns are different from those discussed in previous chapters. The flyweight pattern is an optimization design pattern that's suitable for memory usage minimization. The MVC pattern, on the other hand, is popular in object-orient programming and is designed to separate different parts of a larger application. Finally, the proxy pattern is used to maintain actions that are taken on important objects.

These three patterns will complete our discussion on structural patterns.

In this chapter, we will cover the following topics:

- Implementing the flyweight pattern
- Implementing the model-view-controller pattern
- Applying the proxy pattern

By the end of this chapter, we will have gained an overall understanding of various structural patterns and the use cases of each.

Technical requirements

The code files for this chapter can be found at `https://github.com/PacktPublishing/Advanced-Python-Programming-Second-Edition/tree/main/Chapter23`.

Implementing the flyweight pattern

What is the flyweight pattern? Object-oriented systems can face performance issues due to the overhead of object creation. Performance issues usually appear in embedded systems with limited resources, such as smartphones and tablets. They can also appear in large and complex systems where we need to create a very large number of objects (and possibly users) that need to coexist at the same time. The **flyweight** pattern teaches programmers how to minimize memory usage by sharing resources with similar objects as much as possible.

Whenever we create a new object, extra memory needs to be allocated. Although virtual memory provides us, theoretically, with unlimited memory, the reality is different. If all the physical memory of a system gets exhausted, it will start swapping pages with the secondary storage – usually a **hard disk drive** (**HDD**) – which, in most cases, is unacceptable due to the performance differences between the main memory and the HDD. **Solid-state drives** (**SSDs**) generally have better performance than HDDs, but not everybody is expected to use SSDs. So, SSDs are not going to completely replace HDDs anytime soon.

Apart from memory usage, performance is also a consideration. Graphics software, including computer games, should be able to render 3D information (for example, a forest with thousands of trees, a village full of soldiers, or an urban area with a lot of cars) extremely quickly. If each object in a 3D terrain is created individually and no data sharing is used, the performance will be prohibitive.

As software engineers, we should solve software problems by writing better software, instead of forcing the customer to buy extra or better hardware. The flyweight design pattern is a technique that's used to minimize memory usage and improve performance by introducing data sharing between similar objects (`http://j.mp/wflyw`). A flyweight is a shared object that contains state-independent, immutable (also known as **intrinsic**) data. The state-dependent, mutable (also known as **extrinsic**) data should not be part of the flyweight pattern because this information cannot be shared since it differs per object. If the flyweight pattern needs extrinsic data, it should be provided explicitly by the client code.

An example may help clarify how the flyweight pattern can be used practically. Let's assume that we are creating a performance-critical game, such as a **first-person shooter** (**FPS**). In FPS games, the players (soldiers) share some states, such as representation and behavior. In *Counter-Strike*, for instance, all the soldiers on the same team (counter-terrorists versus terrorists) look the same (representation). In the same game, all the soldiers (on both teams) have some common actions, such as *jump*, *duck*, and so forth (behavior). This means that we can create a flyweight that will contain all of the common data. Of course, the soldiers also have a lot of data that is different per soldier and will not be a part of the flyweight, such as weapons, health, and location.

What are other real-world examples of the flyweight pattern? We will discuss them in the next section.

Real-world examples

Flyweight is an optimization design pattern. Therefore, it is not easy to find a good non-computing example of it. We can think of flyweight as caching in real life. For example, many bookstores have dedicated shelves containing the newest and most popular publications. This is a cache: first, you can look at the dedicated shelves for the book you are looking for, and if you cannot find it, you can ask the bookseller to assist you.

The *Exaile* music player uses flyweight to reuse objects (in this case, music tracks) that are identified by the same URL. There's no point in creating a new object if it has the same URL as an existing object, so the same object is reused to save resources.

Peppy, an XEmacs-like editor that's implemented in Python, uses the flyweight pattern to store the state of a major mode status bar. That's because, unless they're modified by the user, all the status bars share the same properties.

Use cases

Flyweight is all about improving performance and memory usage. All embedded systems (phones, tablets, games consoles, microcontrollers, and so forth) and performance-critical applications (games, 3D graphics processing, real-time systems, and so forth) can benefit from it.

The *Gang of Four* (*GoF*) book lists the following requirements that need to be satisfied to effectively use the flyweight pattern:

- The application needs to use many objects.

- There are so many objects that it's too expensive to store/render them. Once the mutable state is removed (because if it is required, it should be passed explicitly to the flyweight pattern by the client code), many groups of distinct objects can be replaced by relatively few shared objects.

- Object identity is not important for the application. We cannot rely on object identity because object sharing causes identity comparisons to fail (objects that appear different to the client code end up having the same identity).

Now, let's look at our hands-on implementation of the flyweight pattern.

Implementation

Let's see how we can implement the example that we briefly mentioned in the introduction to this section for cars in an area. We will create a small car park to illustrate the idea, making sure that the whole output can be read on a single Terminal page. However, no matter how large you make the car park, the memory allocation stays the same.

Before diving into the code, let's spend a moment noting the differences between memoization and the flyweight pattern. **Memoization** is an optimization technique that uses a cache to avoid recomputing results that were already computed in an earlier execution step. Memoization does not focus on a specific programming paradigm such as **object-oriented programming** (**OOP**). In Python, memoization can be applied to both methods and simple functions. Flyweight is an OOP-specific optimization design pattern that focuses on sharing object data.

First, we need an `Enum` parameter that describes the three different types of cars that are in the car park:

```
CarType = Enum('CarType', 'subcompact compact suv')
```

Then, we will define the class at the core of our implementation: `Car`. The `pool` variable is the object pool (in other words, our cache). Notice that `pool` is a class attribute (a variable that's shared by all instances).

Using the __new__() special method, which is called before __init__(), we are converting the Car class into a metaclass that supports self-references. This means that cls references the Car class. When the client code creates an instance of Car, it passes the type of the car as car_type. The car's type is used to check if a car of the same type has already been created. If that's the case, the previously created object is returned; otherwise, the new car type is added to the pool and returned:

```python
class Car:
    pool = dict()

    def __new__(cls, car_type):
        obj = cls.pool.get(car_type, None)
        if not obj:
            obj = object.__new__(cls)
            cls.pool[car_type] = obj
            obj.car_type = car_type
        return obj
```

The render() method is what will be used to render a car on the screen. Notice how all the mutable information not known by flyweight needs to be explicitly passed by the client code. In this case, a random color and the coordinates of a location (of the *x, y* form) are used for each car.

Also, note that to make render() more useful, it is necessary to ensure that no cars are rendered on top of each other. Consider this as an exercise: if you want to make rendering more fun, you can use a graphics toolkit such as Tkinter, Pygame, or Kivy.

The render() method is defined as follows:

```python
    def render(self, color, x, y):
        type = self.car_type
        msg = f'render a car of type {type} and color \
            {color} at ({x}, {y})'
        print(msg)
```

The main() function shows how we can use the flyweight pattern. The color of a car is a random value from a predefined list of colors. The coordinates use random values between 1 and 100. As we will see shortly, although 18 cars are rendered, memory is only allocated for 3. The last line of the output, which we will see later, proves that when using flyweight, we cannot rely on object identity.

The id() function returns the memory address of an object. This is not the default behavior in Python because, by default, id() returns a unique ID (the memory address of an object as an integer) for each object. In our case, even if two objects appear to be different, they have the same identity if they belong to the same flyweight family (in this case, the family is defined by car_type). Of course, different identity comparisons can still be used for objects of different families, but that is only possible if the client knows the implementation details.

Our example main() function's code is as follows:

```python
def main():
    rnd = random.Random()
    colors = 'white black silver gray red blue brown \
        beige yellow green'.split()
    min_point, max_point = 0, 100
    car_counter = 0

    for _ in range(10):
        c1 = Car(CarType.subcompact)
        c1.render(random.choice(colors),
                  rnd.randint(min_point, max_point),
                  rnd.randint(min_point, max_point))
        car_counter += 1


    ...


    print(f'cars rendered: {car_counter}')
    print(f'cars actually created: {len(Car.pool)}')


    c4 = Car(CarType.subcompact)
    c5 = Car(CarType.subcompact)
    c6 = Car(CarType.suv)
    print(f'{id(c4)} == {id(c5)}? {id(c4) == id(c5)}')
    print(f'{id(c5)} == {id(c6)}? {id(c5) == id(c6)}')
```

Here is the full code listing (the `flyweight.py` file) to show you how the flyweight pattern is implemented and used:

1. First, we need a couple of imports:

    ```python
    import random
    from enum import Enum
    ```

2. The Enum for the types of cars is shown here:

    ```python
    CarType = Enum('CarType', 'subcompact compact suv')
    ```

3. Then, we have the Car class, with its `pool` attribute and the `__new__()` and `render()` methods:

    ```python
    class Car:
        pool = dict()

        def __new__(cls, car_type):
            obj = cls.pool.get(car_type, None)
            if not obj:
                obj = object.__new__(cls)
                cls.pool[car_type] = obj
                obj.car_type = car_type
            return obj

        def render(self, color, x, y):
            type = self.car_type
            msg = f'render a car of type {type} and \
                color {color} at ({x}, {y})'
            print(msg)
    ```

4. In the first part of the `main` function, we define some variables and render a set of cars of the `subcompact` type:

    ```python
    def main():
        rnd = random.Random()
        colors = 'white black silver gray red blue \
            brown beige yellow green'.split()
        min_point, max_point = 0, 100
    ```

```
        car_counter = 0


    for _ in range(10):
        c1 = Car(CarType.subcompact)
        c1.render(random.choice(colors),
                    rnd.randint(min_point, max_point),
                    rnd.randint(min_point, max_point))
        car_counter += 1
```

5. The second part of the `main` function is as follows, which renders another set of cars of the `compact` type:

```
    for _ in range(3):
        c2 = Car(CarType.compact)
        c2.render(random.choice(colors),
                    rnd.randint(min_point, max_point),
                    rnd.randint(min_point, max_point))
        car_counter += 1
```

6. The third part of the `main` function is as follows, this time with `suv` cars:

```
    for _ in range(5):    c3 = Car(CarType.suv)
            c3.render(random.choice(colors),
                        rnd.randint(min_point, max_point),
                        rnd.randint(min_point, max_point))
        car_counter += 1


    print(f'cars rendered: {car_counter}')
    print(f'cars actually created: {len(Car.pool)}')
```

7. Finally, here is the fourth part of the `main` function, where we create three additional cars of the three types:

```
    c4 = Car(CarType.subcompact)
    c5 = Car(CarType.subcompact)
    c6 = Car(CarType.suv)
    print(f'{id(c4)} == {id(c5)}? {id(c4) == id(c5)}')
    print(f'{id(c5)} == {id(c6)}? {id(c5) == id(c6)}')
```

8. We do not forget our usual __name__ == '__main__' trick and good practice, as follows:

```
if __name__ == '__main__':
    main()
```

The execution of the Python flyweight.py command shows the type, random color, and coordinates of the rendered objects, as well as the identity comparison results between flyweight objects of the same/different families:

```
render a car of type CarType.subcompact and color yellow at
(57, 51)
render a car of type CarType.subcompact and color blue at
(10, 61)
render a car of type CarType.subcompact and color gray at
(65, 74)
render a car of type CarType.subcompact and color red at
(10, 19)
render a car of type CarType.subcompact and color green at
(89, 5)
render a car of type CarType.subcompact and color green at
(88, 76)
render a car of type CarType.subcompact and color black at
(0, 18)
render a car of type CarType.subcompact and color silver at
(43, 12)
render a car of type CarType.subcompact and color red at
(25, 71)
render a car of type CarType.subcompact and color blue at
(68, 38)
render a car of type CarType.compact and color white at
(79, 48)
render a car of type CarType.compact and color green at
(18, 93)
render a car of type CarType.compact and color brown at
(71, 43)
render a car of type CarType.suv and color silver at
(2, 71)
```

```
render a car of type CarType.suv and color blue at (70, 42)
render a car of type CarType.suv and color silver at
(100, 98)
render a car of type CarType.suv and color gray at (83, 49)
render a car of type CarType.suv and color brown at (77, 2)
cars rendered: 18
cars actually created: 3
140569248959360 == 140569248959360? True
140569248959360 == 140569298067216? False
```

Do not expect to see the same output since the colors and coordinates are random, and the object identities depend on the memory map.

This program marks the end of our discussion of the flyweight pattern. In the next section, we will learn about the MVC pattern.

Implementing the model-view-controller pattern

The MVC pattern is useful mainly in application development and helps developers improve the maintainability of their applications by avoiding mixing the business logic with the user interface.

One of the design principles related to software engineering is the **separation of concerns** (**SoC**) principle. The idea behind the SoC principle is to split an application into distinct sections, where each section addresses a separate concern. Examples of such concerns are the layers that are used in a layered design (data access layer, business logic layer, presentation layer, and so forth). Using the SoC principle simplifies the development and maintenance of software applications.

The MVC pattern is nothing more than the SoC principle applied to OOP. The name of the pattern comes from the three main components that are used to split a software application: the **model**, the **view**, and the **controller**. MVC is considered an architectural pattern rather than a design pattern. The difference between an architectural and a design pattern is that the former has a broader scope than the latter. Nevertheless, MVC is too important to skip just for this reason. Even if we will never have to implement it from scratch, we need to be familiar with it because all common frameworks use MVC or a slightly different version of it (more on this shortly).

The model is the core component. It represents knowledge. It contains and manages the (business) logic, data, state, and rules of an application. The view is a visual representation of the model. Examples of views include a computer GUI, the text output of a computer terminal, a smartphone's application GUI, a PDF document, a pie chart, a bar chart, and so forth. The view only displays the data; it doesn't handle it. The controller is the link/ glue between the model and view. All communication between the model and the view happens through a controller.

A typical use case for an application that uses MVC, after the initial screen is rendered for the user, is as follows:

1. The user triggers a view by clicking (typing, touching, and so on) a button.

2. The view informs the controller of the user's action.

3. The controller processes user input and interacts with the model.

4. The model performs all the necessary validation and state changes and informs the controller about what should be done.

5. The controller instructs the view to update and display the output appropriately, following the instructions that are given by the model.

This is summarized in the following diagram:

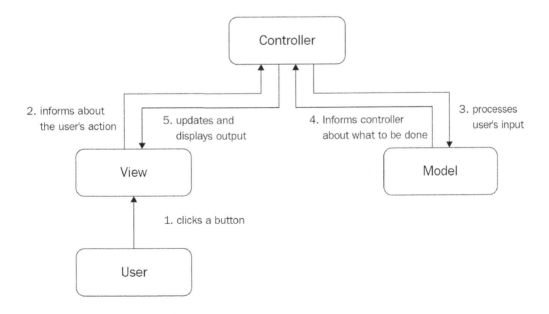

Figure 23.1 — An MVC diagram for a typical computer program

You might be wondering, why is the controller part necessary? Can't we just skip it? We could, but then we would lose a big benefit that MVC provides: the ability to use more than one view (even at the same time, if that's what we want) without modifying the model. To achieve decoupling between the model and its representation, every view typically needs a controller. If the model communicated directly with a specific view, we wouldn't be able to use multiple views (or at least, not in a clean and modular way).

Now, let's see where the MVC pattern is used in the real world.

Real-world examples

As we mentioned previously, MVC is the SoC principle applied to OOP. The SoC principle is used a lot in real life. For example, if you build a new house, you usually assign different professionals to do the following:

- Install the plumbing and electricity
- Paint the house

Another example is a restaurant. In a restaurant, the waiters receive orders and serve dishes to the customers, but the meals are cooked by the chefs.

In web development, several frameworks use the MVC idea:

- The **Web2py** framework (`http://j.mp/webtopy`) is a lightweight Python framework that embraces the MVC pattern. If you have never tried Web2py, I encourage you to do so since it is extremely simple to install. Many examples demonstrate how MVC can be used in Web2py on the project's web page.

- **Django** is also an MVC framework, although it uses different naming conventions. The controller is called view, and the view is called **template**. Django uses the name **Model-Template-View** (**MTV**). According to the designers of Django, the view describes what data is seen by the user, so it uses the name view as the Python callback function for a particular URL. The term *template* in Django is used to separate content from its representation. It describes *how* the data is seen by the user, not *which* data is seen.

In the next section, we will detail the specific use cases of the MVC pattern.

Use cases

MVC is a very generic and useful design pattern. All popular web frameworks (Django, Rails, and Symfony or Yii) and application frameworks (iPhone SDK, Android, and QT) make use of MVC or a variation of it – **model-view-adapter (MVA)**, **model-view-presenter (MVP)**, and so forth. However, even if we don't use any of these frameworks, it makes sense to implement the pattern on our own because of the benefits it provides, which are as follows:

- The separation between the view and model allows graphic designers to focus on the UI part and programmers to focus on development, without them interfering with each other.

- Because of the loose coupling between the view and the model, each part can be modified/extended without them affecting the other. For example, adding a new view is trivial – just implement a new controller for it.

- Maintaining each part is easier because the responsibilities are clear.

When you implement MVC from scratch, ensure that you create smart models, thin controllers, and dumb views.

A model is considered smart because it does the following:

- Contains all the validation/business rules/logic
- Handles the state of the application
- Has access to application data (database, cloud, and so on)
- Does not depend on the UI

A controller is considered thin because it does the following:

- Updates the model when the user interacts with the view
- Updates the view when the model changes
- Processes the data before delivering it to the model/view, if necessary
- Does not display the data
- Does not access the application data directly
- Does not contain validation/business rules/logic

A view is considered dumb because it does the following:

- Displays the data

- Allows the user to interact with it

- Does only minimal processing, usually provided by a template language (for example, using simple variables and loop controls)

- Does not store any data

- Does not access the application data directly

- Does not contain validation/business rules/logic

If you are implementing MVC from scratch and want to find out if you did it right, you can try answering some key questions:

- *If your application has a GUI, is it skinnable? How easily can you change the skin/look and feel of it? Can you give the user the ability to change the skin of your application during runtime?* If these tasks cannot be done easily, it means that something is going wrong with your MVC implementation.

- *If your application has no GUI (for instance, if it's a terminal application), how hard is it to add GUI support? Or, if adding a GUI is irrelevant, is it easy to add views to display the results in a chart (pie chart, bar chart, and so on) or a document (PDF, spreadsheet, and so on)?* If these changes are not trivial (a matter of creating a new controller with a view attached to it, without modifying the model), MVC has not been implemented properly.

If you make sure that these conditions are satisfied, your application will be more flexible and maintainable compared to an application that does not use MVC. We'll look at an example of this in the next section, where we will implement an application to maintain a collection of quotes.

Implementation

I could use any of the common frameworks to demonstrate how to use MVC, but I feel that the picture would be incomplete. So, I have decided to show you how to implement MVC from scratch using a very simple example: a quote printer. The idea is extremely simple. The user enters a number and sees the quote related to that number. The quotes are stored in a quotes tuple. This is the data that normally exists in a database, a file, and so on, and only the model has direct access to it.

Let's consider the following code example:

```
quotes =
(
    'A man is not complete until he is married. Then he is \
      finished.',
    'As I said before, I never repeat myself.',
    'Behind a successful man is an exhausted woman.',
    'Black holes really suck...',
    'Facts are stubborn things.'
)
```

The model is minimalistic; it only has a get_quote() method that returns the quote (string) of the quotes tuple based on its index, n. Note that n can be less than or equal to 0, due to the way indexing works in Python:

```
class QuoteModel:
    def get_quote(self, n):
        try:
            value = quotes[n]
        except IndexError as err:
            value = 'Not found!'
        return value
```

The view has three methods:

- show(), which is used to print a quote (or the message; that is, Not found!) on the screen.
- error(), which is used to print an error message on the screen.
- select_quote(), which reads the user's selection.

This can be seen in the following code:

```
class QuoteTerminalView:
    def show(self, quote):
        print(f'And the quote is: "{quote}"')

    def error(self, msg):
        print(f'Error: {msg}')
```

```
        def select_quote(self):
            return input('Which quote number would you like  \
                to see? ')
```

The controller does the coordination. The __init__() method initializes the model and view. The run() method validates the quoted index that's been given by the user, gets the quote from the model, and passes it back to the view to be displayed, as shown in the following code:

```
class QuoteTerminalController:
    def __init__(self):
        self.model = QuoteModel()
        self.view = QuoteTerminalView()

    def run(self):
        valid_input = False
        while not valid_input:
            try:
                n = self.view.select_quote()
                n = int(n)
                valid_input = True
            except ValueError as err:
                self.view.error(f"Incorrect index '{n}'")
        quote = self.model.get_quote(n)
        self.view.show(quote)
```

Last but not least, the main() function initializes and fires the controller, as shown in the following code:

```
def main():
    controller = QuoteTerminalController()
    while True:
        controller.run()
```

The following is the complete workflow for this example (the mvc.py file):

1. We start by defining a variable for the list of quotes.

2. We implement the model class, QuoteModel.

3. Then, we implement the view class, QuoteTerminalView.

4. Finally, we implement the controller class, `QuoteTerminalController`.

5. At the end of our example code with the `main()` function, we initialize and run the controller.

The following sample execution of the Python `mvc.py` command shows how the program prints out quotes for the user:

```
Which quote number would you like to see? 2
And the quote is: "Behind a successful man is an exhausted
woman."
Which quote number would you like to see? 4
And the quote is: "Facts are stubborn things."
Which quote number would you like to see? 1
And the quote is: "As I said before, I never repeat
myself."
Which quote number would you like to see? 6
And the quote is: "Not found!"
Which quote number would you like to see? 3
And the quote is: "Black holes really suck..."
Which quote number would you like to see? 0
And the quote is: "A man is not complete until he is
married. Then he is finished."
Which quote number would you like to see?
```

Here, we can see that everything is working as intended!

And with that, we will move on to the last topic of this chapter: the proxy pattern.

Applying the proxy pattern

In some applications, we want to execute one or more important actions before accessing an object. This is where the **proxy pattern** comes in. An example is accessing sensitive information. Before we allow any user to access sensitive information, we want to make sure that the user has sufficient privileges. The important action is not necessarily related to security issues. **Lazy initialization** (`http://j.mp/wikilazy`) is another case; we want to delay the creation of a computationally expensive object until the first time the user needs to use it. The idea of the proxy pattern is to help with performing such an action before accessing the actual object.

The proxy design pattern gets its name from the *proxy* (also known as *surrogate*) object, which is used to perform an important action before the actual object is accessed. There are four different well-known proxy types (http://j.mp/proxypat). They are as follows:

- A **remote proxy**, which acts as the local representation of an object that exists in a different address space (for example, a network server).

- A **virtual proxy**, which uses lazy initialization to defer the creation of a computationally expensive object until the moment it is needed.

- A **protection/protective proxy**, which controls access to a sensitive object.

- A **smart (reference) proxy**, which performs extra actions when an object is accessed. Examples of such actions include reference counting and thread-safety checks.

I find virtual proxies very useful, so let's look at an example of how we can implement them in Python right now. In the *Implementation* subsection of this section, you will learn how to create protective proxies.

There are many ways to create a virtual proxy in Python, but I always like focusing on the idiomatic/Pythonic implementations. The code shown here is based on the great answer by Cyclone, a user of the following site: http://stackoverflow.com/ (http://j. mp/solazyinit). To avoid confusion, I should clarify that in this section, the terms *property*, *variable*, and *attribute* are used interchangeably.

First, we must create a `LazyProperty` class that can be used as a decorator. When it decorates a property, `LazyProperty` loads the property lazily (on the first use), instead of instantly. The `__init__()` method creates two variables that are used as aliases to the method that initializes a property. The `method` variable is an alias to the actual method, while the `method_name` variable is an alias to the method's name. To get a better understanding of how the two aliases are used, print their values to the output (uncomment the two commented lines in the following code):

```python
class LazyProperty:
    def __init__(self, method):
        self.method = method
        self.method_name = method.__name__
        # print(f"function overriden: {self.fget}")
        # print(f"function's name: {self.func_name}")
```

The `LazyProperty` class is a descriptor (http://j.mp/pydesc). Descriptors are the recommended mechanisms to use in Python to override the default behavior of its attribute access methods: `__get__()`, `__set__()`, and `__delete__()`. The `LazyProperty` class only overrides `__set__()` because that is the only access method it needs to override. In other words, we don't have to override all the access methods. The `__get__()` method accesses the value of the property the underlying method wants to assign and uses `setattr()` to do the assignment manually.

What `__get()__` does is very neat: it replaces the method with the value! This means that not only is the property lazily loaded, but it can also only be set once. We will see what this means in a moment. Again, uncomment the commented line in the following code to get some extra information:

```python
def __get__(self, obj, cls):
    if not obj:
        return None
    value = self.method(obj)
    # print(f'value {value}')
    setattr(obj, self.method_name, value)
    return value
```

The `Test` class shows how we can use the `LazyProperty` class. There are three attributes: x, y, and _resource. We want the _resource variable to be loaded lazily; thus, we must initialize it to `None`, as shown in the following code:

```python
class Test:
    def __init__(self):
        self.x = 'foo'
        self.y = 'bar'
        self._resource = None
```

The `resource()` method is decorated with the `LazyProperty` class. For demonstration purposes, the `LazyProperty` class initializes the _resource attribute as a tuple, as shown in the following code. Normally, this would be a slow/expensive initialization process (database, graphics, and so on):

```python
@LazyProperty
def resource(self):
    print(f'initializing self._resource which is: \
      {self._resource}')
    self._resource = tuple(range(5)) # expensive
    return self._resource
```

The `main()` function, as follows, shows how lazy initialization behaves:

```
def main():
    t = Test()
    print(t.x)
    print(t.y)
    # do more work...
    print(t.resource)
    print(t.resource)
```

Notice how overriding the `__get()__` access method makes it possible to treat the `resource()` method as a simple attribute (we can use `t.resource` instead of `t.resource()`).

In the execution output of this example (the `lazy.py` file), we can see the following:

- The `_resource` variable is initialized not by the time the `t` instance is created, but the first time that we use `t.resource`.

- The second time `t.resource` is used, the variable is not initialized again. That's why the initialization string that's initializing `self._resource` is shown only once.

Here is the output we get when we execute the Python `lazy.py` command:

```
foo
bar
initializing self._resource which is: None
(0, 1, 2, 3, 4)
(0, 1, 2, 3, 4)
```

There are two basic, different kinds of lazy initialization in OOP. They are as follows:

- **At the instance level**: This means that an object's property is initialized lazily, but the property has an object scope. Each instance (object) of the same class has its own (different) copy of the property.

- **At the class or module level**: In this case, we do not want a different copy per instance, but all the instances share the same property, which is lazily initialized. This case is not covered in this chapter. If you find it interesting, consider it as an exercise.

Now, let's see what real-world examples follow the proxy pattern.

Real-world examples

Chip (also known as **Chip and PIN**) cards (`http://j.mp/wichpin`) offer a good example of how a protective proxy is used in real life. A debit/credit card contains a chip that needs to be read by the ATM or card reader. Once the chip has been verified, a password (PIN) is required to complete the transaction. This means that you cannot make any transactions without physically presenting the card and knowing the PIN.

A bank check, which is used instead of cash to make purchases and deals, is an example of a remote proxy. The check gives access to a bank account.

In software, the `weakref` module of Python contains a `proxy()` method, which accepts an input object and returns a smart proxy to it. Weak references are the recommended way to add reference-counting support to an object.

Use cases

Since there are at least four common proxy types, the proxy design pattern has many use cases, as follows:

- It is used to create a distributed system using either a private network or the cloud. In a distributed system, some objects exist in the local memory, while other objects exist in the memory of remote computers. If we don't want the client code to be aware of such differences, we can create a remote proxy that hides/encapsulates them, making the distributed nature of the application transparent.

- It is used when our application is suffering from performance issues due to the early creation of expensive objects. Introducing lazy initialization using a virtual proxy to create the objects only at the moment they are required can give us significant performance improvements.

- It is used to check if a user has sufficient privileges to access a piece of information. If our application handles sensitive information (for example, medical data), we want to make sure that the user who's trying to access/modify it is allowed to do so. A protection/protective proxy can handle all security-related actions.

- It is used when our application (or library, toolkit, framework, and so forth) uses multiple threads and we want to move the burden of thread safety from the client code to the application. In this case, we can create a smart proxy to hide the thread-safety complexities from the client.

- An **object-relational mapping (ORM)** API is also an example of how to use a remote proxy. Many popular web frameworks, including Django, use an ORM to provide OOP-like access to a relational database. An ORM acts as a proxy to a relational database that can be located anywhere, either at a local or remote server.

Now, let's apply the proxy pattern to build a simple interface that provides example users' information.

Implementation

To demonstrate the proxy pattern, we will implement a simple protection proxy to view and add users. The service provides two options:

- **Viewing the list of users**: This operation does not require special privileges.
- **Adding a new user**: This operation requires the client to provide a special secret message.

The SensitiveInfo class contains the information that we want to protect. The users variable contains the list of existing users. The read() method prints the list of users. The add() method adds a new user to the list.

Let's consider the following code:

```python
class SensitiveInfo:
    def __init__(self):
        self.users = ['nick', 'tom', 'ben', 'mike']

    def read(self):
        nb = len(self.users)
        print(f"There are {nb} users: {' ' \
            .join(self.users)}")

    def add(self, user):
        self.users.append(user)
        print(f'Added user {user}')
```

The `Info` class is a protection proxy of `SensitiveInfo`. The `secret` variable is the message that's required to be known/provided by the client code to add a new user. Note that this is just an example. In reality, you should never do the following:

- Store passwords in the source code
- Store passwords in a cleartext form
- Use a weak (for example, MD5) or custom form of encryption

In the `Info` class, as shown in the following code, the `read()` method is a wrapper to `SensitiveInfo.read()`, and the `add()` method ensures that a new user can only be added if the client code knows the secret message:

```python
class Info:
    '''protection proxy to SensitiveInfo'''

    def __init__(self):
        self.protected = SensitiveInfo()
        self.secret = '0xdeadbeef'

    def read(self):
        self.protected.read()

    def add(self, user):
        sec = input('what is the secret? ')
        self.protected.add(user) if sec == self.secret \
            else print("That's wrong!")
```

The `main()` function shows how the proxy pattern can be used by the client code. The client code creates an instance of the `Info` class and uses the displayed menu to read the list, add a new user, or exit the application. Let's consider the following code:

```python
def main():
    info = Info()

    while True:
        print('1. read list |==| 2. add user |==| 3. \
            quit')
        key = input('choose option: ')
```

```
        if key == '1':
            info.read()
        elif key == '2':
            name = input('choose username: ')
            info.add(name)
        elif key == '3':
            exit()
        else:
            print(f'unknown option: {key}')
```

The following is the sample output of the program when executing the Python `proxy.py` command:

```
1. read list |==| 2. add user |==| 3. quit
choose option: 1
There are 4 users: nick tom ben mike
1. read list |==| 2. add user |==| 3. quit
choose option: 2
choose username: bill
what is the secret? 12345
That's wrong!
1. read list |==| 2. add user |==| 3. quit
choose option: 2
choose username: bill
what is the secret? 0xdeadbeef
Added user bill
1. read list |==| 2. add user |==| 3. quit
choose option: 1
There are 5 users: nick tom ben mike bill
1. read list |==| 2. add user |==| 3. quit
```

Have you already spotted flaws or missing features that could improve our proxy example? I have a few suggestions. They are as follows:

- This example has a very big security flaw. Nothing prevents the client code from bypassing the security of the application by creating an instance of `SensitiveInfo` directly. Improve this example to prevent this situation. One way to do this is to use the `abc` module to forbid direct instantiation of `SensitiveInfo`. *What other code changes are required in this case?*

- A basic security rule is that we should never store cleartext passwords. Storing a password safely is not very hard, so long as we know which libraries to use (`http://j.mp/hashsec`). If you are interested in security, try to implement a secure way to store the secret message externally (for example, in a file or database).

- *The application only supports adding new users, but what about removing an existing user?* Add a `remove()` method.

Summary

In this chapter, we covered three other structural design patterns: flyweight, MVC, and proxy. Throughout this chapter, we learned about the differences between these and the other structural patterns we have discussed. Then, we implemented each of these patterns in hands-on examples. As we saw, the flyweight pattern is designed for memory usage minimization, the MVC pattern maintains a logical organization of different parts of an application, and the proxy pattern is typically used when sensitive information is accessed.

In the next chapter, we will start exploring behavioral design patterns. Behavioral patterns cope with object interconnection and algorithms. The first behavioral pattern we will cover is the chain of responsibility.

Questions

1. What is the main motivation for the flyweight pattern?
2. What is the main motivation for the MVC pattern?
3. What is the main motivation for the proxy pattern?

24

The Chain of Responsibility Pattern

We now cover the **Chain of Responsibility design pattern**, which should be used, as we will see, when we do not know the number and type of requests/events we would need to support. While this may seem vague, this pattern is useful among a wide range of use cases, such as event-based systems, purchase systems, and shipping systems.

In this chapter, we will learn what the Chain of Responsibility pattern is, its benefits, and—as always—how to implement it in a practical Python example. We will discuss the following topics:

- Understanding the Chain of Responsibility pattern
- Real-world examples
- Use cases
- Implementation

Technical requirements

The code files for this chapter can be accessed through this link:

```
https://github.com/PacktPublishing/Advanced-Python-
Programming-Second-Edition/tree/main/Chapter24
```

Understanding the Chain of Responsibility pattern

When developing an application, most of the time, we know which method should satisfy a particular request in advance. However, this is not always the case. For example, think of any broadcast computer network, such as the original Ethernet implementation. In broadcast computer networks, all requests are sent to all nodes (broadcast domains are excluded for simplicity), but only the nodes that are interested in a sent request process it.

All computers that participate in a broadcast network are connected to each other using a common medium such as the cable that connects all nodes. If a node is not interested or does not know how to handle a request, it can perform the following actions:

- Ignore the request and do nothing
- Forward the request to the next node

The way in which the node reacts to a request is an implementation detail. However, we can use the analogy of a broadcast computer network to understand what the Chain of Responsibility pattern is all about. The Chain of Responsibility pattern is used when we want to give multiple objects the chance to satisfy a single request or when we don't know in advance which object (from a chain of objects) should process a specific request.

To illustrate the principle, imagine a chain (linked list, tree, or any other convenient data structure) of objects and the following flow:

1. We start by sending a request to the first object in the chain.
2. The object decides whether it should satisfy the request or not.
3. The object forwards the request to the next object.
4. This procedure is repeated until we reach the end of the chain.

At the application level, instead of talking about cables and network nodes, we can focus on objects and the flow of a request. The following diagram shows how the client code sends a request to all processing elements of an application:

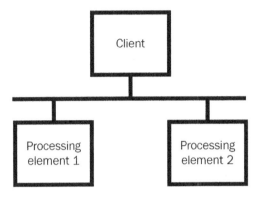

Figure 24.1 – Client code sending a request

Note that the client code only knows about the first processing element, instead of having references to all of them, and each processing element only knows about its immediate next neighbor (called the **successor**), not about every other processing element. This is usually a one-way relationship, which in programming terms means a **singly linked list** in contrast to a **doubly linked list**. A singly linked list does not allow navigation in both ways, while a doubly linked list allows that. This chain organization is used for a good reason. It achieves decoupling between the sender (client) and the receivers (processing elements).

We will see some real-world examples of this pattern in the next section.

Real-world examples

Automated teller machines (ATMs) and, in general, any kind of machine that accepts/returns banknotes or coins (for example, a snack-vending machine) use the Chain of Responsibility pattern.

There is always a single slot for all banknotes, as shown in the following diagram, courtesy of *SourceMaking* (www.sourcemaking.com):

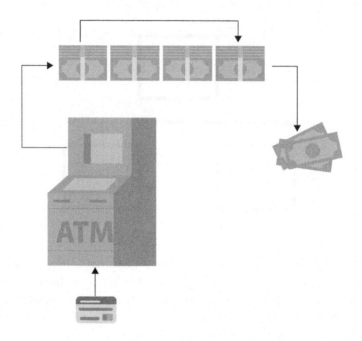

Figure 24.2 – An ATM has a single slot for all banknotes

When a banknote is dropped, it is routed to the appropriate receptacle. When it is returned, it is taken from the appropriate receptacle. We can think of the single slot as a shared communication medium and the different receptacles as processing elements. The result contains cash from one or more receptacles. For example, in the preceding diagram, we see what happens when we request **United States dollars (USD)** $175 from the ATM.

In software, the servlet filters of Java are pieces of code that are executed before a **HyperText Transfer Protocol (HTTP)** request arrives at a target. When using servlet filters, there is a chain of filters. Each filter performs a different action (user authentication, logging, data compression, and so forth) and either forwards the request to the next filter until the chain is exhausted or breaks the flow if there is an error—for example, the authentication failed three consecutive times (j.mp/soservl).

As another software example, Apple's Cocoa and Cocoa Touch frameworks use the Chain of Responsibility to handle events. When a *view* receives an event that it doesn't know how to handle, it forwards the event to its *superview*. This goes on until a *view* is capable of handling the event or the *chain of views* is exhausted (j.mp/chaincocoa).

When is this design pattern useful? Let's discuss that in the next section.

Use cases

By using the Chain of Responsibility pattern, we provide a chance to a number of different objects to satisfy a specific request. This is useful when we don't know which object should satisfy a request in advance. An example is a purchase system. In purchase systems, there are many approval authorities. One approval authority might be able to approve orders up to a certain value—let's say $100. If the order is for more than $100, the order is sent to the next approval authority in the chain that can approve orders up to $200, and so forth.

Another case where the Chain of Responsibility is useful is when we know that more than one object might need to process a single request. This is what happens in event-based programming. A single event, such as a left-mouse click, can be caught by more than one listener.

It is important to note that the Chain of Responsibility pattern is not very useful if all the requests can be taken care of by a single processing element unless we really don't know which element that is. The value of this pattern is the decoupling that it offers. Instead of having a many-to-many relationship between a client and all processing elements (and the same is true regarding the relationship between a processing element and all other processing elements), a client only needs to know how to communicate with the start (head) of the chain.

The following diagram illustrates the difference between **tight** and **loose coupling**:

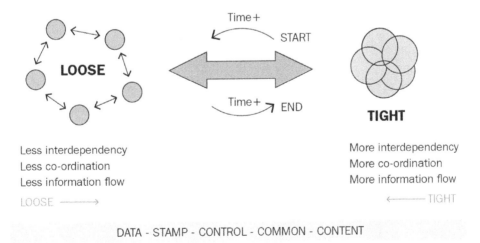

Figure 24.3 – Loose versus tight coupling

The idea behind loosely coupled systems is to simplify maintenance and make it easier for us to understand how they function (j.mp/loosecoup).

We will see that this is the case in the next section, where we implement an event-based system.

Implementation

There are many ways to implement a Chain of Responsibility in Python, but my favorite implementation is the one by Vespe Savikko (https://legacy.python.org/workshops/1997-10/proceedings/savikko.html). Vespe's implementation uses dynamic dispatching in a Pythonic style to handle requests (http://j.mp/ddispatch).

Let's implement a simple event-based system using Vespe's implementation as a guide. Here is a **Unified Modeling Language** (**UML**) class diagram of an event-based system:

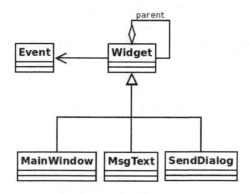

Figure 24.4 – UML class diagram of an event-based system

The Event class describes an event. We'll keep it simple, so in our case, an event has only name, as illustrated in the following code snippet:

```python
class Event:
    def __init__(self, name):
        self.name = name

    def __str__(self):
        return self.name
```

The `Widget` class is the core class of the application. The **parent** aggregation shown in the UML diagram indicates that each widget can have a reference to a `parent` object, which, by convention, we assume is a `Widget` instance. Note, however, that according to the rules of inheritance, an instance of any of the subclasses of `Widget` (for example, an instance of `MsgText`) is also an instance of `Widget`. The default value of `parent` is `None`, as illustrated in the following code snippet:

```python
class Widget:
    def __init__(self, parent=None):
        self.parent = parent
```

The `handle()` method uses dynamic dispatching through `hasattr()` and `getattr()` to decide who is the handler of a specific request (event). If the widget that is asked to handle an event does not support it, there are two fallback mechanisms. If the widget has a parent, then the `handle()` method of the parent is executed. If the widget has no parent but a `handle_default()` method, `handle_default()` is executed, as illustrated in the following code snippet:

```python
def handle(self, event):
    handler = f'handle_{event}'
    if hasattr(self, handler):
        method = getattr(self, handler)
        method(event)
    elif self.parent is not None:
        self.parent.handle(event)
    elif hasattr(self, 'handle_default'):
        self.handle_default(event)
```

At this point, you might have realized why the `Widget` and `Event` classes are only associated (no aggregation or composition relationships) in the UML class diagram. The association is used to show that the `Widget` class knows about the `Event` class but does not have any strict references to it, since an event needs to be passed only as a parameter to `handle()`.

`MainWindow`, `MsgText`, and `SendDialog` are all widgets with different behaviors. Not all these three widgets are expected to be able to handle the same events, and even if they can handle the same event, they might behave differently. `MainWindow` can only handle `close` and `default` events, as illustrated in the following code snippet:

```python
class MainWindow(Widget):
    def handle_close(self, event):
```

```
        print(f'MainWindow: {event}')

    def handle_default(self, event):
        print(f'MainWindow Default: {event}')
```

SendDialog can only handle paint events, as illustrated in the following code snippet:

```
class SendDialog(Widget):
    def handle_paint(self, event):
        print(f'SendDialog: {event}')
```

Finally, MsgText can only handle down events, as illustrated in the following code snippet:

```
class MsgText(Widget):
    def handle_down(self, event):
        print(f'MsgText: {event}')
```

The main() function shows how we can create a few widgets and events and how the widgets react to those events. All events are sent to all the widgets. Note the parent relationship of each widget. The sd object (an instance of SendDialog) has as its parent the mw object (an instance of MainWindow). However, not all objects need to have a parent that is an instance of MainWindow. For example, the msg object (an instance of MsgText) has the sd object as a parent, as illustrated in the following code snippet:

```
def main():
    mw = MainWindow()
    sd = SendDialog(mw)
    msg = MsgText(sd)

    for e in ('down', 'paint', 'unhandled', 'close'):
        evt = Event(e)
        print(f'Sending event -{evt}- to MainWindow')
        mw.handle(evt)
        print(f'Sending event -{evt}- to SendDialog')
        sd.handle(evt)
        print(f'Sending event -{evt}- to MsgText')
        msg.handle(evt)
```

Executing the `python chain.py` command gives us the following output:

```
Sending event -down- to MainWindow
MainWindow Default: down
Sending event -down- to SendDialog
MainWindow Default: down
Sending event -down- to MsgText
MsgText: down
Sending event -paint- to MainWindow
MainWindow Default: paint
Sending event -paint- to SendDialog
SendDialog: paint
Sending event -paint- to MsgText
SendDialog: paint
Sending event -unhandled- to MainWindow
MainWindow Default: unhandled
Sending event -unhandled- to SendDialog
MainWindow Default: unhandled
Sending event -unhandled- to MsgText
MainWindow Default: unhandled
Sending event -close- to MainWindow
MainWindow: close
Sending event -close- to SendDialog
MainWindow: close
Sending event -close- to MsgText
MainWindow: close
```

There are some interesting things that we can see in the output. For instance, sending a down event to `MainWindow` ends up being handled by the default `MainWindow` handler. Another nice case is that although a `close` event cannot be handled directly by `SendDialog` and `MsgText`, all `close` events end up being handled properly by `MainWindow`. That's the beauty of using the *parent relationship* as a fallback mechanism.

If you want to spend some more creative time on the event example, you can replace the dumb `print` statements and add some actual behavior to the listed events. Of course, you are not limited to the listed events. Just add your favorite event and make it do something useful!

Another exercise is to add a `MsgText` instance during runtime that has `MainWindow` as the parent and do the same for an event (add a new event to an existing widget).

Summary

In this chapter, we covered the Chain of Responsibility design pattern. This pattern is useful to model requests and/or handle events when the number and type of handlers aren't known in advance.

Overall, we have learned how to use this design pattern to facilitate loose coupling between the sender and the receiver(s). Some examples that we have seen where this is particularly beneficial include Java's servlet and Apple's Cocoa frameworks.

That's it for the Chain of Responsibility pattern. In the next chapter, we will cover the Command pattern.

Questions

The answers for the following questions can be found in the *Assessments* section at the end of the book.

1. What are the high-level benefits of the Chain of Responsibility pattern?

2. How is the Chain of Responsibility pattern implemented in the Python example of the event-based system we considered?

3. What is an example of a situation in which the Chain of Responsibility pattern is not useful?

25
The Command Pattern

In this chapter, we will cover the **command pattern**. Using this design pattern, we can encapsulate an operation, such as *copy and paste*, as an object. The command pattern is also great for grouping multiple commands. It's useful for implementing macros, multilevel undoing, and transactions. Throughout our discussions, we will learn about the idea of treating an operation as an object and use this command mindset to handle application transactions.

We will discuss the following:

- Understanding the command pattern
- Real-world examples
- Use cases
- Implementation

Technical requirements

The code files for this chapter can be accessed through this link: https://github.com/PacktPublishing/Advanced-Python-Programming-Second-Edition/tree/main/Chapter25.

Understanding the command pattern

Most applications nowadays have an **undo** operation. It is hard to imagine, but undo did not exist in any software for many years. Undo was introduced in 1974 (j.mp/wiundo), but Fortran and Lisp, two programming languages that are still widely used, were created in 1957 and 1958, respectively (j.mp/proghist)! The user had no easy way to fix a mistake. I wouldn't like to have been an application user during those years.

Enough with the history! We want to know how we can implement the undo functionality in our applications, and since you have read the title of this chapter, you already know which design pattern is recommended to implement undo: the command pattern.

The command design pattern helps us encapsulate an operation (undo, redo, copy, paste, and so forth) as an object. What this simply means is that we create a class that contains all the logic and the methods required to implement the operation. The advantages of doing this are as follows (j.mp/cmdpattern):

- We don't have to execute a command directly. It can be executed at will.

- The object that invokes the command is decoupled from the object that knows how to perform it. The invoker does not need to know any implementation details about the command.

- If it makes sense, multiple commands can be grouped to allow the invoker to execute them in order. This is useful, for instance, when implementing a multilevel undo command.

As you can imagine, this pattern has a wide range of use cases in the real world, which we will see in the next section.

Real-world examples

When we go to a restaurant for dinner, we give the order to the waiter. The order pad (usually paper) that they use to write the order is an example of a command. After writing the order, the waiter places it in the queue that is executed by the cook. Each check is independent and can be used to execute many different commands, for example, one command for each item that will be cooked.

As you would expect, we also have several examples in software. Here are two I can think of:

- PyQt is the Python binding of the QT toolkit. PyQt contains a QAction class that models an action as a command. Extra optional information is supported for every action, such as description, tooltip, or shortcut (j.mp/qaction).

- Git Cola (`j.mp/git-cola`), a Git GUI written in Python, uses the Command pattern to modify the model, amend a commit, apply a different election, check out, and so forth (`j.mp/git-cola-code`).

Let's now be more general and discuss when the command pattern will prove useful in the next section.

Use cases

Many developers use the undo example as the only use case of the command pattern. The truth is that undo is the killer feature of the command pattern. However, the command pattern can actually do much more (`j.mp/commddp`):

- **GUI buttons and menu items**: The PyQt example that was already mentioned uses the command pattern to implement actions on buttons and menu items.

- **Other operations**: Apart from undo, commands can be used to implement any operation. A few examples are cut, copy, paste, redo, and capitalize text.

- **Transactional behavior and logging**: Transactional behavior and logging are important to keep a persistent log of changes. They are used by operating systems to recover from system crashes, relational databases to implement transactions, filesystems to implement snapshots, and installers (wizards) to revert canceled installations.

- **Macros**: By macros, in this case, we mean a sequence of actions that can be recorded and executed on demand at any point in time. Popular editors such as Emacs and Vim support macros.

To demonstrate what we have discussed so far, we will implement a file utility management application next.

Implementation

In this section, we will use the command pattern to implement the most basic file utilities:

- Creating a file and optionally writing text (a string) to it
- Reading the contents of a file
- Renaming a file
- Deleting a file

We will not implement these utilities from scratch, since Python already offers good implementations of them in the os module. What we want is to add an extra abstraction level on top of them so that they can be treated as commands. By doing this, we get all the advantages offered by commands.

From the operations shown, renaming a file and creating a file support undo. Deleting a file and reading the contents of a file do not support undo. Undo can actually be implemented on delete file operations. One technique is to use a special trash/wastebasket directory that stores all the deleted files so that they can be restored when the user requests them. This is the default behavior used on all modern desktop environments and is left as an exercise to you.

Each command has two parts:

- **The initialization part**: This is taken care of by the __init__() method and contains all the information required by the command to be able to do something useful (the path of a file, the contents that will be written to the file, and so forth).

- **The execution part**: This is taken care of by the execute() method. We call the execute() method when we want to actually run a command. This is not necessarily right after initializing it.

Let's start with the rename utility, which is implemented using the RenameFile class. The __init__() method accepts the source (src) and destination (dest) file paths as parameters (strings). If no path separators are used, the current directory is used to create the file. An example of using a path separator is passing the /tmp/file1 string as src and the /home/user/file2 string as dest. Another example, where we would not use a path, is passing file1 as src and file2 as dest:

```
class RenameFile:
    def __init__(self, src, dest):
        self.src = src
        self.dest = dest
```

We add the execute() method to the class. This method does the actual renaming using os.rename(). The verbose variable corresponds to a global **flag**, which, when activated (by default, it is activated), gives feedback to the user about the operation that is performed. You can deactivate it if you prefer silent commands. Note that although print() is good enough for an example, normally something more mature and powerful can be used, for example, the logging module (j.mp/py3log):

```
    def execute(self):
        if verbose:
```

```
        print(f"[renaming '{self.src}' to \
            '{self.dest}']")
    os.rename(self.src, self.dest)
```

Our rename utility (`RenameFile`) supports the undo operation through its `undo()` method. In this case, we use `os.rename()` again to revert the name of the file to its original value:

```
def undo(self):
    if verbose:
        print(f"[renaming '{self.dest}' back to \
            '{self.src}']")
    os.rename(self.dest, self.src)
```

In this example, deleting a file is implemented in a function, instead of a class. That is to show it is not mandatory to create a new class for every command that you want to add (more on that will be covered later). The `delete_file()` function accepts a file path as a string and uses `os.remove()` to delete it:

```
def delete_file(path):
    if verbose:
        print(f"deleting file {path}")
    os.remove(path)
```

Back to using classes again. The `CreateFile` class is used to create a file. The `__init__` () method for that class accepts the familiar `path` parameter and a `txt` parameter for the content (a string) that will be written to the file. If nothing is passed as `txt`, the default `hello world` text is written to the file. Normally, the same default behavior is to create an empty file, but for the needs of this example, I decided to write a default string in it.

The definition of the `CreateFile` class starts as follows:

```
class CreateFile:

    def __init__(self, path, txt='hello world\n'):
        self.path = path
        self.txt = txt
```

Then we add an execute() method, in which we use the with statement and Python's open() built-in function to open the file (mode='w' means write mode), and the write() function to write the txt string to it, as follows:

```
def execute(self):
    if verbose:
        print(f"[creating file '{self.path}']")
    with open(self.path, mode='w', encoding='utf-8') \
        as out_file:
        out_file.write(self.txt)
```

The undo action for the operation of creating a file is to delete that file. So, the undo() method, which we add to the class, simply uses the delete_file() function to achieve that, as follows:

```
def undo(self):
    delete_file(self.path)
```

The last utility gives us the ability to read the contents of a file. The execute() method of the ReadFile class uses open() again, this time in read mode, and just prints the content of the file using print().

The ReadFile class is defined as follows:

```
class ReadFile:

    def __init__(self, path):
        self.path = path

    def execute(self):
        if verbose:
            print(f"[reading file '{self.path}']")
        with open(self.path, mode='r', encoding='utf-8') \
            as in_file:
            print(in_file.read(), end='')
```

The `main()` function makes use of the utilities we have defined. The `orig_name` and `new_name` parameters are the original and new names of the file that is created and renamed. A commands list is used to add (and configure) all the commands that we want to execute at a later point. Note that the commands are not executed unless we explicitly call `execute()` for each command:

```python
def main():
    orig_name, new_name = 'file1', 'file2'
    commands = (
        CreateFile(orig_name),
        ReadFile(orig_name),
        RenameFile(orig_name, new_name)
    )

    [c.execute() for c in commands]
```

The next step is to ask the users whether they want to undo the executed commands or not. The user selects whether the commands will be undone or not. If they choose to undo them, `undo()` is executed for all commands in the commands list. However, since not all commands support undo, exception handling is used to catch (and ignore) the `AttributeError` exception generated when the `undo()` method is missing. The code would look like the following:

```python
answer = input('reverse the executed commands? [y/n] ')

if answer not in 'yY':
    print(f"the result is {new_name}")
    exit()

for c in reversed(commands):
    try:
        c.undo()
    except AttributeError as e:
        print("Error", str(e))
```

Using exception handling for such cases is an acceptable practice, but if you don't like it, you can check explicitly whether a command supports the undo operation by adding a **Boolean** method, for example, `supports_undo()` or `can_be_undone()`. Again, that is not mandatory.

Let's see two sample executions using the `python command.py` command line.

In the first one, there is no undo of commands:

```
[creating file 'file1']
[reading file 'file1']
hello world
[renaming 'file1' to 'file2']
reverse the executed commands? [y/n] y
[renaming 'file2' back to 'file1']
Error 'ReadFile' object has no attribute 'undo'
deleting file file1
```

In the second one, we have the undo of commands:

```
[creating file 'file1']
[reading file 'file1']
hello world
[renaming 'file1' to 'file2']
reverse the executed commands? [y/n] n
the result is file2
```

But wait! Let's see what can be improved in our command implementation example. Among the things to consider are the following:

- What happens if we try to rename a file that doesn't exist?
- What about files that exist but cannot be renamed because we don't have the proper filesystem permissions?

We can try improving the utilities by doing some kind of error handling. Checking the return status of the functions in the `os` module can be useful. We could check whether the file exists before trying the delete action, using the `os.path.exists()` function.

Also, the file creation utility creates a file using the default file permissions as decided by the filesystem. For example, in POSIX systems, the permissions are `-rw-rw-r--`. You might want to give the ability to the user to provide their own permissions by passing the appropriate parameter to `CreateFile`. How can you do that? Hint: one way is by using `os.fdopen()`.

And now, here's something for you to think about. I mentioned earlier that a command does not necessarily need to be a class. That's how the delete utility was implemented; there is just a `delete_file()` function. What are the advantages and disadvantages of this approach? Here's a hint: is it possible to put a delete command in the commands list as was done for the rest of the commands? We know that functions are first-class citizens in Python, so we can do something such as the following (see the `first-class.py` file):

```python
import os
verbose = True


class CreateFile:

    def undo(self):
        try:
            delete_file(self.path)
        except:
            print('delete action not successful...')
            print('... file was probably already deleted.')

def main():

    orig_name = 'file1'
    df=delete_file

    commands = [CreateFile(orig_name),]
    commands.append(df)

    for c in commands:
        try:
            c.execute()
        except AttributeError as e:
            df(orig_name)

    for c in reversed(commands):
        try:
            c.undo()
```

```
        except AttributeError as e:
            pass


if __name__ == "__main__":
    main()
```

Running `first-class.py` gives us the following output:

```
[creating file 'file1']
deleting file file1...
deleting file file1...
delete action not successful...
... file was probably already deleted.
```

We see that this variant of the implementation example works as intended, as the second delete throws an error saying that the action was not successful.

With that said, there are some potential improvements to this program that you could think about. First, the code we have is not uniform; we rely too much on exception handling, which is not the normal flow of a program. While all the other commands we implemented have an `execute()` method, in this case, there is no `execute()`.

Furthermore, the delete file utility currently has no undo support. What happens if we eventually decide to add undo support for it? Normally, we add an `undo()` method to the class that represents the command. However, in this case, there is no class. We could create another function to handle undo, but creating a class is a better approach.

Summary

In this chapter, we covered the command pattern. Using this design pattern, we can encapsulate an operation, such as copy and paste, as an object. Using this pattern, we can execute a command whenever we want, and not necessarily at creation time, while the client code that executes a command does not need to know any details about how it is implemented. Moreover, we can group commands and execute them in a specific order.

To demonstrate command, we implemented some basic file utilities on top of Python's `os` module. Our utilities supported undo and had a uniform interface, which makes grouping commands easy.

The next chapter covers the Observer pattern.

Questions

The answers to these questions can be found in the *Assessments* section at the end of the book:

1. What are the high-level benefits of the command pattern?

2. From the perspective of the client of an application, how is the command pattern specifically useful?

3. How is the command pattern implemented in the Python example of file management?

26
The Observer Pattern

We use the observer pattern when we want to be able to inform/notify all stakeholders (an object or a group of objects) when the state of an object changes. An important feature of the observer pattern is that the number of subscribers/observers, as well as who the subscribers are, may vary and can be changed at runtime.

In this chapter, we will learn about this design pattern while comparing it to a similar one we have seen in the past, known as the MVC pattern, and use it to implement a data formatter.

Specifically, we will cover the following topics:

- Understanding the observer pattern
- Real-world examples
- Use cases
- Implementation

Technical requirements

The code files for this chapter can be found at `https://github.com/PacktPublishing/Advanced-Python-Programming-Second-Edition/tree/main/Chapter26`.

Understanding the observer pattern

When we need to update a group of objects when the state of another object changes, a popular solution is offered by the **Model-View-Controller** (**MVC**) pattern. Let's assume that we are using the data of the same *model* in two *views*; for instance, in a pie chart and a spreadsheet. Whenever the model is modified, both views need to be updated. That's the role of the observer pattern.

The observer pattern describes a publish-subscribe relationship between a single object – the publisher, which is also known as the **subject** or **observable** – and one or more objects – the subscribers, also known as **observers**.

In the case of MVC, the publisher is the model, while the subscribers are the views. There are other examples that we will discuss throughout this chapter.

The ideas behind the observer pattern are the same as those behind the separation of concerns principle; that is, to increase decoupling between the publisher and subscribers, and to make it easy to add/remove subscribers at runtime. Let's look at a couple of examples of this.

Real-world examples

In reality, an auction resembles the observer pattern. Every auction bidder has a numbered paddle that is raised whenever they want to place a bid. Whenever the paddle is raised by a bidder, the auctioneer acts as the subject by updating the price of the bid and broadcasting the new price to all bidders (subscribers).

In software, we can cite at least two examples:

- Kivy, the Python framework for developing user interfaces, has a module called **Properties**, which implements the observer pattern. Using this technique, you can specify what should happen when a property's value changes.

- The RabbitMQ library can be used to add asynchronous messaging support to an application. Several messaging protocols are supported, such as HTTP and AMQP. RabbitMQ can be used in a Python application to implement a publish-subscribe pattern, which is nothing more than the observer design pattern (`j.mp/rabbitmqobs`).

In the next section, we will discuss when this design pattern could and should be used.

Use cases

We generally use the observer pattern when we want to inform/update *one or more objects* (observers/subscribers) about a change that happened on *a given object* (subject/publisher/observable). The number of observers, as well as who those observers are, may vary and can be changed dynamically.

We can think of many cases where the observer pattern can be useful. One such use case is **newsfeeds**. With RSS, Atom, or other related formats, you follow a feed, and every time it is updated, you receive a notification about the update.

The same concept exists in social networking. If you are connected to another person using a social networking service, and your connection updates something, you are notified about it. It doesn't matter if the connection is a Twitter user that you follow, a real friend on Facebook, or a business colleague on LinkedIn.

Event-driven systems is another example where the observer pattern is usually used. In such systems, you have *listeners* that *listen* for specific events. The listeners are triggered when an event they are listening to is created. This can be typing a specific key (on the keyboard), moving the mouse, and more. The event plays the role of the publisher, and the listeners play the role of the observers. The key point, in this case, is that multiple listeners (observers) can be attached to a single event (publisher).

Finally, in the next section, we will implement a data formatter.

Implementation

The ideas described here are based on the ActiveState Python Observer code recipe (`https://code.activestate.com/`). There is a default formatter that shows a value in decimal format. However, we can add/register more formatters. In this example, we will add a hex formatter and a binary formatter. Every time the value of the default formatter is updated, the registered formatters will be notified and take action. In this case, the action is to show the new value in the relevant format.

The observer pattern is one of the patterns where inheritance makes sense. We can have a base `Publisher` class that contains the common functionality of adding, removing, and notifying observers. Our `DefaultFormatter` class derives from `Publisher` and adds the formatter-specific functionality. We can also dynamically add and remove observers on demand.

We will begin with the `Publisher` class. The observers are kept in the observer's list. The `add()` method registers a new observer or throws an error if it already exists. The `remove()` method unregisters an existing observer or throws an exception if it does not exist. Finally, the `notify()` method informs all observers about a change. This is shown in the following code block:

```python
class Publisher:
    def __init__(self):
        self.observers = []

    def add(self, observer):
        if observer not in self.observers:
            self.observers.append(observer)
        else:
            print(f'Failed to add: {observer}')

    def remove(self, observer):
        try:
            self.observers.remove(observer)
        except ValueError:
            print(f'Failed to remove: {observer}')

    def notify(self):
        [o.notify(self) for o in self.observers]
```

Let's continue with the `DefaultFormatter` class. The first thing that `__init__()` does is call the `__init__()` method of the base class since this is not done automatically in Python.

A `DefaultFormatter` instance has a name to make it easier for us to track its status. We use **name mangling** in the _data variable to state that it should not be accessed directly. Note that this is always possible in Python but fellow developers have no excuse for doing so since the code already states that they shouldn't. `DefaultFormatter` treats the _data variable as an integer, and the default value is 0:

```python
class DefaultFormatter(Publisher):
    def __init__(self, name):
        Publisher.__init__(self)
```

```
self.name = name
self._data = 0
```

The `__str__()` method returns information about the name of the publisher and the value of the `_data` attribute. `type(self).__name__` is a handy trick to get the name of a class without hardcoding it. It is one of those tricks that makes your code easier to maintain:

```
def __str__(self):
    return f"{type(self).__name__}: '{self.name}' \
        has data =
    {self._data}"
```

There are two `data()` methods. The first one uses the `@property` decorator to give read access to the `_data` variable. Using this, we can just execute `object.data` instead of `object.data()`:

```
@property
def data(self):
    return self._data
```

The second `data()` method is more interesting. It uses the `@setter` decorator, which is called every time the assignment (=) operator is used to assign a new value to the `_data` variable. This method also tries to cast a new value to an integer, and does exception handling in case this operation fails:

```
@data.setter
def data(self, new_value):
    try:
        self._data = int(new_value)
    except ValueError as e:
        print(f'Error: {e}')
    else:
        self.notify()
```

The next step is to add the observers. The functionality of `HexFormatter` and `BinaryFormatter` is very similar. The only difference between them is how they format the value of the data that's received by the publisher – that is, in hexadecimal and binary, respectively:

```python
class HexFormatterObs:
    def notify(self, publisher):
        value = hex(publisher.data)
        print(f"{type(self).__name__}: '{publisher.name}' \
            has now hex data = {value}")


class BinaryFormatterObs:
    def notify(self, publisher):
        value = bin(publisher.data)
        print(f"{type(self).__name__}: '{publisher.name}' \
            has now bin data = {value}")
```

To help us use those classes, the `main()` function initially creates a `DefaultFormatter` instance named `test1` and, afterward, attaches (and detaches) the two available observers. We also have some exception handling to ensure that the application doesn't crash when erroneous data is passed by the user.

The code is as follows:

```python
def main():
    df = DefaultFormatter('test1')
    print(df)

    print()
    hf = HexFormatterObs()
    df.add(hf)
    df.data = 3
    print(df)

    print()
    bf = BinaryFormatterObs()
    df.add(bf)
    df.data = 21
    print(df)
```

Moreover, tasks such as trying to add the same observer twice or removing an observer that does not exist should cause no crashes:

```
print()
df.remove(hf)
df.data = 40
print(df)


print()
df.remove(hf)
df.add(bf)


df.data = 'hello'
print(df)


print()
df.data = 15.8
print(df)
```

Before we run this code and observe the output, let's have a recap on the full code (the `observer.py` file):

1. First, we define the `Publisher` class.
2. Then, we define the `DefaultFormatter` class, along with its special `__init__` and `__str__` methods.
3. We add the `data` property getter and setter methods to the `DefaultFormatter` class.
4. We define our two observer classes.
5. Finally, we take care of the main part of the program.

Executing the `python observer.py` command gives us the following output:

```
DefaultFormatter: 'test1' has data = 0


HexFormatterObs: 'test1' has now hex data = 0x3
DefaultFormatter: 'test1' has data = 3


HexFormatterObs: 'test1' has now hex data = 0x15
```

```
BinaryFormatterObs: 'test1' has now bin data = 0b10101
DefaultFormatter: 'test1' has data = 21


BinaryFormatterObs: 'test1' has now bin data = 0b101000
DefaultFormatter: 'test1' has data = 40


Failed to remove: <__main__.HexFormatterObs object at
0x7fe6e4c9d670>
Failed to add: <__main__.BinaryFormatterObs object at
0x7fe6e4c9d5b0>
Error: invalid literal for int() with base 10: 'hello'
DefaultFormatter: 'test1' has data = 40


BinaryFormatterObs: 'test1' has now bin data = 0b1111
DefaultFormatter: 'test1' has data = 15
```

Here, we can see that as the extra observers are added, the more (and more relevant) output is shown, and when an observer is removed, it is not notified any longer. That's exactly what we want: runtime notifications that we can enable/disable on demand.

The defensive programming part of the application also seems to work fine. Trying to do funny things, such as removing an observer that does not exist or adding the same observer twice, is not allowed. The messages that are shown are not very user-friendly, but I leave it up to you to make them friendlier as an exercise. Runtime failures such as trying to pass a string when the API expects a number are also handled properly without causing the application to crash/terminate.

This example would be much more interesting if it were interactive. Even a simple menu that allows the user to attach/detach observers at runtime and modify the value of DefaultFormatter would be nice because the runtime aspect becomes much more visible. Feel free to do this.

Another nice exercise is to add more observers. For example, you can add an octal formatter, a Roman numeral formatter, or any other observer that uses your favorite representation. Be creative! With this, we have completed our discussion on the observer pattern.

Summary

In this chapter, we covered the observer design pattern, including many examples, such as Kivy, the framework for developing innovative user interfaces, along with its **Properties** concept and module, and the Python bindings of RabbitMQ (we referred to a specific example of RabbitMQ that's used to implement the publish-subscribe, or the observer, pattern).

We also learned how to use the observer pattern to create data formatters that can be attached and detached at runtime to enrich the behavior of an object. Hopefully, you will find the recommended exercises interesting.

This also marks the end of this book. Congratulations on making it to the end, and I hope that the material that's been covered has been helpful for you in taking your Python skills to the next level!

Questions

Answer the following questions to test your knowledge of this chapter:

1. What is the main motivation for the observer pattern?
2. How is the observer pattern different from the MVC pattern when it comes to updating other components of an application when a target component changes?
3. How is the observer pattern implemented in the Python example of value formatters?

Assessments

Chapter 1

1. In the order of importance: functionality, correctness, and efficiency.

2. An `assert` statement raises an error when the condition it checks for is not satisfied. As such, these statements are used in tests, where we determine whether a program computes and outputs values as it is supposed to.

3. A benchmark is a small but representative use case that can be used to estimate the speed of a program. Benchmarks can be used to compare different versions of a program to see if a new implementation leads to an improvement in efficiency.

4. In IPython or Jupyter notebooks, the `timeit` magic command, when placed in front of a code snippet, will run that code several times and record the running time of each run. The output of the command will show summary statistics of the recorded times so that we can estimate the average running time of the code we are interested in.

5. `cProfile` includes the following in its output:

    A. `ncalls`: The number of times the function was called.

    B. `tottime`: The total time spent in the function without considering the calls to other functions.

    C. `cumtime`: The time in the function, including other function calls.

    D. `percall`: The time spent for a single call of the function, which can be obtained by dividing the total or cumulative time by the number of calls.

    E. `filename:lineno`: The filename and corresponding line numbers. This information is not available when calling C extensions modules.

6. The `dis` module analyzes the low-level bytecode and shows how Python code is converted. This is helpful when we are interested in the number of low-level instructions that correspond to a specific statement.

7. Using IPython, we may profile the function as follows:

```
In [1]: %load_ext line_profiler
In [2]: from exercise import close, benchmark
In [3]: %lprun -f close benchmark()
Function: close at line 5
Line #        Hits           Time  Per Hit    % Time  Line
Contents
================================================================
=====
    5                                                     def
close(particles, eps=1e-5):
    6             1            6.0      6.0      66.7      p0,
p1 = particles
    7
    8             1            2.0      2.0      22.2      x_
dist = abs(p0.x - p1.x)
    9             1            1.0      1.0      11.1      y_
dist = abs(p0.y - p1.y)
   10
   11             1            0.0      0.0       0.0
return x_dist < eps and y_dist < eps
```

Perhaps surprisingly, the unpacking and p0 and p1 takes two thirds of the execution time of the `close()` function.

Chapter 2

1. The most appropriate data structure for each of the following use cases is as follows:

    A. Mapping items to another set of items (with set being used in the most general sense): dictionaries.

    B. Accessing, modifying, and appending elements: lists.

    C. Maintaining a collection of unique elements: sets.

    D. Keeping track of the minimum/maximum of a set (in the most general sense): heaps.

    E.   Appending and removing elements at the endpoints of a sequence (in the most general sense): deques.

    F.   Fast searching according to some similarity criterion (used by, for example, autocompletion engines): tries.

2.   Caching is a design where we store expensive results in a temporary location, which can be in memory, on-disk, or a remote location. Memoization is specifically about storing and reusing the results of previous function calls in an application. As such, memoization is a form of caching.

3.   Comprehensions and generators are optimized under the hood, so they are generally more efficient than explicit for loops. They are also more compact in code and are more readable.

4.   A dictionary would be a more appropriate data structure. If the numbers represented the counts, a `Counter` data structure would be the best data structure to use.

Chapter 3

1.   NumPy offers efficient operations on multidimensional arrays, such as array creation, accessing elements (indexing) and slicing along specific axes, and optimized mathematical operations.

2.   Using pandas, you can apply "mapping" operations to data, group, aggregate, and summarize data.

3.   NumPy cannot handle labeled data, while pandas cannot process multidimensional data. `xarray` combines the best features of the two libraries to offer APIs the ability to handle multi-dimensional, labeled data.

Chapter 4

1.   Static types allow the compiler to generate type-specific optimization, making the compiled code more efficient.

2.   A memory view belongs to Cython's interface, which helps it work with different data types such as `byte`, `bytearray`, or `array.array` easier. Specifically, it offers a universal interface that simplifies the process of accessing the values that are stored in these different data types.

3.   To profile Cython, we can use the annotated view to identify hard-to-find interpreter-related calls, as well as the familiar `cProfile` tool.

Chapter 5

1. JIT compilers perform compilation at runtime rather than before running the code. This allows a piece of code that is expected to run many times to become more efficient, as recompilation is no longer necessary.

2. We use the signature of an `nb.jit` function to specify the data types that the function works with, which allows for further optimization for specific numerical data types. When Numba encounters other, unsupported types, it simply registers them as the generic `pyobject` type.

3. Tracing JIT compilation refers to the process of identifying the most intensive loops in a program, tracing the operations involved, and compiling the corresponding optimized, interpreter-free code. This allows us to actively optimize the most inefficient part of our code.

Chapter 6

1. The main components of a typical machine learning pipeline are the predictive model (model assumptions, parameters), the loss function, and the optimization of the model parameters to minimize the loss function.

2. The loss function may be minimized using gradient descent, in which we compute the gradient of the loss with the current values of the model parameters and adjust those values in the opposite direction of the gradient. JAX can compose this gradient loss function using `grad`.

3. In our example, we utilized kernels to create nonlinear features from the features we were given. Naïve implementations of kernels are hard to vectorize, which may lead to inefficient for loops. JAX can automatically vectorize these kernels to address this problem.

Chapter 7

1. At a high level, asynchronous programming aims to avoid idle waiting for unavailable resources. This typically involves interacting with slow and unpredictable resources.

2. A callback is a function that will be called at a given, later time. A future, on the other hand, is a more convenient abstraction that helps us keep track of requested resources and whether they are available. Futures are generally easier to use than callbacks.

3. A reactive application should be responsive, elastic, resilient, and message-driven.

Chapter 8

1. Multithreading cannot possibly speed up Python code due to the **global interpreter lock (GIL)**. In this chapter, we examined different approaches to multiprocessing; that is, running code using multiple processes.

2. Using the `Process` interface, we can have more low-level control by subclassing it. The `Pool` interface, on the other hand, offers a convenient way to distribute tasks across processes using the `apply` and `map` methods.

3. Theano and TensorFlow automatically translate our code into a parallelized version by taking advantage of special operations such as matrix multiplication.

Chapter 9

1. **HTML** stands for **Hypertext Markup Language**, which is the standard and most common language for developing web pages and applications.

2. Most of the communication that's done via the internet (more specifically, the **World Wide Web** (**WWW**)) uses HTTP. In HTTP, request methods are used to convey information on what data is being requested and should be sent back from a server.

3. HTTP response status codes are three-digit numbers that signify the state of communication between a server and its client. They are split into five categories, each indicating a specific state.

4. The `requests` module manages the communication between a Python program and a web server through HTTP requests.

5. A ping test is a tool that's typically used by web administrators to make sure that their sites are still available to clients. A ping test does this by making requests to the websites and analyzing the returned response status code.

6. Both the process of making different requests to a web server and parsing the processing downloaded HTML source code are independent across separate requests.

7. The following considerations should be made when you're developing applications that make concurrent web requests:

    A. The terms of service and data-collecting policies

    B. Error handling

    C. Updating your program regularly

    D. Avoiding over-scraping

Chapter 10

1. Image processing is the task of analyzing and manipulating digital image files to create new versions of the images, or to extract important data from them.

2. The smallest unit of a digital image is a pixel, which typically contains an RGB value: a tuple of integers between 0 and 255.

3. Grayscaling is the processing of converting an image into gray colors by considering only the intensity of each pixel, represented by the amount of light available. It reduces the dimensionality of the image pixel matrix by mapping traditional three-dimensional color data to one-dimensional gray data.

4. Thresholding replaces each pixel in an image with a white pixel if the pixel's intensity is greater than a previously specified threshold, and with a black pixel if the pixel's intensity is less than that threshold. After performing thresholding on an image, each pixel of that image can only hold two possible values, significantly reducing the complexity of image data.

5. Heavy computational number-crunching processes are typically involved when it comes to image processing, as each image is a matrix of integer tuples. However, these processes can be executed independently, which suggests that the whole task should be made concurrent.

6. Some good practices for concurrent image processing are as follows:

    A. Choose the correct method (out of many)

    B. Spawn an appropriate number of processes

    C. Process the input/output concurrently

Chapter 11

1. Communication channels are used to denote both the physical wiring connection between different systems and the logical communication of data that facilitates computer networks. The latter is related to computing and is more relevant to the idea of asynchronous programming. Asynchronous programming can provide functionalities that complement the process of facilitating communication channels efficiently.

2. The media layers contain fairly low-level operations that interact with the underlying process of the communication channel, while the host layers deal with high-level data communication and manipulation.

3. The transport layer is often viewed as the conceptual transition between the media layers and the host layers. It is responsible for sending data along end-to-end connections between different systems.

4. Server-wise, the `asyncio` module combines the abstraction of transport with the implementation of an asynchronous program. Specifically, via its `BaseTransport` and `BaseProtocol` classes, `asyncio` provides different ways to customize the underlying architecture of a communication channel.

5. Together with the `aiohttp` module and, specifically, `aiohttp.ClientSession`, `asyncio` also offers efficiency and flexibility regarding client-side communication processes, via asynchronously making requests and reading the returned responses.

6. The `aiofiles` module, which can work in conjunction with `asyncio` and `aiohttp`, helps facilitate asynchronous file reading/writing.

Chapter 12

1. A lack of (or mishandled) coordination between different lock objects can cause a deadlock, in which no progress can be made, and the program is locked in its current state.

2. In the dining philosophers problem, since each philosopher is holding only one fork with their left hand, they cannot proceed to eat or put down the fork they are holding. The only way a philosopher gets to eat their food is for their neighbor philosopher to put their fork down, which is only possible if they can eat their food; this creates a never-ending circle of conditions that can never be satisfied. This situation is, in essence, the nature of a deadlock, in which all the elements of a system are stuck in place and no progress can be made.

3. A deadlock is also defined by the necessary conditions that a concurrent program needs to have at the same time for a deadlock to occur. These conditions were first proposed by the computer scientist Edward G. Coffman Jr, and are therefore known as the Coffman conditions. These conditions are as follows:

    A. At least one resource has to be in a non-shareable state. This means that the resource is being held by an individual process (or thread) and cannot be accessed by others; the resource can only be accessed and held by a single process (or thread) at any given time. This condition is also known as mutual exclusion.

    B. One process (or thread) exists that is simultaneously accessing a resource and waiting for another that's held by other processes (or threads). In other words, this process (or thread) needs access to two resources to execute its instructions, one of which it is already holding, and the other of which it is waiting for from other processes (or threads). This condition is called hold and wait.

C.   Resources can only be released by a process (or a thread) holding them if there are specific instructions for the process (or thread) to do so. This is to say that unless the process (or thread) voluntarily and actively releases the resource, the resource remains in a non-shareable state. This is the no preemption condition.

D.   The final condition is called circular wait. As its name suggests, this condition specifies that a set of processes (or threads) exists where the first process (or thread) in the set is waiting for a resource to be released by the second process (or thread), which, in turn, needs to be waiting for the third process (or thread); finally, the last process (or thread) in the set is waiting for the first one.

4.   Instead of accessing the resources arbitrarily, if the processes (or threads) are to access them in a predetermined, static order, the circular nature of the way that they acquire and wait for the resources will be eliminated. However, if you place enough locks on the resources of your concurrent program, it will become entirely sequential in its execution, and, combined with the overhead of concurrent programming functionalities, it will have an even worse speed than the purely sequential version of the program.

5.   By ignoring locks, our program resources effectively become shareable among different processes/threads in a concurrent program, thus eliminating the first of the four Coffman conditions: mutual exclusion. Doing this, however, can be seen as misunderstanding the problem completely. We know that locks are utilized so that processes and threads can access the shared resources in a program in a systematic, coordinated way, to avoid mishandling the data. Removing any locking mechanisms in a concurrent program means that the likelihood of the shared resources, which are now free from accessing limitations, being manipulated in an uncoordinated way (and therefore becoming corrupted) increases significantly.

6.   In a livelock situation, the processes (or threads) in the concurrent program can switch their states, yet they simply switch back and forth infinitely, and no progress can be made.

Chapter 13

1.   Starvation is a problem in concurrent systems in which a process (or thread) cannot gain access to the necessary resources to proceed with its execution, which means it cannot make any progress.

2.   Most of the time, a poorly coordinated set of scheduling instructions is the main cause of starvation. Some high-level causes for starvation may include the following:

A.   Processes (or threads) with high priorities dominate the execution flow in the CPU, so low-priority processes (or threads) are not allowed to execute their instructions.

B. Processes (or threads) with high priorities dominate the usage of non-shareable resources, so low-priority processes (or threads) are not allowed to execute their instructions. This situation is similar to the first one but addresses the priority of accessing resources, instead of the priority of execution itself.

C. Processes (or threads) with low priorities are waiting for resources to execute their instructions, but as soon as the resources become available, other processes (or threads) with higher priorities are immediately given access to them, so the low-priority processes (or threads) wait infinitely.

3. Deadlock situations can also lead to starvation, as the definition of starvation states that if a process (or thread) exists that is unable to make any progress because it cannot gain access to the necessary process, the process (or thread) is experiencing starvation. This is also illustrated in the dining philosophers' problem.

4. The readers-writers problem asks for a scheduling algorithm so that readers and writers can access the text file appropriately and efficiently, without mishandling/corrupting the data that's included.

5. The first approach allows for multiple readers to access the text file simultaneously since readers simply read in the text file and do not alter the data in it. The problem with the first approach is that when a reader is accessing the text file and a writer is waiting for the file to be unlocked, if another reader starts its execution and wants to access the file, it will be given priority over the writer, who has already been waiting. Additionally, if more and more readers keep requesting access to the file, the writer will be waiting infinitely.

6. This approach implements the specification that once a writer requests to access the file, no reader should be able to jump in line and access the file before that writer. As opposed to what we see in the first solution to the readers-writers problem, this solution is giving priority to writers and, as a consequence, the readers are starved.

7. This approach implements a lock on both readers and writers. All threads will then be subject to the constants of the lock, so equal priority will be achieved among separate threads.

8. Some common solutions to starvation include the following:

A. Increasing the priority of low-priority threads.

B. Implementing a first-in-first-out thread queue.

C. Implementing a priority queue that also gives gradually increasing priority to threads that have been waiting in the queue for a long time.

D. If a thread has been able to access the shared resource many times, it should be given less priority.

Chapter 14

1. Critical sections indicate shared resources that are accessed by multiple processes or threads in a concurrent application, which can lead to unexpected, and even erroneous, behaviors.

2. A race condition occurs when two or more threads/processes access and alter a shared resource simultaneously, resulting in mishandled and corrupted data.

3. The root cause of a race condition is multiple threads/processes reading in and altering a shared resource simultaneously. When all of the threads/processes finish their execution, only the result of the last thread/process is registered.

4. Since race conditions arise when multiple threads or processes access and write to a shared resource simultaneously, the solution is to isolate the execution of different threads/processes, especially when interacting with the shared resource. With locks, we can turn a shared resource in a concurrent program into a critical section, whose data integrity is guaranteed to be protected.

5. There are several disadvantages to using locks: with enough locks implemented in a concurrent program, the whole program may become entirely sequential; locks don't lock anything.

6. The problems that race conditions raise in real-life systems and applications are as follows:

   A. Security: A race condition can be both exploited as a security vulnerability (to give external agents illegal access to a system) and used as random key generation, for security processes.

   B. Operating systems: A race condition occurring when two agents (users and applications) interact with the same memory space can lead to unpredictable behaviors.

   C. Networking: In networking, a race condition can lead to giving multiple users powerful privileges in a network.

Chapter 15

1. C++ associates a variable with its value by simply writing the value to the memory location of the variable; Python has its variables reference point to the memory location of the values that they hold. For this reason, Python needs to maintain a reference count for every value in its memory space.

2. To avoid race conditions and, consequently, value reference counts from being corrupted, the GIL is implemented so that only one thread can access and mutate the counts at any given time.

3. The GIL effectively prevents multiple threads from taking advantage of the CPU and executing CPU-bound instructions at the same time. This means that if multiple threads that are meant to be executed concurrently are CPU-bound, they will be executed sequentially.

4. There are a few ways to deal with the GIL in your Python applications; namely, implementing multiprocessing instead of multithreading and utilizing other, alternative Python interpreters.

Chapter 16

1. The factory pattern makes it easy to keep track of the objects that are created within a program. Another benefit lies in the separation of code, which creates an object and the code that the object uses.

2. There are two forms of the factory pattern: the factory method and the abstract method. The former is used to handle the creation of a single object, while the latter is a group of factory methods.

3. You should start with the factory method first since it is the simpler of the two. If you find yourself needing many factory methods, then you should start thinking about grouping them into different abstract methods.

Chapter 17

1. The builder pattern helps manage objects that contain many individual components that need to be created sequentially. The pattern allows you to reuse a construction multiple times as well since it decouples an object's construction and the object itself.

2. Many applications, such as HTML page generators, document converters, and UI form creators, are implemented with the builder pattern.

3. The builder pattern uses a director to create an object via multiple steps sequentially, while the factory pattern creates an object in a single step.

Chapter 18

1. The prototype pattern helps us create objects that are based on an existing object (or prototype) via cloning. This can easily be done in Python using the copy function.

2. Objects in a database need to be duplicated many times, depending on the application and its users. This may be an expensive operation without prototypes.

3. The singleton pattern is helpful when we want to implement a class that should only have one instance. This is useful, for example, when we'd like to maintain the global state of a Python program.

4. The singleton pattern may be used to control concurrent access to a shared resource, preventing many concurrency-based bugs and errors.

Chapter 20

1. The decorator pattern specifies the usage and responsibilities of an object dynamically in a transparent and readable way.

2. Python has a built-in decorator feature, allowing programmers to extend the functionalities of a function, method, or class.

3. With the decorator pattern, we can implement memoization with minimal code, which, as we have seen in the main text, helps keep the computation of Fibonacci numbers fast and its code readable.

Chapter 21

1. The bridge pattern is useful when there is a need to share an implementation among different objects without having to implement individual specialized classes. This is typically done with either an abstract class that generalizes the different use cases or the individual specialized classes themselves.

2. The adapter is generally used to make two incompatible interfaces compatible, while the bridge abstracts out the generalization of different classes.

3. We define an abstract content fetcher class, from which two specialized classes inherit: a local file fetcher and a URL fetcher.

Chapter 22

1. The façade pattern helps hide the inner implementation of an application and only exposing the necessary interface. This is particularly important when we are working with a large code base but our user only needs to interact with a small portion of our code.

2. When we need to make a change to an application, the abstraction that the façade pattern provides helps keep the client code separate and safe, which is useful in making the client side unaffected by pending software changes.

3. The operating system class works as a façade, hiding access to the different server classes from client code.

Chapter 23

1. The flyweight pattern is designed to keep memory usage at a minimum by sharing resources among similar objects.

2. The MVC pattern generalizes a common structure among different applications with a model, a view, and a controller. This helps prevent mixing the backend logic with user interfaces.

3. The proxy pattern is useful in requiring the necessary code to be run before an important object is accessed.

Chapter 24

1. The chain of responsibility pattern gracefully handles an unknown number of requests or events that our program needs to process. This is useful in event-based logic such as purchase applications and shipping systems.

2. In our system, if an object does not know how to handle a given request, it passes the request along the chain. As we have seen, a `close` event cannot be handled directly by `SendDialog` and `MsgText` and is passed to `MainWindow`.

3. The chain of responsibility pattern may not be useful if there are multiple requests, but they may be processed by a single object. This renders all the bookkeeping that's done by the pattern useless.

Chapter 25

1. The command pattern helps encapsulate operational logic (copy, paste, undo, redo, and so on) in an object. This leads to better abstraction and management of the logical steps to be taken for each operation, such as grouping multiple operations and implementing macros.

2. The command pattern abstracts out the implementation of the operations that are used, so any client code that executes it does not need to know about the details of their implementation.

3. In our example, we implemented an abstraction on top of various functionalities provided by the `os` module. A particular feature is its undoing function. Moreover, as commands have a consistent interface, grouping them can be done with ease.

Chapter 26

1. The observer pattern maintains a list of objects that are interested in the state of a target object and notifies the former when the latter changes.

2. While the MVC pattern may implement the same function logic of updating views when the model changes, the observer pattern is more effective at maintaining and managing the list of subscribers for a given publisher, making it easy to, for example, add or remove subscribers.

3. We implement data formatters that display an object in different ways. Here, we have multiple subscribing formatters that are interested in a publishing default formatter. When the default formatter is updated, the subscribers are notified and proceed with their respective logic.

Index

C

X

Z

`Packt.com`

Subscribe to our online digital library for full access to over 7,000 books and videos, as well as industry leading tools to help you plan your personal development and advance your career. For more information, please visit our website.

Why subscribe?

- Spend less time learning and more time coding with practical eBooks and Videos from over 4,000 industry professionals

- Improve your learning with Skill Plans built especially for you

- Get a free eBook or video every month

- Fully searchable for easy access to vital information

- Copy and paste, print, and bookmark content

Did you know that Packt offers eBook versions of every book published, with PDF and ePub files available? You can upgrade to the eBook version at `packt.com` and as a print book customer, you are entitled to a discount on the eBook copy. Get in touch with us at `customercare@packtpub.com` for more details.

At `www.packt.com`, you can also read a collection of free technical articles, sign up for a range of free newsletters, and receive exclusive discounts and offers on Packt books and eBooks.

Other Books You May Enjoy

If you enjoyed this book, you may be interested in these other books by Packt:

Python for Geeks

Muhammad Asif

ISBN: 9781801070119

- Understand how to design and manage complex Python projects
- Strategize test-driven development (TDD) in Python
- Explore multithreading and multiprogramming in Python
- Use Python for data processing with Apache Spark and Google Cloud Platform (GCP)
- Deploy serverless programs on public clouds such as GCP
- Use Python to build web applications and application programming interfaces
- Apply Python for network automation and serverless functions
- Get to grips with Python for data analysis and machine learning

Expert Python Programming - Fourth Edition

Michał Jaworski, Tarek Ziadé

ISBN: 9781801071109

- Explore modern ways of setting up repeatable and consistent Python development environments
- Effectively package Python code for community and production use
- Learn modern syntax elements of Python programming, such as f-strings, enums, and lambda functions
- Demystify metaprogramming in Python with metaclasses
- Write concurrent code in Python
- Extend and integrate Python with code written in C and C++

580

Packt is searching for authors like you

If you're interested in becoming an author for Packt, please visit authors. packtpub.com and apply today. We have worked with thousands of developers and tech professionals, just like you, to help them share their insight with the global tech community. You can make a general application, apply for a specific hot topic that we are recruiting an author for, or submit your own idea.

Share Your Thoughts

Now you've finished *Advanced Python Programming*, we'd love to hear your thoughts! Scan the QR code below to go straight to the Amazon review page for this book and share your feedback or leave a review on the site that you purchased it from.

https://packt.link/r/1801814015

Your review is important to us and the tech community and will help us make sure we're delivering excellent quality content.

Made in the USA
Coppell, TX
01 July 2023